Peachtree Bouquet

A Culinary Arrangement

The Junior League of DeKalb County, Georgia

The Junior League of DeKalb County, Inc. is an organization of women committed to promoting voluntarism and to improving the community through the effective action and leadership of trained volunteers. Its purpose is exclusively educational and charitable.

This book contains the favorite recipes of Junior League members and their friends. Each recipe has been tested for accuracy and excellence. We do not claim that all of the recipes are original, only that they are our favorites. We regret that we were unable to include many recipes which were submitted, due to similarity or lack of space.

Copies of Peachtree Bouquet may be obtained from the Junior League Headquarters c/o *Peachtree Bouquet*, 716 West Trinity Place, P.O. Box 183, Decatur, Georgia 30031. Phone (404) 378-4536

International Standard Book Number - 0-9618508-1-7

Library of Congress Catalog Card Number - 87-80377

Printed in the USA by
WIMMER BROTHERS
A Wimmer Company
Memphis • Dallas

Original Cookbook Committee

Chairman
Chris Kendrick

Co-Chairman
Sandy Jernigan

Recipe Chairman
Becky Nicholson

Sustainer Advisor
Barrie Aycock

Committee

Patty Begnaud	Cindy Jollay
Nancy Chambers	Lynne Lock
Jeannie Dyson	Mary Martin
Janet Gallagher	Lisa Pardue
Betsy Harrell	Margaret Scales
Mary Harrington	Barbara Williams

Artist
Helen Schneeberger

Chairmen

Sally Maloof	1987-88
Lynne Lock	1988-89
Susan Roberson	1989-90
Kathy Mulling	1989-90
Barbara Williams	1990-91
Betsy Menneg	1991-92
Carolyn Yelton	1992-93

Funds raised by this cookbook directly support the purpose and community programs of the Junior League of Dekalb County, Inc.

CONTENTS

Introduction 6

Appetizers and Beverages 7
    Appetizers 9
    Beverages 32

Soups 41

Salads 61

Breads 95

Eggs, Pasta, Rice, and Cheese 119
    Eggs 121
    Pasta 124
    Rice 129
    Cheese 132

Entrees
    Fish and Seafood 139
    Meats 165
    Poultry 199

Casseroles 235

Vegetables and Side Dishes 265

Desserts 293

Health and Diet 355

Peachtree Potpourri 377

Acknowledgements 385

Index 389

The peach blossom symbol preceding a recipe title designates a dish which can be prepared quickly and easily.

 The bow preceding a recipe title designates a recipe which can be used as a gift item.

 The balloon preceding a recipe title designates a recipe which children would enjoy or can make themselves.

The flowers of Atlanta are unequaled in their radiant splendor. Delicate dogwoods blooming on Peachtree Street; fragrant magnolias of the "Old South"; azaleas and rhododendron, ablaze with color; roses in a profusion of understated loveliness; and ageless hydrangeas adorned with large clusters of exciting blooms – all are a part of the city's heritage and tradition. When arranged in a bouquet, they present a unique sampling of what Atlanta has to savor.

Peachtree Bouquet, A Culinary Arrangement, likewise presents a sampling of what the city has to savor – international cuisine reflecting the city's cultural expansion and international influence; specialties from restaurants, caterers, and well-known personalities; favorites shared by friends, some truly best-kept secrets; and, of course, traditional Southern-style dishes, legacies from a glorious past. There are selections for family and friends; brunches, luncheons, picnics, and parties; health and diet; and gift-giving. Some are hearty and homestyle, while others are gourmet delights. All are eminently Atlanta's to share in our culinary arrangement, *Peachtree Bouquet.*

ABOUT OUR ARTIST:

Helen Schneeberger (H. Schnee.) was born and educated in Louisville, Kentucky. Painting and drawing have been major interests of hers for most of her life. She is a Signature Member of the Kentucky, Georgia, and Southern Watercolor Societies and maintains a studio and gallery in her Atlanta residence.

Appetizers
and Beverages

Azalea

APPETIZERS AND BEVERAGES

APPETIZERS

COLD

Caviar Pie 9
Cheese Straws 17
Cream Cheese and Bacon Tea
  Sandwiches 10
Elegant and Easy Brie 28
Garlic Olives 24
Glazed Bacon with Walnuts 11
Hidden Treasure 26
Holiday Antipasto 12
Marinated Vegetables 31
Pickled Shrimp 29
Salmon Rolls 28
Shrimp Pizza 30

DIPS

Cheesy Dip Surprise 15
Chili Relleno Dip 23
Clam Dip 19
Divine Dip 22
Groud Beef Dip 23
Hot Nacho Dip 22
Miss Daisey's Crabmeat Dip 20
Onion Rye 21
Rebecca Sauce 27
Tamara Salata 31

HOT

Appetizer Gougère 13
Crab Grass 20
Cranberry Meatballs 9
Easy Fried Cheese 11
Egg Rolls 24
Far East Shrimp Balls 30
Hawaiian Chicken Wings 17
Hot Crabmeat Canapes 19
Italian Cheese Rolls 14
Mushroom Squares 25
Parmesan Onion Canapes 21
Phyllo Pastries 18
Sausage Party Pizzas 26
Sausage Pinwheels 22

SNACKS

Candied Citrus Pecans 16
Glazed Nuts 15

SPREADS AND MOLDS

Asparagus-Lobster Mousse 10
Bacon Ball 11
Delicious Liver Pâté 25
Garlic Cheese Ball 16
Holiday Cheese Ball 13
Hot Crab Spread 20
Olive and Cream Cheese Ball 14
Oyster Log 28
Salmon Mousse 27
Shrimp Mousse 29
Spicy Cheese Ball 14
Strawberry Cheese Ball 16
Tarama Salata 31

BEVERAGES

Amaretto Freeze 32
Champagne Punch 35
Decaffinated Spiced Tea Mix 33
Doris' Banana Punch 33
French Hot Chocolate 34
Ginger's Egg Nog 36
Hot Buttered Rum Mix 32
Hot Florida Tea 39
Hot Mocha Mix 35
Hot Spiced Wine 40
It's Almost Bailey's 40
Kahlua Velvet Frosty 36
Long Island Iced Tea 39
Microwave Cappuccino 34
Orange-Anise Spice Bags 38
Percolator Hot Fruit Tea 37
Pineapple-Champagne Punch 34
Sherry Sour 39
Sneaky Petes 37
Spiced Bourbon-Apple Punch 32
Spiced Iced Tea 38
Tequila-Champagne Punch 38
White Sangria 36

CRANBERRY MEATBALLS
Meatballs with a tangy flavor

Preparation: 30 minutes　　　　　　　　　Baking: 45 minutes
Planning: Can partially prepare ahead　　　　　Servings: 15

2 pounds lean ground beef
2 Tablespoons soy sauce
2 Tablespoons minced
onion
2 eggs
⅓ cup dried parsley
2 cloves garlic
1 cup cornflake crumbs
2 teaspoons salt
¼ teaspoon pepper
1 (16-ounce) can jellied
cranberry sauce
⅓ cup ketchup
2 Tablespoons dark brown
sugar
1 (12-ounce) bottle chili
sauce
1 Tablespoon lemon juice

Combine beef, soy sauce, onion, eggs, parsley, garlic, cornflake crumbs, salt, and pepper; mix well. Shape into balls the size of large olives. Place in large baking dish. Meatballs can be frozen at this point, if desired. Combine cranberry sauce, ketchup, brown sugar, chili sauce, and lemon juice in saucepan; heat, stirring well. Pour sauce over meatballs. Bake, uncovered, at 350 degrees for 45 minutes.

CAVIAR PIE

Preparation: 45 minutes　　　　　　　　　Chilling: 8 hours
Planning: Must partially prepare ahead　　　　Servings: 10

5 hard-cooked eggs
4 Tablespoons butter,
softened
1 teaspoon unflavored
gelatin
1 Tablespoon water
juice of one onion
1 (8-ounce) package cream
cheese, softened
1 cup sour cream
1 (3½-ounce) jar caviar,
drained

Grate eggs; mix eggs with butter. With wet hands, line 7-inch glass pie plate with egg mixture. Chill. Soak gelatin in water and juice of one onion. Combine cream cheese and sour cream with gelatin mixture. Beat until smooth; pour into pie shell. Chill 8 hours or overnight. Just before serving, top with caviar. Serve with crackers.

ASPARAGUS-LOBSTER COCKTAIL MOUSSE

Preparation: 45 minutes
Planning: Must prepare ahead

Chilling: 12 hours
Servings: 35

1½ cups canned asparagus cuts and pieces, undrained
16 ounces lobster meat, cut in small chunks or coarsely shredded, undrained
2 envelopes unflavored gelatin
1 (10¾-ounce) can cream of asparagus soup, undiluted

3 (8-ounce) packages cream cheese
1 teaspoon celery seed
½ cup finely chopped onion
½ cup finely chopped celery
1 (3¼-ounce) can pitted ripe olives, chopped
1 cup mayonnaise
½ teaspoon salt

Drain asparagus and lobster, reserving liquid. Purée asparagus in blender or food processor with ¼ cup of asparagus liquid. Sprinkle gelatin on ½ cup of lobster liquid, ½ cup remaining asparagus liquid, or ½ cup water. Heat soup and cream cheese over low heat, stirring until smooth. Add asparagus purée, gelatin, and remaining ingredients. Pour into oiled 3-quart mold. Chill 12 hours. Serve with crackers.

CREAM CHEESE AND BACON TEA SANDWICHES
Serve at coffee, tea, or brunch

Preparation: 45 minutes

Servings: 12

½ pound bacon
1 (8-ounce) package cream cheese, softened
12 slices whole wheat bread

1 (14-ounce) package bean sprouts
mayonnaise or butter

Fry or microwave bacon until crisp; drain on paper towels. Finely chop or process bacon in food processor. Add cream cheese; mix thoroughly. On 6 slices of bread, spread bacon-cheese mixture. Add layer of bean sprouts. On the other 6 slices, spread mayonnaise or butter; place on top of sprouts making 6 sandwiches. With sharp knife, remove crusts from sandwiches; cut each sandwich cross-wise twice, making four triangles.

GLAZED BACON WITH WALNUTS

Preparation: 10 minutes

Baking: 30 minutes
Servings: 4

1 pound bacon
¼ cup dark brown sugar,
  firmly packed

1 teaspoon all-purpose flour
½ cup chopped walnuts

Preheat oven to 350 degrees. Arrange bacon slices close together but not overlapping on broiler pan or fine wire rack over dripping pan. In bowl, combine brown sugar, flour, and walnuts; sprinkle evenly over bacon. Bake until crisp and brown, about 30 minutes. Drain on paper towels.

 ## BACON BALL ⚔

Preparation: 10 minutes
Planning: Must prepare ahead

Chilling: 2 hours
Servings: 24

1 (1-ounce) package
  ranch-style salad dressing
  mix
2 (8-ounce) packages cream
  cheese, softened

1 (3-ounce) jar real bacon
  bits

Stir dressing mix into cream cheese; roll into a ball. Roll cheese ball in bacon bits. Refrigerate until chilled, about 2 hours. Serve with wheat crackers.

 ## EASY FRIED CHEESE

Preparation: 30 minutes

Frying: 1-2 minutes
Yield: 2 dozen

1 (10-12 ounce) package
  sharp Cheddar cheese, or
  other cheese
¾ cup dry bread crumbs

¾ cup sesame seeds
2 eggs, beaten
sesame seed oil for frying

Cut cheese into bite-size cubes. Combine crumbs and sesame seeds. Dip cheese in egg; coat cheese with crumb mixture. Fry a few at a time in deep hot oil for 1-2 minutes or until lightly browned.

HOLIDAY ANTIPASTO

Preparation: 1 hour
Planning: Must prepare ahead

Marinating: 1 hour
Servings: 8

2 Tablespoons unsalted butter
2 flat anchovy fillets
2 cups sliced fresh mushrooms
1 clove garlic, mashed to paste
2 Tablespoons dry white wine
2 Tablespoons lemon juice, divided
freshly ground pepper
4 ounces Jarlsberg cheese, julienned

4 ounces hard salami, julienned
¼ cup pitted ripe olives, halved
¼ cup minced red onion
3 Tablespoons capers, drained
3 Tablespoons minced fresh parsley
3 Tablespoons olive oil
2 teaspoons wine vinegar

Heat butter in skillet over low heat. Add anchovies and mash to a paste. Add mushrooms and garlic. Sauté, stirring occasionally. Add wine and 1 Tablespoon lemon juice. Increase heat to medium high. Cook for 5 minutes, stirring constantly. Remove from heat; add pepper to taste. Transfer mixture to medium bowl; cool 15 minutes. Add cheese, salami, olives, onion, capers, and parsley. Whisk together oil, vinegar, and remaining 1 Tablespoon lemon juice in small bowl. Pour over mushroom mixture and toss. Cover and marinate at room temperature 30-60 minutes. Antipasto can be stored in refrigerator several days. Return to room temperature 30 minutes before serving. Serve on small rounds of French bread as an appetizer, or as a side dish for a holiday buffet.

APPETIZER GOUGÈRE
This is a great appetizer with wine or fruit

Preparation: 20 minutes
Planning: Can prepare ahead

Baking: 30 minutes
Yield: 2 dozen

1 cup all-purpose flour
1 teaspoon salt
1 cup water
½ cup sweet butter
4 eggs

1½ cups grated Gruyère
cheese
1 teaspoon Dijon mustard
½ teaspoon dry mustard
⅛ teaspoon Tabasco sauce

Sift flour with salt onto waxed paper or plate. Bring water and butter to a boil in medium saucepan. When bubbling, pour into food processor. Pour in flour mixture; beat until mixture pulls away from sides of processor bowl. Add eggs, one at a time, to ensure that pastry stays firm and keeps its shape. Add cheese, mustards, and Tabasco; beat dough 1-2 minutes until glossy and smooth. Remove from processor. Using spoon or pastry bag fitted with plain tip, form a 9-inch circle of dough on moistened parchment paper or waxed paper on baking sheet. Bake at 450 degrees for 10 minutes. Reduce heat to 350 degrees and bake for 10 minutes. Reduce heat to 325 degrees and bake for 10-15 minutes. Remove from oven; pierce with fork to let steam escape. Slice into 24 wedges and serve, or set aside and reheat to crisp at a later time.

HOLIDAY CHEESE BALL

Preparation: 30 minutes
Planning: Must prepare ahead

Chilling: 4 hours
Servings: 24

2 cups grated sharp Cheddar
cheese
2 ounces blue cheese
1 (8-ounce) package cream
cheese

⅛ teaspoon Tabasco sauce
1 Tablespoon grated onion
1 Tablespoon sugar
1 teaspoon salt
½ cup chopped pecans

Bring cheeses to room temperature. Combine all ingredients, except nuts, in large bowl of electric mixer; blend well. Refrigerate, covered, for several hours to allow flavors to mingle and cheese to harden. Form into 1 large ball or divide into 2 or more balls or logs. Roll in chopped nuts.

ITALIAN CHEESE ROLLS

Preparation: 15 minutes

Baking: 10-15 minutes
Servings: 12

**1 cup grated Cheddar
cheese**
1 cup mayonnaise
1 cup butter, softened
1 cup pimientos, drained

**12 bread slices, crusts
removed**
¼ cup melted butter
Italian seasoning for garnish

Combine cheese, mayonnaise, butter, and pimientos; mix well. Spread on bread slices. Roll up jelly-roll style. Place on baking sheet. Brush tops with melted butter; sprinkle with Italian seasoning. Rolls can be refrigerated at this point and baked later. Bake at 400 degrees for 10-15 minutes, or until lighlty toasted.

OLIVE AND CREAM CHEESE BALL
Pretty for the holidays

Preparation: 20 minutes
Planning: Can prepare ahead

Servings: 24

**1 (8-ounce) package cream
cheese, softened**
1 stick butter, softened
½ cup chopped ripe olives
**10 pimiento-stuffed green
olives, chopped**

4 green onion tops, chopped
**½ cup chopped walnuts or
pecans, divided**

Combine cream cheese, butter, olives, onion tops, and ¼ cup chopped nuts. Shape or roll into ball; top with remaining nuts. Refrigerate until ready to serve. Serve with crackers.

SPICY CHEESE BALL

Preparation: 15 minutes
Planning: Must prepare ahead

Chilling: 4 hours
Servings: 12

**1 (8-ounce) package cream
cheese, softened**
4 ounces blue cheese
**1 (2½-ounce) package spicy
beef**

4 fresh green onions
**chopped fresh parsley for
garnish**

Blend cream cheese and blue cheese in bowl, using wooden spoon. Do not use food processor. Chop spicy beef and green onion; add to cheese mixture. Shape into ball; refrigerate a minimum of 4 hours. Cheese ball improves in flavor the longer it is refrigerated. Garnish with fresh parsley, olives, etc. before serving. Serve with crackers.

CHEESY DIP SURPRISE

Preparation: 1 hour
Planning: Can prepare ahead

Servings: 12

2 (8-ounce) packages cream cheese, softened
2 (1-ounce) packages ranch-style salad dressing mix
2 cups grated Muenster cheese

2 cups grated Cheddar cheese
½ cup chopped green onion
1 large tomato, chopped
1 (3¼-ounce) can pitted ripe olives, chopped

Mix cream cheese with powdered dressing; blend thoroughly. Spread on large platter or round pizza pan. Top with grated cheeses, chopped onion, tomato, and ripe olives. Serve with tortilla chips or other strong chip for dipping.

GLAZED NUTS

These are great as holiday gifts for friends and employees

Preparation: 10 minutes
Planning: Can prepare ahead

Baking: 1 hour
Yield: 1 pound

1 egg white
½ cup sugar
½ teaspoon salt
¼ teaspoon ground cinnamon

¼ teaspoon ground nutmeg
¼ teaspoon ground cloves
1 pound unsalted pecans, walnuts, or cashews

Combine all ingredients and mix well. Spread on greased cookie sheet. Bake at 250 degrees for 1 hour. Cool; place in airtight containers.

 ## STRAWBERRY CHEESE BALL

Preparation: 10 minutes   Chilling: 24 hours
Planning: Must partially prepare ahead   Servings: 6

**3 cups grated medium-sharp   1 small onion, grated
  Cheddar cheese   1 cup chopped pecans
1 cup mayonnaise   strawberry jam**

Combine cheese, mayonnaise, onion, and pecans; mix well. Spoon into mold; refrigerate at least 24 hours. Unmold and cover with strawberry jam. Serve with crackers.

GARLIC CHEESE BALL

Preparation: 30 minutes   Chilling: 30 minutes
Planning: Can prepare ahead   Servings: 24

**4 cups grated extra-sharp   2 teaspoons salt
  Cheddar cheese   ⅛ teaspoon cayenne pepper
12 ounces cream cheese,   2 cups finely chopped
  softened   pecans
1 (14-ounce) jar pimientos,   paprika for garnish
  drained and chopped
5 small cloves garlic,
  pressed**

Combine cheese, cream cheese, pimientos, garlic, salt, and cayenne pepper in food processor; process until well blended and smooth. Shape into a ball; chill 30 minutes if mixture will not form a ball. Roll ball in nuts; sprinkle with paprika. Serve with crackers. Cheese ball will keep for up to 1 week in refrigerator.

 ## CANDIED CITRUS PECANS
Makes a pretty gift when wrapped in colored cellophane and tied with a colorful ribbon

Preparation: 40 minutes   Cooking: 20 minutes
Planning: Can prepare ahead   Yield: 3 cups

**2 cups sugar   1 Tablespoon grated orange
¾ cup fresh orange juice   rind
1 teaspoon lemon juice   3 cups pecan halves**

Mix sugar, orange juice, and lemon juice in a 2-quart saucepan. Bring to a boil over medium heat. Reduce heat to low; cook to soft-ball stage, 235 degrees on candy thermometer, or approximately 15-20 minutes. Check frequently to be sure not to overcook. Remove from heat; add rind and pecans. Stir until mixture turns cream color, 7-10 minutes. Pour onto waxed paper. When cool, break apart; store in airtight container.

CHEESE STRAWS

Preparation: 1 hour
Planning: Can prepare ahead

Baking: 12 minutes
Yield: 3 dozen

4 cups grated sharp Cheddar cheese
1 cup butter, softened
3 cups sifted all-purpose flour

1 teaspoon salt
½ teaspoon cayenne pepper

Cream cheese and butter. Add dry ingredients; mix well. Pack into cookie press. Press onto ungreased cookie sheet. Bake at 350 degrees for 10-12 minutes. Transfer to wire racks to cool, or serve warm.

HAWAIIAN CHICKEN WINGS

Preparation: 15 minutes
Planning: Must partially prepare ahead
Marinating: 24 hours

Baking: 1 hour
Yield: 2 dozen

1 cup soy sauce
½ cup pineapple juice
1 cup water
½ cup sugar
1 teaspoon ground ginger

1 teaspoon garlic powder
¼ cup minced onion
⅛ teaspoon pepper
24 chicken wing drumettes

Combine soy sauce, pineapple juice, and water; stir in sugar, ginger, garlic powder, onion, and pepper. Place chicken wings in marinade for at least 24 hours. Bake at 375 degrees for 1 hour. Serve warm in chafing dish.

PHYLLO PASTRIES

Preparation: 30 minutes

Baking: 15 minutes
Servings: 8

**½ (1-pound) frozen phyllo
  pastry, thawed
1½ cups butter, melted**

**Mushroom Filling
Nutty Chicken Filling**

Thaw phyllo according to package directions. Unroll and remove one sheet of pastry; lay pastry on tea towel. Brush carefully with melted butter. Lay another piece of phyllo dough on top. Cut pastries carefully into 3x12-inch strips. Prepare either the Mushroom Filling or the Nutty Chicken Filling. Place 1 Tablespoon of either filling onto one end of a pastry strip; fold dough diagonally over filling, forming a triangle. Continue folding, maintaining a triangle, as though folding a flag. Repeat with other strips. Place on greased baking sheet, seam side up. Brush with melted butter. Bake at 400 degrees for 15 minutes until browned. Remove from oven; drain on wire rack 2-3 minutes. Serve warm.

Mushroom Filling:
**½ pound fresh mushrooms,
  sliced
½ chopped onion**

**½ cup butter
1 teaspoon curry powder**

Sauté mushrooms and onion in butter and curry. Cool completely.

Nutty Chicken Filling:
**2 Tablespoons butter
2½ Tablespoons all-purpose
  flour
1 cup milk**

**½ teaspoon salt
2 boneless chicken breasts,
  cooked and chopped
½ cup chopped nuts**

Melt butter in small saucepan; add flour. Cook over low heat for 2 minutes. Add milk; whisk until thick. Add salt, chicken, and nuts. Cool completely.

CLAM DIP

Preparation: 30 minutes
Planning: Must prepare ahead

Chilling: 8 hours
Servings: 15

1 (6½-ounce) can clams
1 (8-ounce) package cream
cheese, softened
2 Tablespoons half and half

2 Tablespoons mayonnaise
2 Tablespoons sugar
⅛ teaspoon Worcestershire
sauce

Drain clams, reserving liquid; mince. Mix cream cheese, with clams. Add half and half, mayonnaise, and sugar; mix well. Add Worcestershire sauce and small amounts of reserved clam juice until consistency is that of a dip. Refrigerate 8 hours or overnight. Allow to soften just before serving. Add more clam juice to thin again to dip consistency, if needed. Serve with chips or crackers.

HOT CRABMEAT CANAPÉS

Preparation: 45 minutes
Planning: Can partially prepare ahead

Broiling: 1-3 minutes
Yield: 3 dozen

3 dozen slices white bread
½ pound crabmeat
6 Tablespoons mayonnaise
½ teaspoon salt
½ teaspoon monosodium
glutamate
1 Tablespoon grated onion

2 Tablespoons lemon juice
1 Tablespoon
Worcestershire sauce
½ cup grated Parmesan
cheese
paprika for garnish

Cut bread into rounds with biscuit cutter. In skillet, melt small amount of butter; brown one side of bread rounds. Place rounds on baking sheet, toasted side down. Mix crabmeat, mayonnaise, salt, and monosodium glutamate. Blend in onion, lemon juice, Worcestershire sauce, and Parmesan cheese. Pile mixture on toast beds; sprinkle with paprika. At this point, canapés can be refrigerated. Just before serving, broil until bubbly and slightly browned.

MISS DAISEY'S CRABMEAT DIP

Preparation: 15 minutes
Planning: Can prepare ahead

Yield: 2½ cups

1 (8-ounce) package cream cheese, softened
½ cup mayonnaise
1 (7½-ounce) can crabmeat, drained and flaked

½ teaspoon dried dill weed
⅛ teaspoon garlic salt
⅛ teaspoon Worcestershire sauce
1 cup sour cream

Combine cream cheese and mayonnaise; mix thoroughly. Add crabmeat, dill weed, garlic salt, and Worcestershire sauce to cheese mixture; combine thoroughly. Fold in sour cream. Serve with crackers.

 ## CRAB GRASS

Preparation: 20 minutes

Baking: 20 minutes
Servings: 8

½ medium onion, chopped
8 Tablespoons butter
1 (10-ounce) package frozen chopped spinach, cooked and drained

1 (7-ounce) can crabmeat
¾ cup grated Parmesan cheese

Sauté onion in butter until soft; add spinach, crabmeat, and Parmesan cheese. Pour into small to medium baking dish. Bake at 350 degrees for 20 minutes. Serve with sesame rounds or crackers.

HOT CRAB SPREAD

Preparation: 20 minutes

Baking: 15 minutes
Servings: 8

1 (8-ounce) package cream cheese, softened
1 Tablespoon milk
6½ ounces frozen, canned, or fresh crabmeat, drained
2 Tablespoons finely chopped onion

½ teaspoon cream-style horseradish
¼ teaspoon salt
⅛ teaspoon pepper
⅓ cup sliced almonds

Mix cream cheese with milk. Add crabmeat, onion, horseradish, salt, and pepper; spoon into baking dish. Sprinkle with almonds. Bake at 375 degrees for 15 minutes. Serve piping hot with crackers or party rye.

 ## PARMESAN ONION CANAPÉS

Preparation: 15 minutes   Broiling: 2-3 minutes
Planning: Can partially prepare ahead   Yield: 36

1 cup mayonnaise	**1 Tablespoon milk**
1 cup grated Parmesan cheese	**1 loaf sliced cocktail bread, lightly toasted**
½ cup finely chopped onion	

Combine mayonnaise, cheese, onion, and milk; mix thoroughly. Mixture can be refrigerated until ready to use. Just before serving, spread on toast. Place on baking sheet; broil 4 inches from heat for 2-3 minutes, or until golden and bubbly.

ONION RYE

Preparation: 30 minutes   Chilling: 4 hours
Planning: Can partially prepare ahead   Servings: 8

1½ cups mayonnaise	**2 Tablespoons dried parsley**
1½ cups sour cream	**2 (3-ounce) packages dried beef, torn into small pieces**
2 teaspoons beau monde seasoning	
2 teaspoons dried dill weed	**1 round, unsliced loaf onion rye bread**
2 Tablespoons dried minced onion	

Combine mayonnaise and sour cream; mix well. Add seasonings and dried beef. Refrigerate about 4 hours. Immediately before serving, hollow out onion rye loaf, reserving the bread pieces. Pour dip mixture inside crust. Use bread pieces for dipping.

HOT NACHO DIP
A Mexican delight

Preparation: 30 minutes

Baking: 30 minutes
Servings: 12-14

1 pound ground beef
1 medium onion, chopped
1 (16-ounce) can refried
  beans
1 (4-ounce) can chopped
  chiles
2-3 cups grated Cheddar
  cheese

1 (8-ounce) jar hot taco
  sauce
¼ cup chopped green onion
1 cup chopped ripe olives
1 cup sour cream
1 cup guacamole

Brown ground beef and onion; drain thoroughly. Place in bottom of casserole dish. Over meat, layer, in order, beans, chiles, cheese, and taco sauce. Bake at 350 degrees for 25-30 minutes. After baking, add layers of green onion, olives, sour cream, and guacamole. Serve with tortilla chips.

DIVINE DIP
Pretty served in a cored cabbage head

Preparation: 5 minutes
Planning: Must prepare ahead

Chilling: 2 hours
Yield: 1 cup

1 cup mayonnaise
2 Tablespoons prepared
  mustard
1 teaspoon sweet pickle
  juice

2 teaspoons curry powder
⅛ teaspoon sugar

Combine all ingredients in bowl; mix well. Chill thoroughly. Serve as a dip with assorted cold vegetables.

SAUSAGE PINWHEELS

Preparation: 20 minutes

Baking: 20-25 minutes
Yield: 2 dozen

1 (8-ounce) can refrigerated
  crescent rolls

1 pound mild or hot bulk
  sausage

Separate crescent roll dough into 4 rectangles. Brown and drain sausage. Divide the sausage into four equal parts; spread onto the dough rectangles. Roll up each rectangle jelly-roll style, short end to short end. Slice each roll into 6 equal parts. Place on cookie sheet; bake at 375 degrees for 20-25 minutes until golden brown. Serve immediately.

GROUND BEEF DIP

Preparation: 25 minutes   Servings: 24
Planning: Can prepare ahead

1 pound ground beef
½ cup finely chopped onion
1 (6-ounce) can tomato
    paste
½ teaspoon garlic salt

1 Tablespoon
    Worcestershire sauce
2 (8-ounce) packages cream
    cheese

Brown ground beef and onion; drain off fat. Add tomato paste, garlic salt, and Worcestershire sauce; mix thoroughly. Over medium heat, add cream cheese to meat mixture. Continue cooking until cheese is melted and completely blended with meat. Serve in chafing dish with corn chips or tortillas.

 ## CHILI RELLENO DIP

Preparation: 20 minutes   Chilling: 1 hour
Planning: Must prepare ahead   Servings: 10

1 (4-ounce) can chopped
    green chiles
2 large tomatoes, peeled
    and chopped
4 green onions, chopped
1 (3¼-ounce) can pitted ripe
    olives, chopped

3 Tablespoons olive oil
1½ teaspoons vinegar
⅛ teaspoon garlic powder or
    1 clove garlic, pressed
salt and pepper, to taste

Combine all ingredients in bowl; mix well. Refrigerate until cold. Serve with tortilla chips.

EGG ROLLS

Preparation: 45 minutes

Frying: 5-10 minutes
Servings: 12

½ cup finely chopped celery
¾ cup shredded cabbage
½ cup water
3 Tablespoons vegetable oil
½ cup uncooked shrimp, diced
½ cup uncooked pork, ham, beef, veal, or chicken, diced

4 scallions, finely chopped
1 clove garlic, minced
¼ cup soy sauce
12 egg roll skins
vegetable oil for frying

Parboil celery and cabbage in water; drain and set aside. Heat oil in skillet; add shrimp and pork or other meat. Stir fry for 3 minutes, stirring constantly. Add celery, cabbage, scallions, garlic, and soy sauce. Stir fry for 5 minutes, or until meat and shrimp are done. Place 2-3 Table-spoons filling mixture in center of each egg roll skin. Turn ends over edge of filling and roll up. Seal with flour paste. Fry in hot oil until browned.

 # GARLIC OLIVES

Preparation: 10 minutes
Planning: Must prepare ahead

Chilling: several days
Yield: 3 dozen

1 (5¾-ounce) can large pitted ripe olives, undrained
½ cup red wine vinegar
¼ cup vegetable oil
¼ teaspoon crushed red pepper

1 clove garlic, pressed
¼ cup finely chopped onion
1 teaspoon dried whole oregano

Pour olives and their liquid into 1-quart jar; add all other ingred-ients. Cover tightly; shake well. Refrigerate several days, shaking occasionally. Olives will keep indefinitely in the refrigerator.

DELICIOUS LIVER PÂTÈ

Preparation: 30 minutes   Chilling: 2 hours
Planning: Must prepare ahead   Servings: 10

1 medium onion, chopped
1 Tablespoon corn oil
1 pound chicken livers
1 pound hot bulk sausage
½ teaspoon salt
1 teaspoon ground oregano
1 teaspoon ground thyme
⅛ teaspoon cayenne pepper

⅛ teaspoon ground nutmeg
3 Tablespoons chopped
    fresh parsley
1 egg
1 hard-cooked egg yolk,
    sieved
minced parsley for garnish

Sauté onion in oil until tender. Add chicken livers; cook until light in color. Mix in sausage; cook 15 minutes. Add dry seasonings, parsley, and egg. Remove from heat. Grind in food processor for 2 minutes. Pack mixture into two loaf pans. Refrigerate until firm. Remove from pans; garnish with egg yolk and minced parsley. Serve with crackers.

MUSHROOM SQUARES

Preparation: 30 minutes   Baking: 30 minutes
                                                          Servings: 10

2 cups biscuit mix
½ cup cold water
¼ pound bulk sausage,
    browned and drained
¼ cup chopped green onion
    and tops

¾ cup mayonnaise
1 pound fresh mushrooms
2 cups grated Cheddar
    cheese
paprika for garnish

Mix biscuit mix and water with fork; beat 20 times. Press into greased 13x9x2 pan. Combine sausage, onion, and mayonnaise. Wash mushrooms; remove and discard stems. Fill caps with sausage mixture. Place filled caps in rows on dough; sprinkle with cheese and paprika. Cover pan loosely with foil. Bake at 350 degrees for 20 minutes. Remove foil and bake 5-10 minutes longer, or until cheese bubbles. Let stand 15 minutes; cut into squares.

HIDDEN TREASURE

Preparation: 30 minutes   Servings: 12

**1 pound boiled shrimp,
    peeled and deveined**
1 pint cherry tomatoes
**1 (5¾-ounce) can pitted ripe
    olives, drained**
**1 (8-ounce) can whole water
    chestnuts, drained**
**1 (6-ounce) can whole
    mushrooms, drained**
**½ head cauliflower, broken
    into bite-size pieces**

2 teaspoons dry mustard
2 cups mayonnaise
**½ cup horseradish, drained
    well**
**½ teaspoon monosodium
    glutamate**
2 teaspoons lemon juice
½ teaspoon salt

Toss shrimp and vegetables in large bowl. Mix remaining ingredients thoroughly. Pour sauce over shrimp mixture; toss again. Serve with toothpicks.

SAUSAGE PARTY PIZZAS

Preparation: 30 minutes   Baking: 10 minutes
Planning: Can prepare ahead   Yield: 20

1 pound ground beef
**1 pound bulk sausage, mild
    or hot**
1 pound processed cheese
**1 Tablespoon
    Worcestershire sauce**

1 teaspoon ground oregano
1 Tablespoon onion flakes
1 loaf party rye bread

Brown ground beef and sausage; drain well. Stir in cheese, cooking over low heat until melted. Add Worcestershire sauce, oregano, and onion flakes. Spread on rye bread. These may be frozen in plastic bags before baking. When ready to serve, bake at 350 degrees for 10 minutes.

 ## *REBECCA SAUCE*

Preparation: 5 minutes
Planning: Must prepare ahead

Chilling: 2 hours
Yield: 1½ cups

1½ cups sour cream
¼ cup light brown sugar,
  packed

2 Tablespoons Grand
  Marnier
¼ cup chopped raisins

Combine all ingredients in bowl; mix well. Chill. Serve as a dip with a variety of fresh fruits (grapes, strawberries, cantaloupe, pineapple), or as a dressing for fruit salad.

SALMON MOUSSE

An elegant spread from Affairs to
Remember Caterers, Inc. in Atlanta

Preparation: 30 minutes
Planning: Must prepare ahead

Chilling: 2 hours
Servings: 10

½ cup mayonnaise
1 Tablespoon lemon juice
1 Tablespoon grated onion
½ teaspoon Tabasco sauce
¼ teaspoon paprika
1 teaspoon salt

2 cups finely chopped
  salmon
½ cup heavy cream
1 cup cottage cheese
Dill Sauce

Combine mayonnaise, lemon juice, onion, Tabasco, paprika, and salt in a bowl. Add salmon; mix well. Whip cream; fold in salmon mixture. Add cottage cheese; mix thoroughly. Turn into glass serving bowl. Chill completely, about 2 hours. Serve mousse with Dill Sauce.

Dill Sauce:
1 egg
1 teaspoon salt
⅛ teaspoon freshly ground
  pepper
⅛ teaspoon sugar

4 teaspoons lemon juice
1 teaspoon grated onion
2 Tablespoons finely cut
  fresh dill weed
1½ cups sour cream

Beat egg until fluffy and lemon colored. Add remaining ingredients, blending sour cream in last. Chill. Makes about 2 cups.

SALMON ROLLS

Preparation: 10 minutes   Servings: 18

1 (3-ounce) package cream   **1 (3½-ounce) jar black**
   cheese, softened   **lumpfish caviar**
1 teaspoon grated onion   **romaine lettuce leaves**
⅛ teaspoon Tabasco sauce
¼ pound thinly sliced
   smoked salmon

Mix cream cheese, onion, and Tabasco sauce until blended and smooth. With small spatula or knife, spread each slice of salmon with cream cheese mixture. Roll up each slice of salmon jelly-roll style. Cut crosswise into 1-inch pieces. Top each salmon roll with caviar. Arrange salmon rolls on romaine lettuce leaves before serving.

OYSTER LOG

Preparation: 10 minutes   Chilling: 2 hours
Planning: Must prepare ahead   Servings: 12

1 Tablespoon   **1 (3¾-ounce) can smoked**
   Worcestershire sauce   **oysters, drained well**
1 (8-ounce) package cream
   cheese, softened

Add Worcestershire sauce to cream cheese; blend thoroughly. Shape cream cheese into a ball, then roll out flat. Chop oysters. Arrange oysters down center of cream cheese. Fold sides over oysters and pat into a log shape. Chill for at least 2 hours. To serve, slice and serve with crackers.

 # ELEGANT AND EASY BRIE

Preparation: 10 minutes   Chilling: 2 hours
Planning: Must prepare ahead   Servings: 8

1 triangle or circle good   **walnuts or pecans, chopped**
   quality Brie cheese   **and toasted**
apricot preserves

Cut Brie in half horizontally. Spread a generous layer of apricot preserves on one half. Sprinkle generously with toasted nuts. Place other half of Brie on top. Cover and refrigerate until chilled, about 2 hours. Serve with crackers.

PICKLED SHRIMP

Preparation: 1 hour   Chilling: 24 hours
Planning: Must prepare ahead   Servings: 10

2½ pounds raw shrimp   2 teaspoons salt
3½ teaspoons salt   2 Tablespoons capers with
½ cup celery tops   juice
¼ cup pickling spice   2 drops Tabasco sauce
1¼ cups vegetable oil   2 cups sliced onions
¾ cup white vinegar   8 bay leaves

Put shrimp in pot; cover with boiling water. Add salt, celery tops, and pickling spice; boil 5 minutes. Cool. Peel and devein shrimp. Combine oil, vinegar, salt, capers, and Tabasco sauce; set aside. Alternate layers of shrimp and onion in shallow dish; top with bay leaves. Pour oil mixture over shrimp. Refrigerate, covered, at least 24 hours before serving.

SHRIMP MOUSSE

Preparation: 45 minutes   Chilling: 3 hours
Planning: Must prepare ahead   Servings: 16

1 (10¾-ounce) can tomato   1 cup water
  soup, undiluted   ½ cup chopped onion
1 (8-ounce) package cream   1 cup chopped celery
  cheese   2 (6-ounce) cans shrimp
1 cup mayonnaise   fresh parsley sprigs for
1 envelope unflavored   garnish
  gelatin

Heat tomato soup to boiling. Add cream cheese; blend until smooth. Add mayonnaise; blend well. Cool. Add gelatin to water. Add to tomato soup mixture; add onion and celery. Drain, wash, and dry canned shrimp. Add to soup mixture. Pour into greased 5-cup mold. Refrigerate until set. Garnish with parsley and serve with crackers.

FAR EAST SHRIMP BALLS
Serve as an appetizer with a Chinese dinner

Preparation: 1 hour

Frying: 20 minutes
Yield: 2 dozen

1 pound raw shrimp. peeled and deveined
2 Tablespoons bacon drippings
1 slice fresh white bread
1 egg, separated

1 teaspoon salt
2 Tablespoons water
4 water chestnuts, chopped
¼ teaspoon ground ginger
3 cups peanut oil

Preheat oven to 300 degrees. In food processor, process shrimp and drippings into a paste. Break bread into pieces and soak in a small amount of water. Add bread to shrimp paste; mix well. Add egg yolk, salt, water, water chestnuts, and ginger; process. Beat egg whites until foamy; stir into mixture. Heat oil in wok or skillet. Form part of shrimp mixture into balls with 2 wet spoons to prevent mixture from sticking; drop into hot oil. Fry 3-4 minutes, turning gently. Drain on paper towels; keep warm in oven while preparing remaining balls. Dip spoons in water before making new balls.

SHRIMP PIZZA

Preparation: 20 minutes
Planning: Can prepare ahead

Servings: 10

12 ounces cream cheese, softened
2 Tablespoons Worcestershire sauce
1 teaspoon lemon juice
2 Tablespoons mayonnaise
1 small onion, grated

⅛ teaspoon garlic salt
1 cup chili sauce
½ pound shrimp, boiled, peeled, and deveined
chopped fresh parsley for garnish

Beat together cream cheese, Worcestershire sauce, lemon juice, mayonnaise, onion, and garlic salt. Spread into flat dish, approximately 12 inches in diameter. Spread chili sauce evenly over first layer, allowing a crust effect around the edges. Distribute shrimp evenly over chili sauce. Sprinkle with fresh parsley. Arrange crackers around edge to use for dipping or spreading.

TARAMA SALATA
A specialty at Marra's Seafood Grill in Atlanta

Preparation: 20 minutes   Servings: 12

5 slices white bread, crusts removed
1 large onion, peeled and coarsely chopped
1¼ cups Tarama paste (available at gourmet food shops)
4 cups vegetable oil, divided

½ teaspoon chopped garlic
1½ Tablespoons dried parsley
1 teaspoon dried whole oregano
½ teaspoon ground cumin
¼ cup lemon juice

Soak bread in water; squeeze out all water. Combine bread, onion, Tarama paste, and 1 cup oil in food processor; blend until creamy. Add garlic, parsley, oregano, and cumin; blend thoroughly. With food processor running, add 3 cups oil and lemon juice. If dip needs to be thickened, add more oil or bread. If dip needs to be thinned, add cold water. Serve as a spread with sliced fennel bread.

MARINATED VEGETABLES

Preparation: 30 minutes   Marinating: 12 hours
Planning: Must prepare ahead   Servings: 30

3 (10¾-ounce) cans tomato soup, undiluted
1½ cups vegetable oil
1½ cups sugar
2¼ cups apple cider vinegar
3 teaspoons prepared mustard
3 teaspoons Worcestershire sauce
3 teaspoons salt
3 teaspoons pepper

2 (1-pound) cans fingerling carrots, drained
1 pound fresh mushrooms, sliced
1 head cauliflower, separated into flowerets
1 green pepper, cut into rings
1 onion, sliced and separated into rings

Combine soup, oil, sugar, vinegar, mustard, Worcestershire sauce, salt, and pepper; mix thoroughly. Add vegetables to marinade; refrigerate 12 hours or overnight. Drain well before serving. Serve with toothpicks.

31

AMARETTO FREEZE

Preparation: 10 minutes
Planning: Can prepare ahead

Chilling: 1 hour
Servings: 4-6

**1 quart good-quality vanilla
ice cream**
⅓ cup amaretto

⅛ cup Grand Marnier
¼ cup crème de cacao
heavy cream, optional

Position blade in food processor; with machine running, drop ice cream in spoonfuls through feeder tube. Add liqueurs. If too thick or too strong, blend in heavy cream, to taste. Chill or freeze. Serve in liquid or soft frozen form.

 # HOT BUTTERED RUM MIX

*This gift and a bottle of rum make a nice hostess gift when
you have been invited for a winter weekend getaway*

Preparation: 15 minutes
Planning: Must prepare ahead

Yield: 1½ quarts

1 pound butter, softened
1 pound light brown sugar
**1 quart vanilla ice cream,
softened**
2 teaspoons ground nutmeg

**2 teaspoons ground
cinnamon**
**1 pound powdered sugar,
optional**

Beat butter in bowl until creamy. Gradually beat in brown sugar until smooth. Add ice cream, nutmeg, and cinnamon. If a sweeter mix is desired, add powdered sugar. Store in freezer. To serve, mix 1 heaping tablespoon of mix with 1 jigger rum in a mug. Add boiling water. Garnish with nutmeg or cinnamon sticks.

Note: When using as a gift, attach card with serving instructions.

SPICED BOURBON-APPLE PUNCH

Delicious on a cold winter night

Preparation: 20 minutes

Servings: 6

3 cups apple juice
1 Tablespoon raisins
6 sticks cinnamon

6 lemon slices
1 cup bourbon

In saucepan, combine apple juice, raisins, cinnamon, and lemon slices; bring to a boil. Remove cinnamon sticks. Add bourbon; stir gently. Keep warm in crock pot or on stove. Serve warm.

DORIS' BANANA PUNCH
A must punch for your next shower or tea!

Preparation: 30 minutes
Planning: Must prepare ahead

Freezing: 12 hours
Servings: 20

4 cups sugar
1 (12-ounce) can frozen orange juice concentrate
1 (46-ounce) can pineapple juice

5 bananas
½ cup frozen lemon juice
3 (1-liter) bottles ginger ale

Bring 6 cups water and sugar to a boil in saucepan. Boil 5 minutes; cool completely. Add frozen orange juice, 4½ cups water, and pineapple juice to sugar mixture. Purée bananas in blender. Add lemon juice. Add to juice mixture. Pour into 3 large plastic zip-lock bags (easier if plastic bag is put in loaf pan before pouring). Freeze at least 12 hours or up to 3 weeks. Thaw 4-6 hours before serving. Add 1 liter ginger ale to each bag of punch. Pour into punch bowl to serve. A frozen ice ring can be used.

 ## DECAFFINATED SPICED TEA MIX
Makes a terrific holiday gift or hostess gift!

Preparation: 5 minutes
Planning: Can prepare ahead

Yield: 1 quart dry mix

1 (1-pound 2-ounce) jar orange breakfast drink
¾ cup instant decaffinated tea
1 cup sugar

1 large envelope sweetened lemonade mix
1½ teaspoons ground cloves
2 teaspoons ground cinnamon

Mix orange drink mix, tea, sugar, lemonade mix, cloves, and cinnamon in bowl. Store in glass jar. To serve, place 2 heaping teaspoons of mix in mug filled with boiling water.

Note: When using as a gift, attach card with serving instructions.

MICROWAVE CAPPUCCINO

Preparation: 5 minutes

Microwaving: 4 minutes
Servings: 2

**2½ teaspoons light brown
  sugar, firmly packed**
**2 teaspoons instant coffee
  crystals**

1⅓ cups water
¼ cup Grand Marnier
**sweetened whipped cream,
  for garnish**

In 2-cup container or measuring cup, combine sugar, coffee, and water. Cover. Microwave at HIGH (100% power) 2-4 minutes until hot. Stir in liqueur. Pour into mugs. Top with whipped cream sweetened with powdered sugar.

PINEAPPLE-CHAMPAGNE PUNCH

Preparation: 15 minutes
Planning: Must partially prepare ahead

Chilling: 6 hours
Servings: 25

½ pound sugar
1 cup water
1 quart strong tea
1 fifth Jamaican rum
1 fifth bourbon
1 fifth cognac

1 pint Grand Marnier
⅛ teaspoon orange bitters
**1 (20-ounce) can pineapple
  chunks, undrained**
2 fifths champagne

Make sugar syrup by dissolving sugar in water. Have remaining ingredients chilled or chill thoroughly after combining. Mix together tea, liquors, bitters, undrained pineapple, and sugar syrup. Pour into chilled punch bowl. Just before serving, add champagne. Serve in wine glasses or goblets.

FRENCH HOT CHOCOLATE
Lovely for winter company any time of day

Preparation: 15 minutes
Planning: Can partially prepare ahead

Cooking: 10 minutes
Servings: 8

**4 ounces semi-sweet
  chocolate**
¼ cup light corn syrup

½ teaspoon vanilla extract
1 cup heavy cream
8 cups milk

In double boiler, melt chocolate with corn syrup; cool. Stir in vanilla. Add cream and beat until soft peaks form. Chocolate mixture can be refrigerated at this point. To serve, heat milk slowly in saucepan until soft bubbles form around edge. Spoon whipped chocolate mixture into 8 coffee cups; fill each with hot milk. Serve with a spoon.

 ## HOT MOCHA MIX

Preparation: 10 minutes   Yield: 9 cups
Planning: Must prepare ahead

1 cup unsweetened cocoa
2½ cups sugar
2 cups dry non-dairy coffee creamer
2 cups nonfat dry milk powder

½ cup powdered instant coffee
1 vanilla bean, cut into quarters
2 cups miniature marshmallows

Combine ingredients in large, dry bowl; stir until well blended. Pack into 4 jars, making sure a piece of vanilla bean is in each jar. Seal and label. Store in refrigerator at least a week before using to allow vanilla flavor to be absorbed into the mix. To serve, use ⅓ cup mix to 1 cup boiling water.

Note: When using as a gift, attach card with serving instructions.

 ## CHAMPAGNE PUNCH
This recipe can easily be doubled again and again

Preparation: 10 minutes   Servings: 25
Planning: Can partially prepare ahead

4 (12-ounce) cans frozen lemonade concentrate, thawed
4 (750-ML) bottles champagne, chilled

1½ cups cognac
1 (1-liter) bottle club soda
fresh fruit for garnish

Mix lemonade, champagne, and cognac. Add more cognac for an extra punch. Add club soda just before serving. Garnish with an ice ring or fresh fruit, if desired.

GINGER'S EGG NOG
A must for the holidays!

Preparation: 30 minutes   Servings: 18

6 eggs, separated
2 cups sugar, divided
1 teaspoon vanilla extract
1 pint heavy cream
⅔ cup bourbon or rum

⅓ cup Grand Marnier,
 optional
¼ cup amaretto, optional
½ gallon milk
ground nutmeg for garnish

Beat egg whites with ¼ cup sugar and vanilla; set aside. Whip cream, adding ½ cup sugar; set aside. In large bowl, beat egg yolks with 1¼ cups sugar and bourbon or rum. Add Grand Marnier and amaretto, if desired. Slowly add milk, mixing thoroughly. Fold in egg whites. Fold in whipping cream. Garnish each serving with nutmeg.

KAHLUA VELVET FROSTY
Creamy, cold, and refreshing for any occasion

Preparation: 10 minutes   Servings: 6

1 cup Kahlua
1 pint vanilla ice cream

1 cup half and half
⅛ teaspoon almond extract

Combine Kahlua, ice cream, half and half, and extract in blender. Add enough ice cubes to bring mixture to 6-cup level. Blend until smooth.

 # WHITE SANGRIA

Preparation: 10 minutes   Servings: 4

1 orange, thinly sliced
1 lemon, thinly sliced
1 lime, thinly sliced
½ cup Grand Marnier

¼ cup sugar
1 fifth dry white wine
1 (7-ounce) bottle club soda

Mix all ingredients except soda in large pitcher. Before serving, add club soda. Do not add ice.

SNEAKY PETES

Preparation: 20 minutes   Freezing: 12 hours
Planning: Must prepare ahead   Yield: 1½ gallons

2 (1-liter) bottles ginger ale   **2 cups cranberry juice**
2 (12-ounce) cans frozen   **1 cup powdered sugar**
    lemonade concentrate,   **1 fifth gin or vodka**
    thawed   **fresh fruit for garnish**
2 (12-ounce) cans frozen
    orange juice concentrate,
    thawed

Mix all ingredients in large bowl. Transfer thoroughly mixed liquid to containers which have lids and can be placed in freezer. Freeze overnight. To serve, spoon out small amounts of mixture or thaw large container for 20-30 minutes until mixture is somewhat slushy but not completely thawed. Garnish individual servings with fresh fruit.

PERCULATOR HOT FRUIT TEA
This makes the house smell wonderful during a party

Preparation: 15 minutes   Yield: 1 gallon

1 (46-ounce) can pineapple   **½ cup light brown sugar**
    juice   **5 sticks cinnamon**
2 quarts cranberry juice   **3 whole nutmegs**
2 cups apple juice   **2 teaspoons ground ginger**
1 cup orange juice
1 (6-ounce) can frozen
    lemonade concentrate

Pour pineapple juice, cranberry juice, apple juice, orange juice, and lemonade into perculator. Add brown sugar to liquid. Place cinnamon, nutmegs, and ginger in perculator basket. Perk.

 ## ORANGE-ANISE SPICE BAGS

Preparation: 5 minutes   Yield: 1 bag
Planning: Can prepare ahead

½ teaspoon dried orange   **2 whole allspices**
   peel   **cheesecloth**
¼ teaspoon anise seed

Tie all ingredients in center of a double-thickness, 5-inch square piece of cheesecloth.

Note: Give bags as gifts with directions to steep in a 6-ounce cup of hot apple juice.

 ## SPICED ICED TEA

Preparation: 10 minutes   Servings: 16

3 quarts tea   **1 quart ginger ale**
½ cup sugar
1 (12-ounce) can frozen
   lemonade concentrate,
   thawed

Mix together tea, sugar, and lemonade; chill. Add ginger ale just before serving.

TEQUILA-CHAMPAGNE PUNCH
Excellent for brunch!

Preparation: 15 minutes   Chilling: 6 hours
Planning: Must partially prepare ahead   Servings: 64

2 quarts white wine   **2 fifths champagne**
46 ounces pineapple juice   **strawberry halves for garnish**
1 fifth tequila   **oranges slices for garnish**
2 quarts club soda

Chill all ingredients. Mix wine, juice, and tequila in large container. Add soda and champagne just before serving. Float strawberry halves and orange slices in punch for garnish, or freeze fruit in water in ring mold.

LONG ISLAND ICED TEA

Preparation: 5 minutes   Servings: 1

½ ounce rum
½ ounce vodka
½ ounce gin
½ ounce tequila

½ ounce Triple Sec
4 ounces sweet and sour
  mix
cola

Mix liquors with sweet and sour mix. Top with a splash of cola.

SHERRY SOUR

Preparation: 5 minutes   Chilling: 8 hours
Planning: Must prepare ahead   Servings: 6

1 fifth sherry
1 (6-ounce) can frozen
  lemonade concentrate,
  thawed

2 Tablespoons lemon juice
cherries for garnish

Combine sherry, lemonade, and lemon juice; mix well. Refrigerate 8 hours or up to 4 days. Serve in chilled glasses and garnish with a cherry. Add ice, if desired.

HOT FLORIDA TEA

Preparation: 15 minutes   Cooking: 10 minutes
                                                          Servings: 8

1 cup pink grapefruit juice
2½ cups apricot nectar
1 cup water
2 Tablespoons sugar
2 sticks cinnamon, 2 inches
  long

4 lemon slices, ½ inch thick
12 whole cloves
2 teaspoons instant tea

In large saucepan, combine grapefruit juice, apricot nectar, water, sugar, and cinnamon sticks. Stud lemon slices with cloves; add to saucepan. Bring to a boil. Simmer, covered, 10 minutes. Stir in tea. Serve piping hot.

HOT SPICED WINE

Preparation: 20 minutes   Yield: 5 quarts

2 red apples, quartered	**½ cup sugar**
2 Tablespoons cardamon seeds	**1 (6-ounce) can frozen orange juice concentrate, thawed**
4 sticks cinnamon	
2 Tablespoons whole allspice	**1 teaspoon ground nutmeg**
1 gallon port	**1 teaspoon ground cinnamon**
1 fifth bourbon	**cheesecloth**

Tie apples, cardamon, cinnamon, and allspice in a cheesecloth bag. Place wine, bourbon, sugar, and orange juice concentrate in large pan. Stir in nutmeg and cinnamon. Add cheesecloth bag. Heat, being careful not to boil.

IT'S ALMOST BAILEY'S

Preparation: 15 minutes   Chilling: 8 hours
Planning: Must prepare ahead   Servings: 6

1 cup Irish whiskey	**2 Tablespoons chocolate extract**
1 (14-ounce) can sweetened condensed milk	**1 Tablespoon coconut extract**
4 eggs	
2 Tablespoons vanilla extract	**1½ Tablespoons powdered instant coffee or expresso**

In blender, mix all ingredients at low speed until thoroughly blended. Transfer to a bottle with tight cover or good cork. Refrigerate 8 hours, or until ready to serve. Shake well; serve very cold, or over ice.

Soups

Camellia

SOUP

Bouquet Garni 52
COLD
  Cheese Chowder 57
  Chilled Creamy Avocado Soup 60
  Cold Cucumber Soup 54
  Creamy Cucumber-Spinach Soup 55
  Gazpacho Verde 43
  Roasted Pepper and Tomato Soup 58
Homemade Croutons 50
HOT
  Artichoke Soup 51
  Broccoli-Cheese Soup Supreme 44
  Broccoli Chowder 45
  Cheese Chowder 57
  Cheesy Chicken Noodle Soup 47
  Cheesy Microwave Potato Soup 54

Chicken Gumbo 48
Chicken Waterzooi 49
Chunky Corn Chowder 48
Enchilada Soup 50
French Garden Soup 55
Hearty Sausage-Bean Soup 43
Iowa Corn Chowder 47
Minestrone Alphabet Soup with Pesto . . 53
Seafood Soup 56
Sopa De Pollo Y Maíz 46
Split Pea Soup with Smoked Ham 52
Sweet and Sour Soup 44
Trotter's Seafood Soup 56
Turnip Green and Cream Soup 58
Vegetable Medley Soup 59

HEARTY SAUSAGE-BEAN SOUP

Preparation: 30 minutes   Cooking: 1 hour 20 minutes
Planning: Can partially prepare ahead   Servings: 4-5

½ **pound bulk pork sausage**	¾ **teaspoon seasoned salt**
1 medium onion, chopped	¼ **teaspoon garlic salt**
1 (15½-ounce) can kidney beans, undrained	¼ **teaspoon dried whole thyme**
1 (14½-ounce) can tomatoes, coarsely chopped, undrained	¼ **teaspoon black pepper**
	½ **cup chopped green pepper**
1 pint water	**1 medium potato, peeled and diced (1 cup)**
1 bay leaf	

Brown sausage and onion in medium skillet, stirring to crumble meat; drain off excess fat. Pour into large saucepan; stir in kidney beans, tomatoes, water, bay leaf, seasoned salt, garlic salt, thyme, and black pepper. Simmer, covered, 1 hour, stirring occasionally. Soup may be prepared to this point in advance. Add green pepper and potatoes to soup. Simmer, covered, for 20 minutes, or until potatoes are tender. Remove bay leaf before serving.

 ## GAZPACHO VERDE
Simply splendid

Preparation: 15 minutes   Chilling: 12 hours
Planning: Must prepare ahead   Servings: 4-6

1 (10¾-ounce) can cream of celery soup	**2 Tablespoons chopped green pepper**
1⅓ cups water	½ **teaspoon celery salt**
½ **cup sour cream**	**fresh parsley sprigs for garnish**
¼ **cup peeled chopped cucumber**	
2 Tablespoons chopped green onion	

Whisk together soup, water, and sour cream. Add cucumber, green onion, green pepper, and celery salt. Chill 12 hours or up to 2 days. To serve, spoon into chilled bowls and garnish with sprigs of parsley.

BROCCOLI-CHEESE SOUP SUPREME

Preparation: 30 minutes
Planning: Can partially prepare ahead

Cooking: 15 minutes
Servings: 6-8

2½ pounds fresh broccoli
4 cups chicken stock
1 cup chopped onion
4 Tablespoons butter
4 Tablespoons all-purpose flour

1 cup half and half
1 cup grated American or Swiss cheese
⅛ teaspoon ground nutmeg
¼ teaspoon white pepper
½ teaspoon salt

Wash and trim broccoli. Combine with 2 cups chicken stock; cover and cook 7 minutes, or until broccoli is tender crisp. Remove broccoli from stock; cool. Reserve stock. Cut enough 1-inch flowerets from broccoli to measure 2 cups; set aside until serving. Coarsely chop remaining broccoli. In Dutch oven, sauté onion in butter until tender. Blend in flour; cook 1 minute. Gradually add reserved stock and remaining 2 cups stock. Simmer 5 minutes, stirring occasionally. Remove from heat; add chopped broccoli, not flowerets. In blender or food processor, purée broccoli-stock mixture until smooth. Return mixture to Dutch oven. Soup can be prepared in advance to this point, then reheated before continuing. Add half and half, and cheese to puréed broccoli-stock mixture. Cook over low heat until cheese melts, about 10 minutes. Do not boil. Stir in nutmeg, pepper, and salt. Add reserved broccoli flowerets; continue simmering until thoroughly heated.

SWEET AND SOUR SOUP
An unusually good combination of flavors

Preparation: 30 minutes
Planning: Can prepare ahead

Cooking 1 hour 30 minutes
Yield: 10 cups

1 medium head cabbage, coarsely chopped
4 medium onions, sliced
2 Tablespoons salt
1 (15-ounce) can tomato sauce
3 (14½-ounce) cans tomatoes, chopped

4 short ribs of beef or meaty soup bone
juice of 1 lemon
⅛ to ¼ cup sugar
salt and pepper, to taste

Combine cabbage, onion, and salt in large soup pot; steam, covered, over low heat, until cabbage and onion are tender, approximately 10 minutes; stirring occasionally. Stir in tomato sauce and tomatoes. Add ribs; heat soup to boiling. Add lemon juice, sugar, salt, and pepper. Simmer, covered, 1 hour, or until meat is tender. Remove ribs from pot; cut meat from bones; discard bones, fat, and gristle. Return meat to soup; continue cooking 30 minutes more, adding water to thin soup to desired consistency. Ladle into individual bowls to serve. Soup can be frozen.

BROCCOLI CHOWDER

Preparation: 20 minutes   Cooking: 10 minutes
Planning: Can prepare ahead   Servings: 5-6

3-6 slices bacon
¼ cup chopped onion
1 cup thinly sliced carrots
½ cup chopped celery
1 cup chicken broth, fresh or canned
3 Tablespoons all-purpose flour

4 cups milk
1½ cups cooked, coarsely chopped broccoli, fresh or frozen
1 teaspoon salt
⅛ teaspoon pepper
paprika for garnish

Fry bacon in small skillet until crisp; remove bacon, reserving 2 Tablespoons drippings in skillet. Crumble bacon and set aside. Sauté onion in reserved drippings until tender; remove onion from skillet. Combine onion, carrots, celery, and chicken broth in large saucepan. Cook 10 minutes over medium heat. Combine flour with small amount of milk; mix well. Stir flour mixture into broth mixture. Add remaining milk, broccoli, salt, and pepper. Cook over medium heat, stirring constantly, until mixture thickens and is hot, about 10 minutes. Stir in crumbled bacon; garnish each serving with paprika. Soup can be prepared ahead, then reheated to serve. Do not boil when reheating.

SOPA DE POLLO Y MAÍZ

Preparation: 20 minutes

Cooking: 15 minutes

Servings: 4

1 pound boneless chicken breasts, cubed
3 Tablespoons vegetable oil
1 (17-ounce) can cream-style corn
2 jalapeño peppers, seeded and chopped
1 clove garlic, minced
1 cup chicken broth
4 Tablespoons butter
¼ teaspoon salt

¼ teaspoon cayenne pepper
½ teaspoon ground oregano
2 Tablespoons fresh chopped parsley
1 cup cubed Monterey Jack cheese
2 cups half and half
2 tomatoes, peeled, seeded, and diced
2 cups coarsely crumbled tortilla chips

Stir-fry chicken in hot oil until lightly browned and tender. In blender, combine corn, jalapeño peppers, garlic, and broth. Melt butter in large saucepan. Add corn mixture, salt, cayenne pepper, oregano, parsley, and cheese. Cook over low heat for 8-10 minutes, stirring often, until cheese melts. Add half and half and chicken; heat through. Do not boil. To serve, spoon soup into individual bowls and top with tomatoes and crumbled tortilla chips.

 ## *CHEESY CHICKEN NOODLE SOUP*
A combination of simplicity and elegance

Preparation: 10 minutes   Cooking: 10 minutes
Planning: Can prepare ahead   Servings: 3-4

1 (10¾-ounce) can chicken noodle soup, undiluted
1 (10¾-ounce) can cream of onion soup, undiluted
1 cube chicken bouillon, dissolved in 1 cup boiling water
½ cup milk

1 cup grated sharp Cheddar cheese
1 Tablespoon dry sherry
¼ teaspoon ground nutmeg
½ cup frozen or canned English peas, drained
chopped fresh parsley for garnish

Combine soups and dissolved bouillon in saucepan; whisk to blend well. Add milk, cheese, sherry, nutmeg, and peas. Simmer, stirring frequently, until cheese is melted and soup is thoroughly heated, about 10 minutes. To serve, ladle into individual bowls and sprinkle with chopped parsley. Soup can be prepared in advance, then reheated to serve. Do not boil when reheating.

IOWA CORN CHOWDER

Preparation: 40 minutes   Cooking: 10 minutes
                                           Servings: 8

3 potatoes, pared and cubed
5 slices bacon
3 onions, thinly sliced
2 (16½-ounce) cans cream-style corn

2 to 2½ cups milk
2 teaspoons sugar
½ teaspoon salt
¼ teaspoon pepper
4 Tablespoons butter

Cook potatoes 20 minutes, or until done; drain well. Fry bacon in medium skillet until crisp; remove bacon, reserving 1½ Tablespoons drippings in skillet. Crumble bacon; set aside. Sauté onion in reserved drippings for 15 minutes. In large saucepan, combine onion, corn, milk, and sugar. Season with salt and pepper. Add potatoes and butter. Simmer until heated through, about 10 minutes. Sprinkle each serving with crumbled bacon.

CHICKEN GUMBO

Preparation: 20 minutes
Planning: Must prepare ahead

Cooking: 1 hour
Cooling: 5 hours
Servings: 4-6

1 cup chopped onion
1 cup chopped celery
½ cup chopped green bell
  pepper
¼ cup butter
3 Tablespoons all-purpose
  flour
6 cups chicken stock
3 cups chopped chicken

1½ cups sliced okra
¼ cup chopped fresh parsley
3 bay leaves
¼ teaspoon cayenne pepper
1 (14½-ounce) can tomatoes
½ teaspoon salt
¼ teaspoon pepper
hot cooked rice, optional

In large Dutch oven, sauté onion, celery, and green pepper until tender; blend in flour. Stir in chicken stock; simmer 5 minutes. Add chicken, okra, parsley, bay leaves, cayenne pepper, tomatoes, salt, and pepper. Simmer, covered, 1 hour, stirring frequently to prevent sticking. Let stand 5 hours, or refrigerate 1-2 days to further enhance the flavors. Reheat slowly over low heat. Gumbo may be served over hot cooked rice, if desired.

CHUNKY CORN CHOWDER

Preparation: 45 minutes
Planning: Can prepare ahead

Cooking: 22 minutes
Servings: 8-10

3 slices bacon, chopped
1 pound boneless chicken
  breasts, diced
1 medium onion, chopped
2 large stalks celery,
  chopped
4 cups chicken broth,
  divided
4 cups fresh or canned
  whole kernel corn, divided

1 large potato, peeled and
  diced
½ teaspoon salt
1 cup heavy cream
2 Tablespoons chopped
  fresh parsley
⅛ teaspoon white pepper
2 Tablespoons sherry,
  optional

In large Dutch oven, cook bacon until crisp; remove bacon, reserving 2 Tablespoons drippings in pot. Add chicken, onion, and celery to pot; cook 10-15 minutes, or until tender, stirring frequently. Meanwhile, combine 1 cup chicken broth with 2 cups corn; purée in blender. Add puréed corn, remaining 3 cups broth, remaining 2 cups corn, potatoes, and salt to chicken-vegetable mixture. Bring to a boil; reduce heat and simmer, partially covered, for 20 minutes, or until potatoes are tender. Stir in bacon, cream, parsley, white pepper, and sherry; simmer 2-3 minutes. Serve immediately, or refrigerate and reheat for later use.

CHICKEN WATERZOOI

Waterzooi, a national dish of Belgium, was originally made with fish, but is now also prepared with chicken; this version comes from Ghent.

Preparation: 45 minutes

Cooking: 1 hour 45 minutes
Yield: 6 quarts

4 Tablespoons butter
4 leeks, chopped
4 carrots, sliced
4 stalks celery, sliced
4 medium onions, chopped
1 (3½-pound) chicken
1 teaspoon salt
½ teaspoon pepper
8 medium potatoes, peeled
    and cut into large chunks

4 egg yolks
4 Tablespoons half and half
6 Tablespoons dry white
    wine
1 Tablespoon lemon juice
2 sprigs fresh chopped
    parsley

Melt butter in 6-quart pot. Add leeks, carrots, celery, and onion. Cover; cook gently for 5 minutes without browning. Add chicken; cover with cold water; season with salt and pepper. Bring to a boil; simmer 1 hour 20 minutes. Remove chicken from pot; skin and cut into pieces; set aside. Cook potatoes in boiling, salted water. Meanwhile, reduce chicken stock mixture over high heat for 20 minutes. Blend egg yolks, half and half, and wine. Slowly add to reduced stock; reheat without boiling to thicken. Add lemon juice and additional salt and pepper, if desired. Place chicken pieces and potatoes in serving dish. Pour sauce over dish; garnish with parsley.

ENCHILADA SOUP

Preparation: 5 minutes

Cooking: 1¼ hours
Servings: 4

12 (6-inch) corn tortillas, divided
1 small onion, chopped
1 clove garlic, minced
2 Tablespoons vegetable oil
1 (4-ounce) can chopped green chiles, undrained
1 (10¾-ounce) can beef broth, undiluted
1 (10¾-ounce) can chicken broth, undiluted
1 (10¾-ounce) can cream of chicken soup, undiluted

1 cup chopped, cooked chicken
1½ cups water
1 Tablespoon steak sauce
1 teaspoon Worcestershire sauce
1 teaspoon chili powder
⅛ teaspoon pepper
2½-3 cups grated Cheddar cheese
vegetable oil for frying
salt to taste

Cut 3 tortillas into wedges; set aside. Sauté onion and garlic in 2 Table-spoons oil in Dutch oven. Add chiles, beef broth, chicken broth, soup, chicken, water, steak sauce, Worcestershire sauce, chili powder, and pepper; bring to a boil. Cover and simmer for 1 hour. Add tortilla wedges and cheese; simmer, uncovered, 10 minutes. Cut remaining 9 tortillas into wedges; fry in hot oil until crisp. Drain on paper towels; sprinkle with salt. Serve hot with soup.

 ## HOMEMADE CROUTONS
Makes a plain tossed salad a treat!

Preparation: 10 minutes
Planning: Must prepare ahead

Baking: 1 hour
Yield: 2 cups

½ cup butter
1 Tablespoon grated Parmesan cheese
1 teaspoon garlic salt
½ teaspoon paprika

1 Tablespoon dried parsley
1 teaspoon dried whole oregano
2 cups dry bread cubes

Melt butter. Add cheese, garlic, paprika, parsley, and oregano. Pour over bread and toss lightly. Bake at 200 degrees for 1 hour, stirring every 15 minutes. Cool and seal in airtight containers.

Note: Save end pieces of bread, buns, etc. in refrigerator or freezer until there are enough to make croutons.

ARTICHOKE SOUP
An elegant first course for a special dinner

Preparation: 20 minutes   Cooking: 20 minutes
Planning: Can partially prepare ahead   Servings: 4-6

½ cup butter
1 cup chopped onion
½ cup green onion, chopped
2 cloves garlic, chopped
2 dozen oysters, undrained
¼ teaspoon ground thyme
1 bay leaf
1-2 teaspoons creole
** seasoning**

4 drops Tabasco sauce
2 (14-ounce) cans artichoke
** hearts, drained and**
** chopped**
1 (10½-ounce) can chicken
** broth**
1 (10½-ounce) can cream of
** mushroom soup,**
** undiluted**

Combine butter, onion, green onion, and garlic in 4-cup glass measuring cup. Microwave at HIGH (100% power) for 3-4 minutes, or until soft, but not browned. Drain oysters, reserving liquid. In 3-quart casserole dish, combine reserved oyster liquid, onion mixture, thyme, bay leaf, creole seasoning, Tabasco sauce, artichoke hearts, chicken broth, and soup. Soup can be prepared to this point, and cooking completed when ready to serve. Cover with plastic wrap. Microwave at MEDIUM-HIGH (70% power) for 10-12 minutes, or until almost boiling. Stir in oysters and cover with plastic wrap. Microwave at MEDIUM-HIGH (70% power) for 8-10 minutes, or until hot and edges of oysters have curled. Let stand 10 minutes before serving.

BOUQUET GARNI
Adds a special flavor to soups

Preparation: 10 minutes
Planning: Can prepare ahead

Yield: approximately 6 bags

3 Tablespoons dried parsley
3 Tablespoons dried whole
  marjoram
½ bay leaf
1 Tablespoon dried whole
  basil

3 Tablespoons dried whole
  thyme
1 Tablespoon savory
1 teaspoon dried whole
  rosemary
cheesecloth

Crumble all herbs; mix together. Cut cheesecloth into 4-inch squares. Place several tablespoons of herb mix on each square and tie into bags with string. Store in airtight container.

Note: Give several as gifts with a favorite stew or soup recipe, including the directions to add herb packet the last 30 minutes of cooking time.

SPLIT PEA SOUP WITH SMOKED HAM
Velvety smooth, but with the added texture and taste of smoked ham

Preparation: 30 minutes
Planning: Can prepare ahead

Cooking: 2¾ hours
Yield: 3 pints

1 pound split peas
2 smoked ham hocks
3 slices smoked bacon
3 leeks, chopped, white part
  only
1 medium onion, chopped
1 carrot, diced
2 stalks celery, including
  some of leafy tops,
  chopped

1 clove garlic, minced
¼ teaspoon ground thyme
½ teaspoon ground
  marjoram
1 cup dry white wine
8 cups water
salt and white pepper, to
  taste

Rinse peas in water; pick over. In large soup pot, combine peas with all ingredients except salt and pepper. Bring to boil; reduce heat. Simmer, covered, 2½ hours, stirring occasionally. Remove ham hocks and bacon. Cut off meat; set aside. Discard bone, fat, and gristle. Strain soup into 2-quart saucepan. Add meat, season with salt and pepper, and simmer 10 minutes. Add a small amount of water to thin soup to desired consistency. Serve immediately, or soup can be frozen for later use.

MINESTRONE ALPHABET SOUP WITH PESTO
A homestyle and hearty crowd pleaser

Preparation: 45 minutes
Planning: Can partially prepare ahead

Cooking: 45 minutes
Servings: 10

4 slices bacon, diced
2 cups chopped onion
2 (10½-ounce) cans condensed beef broth, undiluted
5½ cups water
2 (14½-ounce) cans tomatoes, undrained
2 medium potatoes, pared and cubed
4 large carrots, pared and sliced

⅛ teaspoon garlic powder
1 teaspoon dried whole basil
1 bay leaf
¼ teaspoon pepper
½ cup uncooked alphabet pasta
2 medium zucchini, sliced
1 (15-ounce) can red kidney beans
Pesto Sauce (see Index)

In large skillet, cook bacon until lightly browned. Remove from skillet; set aside to drain. Add onion to skillet and sauté until tender, about 5 minutes. Transfer onion and bacon to large soup pot. Add beef broth, water, tomatoes and juice, potatoes, carrots, garlic, basil, bay leaf, and pepper. Bring to a boil; reduce heat and simmer, covered, for 30 minutes. Soup can be prepared in advance to this point and reheated to just simmering before continuing. Add alphabet pasta, zucchini, and kidney beans. Continue to simmer, covered, for 15 minutes. Remove bay leaf. Serve with Pesto Sauce.

CHEESY MICROWAVE POTATO SOUP

Preparation: 25 minutes   Cooking: 7½ to 9½ minutes
Planning: Can prepare ahead   Servings: 6

**2 cups finely chopped,
   peeled potatoes
1 cup chopped onion
1½ cups hot water
2 teaspoons instant chicken
   bouillon**

**1 (8-ounce) package
   processed American
   cheese, cubed
6 slices bacon, cooked and
   crumbled**

Combine potatoes, onion, ½ cup hot water, and bouillon in 2-quart microwave safe casserole dish. Cover; microwave at HIGH (100% power) for 3 minutes. Stir mixture; cover and microwave at HIGH (100% power) for 3-5 minutes longer until potatoes are tender. Pour potato mixture into blender. Add remaining 1 cup hot water and cheese. Cover and blend. Soup may be prepared ahead to this point, but cooking time which follows will need to be increased. Return soup mixture to casserole dish. Cover; microwave at HIGH (100% power) for 1½ minutes. To serve, ladle into individual bowls; sprinkle each serving with bacon.

Note: For a chunkier soup, coarsely chop potatoes.

 ## COLD CUCUMBER SOUP

Preparation: 10 minutes   Chilling: 4 hours
Planning: Must prepare ahead   Servings: 6

**3 peeled cucumbers
1 clove garlic
3 cups chicken broth
3 cups sour cream
3 teaspoons white vinegar**

**2 teaspoons salt
fresh dill weed for garnish
thin cucumber slices for
   garnish**

In blender or food processor, blend together cucumber, garlic, and chicken broth until smooth. Gradually add sour cream, vinegar, and salt. Chill. To serve, ladle soup into bowls; garnish each with a sprig of dill weed and a thin cucumber slice.

FRENCH GARDEN SOUP

Preparation: 20 minutes   Cooking: 45 minutes
                                                 Servings: 8

3 Tablespoons butter
1 bunch green onions
1 small onion, chopped
3 potatoes, pared and thinly
   sliced
1 carrot, thinly sliced
5½ teaspoons salt, divided
2 quarts water

¼ cup uncooked long-grain
   rice
½ pound fresh spinach,
   snipped, or 5 ounces
   frozen chopped spinach
⅛ teaspoon pepper
1 cup heavy cream

Melt butter in Dutch oven; sauté onions until tender. Add potatoes, carrot, 1½ teaspoons salt, and water; cover and bring to a boil. Reduce heat and simmer 15 minutes. Stir in rice; cover and simmer 25 minutes. Add spinach; cover and simmer 5 minutes. Stir in remaining 4 teaspoons salt, pepper, and cream. Serve hot.

CREAMY CUCUMBER-SPINACH SOUP
A chilled soup with a rich, hearty flavor

Preparation: 25 minutes   Cooking: 10 minutes
Planning: Must prepare ahead   Chilling: 6 hours
                                                 Servings: 8

½ cup chopped onion
2 Tablespoons unsalted
   butter
2 (14½-ounce) cans chicken
   broth
4 cups diced cucumbers
1 cup chopped fresh spinach

½ cup sliced, pared
   potatoes
1 Tablespoon lemon juice
½ teaspoon salt
¼ teaspoon white pepper
¼ teaspoon ground nutmeg
1 cup half and half

Sauté onion in butter until tender. Add chicken broth, cucumbers, spinach, potatoes, lemon juice, salt, pepper, and nutmeg. Simmer uncovered 8-10 minutes or until potatoes are tender. In small batches, purée soup mixture in blender or food processor until smooth. Stir in half and half. Chill several hours or overnight to blend flavors.

SEAFOOD SOUP

Preparation: 15 minutes   Cooking: 12 minutes
Planning: Can prepare ahead   Servings: 4

**2 Tablespoons unsalted
 butter**
¾ cup chopped onion
1 (16-ounce) can tomatoes
2 cups clam broth
**1 Tablespoon fresh lemon
 juice**
**½ teaspoon red pepper
 sauce**
**¼ teaspoon crushed dried
 thyme or ¾ teaspoon
 chopped fresh thyme**

**1 (7-ounce) can crabmeat,
 drained and flaked, or ½
 pound fresh crabmeat**
½ cup heavy cream
¼ cup dry sherry or marsala
**⅛ teaspoon monosodium
 glutamate**
salt and pepper to taste

In medium saucepan, melt butter; sauté onion until just tender. Add tomatoes, clam broth, lemon juice, pepper sauce, and thyme. Simmer for 10 minutes. Purée mixture in blender or food processor. Return to saucepan; add crabmeat, cream, monosodium glutamate, salt, and pepper. Heat thoroughly. Do not boil. Ladle into individual bowls to serve.

TROTTERS' SEAFOOD SOUP
Recipe provided by Trotters Restaurant in Atlanta

Preparation: 25 minutes   Cooking: 25 minutes
                                                  Servings: 4

**12 Tablespoons unsalted
 butter, softened**
4 large shrimp, peeled
12 sea scallops
6 mushrooms, thinly sliced
**2 Tablespoons finely
 chopped onion**
1 cup fish stock

1 cup dry white wine
2 cups heavy cream
2 teaspoons lemon juice
salt and pepper to taste
**12 mussels, steamed open
 in shells**
**2 teaspoons finely chopped
 fresh parsley**

In large skillet, melt 4 Tablespoons butter. Add shrimp and scallops; brown, stirring constantly. Do not overcook. Add wine and fish stock; bring to a boil. Reduce heat and allow to simmer approximately 3 minutes. Remove from heat and set aside. In saucepan, melt 4 Tablespoons butter. Add mushrooms and onion; sauté until onion is translucent. Remove shrimp and scallops from skillet and set aside. Add fish stock to mushroom-onion mixture; mix thoroughly. Stir in cream and lemon juice. Allow mixture to come to a boil over medium heat. Whip remaining butter into mixture. Season with salt and pepper to taste. Add steamed mussels, shrimp, and scallops; heat thoroughly. Serve soup garnished with chopped parsley.

CHEESE CHOWDER
A versatile soup to serve hot or cold

Preparation: 30 minutes
Planning: Can prepare ahead

Servings: 8

¾ cup unsalted butter, divided
6 Tablespoons all-purpose flour
3 cups milk, room temperature
1 cup half and half, room temperature
1 teaspoon salt
3 cups shredded Cheddar cheese

3 stalks celery, chopped
¼ cup chopped green onion
½ cup chopped carrots
2 cups chicken stock
⅛ teaspoon ground nutmeg
1 Tablespoon Worcestershire sauce
Parmesan cheese for garnish
chopped fresh parsley for garnish

Melt ½ cup butter in 3-quart saucepan. Remove from heat and blend in flour; cook over low heat 1 minute, stirring constantly. Whisk in milk and half and half; boil until mixture thickens, stirring frequently. Add salt. In small batches, stir in cheese, allowing each to melt before continuing. In skillet, melt remaining ¼ cup butter. Add celery, onion, and carrots; stir-fry until tender, about 5-10 minutes. Stir in chicken stock, nutmeg, and Worcestershire sauce. Whisk vegetable-stock mixture into cheese mixture; heat to a boil. Serve hot or cold, garnished with Parmesan cheese and chopped parsley.

Note: Potatoes or crabmeat can be added for an extra flair.

ROASTED PEPPER AND TOMATO SOUP
A unique and tasty blend of flavors

Preparation: 40 minutes
Planning: Must prepare ahead

Cooking: 10-15 minutes
Cooling: 3 hours
Servings: 4-6

4 red bell peppers
2 cups peeled, chopped, and seeded tomatoes or 1 (35-ounce) can tomatoes, drained
3 Tablespoons olive oil
2 cloves garlic, minced
3 cups chicken broth
½ teaspoon salt

¼ teaspoon freshly ground pepper
1½ Tablespoons chopped fresh basil or 1½ teaspoons dried whole basil
2 Tablespoons red wine vinegar

Cut peppers into quarters; remove stems and seeds. Place on foil-lined baking sheet; broil until skins are charred, about 10 minutes. Cover with plastic wrap; let stand 10 minutes. Peel off skins and discard. Combine peppers and tomatoes. Purée in blender in small batches. Heat olive oil in medium saucepan. Add garlic; sauté about 30 seconds. Add tomato-pepper mixture and chicken broth. Simmer 10-15 minutes, stirring occasionally, until slightly thickened. Remove from heat; stir in salt and pepper. Let cool to room temperature. Before serving, blend in basil and vinegar.

TURNIP GREEN AND CREAM SOUP
Reprinted from NEW SOUTHERN COOKING *by Nathalie Dupree*
Published by Alfred A. Knopf, Inc., New York, 1987

Preparation: 30 minutes

Cooking: 25 minutes
Servings: 6-8

3 cups turnip greens, washed and stemmed
4 Tablespoons butter
1 large onion, chopped
1 clove garlic, mashed
8 turnips, peeled and sliced, about 6 cups

2 cups chicken stock
1 cup milk
1 small hot pepper, chopped, or dash Tabasco sauce
salt
freshly ground black pepper

Place the turnip greens in enough boiling water to cover. Boil 5 minutes, remove the greens, and set aside. Return the water you have just boiled the greens in (the "likker") to a boil and reduce to 2-3 cups. Meanwhile, melt the butter in a saucepan. Sauté the onion until soft but not browned. Add garlic, turnips, stock, milk, and the 2 cups of "likker" and continue cooking, covered, until the turnips are tender. Remove the solids and purée in a food processor or blender, then return to the soup. Season to taste with the hot pepper or Tabasco, and salt and pepper, adding more pot "likker" if necessary. Garnish with cooked turnip greens.

VEGETABLE MEDLEY SOUP

Hearty and flavorful; meaty enough for a main dish

Preparation: 30 minutes
Planning: Can partially prepare ahead

Cooking: 40 minutes
Servings: 6

2 Tablespoons vegetable oil
2 Tablespoons butter
1 small onion, chopped
1 pound ground beef
1 small tender eggplant, peeled and diced
1 clove garlic, minced
½ cup sliced carrots
½ cup chopped celery
6 tomatoes, peeled and chopped or 1 (28-ounce) can tomatoes
2 (10½-ounce) cans beef broth
1 teaspoon salt
1 teaspoon sugar
½ teaspoon pepper
½ teaspoon ground nutmeg
½ cup macaroni
2 Tablespoons chopped fresh parsley or 1½ teaspoons dried parsley
grated Parmesan cheese for garnish

Heat oil and butter in large saucepan or Dutch oven. Add onion; sauté for 3 minutes. Add ground beef; cook, draining excess fat. Combine eggplant, garlic, carrots, and celery with ground beef and onion. Blend in tomatoes and beef broth. Add salt, sugar, pepper, and nutmeg. Simmer, covered, 30 minutes. Soup can be prepared to this point in advance, then reheated to complete cooking. Stir in macaroni and parsley; simmer 10 minutes, or until macaroni is tender. Garnish individual servings with grated Parmesan cheese.

CHILLED CREAMY AVOCADO SOUP
Sour cream enhances the flavor and texture of this soup, while insuring that soup will maintain its green color for several hours

Preparation: 40 minutes   Chilling: 3 hours
Planning: Must prepare ahead   Servings: 6

3 Tablespoons unsalted butter
3 Tablespoons all-purpose flour
3 cups chicken broth
3 avocados
1 clove garlic
1 cup sour cream

¼ cup dry vermouth
1½ Tablespoons fresh lemon juice
½ teaspoon white pepper
½ cup cold water
2 scallions, minced
¼ teaspoon cayenne pepper
1 Tablespoon olive oil

Melt butter in medium saucepan. Whisk in flour until smooth; cook over low heat, stirring, for 2 minutes. Add chicken broth; whisk until smooth. Bring mixture to a boil, stirring; reduce heat and simmer 5 minutes. Pour into shallow container and cool in freezer 20-30 minutes. Peel and pit avocados; cut into chunks. In blender or food processor, combine avocados, garlic, and sour cream; purée until smooth. Add half the broth mixture; purée until well blended. Pour into large bowl. Whisk in remaining broth mixture, vermouth, lemon juice, pepper, and cold water. Refrigerate, covered, about 3 hours. In small bowl, combine scallions, cayenne pepper, and olive oil. To serve, ladle soup into bowls, and drop ½ Tablespoon scallion mixture into center of each serving.

Salads

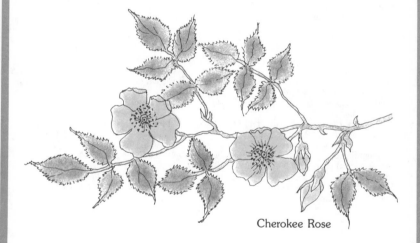

Cherokee Rose

SALADS AND SALAD DRESSINGS

Butter Toasted Croutons 77

FRUIT SALADS

CONGEALED FRUIT

Congealed Cranberry Surprise 84
Frosted Orange Salad 85
Holiday Cranberry Mold 84
Lemon-Lime Soufflé 87
Molded Peaches and Cream 88
Molded Waldorf Salad 89
Pretzel Salad 86
Strawberry Rosé 89
Tangy Lemon Mold 85

FROZEN FRUIT

Frozen Cranberry Dream Salad 83
Frozen Strawberry Yogurt Salad 91
Super Salad 86
Green and Gold Salad 72
Kiwi Orange Salad 90
Orange Marinated Fruit 90
Stuffed Apples 88

MEAT/SEAFOOD SALADS

Beef Salad with Broccoli and
  Asparagus 64
Chicken and Artichoke Rice Salad 63
Ham and Pasta Salad 67
Insalata Romana 65
Main Dish Rice Salad 66
Manuel's Greek Salad 72
Mexican Salad 66
Oriental Chicken Salad 63
Pasta Seafood Salad 69
Smoked Sausage Salad Medley 71
Wild Rice Chicken Salad 64

PASTA/RICE SALADS

Brown Rice-Pecan Salad with Oranges . 80
Chicken and Artichoke Rice Salad 63
Ham and Pasta Salad 67
Linguini Salad 74
Macaroni and Cheese Salad 78
Main Dish Rice Salad 66
Million Dollar Macaroni Salad 78
Pasta Seafood Salad 69

Peloponnesian Pasta Salad 76
Smoked Sausage Salad Medley 71
Wild Rice Chicken Salad 64

VEGETABLE/
TOSSED GREEN SALADS

Bean Medley 68
Broccoli Mold 74
Confetti Potato Salad 79
Corn Salad 71
Crisp Cucumber Pickles 68
Fresh Vegetable Marinade 83
Grecian Potato Salad 73
Greek Tomato and Pepper Salad 82
Green and Gold Salad 72
Hearts of Palm Salad 81
Manuel's Greek Salad 72
Marinated Mushroom Salad 75
Mimosa Salad 77
Mushroom and Leek Salad 75
Potato Salad with Sour Cream Dressing 79
Ripe Olive and Artichoke Salad 76
Strawberry Spinach Salad 91
Tangy English Pea Mold 81
The Georgian Club Caesar Salad
  and Dressing 70
Tree Top Marinade 82

SALAD DRESSINGS

Almond-Honey Dressing 92
Buttermilk-Garlic Dressing 93
Curry Dressing 73
Dill Dressing 67
French Vinaigrette Dressing 94
Ginger Dressing 65
Honey Dressing 92
Honey-Mustard Dressing 93
Manuel's Greek Salad Dressing 72
Mimosa Dressing 77
Oil and Vinegar Dressing 76
Poppy Seed Dressing 91
Sweet and Sour Dressing 94
The Georgian Club Caesar Salad
  Dressing 70

62

CHICKEN AND ARTICHOKE RICE SALAD
By omitting the chicken, this salad is a refreshing side-dish

Preparation: 40 minutes
Planning: Must prepare ahead

Chilling: 4 hours
Servings: 10-12

1 (8-ounce) package
  chicken-flavored
  vermicelli-rice mix
1 (6¼-ounce) package fried
  rice mix with almonds
2 (6-ounce) jars marinated
  artichoke hearts
¾ cup chopped green bell
  pepper

½ cup sliced ripe olives
8 green onions, chopped
3-4 cups diced cooked
  chicken
⅔ cup mayonnaise
½-1 teaspoon curry powder

Cook rice mixes according to package directions, omitting butter; cool. Drain artichoke hearts, reserving marinade, and slice. Add artichokes, pepper, olives, onion, and chicken to rice. Blend together artichoke marinade, mayonnaise, and curry powder. Add to rice salad; toss lightly. Chill several hours before serving.

ORIENTAL CHICKEN SALAD

Preparation: 20 minutes
Planning: Can partially prepare ahead

Servings: 6

½ teaspoon dry mustard
2 Tablespoons sugar
¾ teaspoons salt
¼ cup vegetable oil
1 Tablespoon sesame oil
3 Tablespoons rice vinegar
½ teaspoon white pepper
1 Tablespoon sesame seeds

1 head lettuce, torn into
  pieces
2 to 3 cups cubed cooked
  chicken
1 green onion, finely
  chopped
½ cup pecans, broken into
  pieces

Mix dry mustard, sugar, salt, vegetable oil, sesame oil, rice vinegar, and white pepper to make dressing; reserve. Toast sesame seeds at 350 degrees for 10 minutes, or until golden brown. Ingredients can be prepared ahead to this point. Just before serving, toss lettuce, chicken, onion, pecans, and sesame seeds with salad dressing.

WILD RICE CHICKEN SALAD

Preparation: 1 hour 20 minutes   Chilling: 2-3 hours
Planning: Must prepare ahead   Servings: 6

**1 (6-ounce) package long
grain and wild rice
1 pound boneless chicken
breasts, cooked
½ teaspoon salt
¾ cup mayonnaise
1 Tablespoon milk
2-3 Tablespoons lemon juice
¾ cup seedless red grapes,
cut in halves**

**¾ cup sliced celery
¾ cup coarsely chopped
cashews
2 Tablespoons finely
chopped onion
lettuce leaves, optional
whole seedless grapes for
garnish
whole cashews for garnish**

Prepare rice according to package directions; refrigerate until chilled. Cut chicken into ½-inch cubes. In small bowl, stir together salt, mayonnaise, milk, and lemon juice. In large bowl, combine chicken, grape halves, celery, chopped cashews, onion, and chilled rice; fold in mayonnaise mixture. Refrigerate 2-3 hours. To serve, mound individual salad portions on lettuce leaves; garnish with grapes and cashews.

BEEF SALAD WITH BROCCOLI AND ASPARAGUS

Dinner in a dish - perfect for those warm summer evenings

Preparation: 30 minutes   Chilling: 2 hours
Planning: Must partially prepare ahead   Servings: 4-5

**1 (1½-pound) flank steak
3 cups fresh asparagus,
diagonally sliced into
1½-inch pieces**

**1 bunch broccoli, cut into
bite-size flowerets (4 cups)
Ginger Dressing**

Broil or pan-fry steak to desired doneness. Cool; slice and cut into bite-size pieces. Bring large pot of salted water to rapid boil. Add asparagus; blanch 30 seconds. Remove with slotted spoon or strainer; set aside to cool. Add broccoli to same water; blanch 30 seconds. Drain well and let cool. When ready to serve, toss beef slices with Ginger Dressing. Add vegetables and toss again. Serve at room temperature.

Ginger Dressing:

⅓ cup light soy sauce
¼ cup white vinegar
3 Tablespoons sesame oil
1½-inch piece fresh ginger
   root, peeled and grated

1 teaspoon sugar
white pepper to taste

Combine all ingredients; mix well. Allow to stand several hours to blend flavors.

INSALATA ROMANA

A hearty salad, ideal for buffets, since it can be completely assembled and dressed well in advance of serving

Preparation: 25 minutes
Planning: Can prepare ahead

Servings: 6

⅔ cup olive oil
¼ cup red wine vinegar
1 clove garlic, crushed
3 (7-ounce) cans solid white
   tuna in oil, drained
1 (14-ounce) can artichoke
   hearts, drained and
   quartered
1 (6-ounce) can medium-size
   pitted black olives,
   drained
6 ounces hard salami, sliced
   and cut into julienne
   strips
1 cup small cherry
   tomatoes

1 (7-ounce) jar roasted
   sweet peppers, cut into
   small pieces
1 (3½-ounce) jar capers,
   drained
1 (2-ounce) can anchovy
   fillets, drained
½ cup chopped scallions
2 Tablespoons minced fresh
   parsley, packed

Combine olive oil, vinegar, and garlic; set aside. Place remaining ingredients in large serving bowl. Pour oil and vinegar mixture over salad; mix well. Refrigerate, covered, until ready to serve.

MAIN DISH RICE SALAD

Preparation: 45 minutes Planning: Must partially prepare ahead
Chilling: 2 days Servings: 6-8

1 cup uncooked long-grain white rice
1 cup Italian dressing
1½ cups water
1 cup frozen green peas
4 ounces fresh or canned mushrooms, sliced
5-6 scallions, chopped
1 (8-ounce) can sliced water chestnuts

½ cup green olives, sliced
½ cup black olives, sliced
1 (13¾-ounce) can artichoke hearts, drained and separated
½ cup mayonnaise
1 pound cooked shrimp or chicken, cut into bite-size pieces

Cook rice with Italian dressing and water until done; refrigerate in large bowl until cool. Fold in peas, mushrooms, scallions, water chestnuts, green olives, black olives, artichokes, and mayonnaise. Chill 2 days. When ready to serve, add shrimp or chicken and stir gently.

MEXICAN SALAD

A favorite recipe of Alabama's Head Football Coach, Bill Curry

Preparation: 25 minutes Servings: 6-8

1 pound ground beef
1 (15½-ounce) can kidney beans, drained
¼ teaspoon salt
1 medium onion, chopped
4 tomatoes, chopped
1 head lettuce, torn into pieces

1 avocado, peeled and chopped
1 cup grated Cheddar cheese
½ cup sweet-spicy French dressing
½ to 1 (8-ounce) package tortilla chips, crumbled

In skillet, cook ground beef until browned; drain well and cool slightly. In large bowl, combine ground beef, kidney beans, salt, and onion. Add tomatoes, lettuce, avocado, cheese, and dressing; toss well. Add tortilla chips; serve immediately.

HAM AND PASTA SALAD
A cool summer meal

Preparation: 1 hour   Chilling: 3 hours
Planning: Must prepare ahead   Servings: 6-8

6 ounces small shell pasta,   **2 hard-cooked eggs,**
cooked   **coarsely chopped**
1 pound ham, sliced ½-inch   **2 dill pickles, chopped**
thick, cut into julienne   **½ teaspoon salt**
strips   **Dill Dressing**
¾ cup chopped celery   **fresh dill weed for garnish**
1 small onion, chopped   **tomato wedges for garnish**
¼ cup chopped green bell
pepper

Combine pasta, ham, celery, onion, green bell pepper, eggs, pickles, and salt in large bowl. Toss gently with Dill Dressing. Refrigerate 3 hours or overnight. Before serving, garnish with fresh dill weed and tomato wedges.

Dill Dressing:
2 Tablespoons all-purpose   **¼ cup mayonnaise**
flour   **1 Tablespoon white wine**
1 Tablespoon sugar   **vinegar**
2 teaspoons Dijon mustard   **1½ teaspoons butter**
½ teaspoon salt   **1 Tablespoon minced fresh**
1 egg yolk   **dill weed or 1 teaspoon**
1 cup buttermilk   **dried dill weed**

Combine flour, sugar, mustard, and salt in small saucepan. In small bowl, mix together egg yolk and buttermilk; stir into flour mixture. Cook over medium heat, stirring, until mixture thickens and boils. Boil and stir for 1 minute. Remove from heat and cool 5 minutes. Stir in mayonnaise, vinegar, butter, and dill. Cover and chill until cold.

 ## CRISP CUCUMBER PICKLES
The taste is worth the effort

Preparation: 2½ hours   Cooking: 1 hour
Planning: Must prepare ahead   Yield: 10-12 quarts
Soaking: 19 hours

6 pounds cucumbers   **4 teaspoons alum**
1 (16-ounce) package   **6 pounds sugar**
  pickling lime   **1½ quarts white vinegar**
water, as needed   **4 Tablespoons pickling**
2 (26-ounce) boxes salt   **spice, tied in cloth bag**

Peel, seed, and cut cucumbers into sticks. Soak overnight in lime and water. Remove and rinse. Soak cucumbers in strong salt water for 6 hours. Remove and rinse. Soak cucumbers in clear water 1 hour. Drain. Cook cucumbers for 30 minutes in alum and water. Rinse with hot water. While cooking cucumbers, make syrup of sugar and vinegar; add spice bag. Boil syrup until clear. Put hot cucumbers into hot canning jars; pour hot syrup over cucumbers. Seal.

Note: The secret to success is having everything hot when sealing. Jar lid will pop when sealed.

BEAN MEDLEY

Preparation: 25 minutes   Chilling: 12 hours
Planning: Must partially prepare ahead   Servings: 8

1 cup mayonnaise   **1 (10-ounce) package frozen**
1 teaspoon Worcestershire   **French-style green beans**
  sauce   **1 (10-ounce) package frozen**
1 teaspoon prepared   **English peas**
  mustard   **1 (2¼-ounce) package**
3 Tablespoons vegetable oil   **slivered almonds**
⅛ teaspoon Tabasco sauce   **3 hard-cooked eggs, diced**
1 small onion, minced
1 (10-ounce) package frozen
  lima beans

Combine mayonnaise, Worcestershire sauce, mustard, oil, Tabasco, and onion. Refrigerate 12 hours or overnight. Cook vegetables according to package directions; drain and cool. Add almonds and eggs. Toss with enough dressing to thoroughly coat. Refrigerate until chilled, up to 12 hours.

PASTA SEAFOOD SALAD
A luncheon favorite, locally and nationwide,
from Mortons's of Chicago restaurant in Atlanta

Preparation: 20 minutes   Servings: 1
Planning: Can partially prepare ahead

6 ounces fusilli pasta, cooked and cooled
2 Tablespoons chopped green onion
3 ounces shrimp, cooked and broken into pieces
3 ounces sealegs (crab, lobster), cooked
¼ cup mayonnaise
1 squeeze lemon juice
1 drop Tabasco sauce, or to taste

2 Tablespoons chopped green bell pepper
2 leaves romaine lettuce
2 Tablespoons chopped red bell pepper
1 sprig green onion, sliced
1 sprig fresh parsley
½ lemon for garnish
1 large strawberry for garnish

In small mixing bowl, thoroughly combine fusilli, onion, shrimp, sealegs, mayonnaise, lemon juice, Tabasco, and green pepper. Place lettuce leaves on chilled salad plate and mound salad mixture in center. Sprinkle with chopped red pepper and sliced green onion. Garnish with parsley sprig, lemon, and strawberry.

Note: The ingredients for the desired number of servings can be prepared ahead, then mixed just before serivng.

THE GEORGIAN CLUB
CAESAR SALAD AND DRESSING
*Caesar salad is a favorite selection from Chef
Mohammad Bakhtiari at the Georgian Club in Atlanta*

Preparation: 15 minutes   Servings: 2-3

**salt and freshly ground
  pepper to taste
1 small garlic clove
2 anchovy fillets
½ teaspoon Dijon mustard
1 Tablespoon red wine
  vinegar
2 Tablespoons olive oil
1 egg yolk**

**1 squeeze of lemon juice
1 teaspoon Worcestershire
  sauce
3 cups romaine lettuce
¼ cup grated Parmesan
  cheese
croutons (see Index)
3 ounces cooked shrimp
3 ounces crabmeat**

Sprinkle salt and pepper into wooden bowl. Add garlic; crush into small bits. Add anchovies, mashing until mixture is of pastelike consistency. Mix in mustard, vinegar, olive oil, egg yolk, lemon juice, and Worcestershire sauce. Add romaine lettuce, Parmesan cheese, croutons, shrimp, and crabmeat. Toss together. Serve on chilled salad plates; top with additional croutons. The secret to the refreshing taste of a Caesar salad is that the ingredients are never mixed in advance.

Note: Follow these suggestions to correct salad dressing seasonings
too much vinegar......add more oil and cheese
too much oil.....add more mustard, lemon and Worcestershire sauce
too much Worchestershire......add more lemon and oil
too much mustard......add more oil and lemon

SMOKED SAUSAGE SALAD MEDLEY

Preparation: 45 minutes   Planning: Must prepare ahead
Chilling: 5 hours   Servings: 4

1 cup cooked rice, yellow,   **1 teaspoon onion juice**
  brown, or white   **1 teaspoon garlic powder**
1½ cups diced cooked   **1 teaspoon lemon juice**
  smoked sausage   **1 teaspoon grated onion**
1 cup green peas   **1 teaspoon grated green bell**
1 cup diced celery   **pepper**
1 cup sliced carrots   **1 teaspoon dried parsley**
¾ cup mayonnaise   **1 teaspoon prepared**
½ teaspoon salt   **mustard**
⅛ teaspoon cayenne pepper   **salad greens**

Combine cooled rice, sausage, peas, celery, and carrots. Chill several
hours, or overnight. In small bowl, combine mayonnaise, salt, cayenne
pepper, onion juice, garlic powder, lemon juice, grated onion, green
bell pepper, parsley, and mustard; mix well. One hour before serving,
toss rice mixture with mayonnaise mixture. Refrigerate until ready to
serve. Serve on crisp salad greens.

 ## CORN SALAD

Preparation: 20 minutes   Chilling: 4 hours
Planning: Must partially prepare ahead   Servings: 8

2 (14-ounce) cans whole   **juice of 1 lemon**
  kernel corn, drained   **3 Tablespoons mayonnaise**
4 stalks celery, thinly sliced   **2 Tablespoons sour cream**
1 medium onion, chopped   **½ cup chopped pecans**
1 teaspoon salt   **lettuce leaves**
¼ teaspoon pepper   **paprika for garnish**
1 teaspoon sugar

Combine corn, celery, onion, salt, pepper, sugar, and lemon juice in
medium bowl. Refrigerate, covered, at least 4 hours, or up to 24 hours.
Drain corn mixture. Stir in mayonnaise, sour cream, and pecans. To
serve, spoon salad on lettuce leaves or bed of shredded lettuce;
sprinkle with paprika.

71

MANUEL'S GREEK SALAD
This recipe is from Manuel's Tavern in Atlanta

Preparation: 30 minutes   Servings: 4

1 head curly endive, torn
(6 cups)
½ medium head iceberg
lettuce, torn (3 cups)
2 tomatoes, peeled and
chopped
¾ cup cubed feta cheese
¼ cup ripe olives, pitted and
sliced
¼ cup sliced green onion
fresh parsley for garnish
⅔ cup olive oil or vegetable
oil

⅓ cup white wine vinegar
½ teaspoon salt
½ teaspoon dried whole
oregano, crushed
⅛ teaspoon pepper
½ teaspoon dried whole
basil
1 clove garlic, crushed,
optional
1 (2-ounce) can anchovy
fillets, drained
10 ounces cooked beef, cut
in julienne strips

In mixing bowl, toss together endive and lettuce; mound onto salad plates. Arrange tomatoes, cheese, olives, and onion on greens. Dice parsley and sprinkle on salad. Combine oil, vinegar, salt, oregano, pepper, basil, and garlic in jar. Shake well to blend. Pour dressing over salad. Garnish with anchovies and beef strips.

GREEN AND GOLD SALAD

Preparation: 30 minutes   Servings: 6
Planning: Must partially prepare ahead

1 cucumber, sliced
2 small avocados, peeled
and sliced
1 (20-ounce) can pineapple
chunks, drained

1 (11-ounce) can mandarin
oranges, drained
2 bananas, sliced
lettuce leaves
Curry Dressing

Combine cucumber, avocado, pineapple, oranges, and bananas; mix gently. Spoon individual portions of salad on top of lettuce leaves and serve with chilled Curry Dressing.

Curry Dressing:

½ cup mayonnaise

½ cup sour cream

½ cup chutney

½ teaspoon curry powder

2 Tablespoons olive oil

1 Tablespoon red wine
   vinegar

Combine mayonnaise, sour cream, chutney, curry powder, olive oil, and vinegar in blender; mix until smooth. Chill for 1 hour or up to several days in refrigerator.

GRECIAN POTATO SALAD

Preparation: 30 minutes

Planning: Must prepare ahead

Chilling: 2-3 hours

Servings: 6-8

**3 pounds small new
   potatoes, scrubbed and
   cooked**

**4 scallions, coarsely
   chopped, including some
   of green parts**

**1 cucumber, peeled and
   thinly sliced lengthwise**

**1 medium green bell pepper,
   chopped**

**15 Greek olives, pitted and
   sliced**

**½ pound feta cheese,
   coarsely crumbled**

**2 Tablespoons minced fresh
   mint**

**½ teaspoon dried whole
   oregano**

½ teaspoon salt

¼ teaspoon pepper

½ cup olive oil

**2 Tablespoons fresh lemon
   juice**

assorted garnishes

Drain and cool potatoes. Cut each in half; place in large bowl. Add scallions, cucumber, green pepper, olives, cheese, mint, oregano, salt, and pepper; toss lightly. In small bowl, thoroughly blend olive oil and lemon juice. Pour over salad mixture, tossing gently to coat potatoes. Chill several hours. To serve, spoon salad over lettuce leaves on large serving platter and serve with several of the following garnishes: sliced feta cheese, radish roses, carrot curls, pepper rings, tomato wedges, sliced avocado, sliced pepperoni, anchovy fillets, or shrimp.

BROCCOLI MOLD
A buffet pleaser to serve with turkey

Preparation: 40 minutes
Planning: Must prepare ahead

Chilling: 3 hours
Servings: 8

2 (10-ounce) packages frozen broccoli flowerets
6 hard-cooked eggs, chopped
½ teaspoon salt
1 envelope unflavored gelatin
1 (10½-ounce) can beef consommé

1 cup mayonnaise
2 Tablespoons lemon juice
2 Tablespoons Worcestershire sauce
5-8 drops hot sauce
¼ cup chopped green onion

Cook broccoli according to package directions; drain and cool. Combine with chopped eggs and salt. Soften gelatin in ¼ cup cool consommé. Heat remaining consommé to boiling. Stir in softened gelatin until dissolved. Cool and combine with broccoli-egg mixture; blend in mayonnaise, lemon juice, Worcestershire sauce, hot sauce, and green onions. Pour into lightly oiled 1½-quart mold; chill until firm, about 3 hours.

 # LINGUINI SALAD

Preparation: 20 minutes
Planning: Must prepare ahead

Chilling: 12 hours
Servings: 4-6

1 (8-ounce) package linguini
3 cucumbers, cut into small pieces
3 medium tomatoes, cut into small pieces

½ (2½-ounce) jar of salad seasoning
1 (16-ounce) bottle Italian salad dressing

Cook linguini according to package directions; drain. Combine linguini, cucumbers, and tomatoes in serving bowl. Stir in half jar of salad seasoning. More may be added, if desired. Add Italian dressing and toss until salad is thoroughly coated. Refrigerate, covered, 12 hours or overnight.

 ## MARINATED MUSHROOM SALAD

Preparation: 15 minutes Marinating: 1 hour
Planning: Must prepare ahead Servings: 6-8

¾ cup vegetable oil
¼ cup white vinegar
1½ teaspoons salt
1½ teaspoons dried whole
  tarragon
¼ teaspoon paprika
¼ teaspoon pepper

¼ teaspoon sugar
1 medium onion, thinly
  sliced
½ clove garlic
1 pound mushrooms, sliced
spinach greens and/or other
  salad greens

Combine oil, vinegar, salt, tarragon, paprika, pepper, sugar, onion, and garlic in blender. Cover and blend until liquified. Pour over mushrooms; refrigerate 1 to 4 hours. To serve, toss mushrooms and dressing with salad greens.

MUSHROOM AND LEEK SALAD

Preparation: 15 minutes Marinating: 3 hours
Planning: Must prepare ahead Servings: 6

8 leeks, washed and thinly
  sliced, white part only
12 ounces fresh
  mushrooms, sliced
1 clove garlic
½ cup vegetable oil
¼ cup olive oil
3-4 Tablespoons red wine
  vinegar

¼ cup chopped green onions
  or leek tops
¼ cup chopped fresh parsley
½ teaspoon salt
¼ teaspoon pepper
2 Tablespoons chopped
  pimientos
lettuce leaves

Steam mushrooms and leeks until tender, about 5 minutes. In food processor or blender, combine garlic, oils, vinegar, green onion, parsley, salt, and pepper. Blend, then add pimientos. Pour over leeks and mushrooms; chill 3 hours. Serve on a bed of lettuce.

RIPE OLIVE AND ARTICHOKE SALAD

Preparation: 30 minutes   Servings: 6
Planning: Can partially prepare ahead

1 head Bibb or leaf lettuce
1 (6-ounce) jar marinated
   artichoke hearts, drained
   and quartered
½ (10-ounce) can pitted ripe
   olives, drained and halved
2 Tablespoons lemon juice

1 teaspoon dried dill weed
¼ cup olive oil
salt and pepper to taste
½ cup croutons (see Index)
¼ cup freshly grated
   Parmesan cheese

Tear lettuce into bite-size pieces. Toss with artichoke hearts and olives. Just before serving, combine lemon juice, dill weed, olive oil, salt, and pepper; toss with salad. Add croutons and Parmesan cheese. Toss again.

PELOPONNESIAN PASTA SALAD

Preparation: 30 minutes   Chilling: 2 hours
Planning: Must prepare ahead   Servings: 6-8

½ pound cooked tri-color
   spiral noodles (tomato,
   spinach and regular blend)
1 medium onion, finely
   chopped
½ pound feta cheese, finely
   crumbled

2-3 tomatoes, seeded and
   cut into wedges
1 cup pitted black olives,
   sliced
Oil and Vinegar Dressing

In large serving bowl, combine cooked noodles, onion, feta cheese, tomatoes, and olives. Pour Oil and Vinegar Dressing over salad mixture; toss gently. Refrigerate until chilled, about 2 hours.

Oil and Vinegar Dressing:
6 Tablespoons olive oil
3 Tablespoons red wine
   vinegar

1 teaspoon Dijon mustard
⅛ teaspoon salt
⅛ teaspoon pepper

Whisk together olive oil, vinegar, mustard, salt, and pepper.

MIMOSA SALAD

Preparation: 30 minutes
Planning: Must partially prepare ahead

Servings: 6

2 heads Bibb lettuce
1 head Boston lettuce
1 head leaf lettuce
5 hard-cooked eggs, sieved
Butter Toasted Croutons
¼ cup finely chopped
  toasted pecans
Mimosa Dressing

Line 6 salad plates with leaves from one head Bibb lettuce. Tear remaining lettuce heads into bite-size pieces and divide evenly among plates. Sprinkle with sieved eggs and Butter Toasted Croutons; top with pecans. Just before serving, spoon Mimosa Dressing generously over each salad.

Butter Toasted Croutons:
4 slices day-old bread
¼ cup olive oil
¼ cup butter
garlic salt to taste

Trim crust from bread; cut bread into tiny cubes. Heat together oil, butter, and garlic salt. Fry bread cubes to a golden color. Drain on paper towel.

Mimosa Dressing:
¼ cup olive oil
¼ cup wine vinegar
1 teaspoon salt
½ teaspoon garlic salt
½ teaspoon white pepper or
  3 dashes hot sauce
1 small sweet onion, thinly
  sliced
1 teaspoon dried whole
  oregano
1 teaspoon grated Parmesan
  cheese, optional
1 Tablespoon water

Combine all ingredients in screw-top jar; shake gently to mix. Prepare well in advance of serving to allow dressing to marinate to tangy goodness.

MACARONI AND CHEESE SALAD
A flavorful variation of a traditional favorite

Preparation: 30 minutes
Planning: Must prepare ahead

Chilling: 4 hours
Servings: 6-8

1 (7¼-ounce) package macaroni and cheese
2 cups shredded cabbage
½ cup chopped green bell pepper
¼ cup chopped red onion
3 hard-cooked eggs, chopped

½ cup mayonnaise
¼ cup sour cream
1 Tablespoon prepared mustard
½ teaspoon salt
⅛ teaspoon pepper

Prepare macaroni and cheese according to package directions. Combine macaroni and cheese, cabbage, green pepper, onion, and eggs. Combine mayonnaise, sour cream, mustard, salt, and pepper; mix well. Add to macaroni mixture; stir gently. Pour into 1½ quart bowl. Chill 4 hours, or overnight.

MILLION DOLLAR MACARONI SALAD

Preparation: 20 minutes
Planning: Must prepare ahead

Chilling: 4 hours
Servings: 6-8

2 cups uncooked macaroni
½ cup mayonnaise
1½ teaspoons prepared mustard
1 Tablespoon sugar
¾ teaspoon salt
½ teaspoon white pepper
⅛ teaspoon cayenne pepper

2 Tablespoons white vinegar
½ cup half and half
2 Tablespoons butter, melted
⅓ cup chopped celery
⅔ cup chopped onion
⅓ cup chopped green bell pepper

Cook macaroni according to package directions; drain but do not rinse or cool. In small mixing bowl, combine mayonnaise, mustard, sugar, salt, white pepper, cayenne, and vinegar. Slowly mix in half and half. Add butter; stir until blended. Toss dressing with macaroni; add celery, onion, and green pepper. Toss again until salad is thoroughly coated. Refrigerate, covered, 4 hours or overnight.

CONFETTI POTATO SALAD
A picnic pleaser

Preparation: 1 hour   Chilling: 7 hours minimum
Planning: Must prepare ahead   Servings: 8-10

6 cups pared, cubed, cooked ¾ cup mayonnaise
   potatoes   2 teaspoons prepared
½ cup finely chopped onions   mustard
1 cup chopped celery   1½ teaspoons lemon juice
½ cup thinly sliced radishes 1 teaspoon salt
½ cup shredded carrots   ⅛ teaspoon pepper
⅓ cup herbs and spices   1 cup cubed cucumber
   salad dressing   6 hard-cooked eggs, sliced

In large bowl, combine potatoes, onion, celery, radishes, and carrots; toss gently with salad dressing. Refrigerate, covered, several hours or overnight, stirring gently once or twice. Mix together mayonnaise, mustard, lemon juice, salt, and pepper. Toss lightly with potato mixture. Gently stir in cucumber and eggs. Chill 1 to 4 hours before serving.

POTATO SALAD WITH SOUR CREAM DRESSING
This recipe comes from the Peasant Uptown restaurant in Atlanta

Preparation: 35 minutes   Chilling: 4 hours
Planning: Must prepare ahead   Servings: 6

2½ pounds red potatoes,   ½ teaspoon black pepper
   unpeeled, sliced ⅜-inch   1½ Tablespoons red wine
   thick   vinegar
1½ teaspoons salt, divided   2 Tablespoons finely
1 cup mayonnaise   chopped fresh chives
⅓ cup sour cream

In large, heavy pot, bring 4 quarts water to a rolling boil; add 1 teaspoon salt. Add potatoes; cook until just barely tender. Drain; let cool. Combine mayonnaise, sour cream, ½ teaspoon salt, pepper, vinegar. and chives. Toss with potatoes. Refrigerate, covered, until ready to serve.

BROWN RICE-PECAN SALAD WITH ORANGES
*The brown rice lends a chewy texture
and appealing nutlike flavor to this salad*

Preparation: 1 hour
Planning: Must prepare ahead

Chilling: 2 hours
Servings: 6

1 orange
2½ cups chicken stock or
chicken broth
1 cup uncooked long-grain
brown rice, washed and
drained
1 Tablespoon unsalted
butter
1 teaspoon salt, divided
3 Tablespoons fresh lemon
juice
2 Tablespoons olive or
vegetable oil
1 cup finely chopped celery
3 Tablespoons minced
scallions with tops

3 Tablespoons chopped
fresh parsley
¼ cup sour cream
2 teaspoons Dijon mustard
¼ teaspoon freshly ground
pepper
½ cup pecans, coarsely
chopped
Boston or romaine lettuce
leaves
½ cup pecan halves
cherry tomatoes for garnish
orange slices for garnish

Peel orange removing all white pith. Slice into segments, removing and discarding membranes. Cut each segment in half crosswise; reserve. Heat stock in heavy medium saucepan to boiling; add rice, butter, and ½ teaspoon salt. Reduce heat; simmer, covered ,until rice is tender and all liquid is absorbed, about 45 minutes. When rice is cooked, transfer to large bowl; sprinkle with lemon juice and oil; toss well. Add celery, scallion, parsley, sour cream, mustard, ½ teaspoon salt, and pepper; toss well. Stir in pecans and reserved orange pieces. Refrigerate, covered until flavors are blended, about 2 hours. To serve, arrange lettuce leaves on platter. Spoon rice salad over lettuce, shaping into a mound. Top with pecan halves; garnish with cherry tomatoes and halved orange slices.

HEARTS OF PALM SALAD

Preparation: 30 minutes
Servings: 8

Chilling: 1 hour

1 head red leaf lettuce
1 head Boston or Bibb
  lettuce
1 Tablespoon vegetable oil
½ cup slivered almonds
1 (14-ounce) can hearts of
  palm, drained and cut
  crosswise into bite-size
  pieces

½ pound mushrooms, sliced
French Vinaigrette Dressing
  (see Index)

Wash lettuces, drain well; tear into bite-size pieces. Heat oil in small skillet over medium heat. Add almonds and cook until slightly brown, stirring constantly. Drain on paper towel; cool. Toss together lettuces, hearts of palm, and mushrooms; chill. Just before serving, add almonds to salad; toss. Add French Vinaigrette Dressing, a spoonful at a time, and toss until greens are lightly coated.

 ## TANGY ENGLISH PEA MOLD

Preparation: 20 minutes
Planning: Must prepare ahead

Chilling: 4 hours
Servings: 8-10

1 (3-ounce) package lemon
  gelatin
½ cup boiling water
4 Tablespoons vinegar
1 teaspoon salt
1 (17-ounce) can small
  garden peas, drained,
  reserving ¼ cup liquid

1 teaspoon prepared
  mustard
1 cup mayonnaise
1 cup chopped celery
1 Tablespoon chopped
  onion
1 Tablespoon chopped green
  bell pepper

Dissolve gelatin in boiling water. Add vinegar, salt, and reserved liquid from peas. Whisk in mustard and mayonnaise; add peas, celery, onion, and green bell pepper. Pour into lightly oiled mold; refrigerate until firm.

GREEK TOMATO AND PEPPER SALAD

Preparation: 20 minutes
Planning: Must prepare ahead

Marinating: 2-6 hours
Servings: 6

½ **cup olive oil**
2 **Tablespoons red wine**
  vinegar
1 **teaspoon salt**
½ **teaspoon black pepper**
¾ **teaspoon dried thyme**
½ **pound cherry tomatoes,**
  each halved or quartered
½ **red bell pepper, cut into**
  ⅛-inch strips

½ **green bell pepper, cut**
  into ⅛-inch strips
1 **small red onion, thinly**
  sliced
1 **cup pitted black olives,**
  sliced
¼ **pound feta cheese,**
  coarsely crumbled

Combine oil, vinegar, salt, black pepper, and thyme in 2½-quart serving dish. Add tomatoes, red and green peppers, onion, olives, and cheese; toss well. Refrigerate, covered, for 2 to 6 hours. Toss again before serving.

TREE TOP MARINADE

Preparation: 30 minutes
Planning: Must prepare ahead

Marinating: 2 hours
Servings: 8-10

½ **cup mayonnaise**
⅓ **cup vegetable oil**
⅓ **cup vinegar**
¼ **cup sugar**
½ **teaspoon salt**
¼ **teaspoon pepper**
1 **head cauliflower**

1 **bunch broccoli**
1 **large sweet onion, thinly**
  sliced
8 **ounces fresh mushrooms,**
  sliced
4 **slices bacon, cooked and**
  crumbled

Combine mayonnaise, oil, vinegar, sugar, salt, and pepper in pint jar. Close lid; shake until mixed thoroughly. Tear cauliflower and broccoli into bite-size flowerets. Combine flowerets, onion, and mushrooms. Pour marinade over vegetables; toss lightly until coated. Refrigerate, covered, at least 2 hours, or as long as 2 days. Before serving, drain off excess dressing; top with crumbled bacon.

FRESH VEGETABLE MARINADE
An unusual marinade; sweet and tangy

Preparation: 30 minutes
Planning: Must prepare ahead

Marinating: 3 hours
Servings: 8-10

1 small onion, grated
1 cup sugar
2 teaspoons dry mustard
½ cup vinegar
1½ cups vegetable oil
2 Tablespoons poppy seeds

4 stalks broccoli
1 small head cauliflower
8 large mushrooms, sliced
1 medium green bell pepper, chopped
3 stalks celery, chopped

Combine onion, sugar, mustard, vinegar, oil, and poppy seeds in quart jar. Close lid; shake until mixed thoroughly. Tear broccoli and cauliflower into bite-size flowerets. Combine flowerets, mushrooms, pepper, and celery. Pour marinade over vegetables; toss lightly until coated. Refrigerate, covered, at least 3 hours, or up to 2 days, before serving.

FROZEN CRANBERRY DREAM SALAD

Preparation: 25 minutes
Planning: Must prepare ahead

Freezing: 4 hours
Servings: 8

1 (1-pound) can whole
  cranberry sauce
2 Tablespoons sugar
1 (8-ounce) package cream
  cheese, softened
1 cup heavy cream, whipped

1 cup vanilla yogurt
1 (8¼-ounce) can crushed
  pineapple, drained
lettuce leaves
mayonnaise or yogurt for
  garnish

In mixing bowl, blend together cranberry sauce, sugar, and cream cheese. Fold in whipped cream, yogurt, and pineapple. Oil 8-inch square dish with mayonnaise and fill with salad mixture. Cover and freeze overnight. To serve, let salad stand for 10 minutes, then cut into squares. Serve on lettuce leaves; garnish with mayonnaise or yogurt.

HOLIDAY CRANBERRY MOLD

Preparation: 25 minutes

Planning: Must prepare ahead

Chilling: 6 hours

Servings: 8

2 envelopes unflavored gelatin
½ cold water
½ cup pecans
2 cups raw cranberries
4 stalks celery, cut in half

¾ cup sugar
½ teaspoon grated lemon rind
1 cup red wine
2 Tablespoons lemon juice
½ cup mayonnaise

In saucepan, soften gelatin in cold water. In food processor, chop pecans; set aside. Add cranberries and celery; chop finely. Stir sugar and lemon rind into cranberry-celery mixture. Heat wine in small saucepan. Add wine to softened gelatin and stir until dissolved. Stir in pecans, cranberry-celery mixture, lemon juice, and mayonnaise. Pour into lightly oiled 1-quart mold; chill until set.

 ## CONGEALED CRANBERRY SURPRISE
Delightfully delicious and not too sweet

Preparation: 20 minutes

Planning: Must prepare ahead

Chilling: 4 hours

Servings: 9

1 (3-ounce) package raspberry gelatin
1 cup boiling water
1 (14-ounce) jar cran-orange relish

1 cup sour cream
1 cup chopped pecans
2 bananas, diced
½ cup sour cream for garnish

Dissolve gelatin in boiling water. Stir in cran-orange relish, sour cream, pecans, and bananas. Pour into 9-inch square dish. Chill until firm. When ready to serve, ½ cup sour cream may be spread over gelatin.

TANGY LEMON MOLD

Preparation: 20 minutes
Planning: Must prepare ahead

Chilling: 4 hours
Servings: 6

1 envelope unflavored
  gelatin
¼ cup cold water
½ cup boiling water
2 (3-ounce) packages cream
  cheese, softened
3 Tablespoons sugar

1 cup half and half
1 (6-ounce) can frozen
  lemonade concentrate,
  thawed
grated rind of 1 lemon
1 pint fresh strawberries,
  sliced, optional

Soften gelatin in cold water, then dissolve in boiling water. In another bowl, blend cream cheese and sugar; gradually add half and half. Combine gelatin with cream cheese mixture. Add lemonade and blend; stir in grated lemon rind. Pour into lightly oiled 1-quart ring mold. Refrigerate until firm. Unmold and fill center with strawberries, if desired.

FROSTED ORANGE SALAD

Preparation: 25 minutes
Planning: Must prepare ahead

Chilling: 4 hours
Servings: 6-8

1 (10-ounce) can mandarin
  oranges, drained, reserving
  juice
1 (3-ounce) package orange
  gelatin
1 cup orange sherbert,
  softened

1 (6-ounce) can frozen
  orange juice concentrate,
  thawed
orange slices for garnish
strawberries for garnish

Combine reserved mandarin orange juice with water to make one cup; heat to boiling. Stir in gelatin to dissolve. Add mandarin oranges, orange sherbert, and orange juice concentrate; mix thoroughly. Pour into mold rinsed in cold water; refrigerate until firm. Garnish with orange slices and strawberries.

PRETZEL SALAD
An unusual blend of textures and flavors

Preparation: 1 hour   Chilling: 6 hours
Planning: Must prepare ahead   Servings: 12-15

1 stick butter, melted
1 cup crushed pretzels
3 Tablespoons sugar
1 cup crushed pecans
1 (8-ounce) package cream
  cheese, softened
1 (8-ounce) carton non-dairy
  whipped topping

1 cup powdered sugar
1 (6-ounce) package
  strawberry gelatin
2 cups hot water
1 (16-ounce) package frozen
  strawberries
whipped topping for garnish,
  optional

Combine melted butter, pretzels, sugar, and pecans. Pat into bottom of 13x9x2 pan. Bake at 350 degrees for 10 minutes; cool. Beat together cream cheese, whipped topping, and powdered sugar. Spread on top of pretzel mixture. Refrigerate 30 minutes, or until completely chilled. Dissolve gelatin in boiling water. Add strawberries; stir until gelatin begins to thicken and cool. Pour over cream cheese mixture. Refrigerate, covered, until firm. Before serving, top with additional whipped topping, if desired.

Note: Prepare pretzel salad the night before or the day of serving so the pretzel layer will remain crisp.

 ## *SUPER SALAD*
This is so easy and always gets positive comments from all ages!

Preparation: 5 minutes   Servings: 8
Planning: Must prepare ahead

1 (21-ounce) can strawberry
  pie filling
1 (14-ounce) can sweetened
  condensed milk
1 (20-ounce) can crushed
  pineapple, drained

1 (9-ounce) carton whipped
  topping
red food coloring, optional

Empty pie filling into bowl. Add sweetened condensed milk and crushed pineapple. Fold in whipped topping. Stir in a few drops of red food coloring, if desired. Spoon into a 13x9x2 pan or paper-lined muffin tins. Freeze.

LEMON-LIME SOUFFLÉ
Light, luscious, and well worth the effort

Preparation: 35 minutes
Planning: Must prepare ahead

Chilling: 4 hours
Servings: 12

1 lemon
1 lime
½ cup water
2 teaspoons unflavored
  gelatin
1 (3-ounce) package lime
  gelatin
1 (6-ounce) can frozen
  limeade concentrate,
  thawed

6 eggs, separated
½ teaspoon cream of tartar
1½ cups heavy cream,
  whipped
1 cup sugar
kiwi slices for garnish
strawberries for garnish

Grate lemon and lime; reserve peel. Squeeze juice from lemon and lime and combine to equal ½ cup. Heat lemon-lime juice with ½ cup water; add gelatins and stir until dissolved. Stir limeade concentrate into gelatin mixture. Chill in freezer until consistency of unbeaten egg white, about 15-20 minutes. Meanwhile, mix egg whites and cream of tartar; beat until stiff. In another bowl, beat egg yolks and sugar at medium speed for 3 minutes; add gelatin mixture. Reduce mixer speed and add whipped cream, and grated lemon and lime peel. Gently fold in egg whites by hand. Pour mixture into soufflé dish; chill 3-4 hours. Before serving, garnish with kiwi slices and strawberries.

Note: Lemon-Lime Soufflé is best if prepared the day of serving, as it tends to lose its light texture if refrigerated too long.

MOLDED PEACHES AND CREAM
A Peach State summertime favorite

Preparation: 45 minutes
Planning: Must prepare ahead

Chilling: 6 hours
Servings: 12

1 (3-ounce) package peach gelatin
1 cup boiling water
¾ cup cold water
3 cups sliced peaches
1 banana, sliced
1 envelope unflavored gelatin

3 Tablespoons cold water
½ cup half and half
1 (8-ounce) package cream cheese, softened
1 cup heavy cream
½ cup plus 2 Tablespoons sugar
1 cup puréed peaches

Dissolve peach gelatin in 1 cup boiling water. Add ¾ cup cold water and mix well. Chill until slightly thick, about 20 to 30 minutes. Stir peach and banana slices into peach gelatin mixture. Pour into lightly oiled 8-cup mold. Chill until set. Soften unflavored gelatin in 3 Tablespoons cold water. Scald half and half; blend into unflavored gelatin mixture. With electric mixer, beat cream cheese. Add cream, sugar, and pureed peaches; mix well. Add to unflavored gelatin mixture; stir well. Pour over peach and banana gelatin layer. Chill until firm.

 ## STUFFED APPLES

Preparation: 5 minutes

Planning: Can prepare ahead
Yield: 2 large or 8 small

2 large apples, cored
3 Tablespoons chunky peanut butter

1 Tablespoon chocolate chips
1 Tablespoon raisins

Mix peanut butter, chips, and raisins; fill cored apples. May slice for smaller servings.

STRAWBERRY ROSÉ

Preparation: 1 hour 25 minutes
Planning: Must prepare ahead

Chilling: 3 hours
Servings: 9

1 (6-ounce) package
strawberry gelatin
1 cup boiling water
1 cup rosé wine
2 (10-ounce) packages
frozen sliced strawberries,
thawed

1 (8-ounce) can crushed
pineapple, drained
3 bananas, mashed
1 cup chopped nuts
1 cup sour cream

Dissolve gelatin in boiling water. Add wine; mix well. Fold in strawberries, pineapple, bananas, and nuts. Spoon half of mixture into 8-inch
square dish. Chill until thickened, about 1 hour. Spread sour cream
evenly over gelatin. Spoon remaining gelatin mixture over sour cream
layer. Chill until firm.

MOLDED WALDORF SALAD

Preparation: 30 minutes
Planning: Must prepare ahead

Chilling: 4 hours
Servings: 10

2 eggs, well beaten
$\frac{1}{2}$ cup sugar
$\frac{1}{8}$ teaspoon salt
$\frac{1}{4}$ cup lemon juice
$\frac{1}{2}$ cup crushed pineapple,
well drained, reserving $\frac{1}{2}$
cup juice
$\frac{1}{2}$ envelope unflavored
gelatin

$\frac{1}{4}$ cup cold water
$\frac{1}{2}$ cup finely chopped celery
$\frac{1}{2}$ cup broken pecans or
walnuts
2 apples, unpeeled, finely
chopped
$\frac{1}{2}$ cup heavy cream,
whipped

Combine beaten eggs, sugar, salt, lemon juice, and $\frac{1}{2}$ cup reserved
pineapple juice in double boiler. Cook over hot water, stirring constantly, until thickened. Soften unflavored gelatin in $\frac{1}{4}$ cup cold water.
Combine gelatin with egg mixture; cool. Add celery, pineapple, nuts,
and apples; fold in whipped cream. Pour mixture into lightly oiled 5-
cup mold; chill until firm.

ORANGE MARINATED FRUIT
*This recipe from Atlanta caterer, Joyce Gould,
is especially good when there is a shortage of fresh fruit*

Preparation: 20 minutes
Planning: Must prepare ahead

Chilling: 12 hours
Servings: 24

**1 (12-ounce) can frozen
orange juice concentrate**
**1-2 cantaloupes, peeled and
cubed**
**1 (20-ounce) can pineapple
chunks, drained**
**2 (16-ounce) cans peaches,
drained and cut into
bite-size pieces**

**3-4 red apples, unpeeled,
cored, and cut into
bite-size pieces**
**2 (16-ounce) cans mandarin
oranges, drained**
lettuce leaves, optional

Thaw orange juice concentrate. Combine fruit in large serving bowl.
Pour undiluted concentrate over fruit and toss gently. Chill overnight.
Fruit can be served in stemmed glasses, or drained and served on
lettuce leaves.

KIWI ORANGE SALAD

Preparation: 30 minutes

Servings: 6

**½ cup whole blanched
almonds**
**6 Tablespoons walnut,
safflower, or vegetable oil**
**2 Tablespoons red wine or
sherry vinegar**
**salt and freshly ground
pepper to taste**
3 kiwis, peeled and sliced

**2 large oranges, peeled and
sectioned**
**2 stalks celery, cut
diagonally into 1-inch
pieces**
**1 head Boston or ½ head
romaine lettuce, torn into
pieces**

Toast almonds in 350 degree oven for about 15 minutes; let cool.
Combine walnut oil and vinegar; season with salt and pepper. Toss
dressing with almonds, kiwis, orange sections, celery, and lettuce.
Serve immediately.

STRAWBERRY SPINACH SALAD
A delightfully different spinach salad

Preparation: 30 minutes
Planning: Can partially prepare ahead

Chilling: 1 hour
Servings: 6

1 pound fresh spinach
1 pint fresh strawberries,
  halved or sliced
½ cup walnut pieces for
  garnish

½ cup crumbled blue cheese
  for garnish
Poppy Seed Dressing

Wash and spin dry spinach; remove stems and tear into bite-size pieces. In salad bowl, combine spinach and strawberries. Add walnut pieces and/or blue cheese for garnish. Toss with Poppy Seed Dressing just before serving. Store remaining dressing in refrigerator.

Poppy Seed Dressing:
½ cup sugar
2 Tablespoons sesame seeds
1 Tablespoon poppy seeds
1½ teaspoons minced onion
¼ teaspoon Worcestershire
  sauce

¼ teaspoon paprika
¼ cup cider vinegar
½ cup vegetable oil

Mix together sugar, sesame seeds, poppy seeds, onion, Worcestershire sauce, paprika, and vinegar in pint jar. Shake well until sugar is dissolved; add oil and shake again. Refrigerate for 1 hour or more.

 ## FROZEN STRAWBERRY YOGURT SALAD

Preparation: 15 minutes
Planning: Must prepare ahead

Freezing: 3 hours
Servings: 8-10

1 cup strawberry yogurt
¼ cup honey
4 ounces cream cheese,
  softened

1 (8-ounce) can crushed
  pineapple, drained

Mix yogurt, honey, cream cheese, and pineapple. Pour into muffin tins and freeze. Remove from freezer 10-15 minutes before serving.

 ## ALMOND-HONEY DRESSING

Preparation: 5 minutes   Planning: Can prepare ahead
Chilling: 30 minutes   Yield: 1 cup

**1 (8-ounce) package cream   2 Tablespoons honey
  cheese, softened   ½ teaspoon almond extract
¼ cup milk**

Combine cream cheese, milk, honey, and almond extract in blender; mix until smooth. Refrigerate until chilled. Dressing can be served with a fruit salad or used as a dip for a fresh fruit appetizer or dessert.

HONEY DRESSING

Preparation: 15 minutes   Yield: 2 cups
Planning: Can prepare ahead

**¼ to ⅔ cup sugar   ⅓ cup honey
1 teaspoon dry mustard   ⅓ cup white vinegar
1 teaspoon paprika   1 Tablespoon lemon juice
1 teaspoon celery seed   1 teaspoon grated onion
¼ teaspoon salt   1 cup vegetable oil**

In small mixing bowl, combine sugar, mustard, paprika, celery seed, and salt. Stir in honey, vinegar, lemon juice, and onion. Very slowly, pour oil into mixture, beating constantly with electric mixer. Serve immediately or store in refrigerator for up to 1 month. Dressing should be shaken well or beaten before each use. Serve with a Bibb lettuce and mandarin orange salad.

 ## HONEY-MUSTARD DRESSING

Preparation: 5 minutes   Yield: 1 cup
Planning: Can prepare ahead

¾ cup mayonnaise   **3 Tablespoons honey**
1 Tablespoon prepared
   mustard

In mixing bowl, whisk together all ingredients until smooth. Use immediately or store in covered container in refrigerator. Dressing can be tossed with salad greens or served as a dip for chicken nuggets, raw vegetables, or fried vegetables.

Note: Mix with a combination of romaine, red leaf lettuce, mushrooms, red onion rings, and slices of yellow squash for a savory salad.

 ## BUTTERMILK-GARLIC DRESSING
A spicy combination of bold flavors

Preparation: 10 minutes   Planning: Must prepare ahead
Chilling: 8 hours   Yield: 4 cups

2 cups mayonnaise   **2 Tablespoons vinegar**
⅓ cup buttermilk   **1½ teaspoons lemon juice**
⅓ cup vegetable oil   **1½ teaspoons honey**
¼ cup water   **¾ teaspoon dry mustard**
1½ Tablespoons garlic   **½ teaspoon salt**
   powder   **¼ teaspoon white pepper**

Whisk together mayonnaise and buttermilk; stir in remaining ingredients. Refrigerate, covered, at least 8 hours.

93

 ### SWEET AND SOUR DRESSING
A favorite to toss with a spinach salad

Preparation: 5 minutes   Yield: 2½ cups
Planning: Can prepare ahead

1 cup vegetable oil
¾ cup sugar
¼ cup cider vinegar
⅓ cup ketchup

2 teaspoons Worcestershire
sauce
1 medium onion, chopped
salt to taste

Mix all ingredients in electric blender. Refrigerate in tightly closed jar up to 2 weeks. When ready to serve, shake well to blend.

Note: For Korean salad, toss dressing with a combination of fresh spinach leaves, sliced water chestnuts, bean sprouts, hard-cooked egg slices, and crumbled, cooked bacon.

FRENCH VINAIGRETTE DRESSING
This tangy blend of flavors goes well with any mixture of greens

Preparation: 15 minutes   Yield: 1½ cups
Planning: Can prepare ahead

¼ cup chopped fresh parsley
1 clove garlic, finely minced
½ cup olive oil
½ cup vegetable oil
2 Tablespoons lemon juice
4 Tablespoons red wine
vinegar

2 Tablespoons Dijon
mustard
1 teaspoon sugar
¼ teaspoon salt
⅛ teaspoon freshly ground
pepper

Combine all ingredients in pint jar; mix well. To prepare dressing in food processor, place unchopped parsley in bowl, with knife blade positioned. With processor on, drop whole garlic clove through tube and finely mince parsley and garlic. Add remaining ingredients and process for 3 seconds. This dressing will keep in refrigerator indefinitely.

Breads

Amaryllis

BREADS

Basic Steps to Making Bread 97

BISCUITS

Cheese Biscuits 111
Quick Biscuits 111

COFFEECAKES AND SWEET BREADS

Apricot and Prune Coffeecake 116
Bishops Bread 107
Dandy-Quicky Doughnuts 102
Pluck It Cake 112
Cheese French Bread 99
Corn Sticks 110
Fabulous French Toast 117
Five Minute Microwave Croutons 117
Herb Butter 118

MUFFINS

Ice Cream Muffins 98
Peach Muffins 108
Pineapple Bran Muffins 109
Six Week Bran Muffins 110
Sweet Potato Muffins 108
Pretzels, Soft 118

QUICK BREADS

Chocolate Zucchini Bread 100
Cranberry Orange Tea Bread 101
Ham and Cheese Bread 101
Herb Tomato Bread 103
Irish Raisin Bread 104
Poppy Seed Bread 105
Strawberry Bread 106

ROLLS

Butter Rolls 114
Fan Up Rolls 112
Honey Wheat Rolls 113
Sweet Roll's From Herren's 115

YEAST BREAD

Brown Bread 99
Cheese Bread Sticks 100
Herb Cheese Bread 98
Proscuitto and Onion Bread 106
Spinach Bread 104
The Market's Crusty Bread 102
White Batter Bread 103

BASIC STEPS TO MAKING BREAD

Just by understanding a few simple procedures, you will have the confidence of a professional baker and will find that making bread can be fun.

1.   Kneading - Lightly flour work surface with your hands. Turn dough onto surface and shape into a ball. Press ball flat with the palms of your hands. Fold it over toward you; then, with the heels of your hands, push down and away. Turn it one-quarter of the way around and repeat. Keep folding, pushing and turning until dough looks smooth and no longer feels sticky. This will take anywhere from 5 to 15 minutes. To test whether dough has been kneaded enough, make an indentation in it with your finger and see if it springs back. Sometimes blisters will form on surface of dough and break, which is another sign that kneading is sufficient.

2.   Rising - Grease inside of bowl lightly. Press top of dough in bowl, then turn dough over. Cover dough with a clean towel and set bowl in a warm place, free from drafts, for dough to rise until double in size.

3.   Testing for double in size - Press dough with the tip of your finger, making a dent about ½-inch deep. If dent disappears, let dough rise a little longer and then test again. If dent remains, dough has risen enough and is ready to punch down.

4.   Punching down - Punch dough down by pushing your fist deep into center of dough. Fold edges of dough into the center and turn ball of dough over completely.

5.   Shaping - After punching down, divide dough into required number of portions by cutting with large sharp knife. To make round loaves or rolls, pull edges of dough under until ball is rounded and smooth; then place on greased baking pan.

6.   Testing for lightness - After shaping, allow dough to rise until double in size. To tell if it has risen enough, press dough lightly near the bottom or edge with your finger. If dent remains, dough has risen enough and is ready for baking.

7.   Testing to see if bread is done - Tap top of loaf with your knuckles. When done, loaf will sound hollow. There will also be a hollow sound when bottom of pan is tapped. Bread will have shrunk slightly from sides of pan.

HERB CHEESE BREAD
No kneading necessary with this yeast bread

Preparation: 15 minutes
Planning: Can prepare ahead
Rising: 1-1½ hours

Baking: 35-40 minutes
Yield: 1 10-inch round of bread

**1-2 Tablespoons sesame
  seeds**
**2½ cups all-purpose flour,
  divided**
2 Tablespoons sugar
1 teaspoon salt
½ cup milk
½ cup water
2 packages dry active yeast

1 egg, beaten
¼ cup butter, melted
¼ cup butter
**½ teaspoon Italian
  seasoning**
½ Tablespoon garlic powder
**1 cup (4 ounces) grated
  Cheddar cheese**

Grease 10-inch bundt pan. Sprinkle sides and bottom of pan with sesame seeds. Combine 1½ cups flour, sugar, and salt. Heat milk and water to just warm; add yeast to warm mixture; dissolve. Add egg to yeast mixture; pour yeast mixture into flour mixture; beat well. Add melted butter and remaining flour; mix well. Mix ¼ cup butter, Italian seasoning, garlic powder, and Cheddar cheese. Spoon half of dough mixture into pan. Spread cheese mixture over dough. Add remaining dough, spreading evenly. Let rise, covered, 1 to 1½ hours. Bake at 350 degrees for 35-40 minutes. When done, invert and remove from pan. Serve warm. After baking, bread can be frozen.

 ## *ICE CREAM MUFFINS*

Preparation: 5 minutes

Baking: 12 minutes
Yield: 6 muffins

**1 cup vanilla ice cream,
  softened**

1 cup self-rising flour

Mix softened ice cream and flour. Spoon into 6 greased muffin tins. Bake at 425 degrees for 10-12 minutes.

BROWN BREAD
Hiivaleipa, a Finnish bread recipe

Preparation: 20 minutes
Rising: 1¾ hours

Baking: 25-30 minutes
Yield: 2 small loaves

½ cup hot water
2 Tablespoons butter
1 Tablespoon sugar
2 teaspoons salt
1 package dry active yeast
½ cup warm water

2 cups whole wheat flour or
   rye flour
½-1 cup unbleached
   all-purpose flour
melted butter

Mix hot water, butter, sugar, and salt; set aside to cool to lukewarm. Dissolve yeast in ½ cup warm water; let sit 5 minutes, then blend into cooled mixture. With blade in place, put whole wheat flour into work bowl of food processor; turn on/off to aerate. Add liquid; turn on/off to combine. Add white flour gradually, until satiny smooth and not sticky. Place dough in buttered bowl; brush top with melted butter. Cover with towel and allow to rise in warm place until double in size, about 1 hour. Punch down dough, kneading lightly; divide dough in half. Shape each half into a round flat loaf; place on lightly greased baking sheet. Cover; allow to rise about 45 minutes, or until nearly doubled in size. Bake at 400 degrees for 25-30 minutes, or until crust is light brown.

 ## CHEESE FRENCH BREAD
A tasty change from garlic bread

Preparation: 5 minutes
Planning: Can partially prepare ahead

Baking: 10 minutes
Yield: 1 loaf

1 loaf French bread
1 stick butter, softened
½ cup mayonnaise
2 cups grated mozzarella
   cheese

½ cup chopped green onion
1 (3¼-ounce) can black
   olives, chopped
½ Tablespoon garlic powder

Slice French bread in half, lengthwise. Mix butter, mayonnaise, cheese, green onion, olives, and garlic powder; spread evenly over each bread half. Bread can be refrigerated at this point until ready to bake. Bake at 350 degrees for 10 minutes, or until cheese melts. Serve hot.

CHEESE BREAD STICKS

Preparation: 30 minutes
Planning: Can prepare ahead

Baking: 20 minutes
Yield: 30 breadsticks

2 packages dry active yeast
1½ cups warm water
2 Tablespoons sugar
½ cup vegetable oil or olive oil
4-4½ cups all-purpose flour

1 teaspoon salt
3 egg whites, slightly beaten
coarse salt for garnish
grated Parmesan cheese for garnish

Preheat oven to 375 degrees. Add yeast to warm water; add sugar. Set aside until yeast mixture activates and foam forms on top. Add oil. Slowly sift in flour and salt, mixing to make a smooth dough. Roll out 60 pieces of dough to the size of pencils; twist 2 pieces together. Brush with egg whites; sprinkle with baker's salt and Parmesan cheese. Bake on greased cookie sheet for 20 minutes.

Note: Olive oil gives the bread sticks a distinctive Italian flavor.

 # CHOCOLATE ZUCCHINI BREAD
Yummy and delicious!

Preparation: 5 minutes
Planning: Can prepare ahead

Baking: 30-40 minutes
Yield: 2 loaves

½ cup butter, softened
¼ cup vegetable oil
1¾ cups sugar
1 teaspoon vanilla extract
2 eggs
½ cup sour cream
2 cups shredded zucchini
2½ cups all-purpose flour

4 Tablespoons cocoa
½ teaspoon salt
¼ cup chocolate chips
1 teaspoon baking soda
½ teaspoon ground cloves
½ teaspoon ground cinnamon

Preheat oven to 350 degrees. Cream butter, oil, sugar, vanilla, eggs, and sour cream. Add zucchini; mix. In separate bowl, mix flour, cocoa, salt, chocolate chips, baking soda, cloves, and cinnamon. Blend with zucchini mixture. Pour batter into 2 greased and floured loaf pans. Bake for 30-40 minutes. These loaves freeze well.

CRANBERRY ORANGE TEA BREAD
A terrific holiday treat! Tastes great with turkey.

Preparation: 15 minutes
Planning: Can prepare ahead

Baking: 1 hour
Yield: 1 loaf

1 cup sugar
2 cups all-purpose flour
1½ teaspoons baking powder
½ teaspoon baking soda
1 teaspoon salt
4 Tablespoons butter, softened

¾ cup orange juice
1 egg, beaten
1 Tablespoon grated orange rind
½ cup chopped nuts, optional
1 cup chopped fresh cranberries

Preheat oven to 350 degrees. Mix sugar, flour, baking powder, baking soda, and salt. Cut in butter with pastry blender or 2 knives to make very fine crumbs. Combine orange juice, and egg; add to crumb mixture all at once; stir to moisten. Fold in orange rind, nuts, and cranberries. Avoid over mixing. Spread in greased 9x5x3 loaf pan. Bake for about 1 hour, or until loaf is browned and a skewer inserted in the center comes out dry. Cool before slicing. This loaf freezes well.

HAM AND CHEESE BREAD

Preparation: 15 minutes
Planning: Can prepare ahead

Baking: 35 minutes
Yield: 6-8 wedges

2 cups biscuit mix
1 cup chopped cooked ham
⅔ cup milk
2 eggs, beaten
2 green onions, chopped
2 Tablespoons corn oil

½ teaspoon Dijon mustard
1½ cups (6 ounces) shredded extra sharp Cheddar cheese, divided
3 Tablespoons butter
2 Tablespoons sesame seeds

Combine biscuit mix, ham, milk, eggs, onion, corn oil, mustard, and ¾ cup cheese in medium bowl; stir well. Pour batter into greased 10-inch pie pan. Drizzle butter over top. Bake at 375 degrees for 30 minutes. Top with remaining ¾ cup cheese and 2 Tablespoons sesame seeds. Bake an additional 5 minutes. Cut into wedges and serve. After baking, this bread can be frozen and reheated when ready to serve.

THE MARKET'S CRUSTY BREAD
From the E. 48th Street Market, Italian Food
Specialists, in Dunwoody, Georgia

Preparation: 30 minutes
Planning: Can prepare ahead
Rising: 20 minutes

Baking: 20 minutes
Yield: 2 loaves

1½ cups warm water
½ Tablespoon salt
1½ Tablespoons dry active
yeast

4 cups unbleached or white
flour

Combine water, salt, and yeast in mixing bowl; stir to dissolve yeast. Allow to sit 5-10 minutes in warm, draft-free area, until mixture starts to bubble. Stir in small quantities of flour with wooden spoon until dough no longer sticks to sides of bowl. Some flour will be left. Turn dough onto well floured surface. Coat hands and dough with additional flour; shape dough into an oval. Cut dough into 2 pieces; working quickly, shape dough into a long loaf shape by gently rolling dough. Lay each loaf on well-greased cookie sheet. Cover with towel; allow to sit in warm place for 20 minutes. Preheat oven to 450 degrees. Make 3 slashes with sharp knife along top of each loaf. Spray each loaf with salted water. Bake on middle rack of oven for 20 minutes. Cool bread on wire rack. After baking, loaves may be frozen.

 # DANDY-QUICKY DOUGHNUTS

Preparation: 10 minutes

Cooking: 5 minutes
Yield: 5-10 doughnuts

1 can refrigerated rolls
(allow 1 roll per child)

¼ cup vegetable oil
½ cup powdered sugar

Open can of rolls and separate; cut hole in center of each roll. Heat oil to sizzling in electric skillet. Gently drop the cut rolls and holes into oil. Turn over when one side is brown; remove when golden brown. Drain on paper towels. Pour sugar into paper bag; add doughnuts and shake to coat. Serve immediately.

HERB TOMATO BREAD
Tastes like pizza!

Preparation: 15 minutes

Baking: 20-25 minutes
Yield: 12 large or 16 small squares

⅔ cup milk
2 cups biscuit mix
3 medium tomatoes, peeled
  and sliced
paprika for garnish
1 medium onion, minced
2 Tablespoons butter,
  softened

¾ cup sour cream
⅓ cup mayonnaise
1 cup grated Cheddar
  cheese
¾ teaspoon salt
¼ teaspoon pepper
¼ teaspoon dried oregano

Preheat oven to 400 degrees. Stir milk into biscuit mix. Knead on well-floured board or beat 12 times. Pat dough into bottom and ¼-inch up sides of greased, 13x9x2 pan. Arrange tomato slices over dough; sprinkle with paprika. Mix remaining ingredients until smooth and creamy enough to spread. Spoon topping mixture over tomato slices. Bake for 20-25 minutes. Let stand 10 minutes before cutting into squares.

WHITE BATTER BREAD

Preparation: 15 minutes
Rising: 45 minutes

Baking: 45 minutes
Yield: 1 loaf

1 package dry active yeast
1¼ cups very warm water
2 Tablespoons sugar
2 teaspoons salt

2 Tablespoons butter,
  softened
3 cups white or unbleached
  all-purpose flour

Preheat oven to 375 degrees. Dissolve yeast in warm water with sugar and salt; stir in butter. Add half the flour; beat well with mixer or wooden spoon. Add remaining flour; beat well. Let rise, covered, until double in bulk, about 45 minutes. Stir batter down; spread evenly in greased 9x5x3 loaf pan. Let dough rise again until it reaches within 1 inch of top of pan. Bake for about 45 minutes, or until richly browned. Brush top with butter; cool on rack before cutting.

103

IRISH RAISIN BREAD
A Saint Patrick's Day must!

Preparation: 15 minutes
Planning: Can prepare ahead

Baking: 50 minutes
Yield: 2 loaves

1 cup butter, softened	⅛ teaspoon ground allspice
2 cups sugar	⅛ teaspoon ground nutmeg
4 eggs, beaten	2 cups raisins
4 cups all-purpose flour	2 cups applesauce
2 teaspoons baking powder	¼ teaspoon salt
1½ teaspoons baking soda	1 teaspoon lemon juice
1 teaspoon ground cinnamon	1 teaspoon vanilla extract

Preheat oven to 350 degrees. Cream butter and sugar; add beaten eggs. Sift in flour, baking powder, baking soda, cinnamon, allspice, and nutmeg. Let raisins stand in hot water for 5 minutes; drain and pat dry. Add raisins and applesauce to flour mixture. Add salt, lemon juice, and vanilla; mix. Place dough in 2 greased loaf pans. Bake for 50 minutes, or until done. Cool. These loaves freeze well.

SPINACH BREAD
Friends will think you have baked all day

Preparation: 20 minutes
Planning: Can prepare ahead

Baking: 30 minutes

Yield: 1 loaf

1 (13¾-ounce) package hot roll mix	3 garlic cloves, split
2 (10-ounce) packages frozen, chopped spinach	2 Tablespoons vegetable oil
	⅛ teaspoon salt
	⅛ teaspoon pepper

Preheat oven to 325 degrees. Prepare hot roll mix according to package directions; let rise. Cook frozen spinach; drain thoroughly and remove all excess moisture. In saucepan, sauté garlic in oil until light brown. Add spinach; cook 10 minutes. Add salt and pepper. Remove garlic. On floured surface, roll dough into a 9x13 rectangle. Spread spinach over dough. Roll up lengthwise for a long loaf with smaller slices or crosswise for a shorter loaf with larger slices. Use water to seal edges. Place on cookie sheet, seam side down. Pierce top with fork tines. Bake for 30 minutes, or until golden brown. Rub top crust with small amount of butter. Serve warm. After baking, loaf can be frozen.

 ## POPPY SEED BREAD

Preparation: 15 minutes   Baking: 50-60 minutes
Planning: Can prepare ahead   Yield: 2 loaves

3 cups minus 2 Tablespoons   **1½ teaspoons almond**
  self-rising flour   **extract**
2⅓ cups sugar   **1½ teaspoons butter**
3 eggs   **flavoring**
1½ cups milk   **2 Tablespoon poppy seeds**
1⅛ cups vegetable oil   **Glaze**
1½ teaspoons vanilla extract

Preheat oven to 325 degrees. In large bowl mix all ingredients together; batter will be runny. Pour into two greased and floured 9x5x3 loaf pans. Bake for 50-60 minutes. Cool 15 minutes. Pour an equal amount of glaze on each loaf. Cool completely before removing from pans. These loaves freeze well.

Glaze:
½ teaspoon vanilla extract   **¼ cup orange juice**
½ teaspoon almond extract   **¾ cup sugar**
½ teaspoon butter flavoring

Stir together all ingredients.

PROSCUITTO AND ONION BREAD
A no-knead yeast bread

Preparation: 30 minutes
Planning: Can prepare ahead
Rising: 1 hour

Baking: 25-30 minutes
Yield: 1 loaf

1 package dry active yeast
¼ cup warm water
1 cup plus 1 Tablespoon
   milk, divided
½ cup butter
2 eggs, well beaten
½ teaspoon salt

2 ounces proscuitto,
   chopped
2 Tablespoons minced
   onion
4 cups all-purpose flour
2 Tablespoons sesame seeds

In large bowl, stir yeast in water; let stand 5 minutes to dissolve. In small saucepan, heat 1 cup milk with butter over low heat until luke warm. Butter does not have to melt. Add warm milk, eggs, salt, proscuitto, and onion to yeast. Add flour; beat with spoon until ingredients are well blended and dough pulls away cleanly from spoon. Grease 1-½ quart round baking dish. Scrape dough into dish; spread out evenly. Brush top of dough with remaining 1 Tablespoon milk; sprinkle with sesame seeds. Let dough rise, uncovered, in warm place until it comes to top of baking dish, about 1 hour. Preheat oven to 350 degrees. Bake for 25-30 minutes, or until bread is light brown and sounds hollow when top is tapped. Remove from pan; cool slightly. Serve warm. After baking, loaf can be frozen, then reheated before serving.

 ## STRAWBERRY BREAD

Preparation: 5 minutes
Planning: Can prepare ahead

Baking: 1¼ hours
Yield: 2 loaves

3 cups all-purpose flour
2 cups sugar
3 teaspoons ground
   cinnamon
1 teaspoon baking soda
1 teaspoon salt

1 cup vegetable oil
4 eggs, beaten
2 (10-ounce) packages
   frozen strawberries,
   thawed
1¼ cups chopped nuts

Preheat oven to 350 degrees. Combine flour, sugar, cinnamon, baking soda, and salt in large bowl. Add oil and eggs; mix well. Stir in berries and nuts. Pour batter into two greased and floured 9x5x3 loaf pans; bake for 1 hour 15 minutes. These loaves freeze well.

BISHOPS BREAD

This recipe is from the head dietician for John D. Rockefeller in the early 1930's. It was said that Bishops Bread was always served for afternoon tea.

Preparation: 20 minutes   Baking: 40 minutes
Planning: Can prepare ahead   Yield: 18-20 squares

2 cups light brown sugar   **1 teaspoon ground nutmeg**
½ cup butter   **2 eggs**
1 cup chopped pecans   **2 teaspoons baking powder**
3 cups all-purpose flour,   **½ teaspoon salt**
** divided**   **1 teaspoon baking soda**
1 teaspoon ground allspice   **1 cup buttermilk or sour**
1 teaspoon ground   ** milk**
** cinnamon**

Preheat oven to 350 degrees. Cream brown sugar and butter. Add nuts, 1 cup flour, allspice, cinnamon, and nutmeg; mix well. Remove 1 cup of mixture and refrigerate. To remainder of mixture, add eggs. Sift together 2 cups flour, baking powder, salt, and baking soda. Add flour mixture and buttermilk alternately to egg mixture. Pour into greased 12x8x2 pan. Sprinkle top with reserved 1 cup of spice mixture. Bake for 40 minutes. Remove from oven; cool before cutting into squares. Bread will keep 1 week or can be frozen.

PEACH MUFFINS
Perfect for ripe Georgia peaches; a summertime treat

Preparation: 15 minutes

Baking: 20-25 minutes
Yield: 12 muffins

⅓ cup butter, softened
1 cup sugar, divided
1 egg
1½ cups all-purpose flour
1½ teaspoons baking
  powder
½ teaspoon salt

¼ teaspoon ground nutmeg
½ cup milk
½ cup chopped peaches
1 teaspoon ground
  cinnamon
½ cup butter, melted

Preheat oven to 350 degrees. Cream butter and ½ cup sugar. Add egg; mix. Combine flour, baking powder, salt, and nutmeg; stir flour mixture into butter mixture alternately with milk. Stir in peaches. Fill greased muffin cups ⅔ full. Bake for 20-25 minutes. Mix ½ cup sugar with cinnamon. When muffins are done, immediately dip tops into melted butter, then into cinnamon-sugar mixture.

 ## SWEET POTATO MUFFINS

Preparation: 15 minutes
Planning: Can prepare ahead

Baking: 25 minutes
Yield: 12 muffins

1 cup all-purpose flour,
  sifted
1 teaspoon baking powder
¼ teaspoon baking soda
½ teaspoon salt
½ teaspoon ground
  cinnamon
½ teaspoon ground nutmeg
½ cup chopped pecans or
  walnuts

½ cup cooked mashed sweet
  potatoes (approximately 1
  large or 2 small)
¼ cup sugar or honey
¼ cup milk
1 egg
2 Tablespoons butter,
  melted

Preheat oven to 350 degrees. In medium bowl, sift together flour, baking powder, baking soda, salt, cinnamon, and nutmeg. Add pecans; set aside. Combine sweet potatoes, sugar, milk, egg, and butter in mixing bowl. Add to flour mixture; stir until well moistened. Line muffin tins with paper baking liners; fill each ⅔ full. Bake for 25 minutes. Muffins can be frozen after baking.

PINEAPPLE BRAN MUFFINS
Good and nutritious

Preparation: 40 minutes
Planning: Can prepare ahead

Baking: 20 minutes
Yield: 20 small muffins,
15-18 large muffins

½ stick butter, softened
⅓ cup firmly packed dark
  brown sugar
¼ cup plus 2 Tablespoons
  honey, divided
1 Tablespoon cold water
½ cup all-purpose white or
  whole wheat flour, sifted
½ cup plus 2 Tablespoons
  cake flour, sifted
⅔ cup sugar 3 cups all-bran
  cereal flakes

½ teaspoon salt
½ teaspoon baking soda
½ teaspoon ground
  cinnamon
2 large eggs
¼ cup vegetable oil
¼ cup crushed pineapple,
  well drained
¼ cup honey
1½ cups buttermilk
½ cup seedless raisins

Preheat oven to 400 degrees. Cream butter and brown sugar in small mixing bowl until mixture is very light and creamy. Add 2 Tablespoons honey and cold water; continue beating until very fluffy. Spoon mixture into greased muffin tins or paper baking liners placed in muffin tins, about 2 teaspoons per muffin cup. Set prepared muffin cups aside. Sift flours, sugar, salt, baking soda, and cinnamon in large mixing bowl. Add eggs, oil, ¼ cup honey, pineapple, bran flakes, and buttermilk; beat until batter is well blended. Stir in raisins. Fill prepared muffin cups ¾ full. Bake about 20 minutes, or until muffins are firm to touch. Turn muffins out of pan immediately onto rack to cool. Serve warm or reheat to serve.

 ## SIX WEEK BRAN MUFFINS

Preparation: 10 minutes
Planning: Can prepare ahead

Baking: 15-20 minutes
Yield: 36 muffins

**1 (15-ounce) package raisin
  bran cereal**
3 cups sugar
5 cups all-purpose flour
2 teaspoons salt
5 teaspoons baking soda

raisins, optional
2 teaspoons pumpkin spice
4 eggs
1 cup vegetable oil
1 quart buttermilk

Preheat oven to 400 degrees. Mix cereal, sugar, flour, salt, baking soda, raisins, and pumpkin spice in bowl. Add eggs, oil, and buttermilk; mix well. At this point, batter can be refrigerated in a covered container for up to six weeks. Fill greased muffin cups ⅔ full. Bake for 15-20 minutes.

Note: To save time and make muffins uniform in size, use an ice cream scoop to measure muffin batter.

CORN STICKS
*Authentic Georgia corn sticks from a true
southern restaurant, Pittypat's Porch*

Preparation: 30 minutes
Planning: Can prepare ahead

Baking: 10-15 minutes
Yield: 4 dozen

5 eggs
5 cups buttermilk
**7½ Tablespoons butter,
  melted**
2½ teaspoons sugar

5 teaspoons salt
5 cups plain corn meal
2½ teaspoons baking soda
**7½ teaspoons baking
  powder**

Preheat oven to 450 degrees. Beat eggs until light. Add buttermilk, butter, sugar and salt; blend well. Carefully blend in corn meal. Dissolve baking soda in 3 Tablespoons cold water; add to corn meal mixture. Sift baking powder; add to corn meal mixture. Stir well. Pour into greased and heated corn stick pans. Bake for 10-15 minutes until lightly browned.

CHEESE BISCUITS
A cheese lover's delight

Preparation: 10 minutes

Baking: 12-15 minutes

Planning: Must partially prepare ahead

Yield: 100 biscuits

Chilling: 1 hour

2 cups all-purpose flour or 1 cup whole wheat flour plus 1 cup white flour
2 teaspoons salt
⅛ teaspoon freshly ground pepper

⅛ teaspoon cayenne pepper
½-1 teaspoon dry mustard
2 sticks unsalted butter, softened
2 cups firmly packed grated sharp Cheddar cheese

Preheat oven to 375 degrees. Mix flour, salt, pepper, cayenne, and mustard. Add butter and cheese; blend until dough is smooth. Add more ground pepper and cayenne, if desired. Form dough into rolls about 1 inch in diameter; refrigerate about 1 hour or freeze. Slice chilled or frozen dough rolls into biscuits a little less than ¼-inch thick. Arrange on baking sheets; bake 12-15 minutes, until very lightly browned and centers are just barely firm to the touch. Let cool a few seconds before removing from baking sheets. Baked biscuits can be frozen.

Note: Vary the seasonings by adding 1 to 2 Tablespoons sesame seeds or poppy seeds to the dough; vary the cheeses by substituting any hard cheese, such as Parmesan, Gouda, or Edam, or by using a mixture of cheeses.

 # QUICK BISCUITS

Preparation: 10 minutes

Baking: 15-20 minutes

Yield: 6 biscuits

1 cup self-rising flour
2 Tablespoons mayonnaise

⅔ cup milk

Combine flour and mayonnaise; add milk, stirring well. Drop batter into well-greased muffin tin. Bake at 350 degrees for 15-20 minutes, until lightly browned.

FAN UP ROLLS

Preparation: 30 minutes

Baking: 12 minutes
Yield: 10 muffins

2 cups all-purpose flour
½ teaspoon salt
4 teaspoons baking powder
½ teaspoon cream of tartar
1 cup plus 3 Tablespoons sugar, divided

½ cup butter, softened
⅔ cup milk
1-2 Tablespoons ground cinnamon
½ cup butter, melted

Preheat oven to 425 degrees. Place flour, salt, baking powder, cream of tartar, and 3 Tablespoons sugar in bowl. With fork or pastry blender, cut in ½ cup butter; add milk all at once. Mix with fork or pastry blender until dough has the consistency to knead. Knead for 2 minutes, forming a ball when complete. Cut dough in half. Roll half of dough into ¼-inch thick 10x10 square. Combine 1 cup sugar and cinnamon. With pastry brush spread melted butter on dough; sprinkle with cinnamon mixture. Cut five 2-inch strips from dough; stack one on top of the other to make a 10x2x2-inch piece. Cut into 2-inch pieces, turn sideways in greased muffin pan. Repeat with remaining half of dough. Dab each top with remaining melted butter; bake for 12 minutes.

PLUCK IT CAKE
Just "pluck" off the pieces to eat!

Preparation: 20 minutes

Baking: 50-55 minutes
Servings: 24

3 (11-ounce) cans buttermilk biscuits
1½ sticks butter
1½ cups light brown sugar

1 cup chopped nuts
½ teaspoon ground cinnamon
1 teaspoon ground nutmeg

Preheat oven to 300 degrees. Cut each biscuit into quarters. Put half of quartered biscuits into greased bundt pan. Melt butter; remove from heat. Add sugar, nuts, cinnamon, and nutmeg; mix well. Pour half of mixture over biscuits. Put remaining quartered biscuits on top; cover with remaining butter mixture. Bake for 50-55 minutes. Remove pan from oven and cover with foil for 20 minutes. Invert pan on serving plate and "pluck" away.

HONEY WHEAT ROLLS
An easy yeast bread; the food processor does the kneading!

Preparation: 15 minutes

Planning: Can prepare ahead

Rising: 1½ hours

Baking: 20 minutes

Yield: 12 rolls

1 package dry active yeast
1 teaspoon sugar
1 cup warm water
1½ cups whole wheat flour
1½ cups white or
   unbleached all-purpose
   flour, divided

1 teaspoon salt
2 Tablespoons honey
1 egg
1 Tablespoon water
butter

Combine yeast and sugar in 1 cup warm water; let sit for 5-10 minutes. With blade in place, put whole wheat flour and 1 cup white flour in work bowl of food processor. Add salt; throughly mix. Add honey and yeast mixture; turn machine on/off quickly 3 to 4 times. Process mixture continuously until it forms a ball. At this point, stop food processor and touch dough to see if it needs the other ½ cup flour. If it is wet and sticky, add about ¼ cup flour. Run processor for 15 seconds, or until dough forms a ball again. When it does, stop processor and feel dough. If still wet and sticky, add remaining flour. If "tacky", but not wet, enough flour has been added and processor can be turned on again and allowed to run continuously. Count 60 revolutions of dough; stop processor. Turn dough out into a buttered bowl. Coat dough evenly all over. Cover with a damp towel and let rise in warm place for 1 hour, or until double in size. Punch down and divide into 12 balls. Place shaped balls onto greased baking sheet. Let rise in warm place until double in size, about 30 minutes. Preheat oven to 375 degrees. Beat egg with 1 Tablespoon water; brush rolls with mixture; bake for 20 minutes. After baking rolls can be frozen.

BUTTER ROLLS

An easy yeast bread; the food processor does the kneading for you

Preparation: 30 minutes
Planning: Can prepare ahead
Rising: 2 hours

Baking: 20 minutes
Yield: 12 rolls

1 package dry active yeast
¼ cup warm water
2½ to 3 cups all-purpose flour
¼ cup sugar
1 teaspoon salt
1 egg
¼ cup milk, room temperature

½ stick butter, softened and cut into Tablespoon-size pieces
1 egg, beaten
1 Tablespoon water
poppy or sesame seeds for garnish

Sprinkle yeast over water and stir; set aside. With blade in place, put 2 cups flour in work bowl of food processor; add sugar and salt, turning on/off once to combine. Add dissolved yeast, egg, and milk; process until combined. Add butter; process until combined. Gradually add remaining flour until dough is kneaded and no longer sticky. It should become smooth and satiny. Place dough in buttered bowl and cover. Allow dough to rise until double in size, about 1 hour. Punch down dough. Dough can be kept unshaped and well covered for up to 3 days in refrigerator. When ready to bake, preheat oven to 375 degrees. Pinch off enough dough for one roll. Shape as desired; place on buttered baking sheet. Repeat for other rolls, placing them about 1 inch apart on sheet. Allow to rise about 1 hour. Combine egg with 1 Tablespoon water; brush shaped rolls with mixture. Sprinkle with poppy or sesame seeds. Bake for 20 minutes. After baking, rolls can be frozen.

SWEET ROLLS FROM HERREN'S

Herren's Restaurant in Atlanta is well-known for these cinnamon rolls

Preparation: 30 minutes
Planning: Can partially prepare ahead
Rising: 2 hours

Baking: 18-20 minutes
Yield: 60 rolls

1 cup milk
¼ cup butter
2¼ cups sugar, divided
1½ teaspoons salt
2 packages dry active yeast
¼ cup warm water

4 cups all-purpose flour,
   sifted
4 Tablespoons ground
   cinnamon
½-1 cup melted butter

Let milk come to a boil in heavy saucepan. Add butter, ¼ cup sugar, and salt; cool. Meanwhile, soften yeast in water; stir into milk mixture. Add flour, half at a time, beating well. Turn out onto floured board; allow to sit for 15 minutes then knead until smooth. Place dough in buttered bowl, cover with cloth, let rise until double in size. Roll out dough onto floured board to about ¼-inch thick; cut into rough 8-inch squares. Mix cinnamon with 2 cups sugar. Brush 1 square at a time with melted butter, then sprinkle cinnamon-sugar mixture over entire surface. Starting at one side of square, roll up into tube. Roll tube back and forth until it is 12-16 inches long. Cut tube into slices approximately ½-inch wide; place flat into pan that has been brushed with melted butter and sprinkled thoroughly with cinnamon-sugar mixture. Sides of rolls should touch but not be overpacked. Repeat with remaining squares. Use 3 or 4 (6-8-inch) aluminum pans to allow for staggered baking during the meal or for baking at a later time. Brush tops with melted butter and sprinkle cinnamon sugar mixture generously over entire surface. Let stand at room temperature for 1 hour. Bake at 350 degrees for 18-20 minutes, or cover with aluminum foil and refrigerate. Allow 30 minutes for rolls to return to room temperature after removing from refrigerator.

APRICOT AND PRUNE COFFEECAKE

Preparation: 30 minutes
Planning: Can prepare ahead

Baking: 60 minutes
Yield: 1 10-inch coffeecake

¾ cup light brown sugar, packed
¾ cup plus 3 Tablespoons butter, softened, divided
3 cups plus 3 Tablespoons all-purpose flour, divided
1½ teaspoons ground cinnamon
½ cup finely chopped toasted nuts
1½ teaspoons baking powder

¾ teaspoon baking soda
¼ teaspoon salt
1¼ cups sugar
4 eggs
1½ teaspoons vanilla extract
1 cup sour cream
1 cup pitted dried prunes, coarsely chopped
1 cup dried apricots, coarsely chopped
2 Tablespoons powdered sugar

Preheat oven to 350 degrees. Combine brown sugar, 3 Tablespoons butter, 3 Tablespoons flour, and cinnamon; mix with fork until crumbly; add chopped nuts; set aside. Grease and lightly flour 10-inch tube pan. On waxed paper, sift together 3 cups flour, baking powder, soda, and salt; set aside. Beat ¾ cup butter in large bowl with electric mixer at medium speed until fluffy. Gradually beat in sugar and eggs, one at a time, until very light and fluffy, about 3 minutes. Add vanilla. Divide flour mixture into four parts. At low speed, alternately beat in flour mixture and sour cream, beginning and ending with flour mixture. Beat just until smooth, about 1 minute. Gently fold in prunes and apricots. Turn ⅓ batter into prepared pan. Sprinkle with half cinnamon-nut mixture; repeat layers, ending with batter. Bake 55-60 minutes, or until toothpick inserted in center of cake comes out clean. Let cool in pan on wire rack 20 minutes. Remove to platter; sift powdered sugar over cake.

FABULOUS FRENCH TOAST

Preparation: 20 minutes   Cooking: 20 minutes
Planning: Must partially prepare ahead   Servings: 4
Chilling: 12 hours

1 loaf unsliced white or French bread
1 cup milk
¼ cup sugar
4 eggs, beaten
1 teaspoon vanilla extract
¼ teaspoon salt
¼ cup bacon grease or vegetable oil
powdered sugar for garnish
maple syrup

Slice bread into ¾-inch slices. Heat milk; add sugar, stirring to dissolve. Remove from heat; cool slightly. Add eggs, vanilla, and salt; mix well. Dip each bread slice into liquid mixture until well coated. Place in flat baking dish; pour remaining liquid over bread. Refrigerate, covered, overnight. In heavy skillet, sauté bread in very hot bacon grease until golden on both sides; sprinkle with powdered sugar. Serve hot with maple syrup.

Note: For variety, add 2 Tablespoons Grand Marnier to milk, decrease sugar to 1 Tablespoon, and vanilla to ½ teaspoon.

 ## FIVE MINUTE MICROWAVE CROUTONS
A great crunchy topping for soups and salads

Preparation: 5 minutes   Cooking: 5 minutes
Planning: Can prepare ahead   Yield: 2 cups

¼ cup butter
2 teaspoons salad seasoning
4 cups (¾-inch cubes) French bread

Microwave butter in 2-quart shallow baking dish at HIGH (100% power) for 55 seconds, or until melted; stir in salad seasoning. Add bread cubes; stir to gently coat. Microwave at HIGH (100% power) 4½ to 5 minutes, stirring 2 or 3 times; cool; croutons will crisp as they cool. Store in airtight container.

Note: Salad seasoning can be found in jars in the supermarket spice section.

SOFT PRETZELS

Preparation: 15 minutes
Planning: Must partially prepare ahead
Rising: 30-60 minutes

Chilling: 2-24 hours
Baking: 15 minutes
Yield: 32 pretzels

2 cups warm water
2 packages dry active yeast
½ cup sugar
2 teaspoons salt
¼ cup butter, softened
1 egg

6½-7½ cups all-purpose flour
1 egg yolk
2 Tablespoons water
coarse salt for garnish

Pour warm water into large bowl. Sprinkle in yeast; stir until dissolved. Add sugar, salt, butter, egg, and 3 cups of flour; beat until smooth. Add enough additional flour to make a stiff dough. Cover bowl tightly; refrigerate 2 to 24 hours. Turn dough onto lightly floured board. Divide dough in half. Cut each half into 16 pieces. Roll each piece into pencil shape, about 20-inches long. Shape into pretzels. Place on lightly greased baking sheet. Blend together egg yolk and water. Brush pretzels with egg yolk mixture. Sprinkle with coarse salt. Let rise in warm place, free from draft, until double in size, about 30-60 minutes. Bake at 400 degrees for 12-15 minutes. Cool on wire racks. Pretzels are delicious served with mustard or cream cheese.

 ## *HERB BUTTER*

Delicious and fun to serve with homemade bread or rolls

Preparation: 5 minutes
Planning: Can prepare ahead

Yield: ½ cup

½ cup butter, softened
1 Tablespoon chopped fresh parsley
1 Tablespoon chopped fresh basil

1 Tablespoon chopped fresh chives
⅛ teaspoon garlic powder

Cream butter with parsley, basil, chives, and garlic powder. Serve on thick slices of bread. Herb butter can be refrigerated for up to 2 weeks.

Eggs, Pasta, Rice, and Cheese

Morning Glory

EGGS, PASTA, RICE AND CHEESE

EGGS AND CHEESE

Blue Cheese Soufflé 133
Brunch Eggs 121
Brunch Puff 134
Cheese Blintzes 134
Cheese Strata 136
Creole Eggs 122
Easy Swiss Cheese Pie 138
Fancy Egg Scramble 123
Feta Cheese Tart 137
Herb Cheese Grits 132
Irrestible Spinach Quiche 135
Queso 138
Shrimp-Eggs 122
Willard Scott's Cheese Grits Soufflé 132
Swiss Cheese Soufflé 133

PASTA

Baked Rotelle with Ground Beef 125

Deluxe Macaroni and Cheese 136
Fettuccini with Asparagus 124
Fussilli Pescatore 129
Macaroni with Wine and Cheese 135
Pasta with Clam Sauce 126
Pesto and Pasta 126
Shrimp and Fresh Basil Pasta 127
Spinach Fettuccini 124
Vegetable Pasta Medley 128

RICE

Brazillian Rice 129
Fruited Curry Rice Mix 130
Rice with Thyme 131
Rice with Green Chiles 128
Risotto-"Italian Rice" 130
Wild Rice with Mushrooms and
    Almonds 131

BRUNCH EGGS
Great for company

Preparation: 45 minutes

Baking: 30 minutes
Servings: 12

12 eggs, hard-cooked
½ cup mayonnaise
1 Tablespoon grated onion
½ teaspoon dry mustard
⅛ teaspoon curry powder
⅓ cup bacon bits

2 cups Cream Sauce
1 (4-ounce) can sliced
  mushrooms, drained
1½ cups grated sharp
  Cheddar cheese

Split eggs lengthwise and remove yolks. Place yolks in mixing bowl; add mayonnaise, onion, mustard, curry, and bacon bits. Mix until smooth. Stuff the 24 egg whites with mixture. Place eggs in greased 13x9x2 baking dish. Cover eggs with 2 cups cream sauce. Sprinkle mushrooms over cream sauce. Top with grated cheese. Bake at 350 degrees for 30 minutes.

Cream Sauce:

4 Tablespoons lightly salted
  butter
4 Tablespoons all-purpose
  flour

2 cups hot milk
¼ teaspoon salt
¼ teaspoon paprika

Melt butter over low heat; stir in flour until smooth. Slowly stir in milk, salt, and paprika. Cook and stir sauce with wire whisk until smooth and boiling.

CREOLE EGGS

A specialty of caterer Jean Benton
of Benton and Associates, Inc. in Atlanta

Preparation: 10 minutes
Baking: 15 minutes

Cooking: 45 minutes
Servings: 10-12

1 large green bell pepper,
  coarsely chopped
2 medium onions, coarsely
  chopped
2 Tablespoons butter
2 (14½-ounce) cans whole
  tomatoes, undrained
1 (16½-ounce) can early
  peas, drained

salt and pepper, to taste
1 teaspoon chili powder
8 eggs, hard-cooked
2 cups White Sauce (see
  Index)
1 cup buttered breadcrumbs

Sauté pepper and onion in butter; add tomatoes. Cook for 30 minutes.
Stir in peas; cook 15 more minutes. Add salt, pepper, and chili powder;
set aside. Slice eggs in half lengthwise. In bottom of greased 13x9x2
dish, layer half of tomato mixture, half of the sliced eggs; cover with
half of White Sauce. Repeat layers. Top with buttered breadcrumbs.
Bake at 350 degrees for 15 minutes.

SHRIMP EGGS

Preparation: 30 minutes

Cooking: 10 minutes
Servings: 4-6

6 eggs, hard-cooked
1 teaspoon lemon juice
½ teaspoon finely chopped
  onion
⅛ teaspoon salt

1 cup chopped cooked
  shrimp
Parmesan Cheese Sauce
2 Tablespoons dried parsley

Halve cooked eggs; remove yolks. In medium bowl, mash yolks; add
lemon juice, onion, and salt. Stir in shrimp and 1 Tablespoon cheese
sauce. Stuff egg whites with shrimp mixture. Arrange in chafing dish;
spoon remaining cheese sauce over eggs and sprinkle with parsley.

Parmesan Cheese Sauce:
4 Tablespoons butter
3 Tablespoons all-purpose
  flour
¾ cup chicken broth

¾ cup half and half
2 egg yolks, beaten
⅓ cup grated Parmesan
  cheese

Melt 4 Tablespoons butter in saucepan. Stir in flour. Add chicken broth and half and half; bring to a boil and cook 2 minutes. Add a small amount of sauce to egg yolks; stir yolks back into sauce. Stir in Parmesan cheese and cook an additional 4 minutes. Keep warm.

FANCY EGG SCRAMBLE
A new twist to the morning egg

Preparation: 40 minutes

Baking: 30 minutes
Servings: 10

1 cup diced Canadian bacon
1 cup sliced fresh
  mushrooms
¼ cup chopped green onion
3 Tablespoons butter
12 eggs, beaten

Cheddar Cheese Sauce
4 teaspoons melted butter
3 slices soft bread,
  crumbled
⅛ teaspoon paprika

In large skillet, cook bacon, mushrooms, and onion in butter until onion is tender, but not brown. Add eggs and scramble until just set. Fold eggs into cheese sauce and put into large baking dish. Combine 4 teaspoons melted butter, bread crumbs, and paprika; sprinkle over eggs. Bake at 350 degrees for 30 minutes.

Cheddar Cheese Sauce:
2 Tablespoons butter
2 Tablespoons all-purpose
  flour
1½ teaspoons salt

⅛ teaspoon pepper
2 cups milk
1 cup grated Cheddar
  cheese

In small saucepan, melt butter; blend in flour, salt, and pepper. Add milk; cook and stir until bubbly. Stir in cheese until melted.

FETTUCCINI WITH ASPARAGUS

Preparation: 30 minutes

Cooking: 25 minutes

Servings: 8

1¾ pounds asparagus, peeled, trimmed, and cut into 2-inch pieces
½ pound fresh mushrooms, thinly sliced
2 red bell peppers, cored and cut in julienne strips
8 Tablespoons butter, divided

3 cups heavy cream
12 ounces fettuccini, fresh or dried
¼ pound prosciutto, cut in julienne strips
salt and pepper, to taste
1½ cups grated Parmesan cheese, divided

Cook asparagus in large pot of boiling water, uncovered, for 3-4 minutes, just until tender crisp. Drain; run under cold water. Drain; set aside. Sauté mushrooms and red pepper in 4 Tablespoons butter; set aside. Twenty minutes before serving, heat cream in heavy saucepan over medium heat until simmering; reduce heat and continue to cook until reduced and slightly thickened, about 15 minutes. Meanwhile, cook pasta; rinse. Toss with remaining 4 Tablespoons butter. Add asparagus, red pepper, mushrooms, prosciutto, and cream; toss well. Add salt and pepper to taste. Sprinkle with ¾ cup Parmesan cheese. Serve immediately, and pass remaining ¾ cup Parmesan cheese with the fettuccini.

SPINACH FETTUCCINI

Preparation: 20 minutes

Cooking: 30 minutes

Servings: 6

2 small zucchini, sliced
2 carrots, sliced
1 cup sliced, fresh mushrooms
4 green onions, chopped
¼ cup butter
1 clove garlic, minced
½ teaspoon dried whole basil
½ teaspoon salt

¼ teaspoon pepper
8 ounces spinach fettuccini
1 cup diced chicken, optional
1 (19-ounce) can chick peas, drained
1 cup grated Parmesan cheese
2 egg yolks
1 cup heavy cream

In skillet, sauté vegetables in butter; stir in garlic, basil, salt, and pepper. When vegetables are tender, set aside. Cook fettuccini according to package directions; drain. Combine vegetables, chicken, peas, and fettuccini, tossing gently. Simmer; stir in Parmesan cheese. Beat egg yolks and cream until foamy. Add to fettuccini mixture and cook until thickened.

BAKED ROTELLE WITH GROUND BEEF

Preparation: 30 minutes

Baking: 50 minutes
Servings: 6-8

½ pound rotelle or other
   twisted noodles
1 pound lean ground beef
2 medium onions, chopped
1 clove garlic, minced
1 (35-ounce) can tomatoes
½ cup tomato paste
1 cup dry red wine
½ teaspoon paprika
1 Tablespoon salt

1 bay leaf
⅛ teaspoon dried thyme
1 teaspoon ground
   marjoram
1 teaspoon Worcestershire
   sauce
½ teaspoon Tabasco sauce
2 cups White Sauce
¼ cup freshly grated
   Parmesan cheese

Cook noodles according to package directions; drain. Sauté ground beef, onion, and garlic until beef is brown and crumbly and onion is tender. Add tomatoes, tomato paste, wine, paprika, salt, bay leaf, thyme, marjoram, Worcestershire sauce, and Tabasco. Simmer 15-20 minutes. In 2½-quart casserole dish, mix noodles with tomato-beef mixture until well blended. Pour white sauce over casserole; bake at 375 degrees for 40 minutes. Top with Parmesan cheese; bake an additional 10 minutes.

White Sauce:
2 Tablespoons butter
2 Tablespoons all-purpose
   flour

2 cups milk
½ teaspoon salt
½ teaspoon white pepper

Melt butter in small saucepan; stir in flour until well blended. Add milk, stirring constantly, until sauce thickens. Add salt and pepper.

PASTA WITH CLAM SAUCE

Preparation: 5 minutes   Cooking: 20 minutes
                                                        Servings: 6

**3 (10-ounce) cans baby
    clams**
olive oil for sautéing
2 Tablespoons butter
6 cloves garlic, minced

**4 Tablespoons chopped
    fresh parsley, divided
    (Italian flat leaf preferred)**
1½ pounds linguini, cooked

Strain clam juice from clams. In saucepan, heat clam juice until liquid is reduced by half. Cover bottom of medium skillet with olive oil; add butter, garlic, and 2 Tablespoons parsley. Cook over low heat until garlic is transparent. Add clam juice; increase heat and let mixture come to a boil. Add clams and remaining 2 Tablespoons parsley; cook until clams are just heated through. Do not overcook or clams will be tough. Meanwhile cook linguini according to package directions. Pour clam sauce over hot, drained linguini.

PESTO AND PASTA

Preparation: 15 minutes   Cooking: 12 minutes
Planning: Can partially prepare ahead   Servings: 2

**½ cup snipped fresh basil,
    firmly packed**
¼ cup snipped fresh parsley
**¼ cup grated Parmesan
    cheese**
**2 Tablespoons pine nuts,
    walnuts, or pecans,
    chopped**

1 clove garlic, halved
2 Tablespoons olive oil
**2 Tablespoons butter,
    softened**
salt and pepper, optional
**4-6 ounces linguini or other
    pasta**

Put basil, parsley, Parmesan cheese, nuts, garlic, oil, and butter in blender or food processor; blend until smooth. Season with salt and pepper, if desired. Pesto can be stored in screw-top jar in refrigerator for up to 1 week or frozen for up to 6 months. Meanwhile, cook pasta according to package directions until al dente. Drain, reserving liquid. Stir 2-4 Tablespoons hot, reserved liquid into pesto until desired consistency. Toss with hot, cooked pasta. Serve warm or chilled.

Note: If fresh basil is not available, 2 teaspoons dried basil can be substituted; increase parsley to ¾ cup or use ¾ cup shredded fresh spinach.

SHRIMP AND FRESH BASIL PASTA
Compliments of John Wilson, Corporate Executive Chef at The Mansion restaurant in Atlanta

Preparation: 20 minutes

Cooking: 30 minutes
Servings: 4

1 shallot, finely diced
2 cloves garlic, minced
3 Tablespoons butter
1 bunch fresh basil, finely chopped with large stems removed
½ cup white wine
1 Tablespoon roux
1 Tablespoon tomato paste
1 cup heavy cream

salt and white pepper, to taste
1 pound mixed fresh linguini or fettucini (spinach, tomato, egg or other flavors)
20 medium raw shrimp, peeled, deveined and butterflied
grated Parmesan cheese for garnish

Sauté shallot and garlic in 1 Tablespoon butter over medium heat for 3 minutes. Add basil, mix well; cook 1 minute. Add white wine; reduce by ⅓. Whisk in roux and tomato paste until well blended; simmer over low heat for 5 minutes. Add cream; bring to a boil; add salt and pepper to taste. Simmer 5 minutes; set aside. Meanwhile cook pasta in 4 quarts boiling salted water, stirring frequently, until al dente, about 3-5 minutes. Melt remaining 2 Tablespoons butter in saucepan. Over high heat, add shrimp and season lightly with salt and pepper. Cook, shaking pan frequently to keep shrimp moving, for 2 minutes or until shrimp are pink and firm. Drain excess butter from pan. Add basil sauce to shrimp; heat 2 minutes. Drain pasta; divide among 4 serving dishes. Arrange 5 shrimp on top of pasta and pour sauce over shrimp. Sprinkle with Parmesan cheese and serve immediately.

VEGETABLE PASTA MEDLEY
Excellent!

Preparation: 30 minutes

Cooking: 30 minutes
Servings: 6

1 pound broccoli
2 small zucchini
½ pound asparagus
1 pound linguini, preferably fresh
1 clove garlic, crushed
1 pint cherry tomatoes, halved
¼ cup olive oil
¼ cup chopped fresh basil or 1 teaspoon dried whole basil, crumbled

½ pound mushrooms, sliced
½ cup frozen green peas
½ cup chopped fresh parsley
1½ teaspoons salt
¼ teaspoon black pepper
¼ teaspoon crushed red pepper
¼ cup butter
¾ cup heavy cream
⅔ cup freshly grated Parmesan cheese

Wash and trim broccoli, zucchini, and asparagus. Cut broccoli into bite-size pieces; cut zucchini into thin slices; cut asparagus into 1-inch pieces. Cook in boiling, salted water until tender crisp. Drain; put in large bowl. Cook and drain linguini. Sauté garlic and tomatoes in oil in large skillet for 2 minutes. Stir in basil and mushrooms; cook 3 minutes. Stir in peas, parsley, salt, and black and red pepper; cook 1 minute more. Add mixture to vegetables in bowl. Melt butter in sauce skillet; stir in cream and cheese. Cook over medium heat, stirring constantly, until smooth. Add linguini; toss to coat. Stir in vegetables; heat gently just until hot.

 ## RICE WITH GREEN CHILES

Preparation: 15 minutes

Baking: 45 minutes
Servings: 8

2 (10¾-ounce) cans cream of celery soup, undiluted
2 cups sour cream
2 (4-ounce) cans chopped mild green chiles

4 cups cooked instant rice
2 cups grated sharp Cheddar cheese, divided

Mix soup, sour cream, chiles, rice, and 1⅔ cups cheese. Pour into greased 1½-quart casserole dish. Top with remaining ⅓ cup cheese. Bake, uncovered, at 375 degrees for 45 minutes.

FUSSILLI PESCATORE
Compliments of Luigi Bosco, Bosco's Ristorante Italiano in Atlanta

Preparation: 15 minutes

Cooking: 25 minutes
Servings: 2

½ pound fussilli
1 Tablespoon butter
4 cups marinara sauce,
  divided
½ cup olive oil
4-6 shrimp (16-20 count
  size), peeled and deveined
8 sea scallops (30-40 count
  size)
8 mussels

10 ounces Gulf snapper, in
  chunks
6 littleneck clams
1 teaspoon chopped fresh
  garlic
⅛ teaspoon fresh basil
⅛ teaspoon fresh Italian
  parsley
½ cup dry white wine
salt and pepper, to taste

Cook fussilli in boiling salted water for 8 minutes; drain. Sauté fussilli in butter and 1 cup marinara sauce for 1 minute; set aside. Heat ½ cup olive oil in sauté pan until very hot; add shrimp, scallops, mussels, snapper, clams, and garlic. Sauté for 3 minutes. Add basil, parsley, wine, remaining 3 cups marinara sauce, and salt and pepper to taste; simmer for 8 minutes. Combine fussilli and seafood mixture. Serve immediately.

BRAZILLIAN RICE

Preparation: 20 minutes

Baking: 1 hour
Servings: 6

¼ red bell pepper, chopped
¼ green bell pepper,
  chopped
1 carrot, grated
2 Tablespoons grated onion
2 Tablespoons corn oil

1 cup uncooked long-grain
  rice
⅛ teaspoon salt
1 (10¾-ounce) can chicken
  broth
10¾ ounces water

Sauté peppers, carrot, and onion in oil until tender. Add rice to vegetables; stir until oil is absorbed. Transfer mixture to greased casserole dish. Add salt, broth, and water. Bake, covered, at 350 degrees for 1 hour.

 ## FRUITED CURRY RICE MIX

Preparation: 10 minutes
Planning: Can prepare ahead

Yield: 1 gift package (enough for 4 cups cooked rice)

1 cup uncooked long-grain rice
¼ cup mixed dried fruit, chopped
¼ cup slivered almonds
2 Tablespoons light raisins

1 Tablespoon minced dry onion
1-2 teaspoons curry powder
2 beef bouillon cubes, crushed
½ teaspoon salt

Mix all ingredients. To cook, combine rice mixture in saucepan with 2½ cups water and 2 Tablespoons butter. Cover tightly and bring to a boil. Reduce heat and simmer 20 minutes. Do not lift cover while simmering. Makes 4 cups cooked rice.

Note: When using as a gift, attach card with cooking instructions.

RISOTTO - "ITALIAN RICE"

Preparation: 10 minutes

Cooking: 20 minutes
Servings: 10

4 Tablespoons olive oil
6 Tablespoons butter, divided
1 large onion, finely chopped
1 large clove garlic, minced or pressed

2 cups uncooked white rice
⅛ teaspoon saffron, optional
7½ cups chicken or beef broth
1 cup freshly grated Parmesan cheese

Put olive oil and 4 Tablespoons butter into heavy 3- or 4-quart pan. Over medium heat, add onion and cook until golden, stirring well. Add garlic and rice; stir until rice looks milky, about 3 minutes. Stir in saffron and broth. Cook, uncovered, stirring occasionally, until mixture boils. Reduce heat so rice boils gently. Cook, uncovered, 20-25 minutes. Toward end of cooking time, stir rice. Turn off heat; stir in cheese and remaining 2 Tablespoons butter.

130

WILD RICE WITH MUSHROOMS AND ALMONDS

Preparation: 30 minutes

Baking: 1½ hours
Servings: 8

1 cup uncooked wild rice
¼ cup butter
½ cup slivered almonds
2 Tablespoons snipped chives or chopped green onions

½ cup chopped mushrooms
3 cups chicken broth

Wash and drain wild rice. Melt butter in large skillet; add rice, almonds, chives, and mushrooms. Cook, stirring until almonds are golden brown, about 20 minutes. Pour rice mixture into ungreased 1½-quart casserole dish. Heat chicken broth to boiling; stir into rice mixture. Bake, covered tightly, at 325 degrees for 1 to 1½ hours, or until liquid is absorbed and rice is fluffy.

 ## RICE WITH THYME

Preparation: 15 minutes

Baking: 1 hour
Servings: 6

3 Tablespoons butter
⅓ cup chopped onion
⅔ cup sliced mushrooms
1 cup uncooked long-grain rice

⅛ teaspoon dried thyme
1 (10¾-ounce) can beef broth
10¾ ounces water

Melt butter in saucepan. Add onion and mushrooms; sauté until tender. Add rice and thyme; stir until rice looks milky. Transfer to 1½-quart casserole dish; add broth and water. Bake, covered, at 350 degrees for 1 hour.

Note: Chicken broth can be substituted for beef broth, and mushrooms and thyme deleted, for another tasty rice dish.

HERB CHEESE GRITS

Preparation: 45 minutes

Baking: 1 hour 10 minutes
Servings: 8

1½ cups grated Cheddar
    cheese
1 clove garlic, minced
½ cup butter
2 cups hot cooked grits (not
    instant)
3 eggs, beaten

2 cups milk
¼ teaspoon dried tarragon
¼ teaspoon ground
    marjoram
⅛ teaspoon ground sage
½ cup freshly grated
    Parmesan cheese

Add cheese, garlic, and butter to freshly cooked hot grits. Allow cheese and butter to melt. When mixture cools, add eggs, milk, tarragon, marjoram, and sage. Place in 2-quart casserole dish. Bake at 325 degrees for 1 hour. Sprinkle with Parmesan cheese and bake an additional 10 minutes.

WILLARD SCOTT'S CHEESE GRITS SOUFFLÉ
Willard Scott, of NBC's Today Show, shares
one of his favorite recipes

Preparation: 20 minutes

Baking: 45 minutes
Servings: 8

1 cup quick-cooking grits
4½ cups water
1 teaspoon salt
6 Tablespoons butter
1 stick garlic cheese
2 eggs, beaten

¼ cup milk
salt and pepper, to taste
1 cup crushed corn flakes
2 Tablespoons butter,
    melted

Cook grits in salted water. When done, stir in butter and cheese. Allow to cool. Mix eggs and milk; season with salt and pepper. Stir in grits. Pour into buttered casserole dish; top with corn flakes mixed with butter. Bake, covered, at 350 degrees for 40-45 minutes.

SWISS CHEESE SOUFFLÉ
A specialty of The Hedgerose Heights Inn in Atlanta

Preparation: 1 hour

Baking: 30 minutes
Servings: 4

4 Tablespoons unsalted butter
¼ cup all-purpose flour
1¼ cups milk, heated
5 eggs, separated, room temperature
½ cup freshly grated Swiss Gruyère cheese
½ cup freshly grated Swiss cheese or Appenzeller
¼ teaspoon salt
⅛ teaspoon ground nutmeg
⅛ teaspoon freshly ground pepper
⅛ teaspoon paprika

Preheat oven to 375 degress. Melt butter in medium saucepan over low heat. Add flour; cook, stirring constantly, until smooth. Add milk; cook over medium heat, stirring constantly, until thick and bubbly. Whisk egg yolks in small bowl and slowly whisk into milk mixture. Add cheeses, salt, nutmeg, pepper, and paprika. Cool mixture to room temperature. Beat egg whites until stiff; fold into cheese mixture. Pour into well-buttered 1½-quart soufflé dish. Bake 30 minutes until golden brown. Serve immediately with a salad for a luncheon or as a hot appetizer.

BLUE CHEESE SOUFFLÉ

Preparation: 30 minutes

Baking: 40 minutes
Servings: 6

3 Tablespoons butter
¼ cup flour
½ teaspoon salt
pepper
1½ cups milk
1 cup crumbled blue cheese
6 eggs, separated
1 Tablespoon caraway seeds, optional

Melt butter; blend in flour, salt and pepper. Stir in milk; bring to a boil. Cook 5 minutes, stirring constantly. Add cheese. Add egg yolks one at a time, beating well after each addition. Add caraway seeds, if desired. Cool. Stiffly beat egg whites. Fold ⅓ whites into cheese mixture; very gently fold cheese into remaining whites. Turn into buttered and floured 2-quart soufflé dish. Bake at 375 degrees for 30 to 40 minutes.

BRUNCH PUFF

Preparation: 30 minutes
Planning: Can partially prepare ahead

Cooking: 50 minutes
Servings: 8

12 slices bacon
2 medium onions, sliced
12 slices white or wheat
bread, quartered
2 cups grated Swiss cheese

8 eggs
4 cups milk
1½ teaspoons salt
¼ teaspoon pepper

Cook bacon until crisp; drain and crumble. Cook onion in bacon drippings until soft. Spread half of bread in bottom of greased 13x9x2 pan. Sprinkle with half of crumbled bacon, onion, and cheese. Repeat layers. Combine eggs, milk, salt, and pepper; pour over top layer in pan. The casserole can be prepared to this stage in advance and stored in refrigerator until 1 hour before serving. Bake at 350 degrees for 45-50 minutes until set and puffed.

CHEESE BLINTZES

Preparation: 1 hour
Planning: Can prepare ahead

Baking: 20 minutes
Yield: 40 blintzes

1 loaf fresh white bread (20
slices)
1 (8-ounce) package cream
cheese, softened
1 egg yolk
1 cup sugar

3 teaspoons ground
cinnamon
1 stick butter, melted
1 cup sour cream
fresh parsley sprig for
garnish

Trim crust from bread. Flatten bread with rolling pin. Thoroughly combine cream cheese and egg yolk. Spread bread slices with cream cheese mixture and roll up jelly-roll style. After spreading and rolling all 20 slices of bread, cut each roll in half making 40 blintzes. Combine sugar and cinnamon. Dip blintzes in butter to coat and roll in sugar mixture. Bake at 350 degrees for 20 minutes. Serve with sour cream decorated with fresh parsley. Blintzes can be frozen and thawed before baking.

IRRESISTIBLE SPINACH QUICHE

Preparation: 30 minutes   Baking: 45 minutes
Planning: Can prepare ahead   Servings: 12

2 (9-inch) frozen pie shells
1 (10-ounce) package frozen
** chopped spinach, cooked**
** and drained**
1 medium onion, chopped
2 Tablespoons butter
5 eggs
1 (13-ounce) can evaporated
** milk**

salt and pepper to taste
2 cups grated Swiss cheese
½ cup grated Parmesan
** cheese, divided**
4 pieces bacon, cooked and
** crumbled**

Prebake pie shells at 400 degrees for 5 minutes. In skillet, sauté spinach and onion in butter. In bowl, beat eggs, milk, salt, pepper, Swiss cheese, and ¼ cup Parmesan cheese. Pour mixture into lukewarm spinach. Add bacon. Stir and pour into pie shells. Sprinkle remaining ¼ cup Parmesan cheese on top. Bake at 350 degrees for 45 minutes. This dish can be frozen after baking and reheated to serve.

 ## MACARONI WITH WINE AND CHEESE

Preparation: 30 minutes   Cooking: 15 minutes
                                              Servings: 6

2 cups seashell macaroni
¼ cup finely chopped onion
3 Tablespoons butter
3 Tablespoons all-purpose
** flour**
½ teaspoon salt

½ teaspoon pepper
1 cup heavy cream
⅓ cup dry white wine
2 cups grated sharp Cheddar
** or Swiss cheese**

Cook macaroni; drain. Sauté onion in butter until tender. Stir in flour, salt, and pepper. Slowly add cream and wine; stir until mixture thickens. Add cheese and stir until melted. Combine sauce and macaroni; place in buttered casserole. Bake at 350 degrees for 15 minutes, until hot and bubbly.

CHEESE STRATA
Wonderful early morning treat

Preparation: 30 minutes
Planning: Must partially prepare ahead

Chilling: 12 hours
Baking: 1 hour
Servings: 8

16 slices white bread
8 slices Canadian bacon
8-10 slices sharp Cheddar cheese
6 eggs, beaten
½ teaspoon salt
¼ teaspoon pepper
½ teaspoon dry mustard
¼ cup minced onion
¼ cup chopped green bell pepper

2 teaspoons Worcestershire sauce
3 cups milk
⅛ teaspoon cayenne pepper
1 stick butter, melted
2 cups crushed potato chips

Trim crust from bread. In greased 13x9x2 dish, layer, in order, the following ingredients: 8 slices bread, bacon, sliced cheese, and 8 slices bread. There will be 8 individual cheese stratas. Mix eggs, salt, pepper, mustard, onion, green pepper, Worcestershire sauce, milk, and cayenne pepper; pour over stratas. Refrigerate 12 hours or overnight. Mix melted butter and potato chips; sprinkle over mixture. Bake at 350 degrees for 1 hour.

 ## DELUXE MACARONI AND CHEESE

Preparation: 25 minutes

Cooking: 20 minutes
Servings: 12

1 (8-ounce) package macaroni, cooked
1 cup mayonnaise
1 (4½-ounce) can mushrooms, drained and chopped
4 cups grated sharp Cheddar cheese
¼ cup chopped pimientoes

1 (10¾-ounce) can cream of mushroom soup, undiluted
¼ cup chopped onion
¼ cup chopped green bell pepper
1 cup crushed saltine crackers
3 Tablespoons butter

Cook macaroni according to package directions. Mix cooked macaroni, mayonnaise, mushrooms, cheese, pimientoes, soup, onion, and pepper. Pour into greased 13x9x2 dish. Sprinkle crushed crackers on top and dot with butter. Bake at 375 degrees for 20-30 minutes.

FETA CHEESE TART
A favorite at the Peasant Uptown restaurant in Atlanta

Preparation: 30 minutes   Baking: 1½ hours
                                                              Servings: 8

pastry for 10-inch tart pan
1 egg, beaten with 1 Tablespoon water
1 pound fresh mushrooms, halved (quartered if large)
4 Tablespoons butter, divided
3 medium tomatoes, each cut into 8 wedges

½ pound fresh spinach
2 ounces feta cheese, crumbled, divided
1 Tablespoon dried whole oregano
2-3 eggs, to make ½ cup
1½ cups heavy cream
½ teaspoon salt
1 teaspoon pepper

Prepare pastry and place in tart pan. Prick bottom and sides; brush with egg wash. Bake at 300 degrees for 20 minutes or until golden brown. Set aside to cool. Sauté mushrooms in 2 Tablespoons butter 8-10 minutes; drain and set aside. Sauté tomatoes in remaining 2 Tablespoons butter, just until they render their juice and do not look raw; drain well and set aside. Without adding any liquid, toss spinach in small saucepan over medium heat until wilted. Layer ingredients in pastry shell as follows: 1 ounce feta cheese, mushrooms, tomatoes, spinach, oregano, and remaining 1 ounce feta cheese. Whisk eggs with cream; add salt and pepper. Pour egg mixture over tart, whisking while pouring. Bake at 325 degrees for 1½ hours, rotating pan for even browning after 45 minutes. Allow to cool 30 minutes before serving.

QUESO

Preparation: 20 minutes
Cooking: 10 minutes

Baking: 10 minutes
Servings: 18-20 tortillas

1 pound white melting
  cheese (Monterey Jack,
  mozzarella, havarti, etc.)
3 Tablespoons vegetable oil
1 large yellow onion,
  chopped

½ cup green bell pepper,
  chopped
1 pound mushrooms, sliced
½ cup heavy cream
flour tortillas

Preheat oven to 200 degrees. Grate cheese; place in large, shallow, oven-proof dish. Bake for 10 minutes, allowing cheese to slowly melt. The cheese will separate and become rubbery if oven is too hot. Heat oil in large frying pan. Sauté onion and pepper 3-4 minutes. Stir in mushrooms; cook 4-5 minutes more. Remove melted cheese from oven. Gradually stir in cream. Slowly add sautéed mixture until thoroughly blended. Serve immediately by spreading on hot, fresh flour tortillas.

Note: Queso can be made with any cheese that becomes stringy when melted or a combination of those listed in ingredients.

 ## EASY SWISS CHEESE PIE

Preparation: 15 minutes
Planning: Can prepare ahead

Baking: 1 hour
Servings: 6

1 scant cup milk
3 eggs
1½ cups cubed Swiss
  cheese
1 Tablespoon all-purpose
  flour

1 Tablespoon vegetable oil
1 teaspoon chopped chervil
  or dried parsley
1 small onion, chopped,
  optional
¼ cup sesame seeds

Measure milk, eggs, cheese, flour, oil, and chervil into blender. Blend until mixture is smooth. Pour into buttered pie dish. Sprinkle onion and seasame seeds on top. Bake at 300 degrees for 1 hour. This can be frozen after baking and reheated to serve.

Fish and Seafood

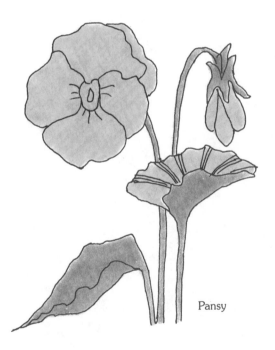

Pansy

FISH AND SEAFOOD

Bone's Seafood Seasoning 164
CRAB
  Chicago-Style Crab 142
  Crab Avocado 142
  Pearls' Fried Crabmeat Puffs 144
  Trotters' Linguini with Crabmeat 143
CRAWFISH
  Crawfish Monica 146
  Crawfish Soufflé 145
FISH
  Baked Stuffed Snapper 162
  Crunchy Fried Fish 141
  Delicious Baked Fish 160
  Grilled Amberjack 141
  Grilled Marinated Tuna with Fresh
    Ginger and Soy-Butter Sauce 163
  Red Snapper Almondine 161
  Salmon in Foil 148
  Stuffed Fish Fillets 149
  Zesty Grilled Swordfish 164
LOBSTER
  Thermidor 150

OYSTER
  New Orleans Oyster Sandwich 147
  Oysters Rockefeller Casserole 146
  Scalloped Oysters 148
SCALLOPS
  Scallops in Herb Sauce 151
SHRIMP
  Barbara Dooley's Stir-Fry Shrimp with
    Fried Rice 159
  Bone's Beer-Battered Shrimp 153
  Frogmore Stew 155
  Parmesan Shrimp Scampi 158
  Shrimp a La Grecque 157
  Shrimp Creole 154
  Shrimp Manallé 156
  Shrimp Perlo 156
SEAFOOD COMBINATIONS
  Curried Seafood Salad 160
  Seafood Pecan 158
  Seafood Stew 154
  Seafood Supreme 152

GRILLED AMBERJACK
From the Peasant Uptown restaurant in Atlanta

Preparation: 10 minutes
Planning: Must partially prepare ahead

Marinating: 12 hours
Grilling: 10 minutes
Servings: 8

8 (6-8-ounce) amberjack
fillets
½ cup Hoisin sauce

¼ cup dry vermouth
1 Tablespoon sugar

Place amberjack fillets on large platter. Combine Hoisin sauce, vermouth, and sugar; brush over both sides of fillets. Cover with plastic wrap; marinate in refrigerator overnight. Preheat grill to medium-hot. Grill fillets 4-5 minutes on each side, or until fish flakes with fork.

Wine suggestions: Moulin-a-Vent
Gewurztraminer - Alsace

CRUNCHY FRIED FISH

Preparation: 15 minutes
Planning: Can partially prepare ahead

Frying: 10 minutes
Servings: 6

2 pounds fish fillets,
flounder, snapper, or sole
salt and pepper to taste
1 cup all-purpose flour
2 teaspoons baking
powder

1 teaspoon salt
1 egg yolk
1 cup lukewarm water
1 Tablespoon vegetable oil
1 egg white, stiffly beaten
vegetable oil for frying

Thoroughly wash and dry fillets; sprinkle with salt and pepper to taste. Combine flour, baking powder, and salt in bowl; drop egg yolk in center. Add water and oil; stir well. Fold egg white into batter. Dip fillets in batter; fry in ¼-inch oil heated to 370 degrees until golden on both sides. Drain on paper towels.

Wine suggestions: Macon Villages
Chenin Blanc (dry)

141

CRAB AVOCADO

Preparation: 45 minutes   Chilling: 6 hours
Planning: Must partially prepare ahead   Servings: 8-10

Avocado Mold:
1 cup cold water
3 envelopes unflavored
   gelatin
3 avocados, mashed
1 cup sour cream
1 cup mayonnaise
1 small onion, grated
¼ cup lemon juice
1 teaspoon salt

Crab Salad:
4 (6½-ounce) cans white
   crabmeat
⅓ cup chopped pimientos
½ cup finely chopped celery
½ cup finely chopped
   scallions
½ to ¾ cup mayonnaise
⅛ teaspoon salt
⅛ teaspoon pepper

Pour cold water in top of double boiler. Add gelatin; stir until dissolved. Refrigerate gelatin for about 1 hour. Combine avocados, sour cream, mayonnaise, onion, lemon juice, and salt; add to thickened gelatin. Rinse ring mold in cold water; spoon avocado-gelatin mixture into mold. Refrigerate, covered, several hours or overnight. Rinse crabmeat in cold water and remove any cartilege. Add remaining ingredients, blending well. Refrigerate, covered, several hours or overnight. When ready to serve, unmold avocado mixture and spoon crabmeat salad into center. Serve with warm croissants for a wonderful meal.

Wine suggestions: Chardonnay - Raymond, Grgich Hills
                     Meursult

CHICAGO-STYLE CRAB
Makes a lovely luncheon or buffet dish

Preparation: 10 minutes   Baking: 15 minutes
Planning: Can partially prepare ahead   Servings: 3-4

1 pound imitation shredded
   crabmeat
1 stick butter, softened
1 cup soft bread crumbs
2 Tablespoons minced
   onion

2 cloves garlic, minced
2 Tablespoons minced fresh
   parsley
½ teaspoon salt
¼ teaspoon dried tarragon
2 Tablespoons sherry

Arrange crabmeat in shallow, buttered casserole or au gratin dish. Combine butter, bread crumbs, onion, garlic, parsley, salt, tarragon, and sherry. Sprinkle crumb mixture over crabmeat. Can prepare dish ahead to this point and refrigerate. Bring to room temperature before baking. Bake at 350 degrees for 15 minutes, or until crumbs are browned. Enjoy a tossed salad and fresh bread with this meal.

Wine suggestions: Riesling - Mosel
Meursault

TROTTERS' LINGUINI WITH CRABMEAT
A luxurious meal from Trotter's Restaurant in Atlanta

Preparation: 30 minutes
Planning: Can partially prepare ahead

Cooking: 20 minutes
Servings: 4

2 quarts water
½ teaspoon olive oil
2 teaspoons salt
1 pound fresh linguini
3 Tablespoons olive oil
3 cloves garlic, pressed
1 teaspoon cayenne pepper
1 pound fresh lump crabmeat

4 cups clam juice
1 cup dry white wine
½ cup clarified butter
salt and white pepper to taste
4 Tablespoons chopped fresh parsley, divided

Bring water to a boil in large pot. Add ½ teaspoon olive oil and salt; stir in pasta. Cook until tender, but still firm; drain immediately. Heat 3 Tablespoons olive oil in large skillet. Add garlic and cayenne pepper; heat thoroughly. Add crabmeat, clam juice, and wine to pan; continue to stir. Add clarified butter, salt, and pepper. Allow mixture to come to a boil over medium-high heat. Continue to boil, reducing liquid to half original amount. After reduced, mix in 3 Tablespoons chopped parsley. Arrange cooked linguini in large soup bowls; pour crabmeat and sauce over pasta. Garnish with remaining 1 Tablespoon parsley before serving.

Wine suggestions: Chardonnay - Sonoma Cutrer, Acacia
Meursault - Premier Cru

PEARLS' FRIED CRABMEAT PUFFS
A wonderful main dish or appetizer
from Pearl's Fish Cafe in Atlanta

Preparation: 45 minutes   Frying: 5 minutes
Planning: Can partially prepare ahead   Servings: 6

**1 pound fresh lump
  crabmeat
1 pound fresh crab claw
  meat
3 Tablespoons mayonnaise
½ bunch green onions,
  minced
1 small green bell pepper,
  minced**

**½-1 teaspoon lemon juice
1 stalk celery, minced
⅛ teaspoon salt
⅛ teaspoon white pepper
Beer Batter
vegetable oil frying
Honey-Mustard Sauce**

Clean crabmeat thoroughly, picking out shells; squeeze out all liquid. Combine crabmeat, mayonnaise, green onion, pepper, lemon juice, celery, salt and white pepper in large bowl. Mix thoroughly with hands. Roll mixture into 2- or 3-ounce balls, as preferred; squeeze together firmly. Dip crabmeat balls into Beer Batter, coating well. Place gently into hot oil; deep fry until golden brown. Serve with Honey-Mustard Sauce for dipping.

Beer Batter:
**1 (12-ounce) bottle beer, not
  light
2 large eggs**

**6½ ounces vegetable oil
1¼ cups all-purpose flour**

Combine beer, eggs, and vegetable oil in mixing bowl. Mix at low speed, adding flour gradually. Continue whipping until thoroughly mixed, and batter is smooth.

Honey-Mustard Sauce:
**¼ cup Dijon mustard
¼ cup honey
3 Tablespoons red wine
  vinegar**

1½ cups mayonnaise

Combine mustard, honey, and red wine vinegar in mixing bowl; mix thoroughly at medium speed. Add mayonnaise gradually; continue whipping until sauce is smooth.

Wine suggestions: Chardonnay - Innisfree, Stratford
Puilly Fuisse

CRAWFISH SOUFFLÉ
A specialty from Anthonys Restaurant in Atlanta

Preparation: 45 minutes

Baking: 15 minutes
Servings: 4-6

½ stick butter
2 Tablespoons minced celery
2 Tablespoons chopped onion
2 Tablespoons chopped green onion
2 Tablespoons chopped red bell pepper

½ teaspoon salt
½ teaspoon pepper
2½ cups shrimp stock
1½ cups all-purpose flour
4 egg yolks
6 egg whites
1½ cups chopped cooked crawfish or bay shrimp

Melt butter in large skillet. Combine celery, onion, green onion, and bell pepper; add salt and pepper. Sauté for 3 minutes, or until tender. Add shrimp stock; simmer 15 minutes. Add flour, ¼ cup at a time, beating with wooden spoon until mixture thickens and leaves sides of pan. Cook 5 minutes, stirring constantly. Beat in egg yolks, one at a time, with wooden spoon. Cool. Beat egg whites until stiff. Fold ¼ of egg whites into vegetable mixture to thin. Add crawfish; fold in remaining egg whites. Spoon into buttered individual soufflé dishes. Bake at 350 degrees for 15 minutes. Crawfish Soufflé is good served with a sherry sauce.

Wine suggestions: Alsace Riesling
Sylvaner

CRAWFISH MONICA
Cajun food lovers will love this!

Preparation: 20 minutes

Cooking: 20-30 minutes
Servings: 4

1 pound pasta (rotelle was used for New Orleans Jazz Festival)
1 stick butter
¾ cup chopped green onions

1 Tablespoon Cajun Seafood Magic
1 pound crawfish tails, peeled
2 cups half and half

Cook pasta according to package directions; drain. Chill by running under cold water; drain thoroughly. Melt butter in large saucepan and sauté onions for 2-3 minutes. Add Cajun Magic and crawfish tails; sauté 1 minute. Add half and half; cook for 5-10 minutes over medium heat until sauce thickens. Add pasta to pan, tossing well. Serve immediately.

Wine suggestion: Gewurztraminer

OYSTERS ROCKEFELLER CASSEROLE

Preparation: 20 minutes
Planning: Can partially prepare ahead

Baking: 40 minutes
Servings: 8

1 quart raw oysters
1 medium onion, chopped
1 stalk celery, chopped
1 stick butter
½ cup chopped fresh parsley
1 (10-ounce) package frozen chopped spinach, thawed, drained

¼ cup Worcestershire sauce
½ cup seasoned bread crumbs
salt and pepper to taste
1 cup grated sharp Cheddar cheese
seasoned bread crumbs for topping

146

Drain oysters. Sauté onion and celery in butter for 5 minutes. Add parsley, spinach, Worcestershire sauce, bread crumbs, salt, and pepper. Grease shallow casserole dish; arrange oysters in single layer; cover with spinach mixture. Casserole can be prepared ahead to this point. When ready to serve, bake at 350 degrees for 30 minutes. Remove; sprinkle with cheese and a thin layer of bread crumbs. Return to oven; bake an additional 10 minutes.

Wine suggestions: Chardonnay - Chalone, Kalim
Chablis - Premier Cru

NEW ORLEANS OYSTER SANDWICH
This recipe contributed by Decatur, Georgia artist Wayland Moore

Preparation: 20 minutes

Toasting: 5 minutes
Servings: 2

1 (10-inch) length of French or Italian bread, or 2 Kaiser or small hero rolls
2 Tablespoons butter, softened
4 thin slices bacon, diced
1 (8-ounce) container shucked oysters, drained

2 teaspoons all-purpose flour
½ cup shredded iceberg lettuce
4 slices tomato
2 Tablespoons chili sauce
½ teaspoon horseradish

Preheat oven or toaster-oven to 375 degrees. Split bread in half lengthwise and scoop out most of the soft insides, leaving a ½-inch thick shell. Butter shells; toast about 5 minutes, until butter melts and bread is warm. Meanwhile, in small skillet, fry bacon 2-3 minutes over moderately high heat until lightly browned. Dry oysters with paper towels and dust with flour. Add to skillet; cook 2 minutes, stirring. Drain on paper towels. Place lettuce on bottom of loaf; top with oysters, bacon, and tomato. Mix chili sauce and horseradish; spread over loaf. Close the sandwich and cut in half to serve.

Wine suggestions: Sauvignon Blanc - Kenwood, Groth
Pouilly Fume

SCALLOPED OYSTERS

Preparation: 15 minutes   Baking: 35 minutes
Planning: Can partially prepare ahead   Servings: 4

½ cup dry bread crumbs   **⅛ teaspoon salt**
1 cup cracker crumbs   **⅛ teaspoon pepper**
½ cup butter, melted   **4 Tablespoons oyster liquid**
1 pint oysters   **2 Tablespoons heavy cream**

Mix bread and cracker crumbs; stir in butter. Layer ⅓ of crumbs in bottom of shallow, buttered baking dish. Cover with half the oysters; sprinkle with salt and pepper. Add half of oyster liquid and cream. Repeat layers, ending with remaining crumbs. Can be prepared to this point in advance. When ready to serve, bake at 450 degrees for 35 minutes.

Note: This recipe can be doubled, but a large enough dish must be used so that there are never more than 2 layers of oysters. If 3 layers are used, the middle layer will be underdone. Oysters should be crowded together.

Wine suggestions: Chardonnay - Acacia, Deloach
                     Puligny Montrachet

SALMON IN FOIL
Elegant and easy!

Preparation: 15 minutes   Baking: 20 minutes
Planning: Can partially prepare ahead   Servings: 4

4 salmon fillets   **1 onion, thinly sliced**
salt and pepper to taste   **1 stick butter, cut into 8**
1 (10-ounce) package frozen   **pieces**
   artichoke hearts   **hollandaise sauce, optional**
1 lemon, thinly sliced

Preheat oven to 375 degrees. Rinse salmon and pat dry. Place each fillet in center of a 12x12-inch lightly oiled aluminum foil square. Season salmon with salt and pepper. Divide artichoke hearts, lemon slices, and onion evenly and place equal amounts of each on salmon fillets. Top with two squares of butter on each fillet. Seal foil securely. Can be prepared to this point in advance. When ready to bake, bake 20 minutes. Serve with hollandaise sauce for a special treat.

Wine suggestions: Chardonnay - Stratford, Kendall Jackson
Meursault

STUFFED FISH FILLETS

Preparation: 20 minutes   Baking: 20-30 minutes
Planning: Can partially prepare ahead   Servings: 4-6

⅓ cup finely chopped celery
2 Tablespoons finely
  chopped onion
⅔ cup butter, divided
1 cup herb stuffing
1 Tablespoon lemon juice
1 teaspoon minced fresh
  parsley

½ cup flaked crabmeat,
  optional
2 pounds fish fillets,
  flounder or sole
½ teaspoon dried dill weed

Preheat oven to 350 degrees. In saucepan, sauté celery and onion in ⅓ cup butter until soft. Add stuffing, lemon juice, parsley, and crabmeat; set aside. Place half of fillets in large, lightly oiled baking pan. Top with stuffing mixture. Layer remaining fillets on top of stuffing. Melt butter; add dill weed. Spoon over stuffed fish fillets. Bake for 20-30 minutes, basting often with butter and dill weed from pan.

Wine suggestions: Chardonnay - Beringer, Raymond
Chablis Premier Cru

LOBSTER THERMIDOR
From The Abbey Restaurant in Atlanta,
a luxurious meal and well worth the effort

Preparation: 1½ hours   Cooking: 20 minutes
Planning: Can partially prepare ahead   Servings: 4

**4 (1½ pound) live Maine
  lobsters
2 Tablespoons clarified
  butter
1 large shallot, finely diced
½ pound fresh mushrooms,
  thinly sliced
2 ounces dry white wine
1 ounce cognac**

**1 ounce sherry
1 cup heavy cream
1½ Tablespoons Dijon
  mustard
salt and white pepper to
  taste
1 cup hollandaise sauce,
  optional**

Place 1 inch water in pot large enough to easily accomodate the 4 lobsters. Bring to a vigorous boil. Add lobsters and cover immediately. When the water returns to a boil, continue to cook lobsters, covered, for 4 minutes. Remove lobsters; allow to cool to room temperature. Beginning 1 inch from tail, cut rectangular-shaped hole in back of lobster with lobster or poultry shears, going about halfway up main body cavity. Remove tail meat in one piece by slipping fingers under meat and loosening the bottom. The meat will only be half cooked. Remove vein running along bottom of tail and remove coral and roe from base of tail, reserving for another purpose. Cut tail into several large pieces and reserve. Remove claws from body by twisting them off. Crack claws with nut cracker and remove claw meat. Add to reserved tail meat. Repeat this operation until all four lobsters have been shelled. Rinse out body cavity; drain shells until ready to use.

Preheat oven to 350 degrees. Heat large saucepan until very hot; add clarified butter. Add shallots and mushrooms; sauté over high heat for 2 minutes. Add white wine, cognac, and sherry; reduce over high heat for 2 minutes, or until pan is nearly dry. Add cream and bring to a boil. Add mustard; whisk with wire whisk until completely dissolved in sauce. Add semi-cooked lobster meat and simmer over medium heat for 3-4 minutes, or until lobster pieces are cooked through. Do not

overcook because lobster will become very tough and rubbery. Season to taste with salt and white pepper. Arrange lobster bodies on cookie sheet and warm in oven while lobster is cooking in sauce. Spoon lobster into shells, dividing it equally among the shells. Top with hollandaise sauce, if desired, and serve immediately.

Wine suggestions: Chardonnay - Simi Reserve
Chassange Montrachet, Meursault

SCALLOPS IN HERB SAUCE

Preparation: 30 minutes
Planning: Can prepare ahead

Cooking: 10 minutes
Servings: 2

1 pound sea or bay scallops, rinsed and drained
²/₃ cup white wine
¹/₃ cup water
¹/₄ teaspoon freshly ground pepper
2 Tablespoons butter
1 Tablespoon all-purpose flour
¹/₂ teaspoon finely snipped fresh tarragon

¹/₂ teaspoon finely snipped fresh chives
¹/₂ teaspoon finely snipped fresh parsley
¹/₂ teaspoon finely snipped fresh dill weed
²/₃ cup half and half
hot cooked fettucini

Cut sea scallops in quarters; bay scallops can be left whole. Bring wine, water, and pepper to a boil in saucepan. Add scallops; simmer, covered, 6 minutes, or until tender, remove scallops with slotted spoon, reserving liquid. Melt butter in saucepan. Blend in flour to form a smooth paste. Slowly stir in reserved liquid; stir until sauce is smooth. Add herbs and gently simmer 2-3 minutes. Blend in cream. Return scallops to sauce to heat through. Serve over hot, cooked fettucini.

Wine suggestions: Sauvignon Blanc - Clos du Bois, Stratford
Sancere

SEAFOOD SUPREME

Preparation: 1½ hours   Baking: 45 minutes
Planning: Can prepare ahead   Servings: 10-12

3 pounds seafood (shrimp, crabmeat, and lobster)
1 pint sea scallops
¾ cup butter
1 Tablespoon lemon juice
½ pound mushrooms, sliced
¾ cup all-purpose flour
3 cups milk or half and half
2 cups grated Gruyère cheese

¼ teaspoon salt
¼ teaspoon pepper
¼ teaspoon dry mustard
2 teaspoons tomato paste
2 (10-ounce) packages frozen artichoke hearts, thawed

Cook and clean seafood; set aside. Sauté scallops in butter and lemon juice. Add mushrooms; cook until mushrooms are barely limp. Place scallop and mushroom mixture in large bowl. Let cool slightly. Mix flour and milk; cook over medium heat, stirring constantly, until slightly thickened. Add Gruyère cheese and blend. Pour cheese sauce over scallop mixture. Add rest of seafood to scallop-Gruyère cheese mixture. Add salt, pepper, mustard, and tomato paste; mix thoroughly. Place artichoke hearts on bottom of large buttered casserole dish. Pour seafood mixture over artichoke hearts. Can be refrigerated at this point until ready to bake. Bake at 350 degrees for 45 minutes.

Wine suggestions: Chardonnay - Chateau Montelena, Simi Reserve
Puligny Montrachet
Corton Charlemagne

BONE'S BEER-BATTERED SHRIMP

This recipe comes from Bone's Steak and Seafood restaurant in Atlanta

Preparation: 45 minutes

Frying: 15 minutes
Servings: 6

2 eggs
½ cup beer
1¼ cups all-purpose flour
1 Tablespoon baking powder
Bone's Seafood Seasoning,
**   to taste (see Index)**

4 dozen large, fresh raw
**   shrimp, peeled and**
**   deveined, tails intact**
6 ounces grated coconut
shortening for frying
orange slices for garnish

In large bowl, mix eggs, beer, flour, baking powder, and Bone's Seafood Seasoning; batter should have the consistency of whipping cream. Dip shrimp in batter to coat, then dip into grated coconut. In large skillet, heat 2 inches of shortening until very hot. Add shrimp one at a time. Deep fry until golden brown. Serve with Sweet and Tangy Dipping Sauce that has been placed in small bowl in middle of individual serving plate. Put fried shrimp in circle around bowl. Garnish with fresh orange slices.

Sweet and Tangy Dipping
**   Sauce:**
2 cups orange marmalade
6 Tablespoons Dijon
**   mustard**

6 Tablespoons horseradish

Blend together all ingredients.

Wine suggestions: Chardonnay - Pine Ridge, Sonama Cutrer
                    Pouilly Fuisse

SHRIMP CREOLE

Preparation: 30 minutes   Cooking: 15 minutes
Planning: Can partially prepare ahead   Servings: 6

¼ **cup butter**
¾ **cup chopped celery**
¼ **cup chopped onion**
¼ **cup chopped green bell**
    pepper
1 **(16-ounce) can tomatoes,**
    undrained
¼ **teaspoon ground thyme,**
    optional

1 **bay leaf**
1 **teaspoon salt**
¼ **cup chili sauce**
½ **teaspoon pepper**
1 **teaspoon Worcestershire**
    sauce
2 **cups cooked shrimp,**
    peeled and deveined
hot cooked rice

Melt butter in large skillet; add celery, onion, and green pepper. Cook until vegetables are tender. Add tomatoes, thyme, bay leaf, salt, chili sauce, pepper, and Worcestershire sauce. Simmer until slightly thickened. Add shrimp and heat thoroughly. Remove bay leaf; serve at once over fluffy rice.

Wine suggestions: Chardonnay - Simi Reserve, Chalone
                    Corton Charlemagne

SEAFOOD STEW

Preparation: 45 minutes   Cooking: 1 hour
Planning: Can partially prepare ahead   Servings: 10-12

¼ **cup diced onion**
½ **cup diced celery**
½ **cup diced carrots**
3 **Tablespoons olive oil**
3 **Tablespoons butter**
2 **cloves garlic, minced**
2 **(28-ounce) cans tomatoes,**
    crushed
2 **bay leaves**
1 **teaspoon dried whole**
    oregano
1 **teaspoon dried basil**

⅛ **teaspoon cayenne pepper**
1 **teaspoon Worcestershire**
    sauce, optional
4-6 **drops Tabasco sauce,**
    optional
1 **cup dry white wine**
2 **(8-ounce) bottles clam**
    juice
3 **pounds seafood (shrimp,**
    crabmeat, fish, scallops)
1 **dozen clams**

Sauté onion, celery, and carrots in oil and butter for 5 minutes. Add garlic, tomatoes, bay leaves, oregano, basil, cayenne, Worcestershire sauce, and Tabasco sauce. Cook sauce 20 minutes. Stew can be made ahead to this point. Add wine, clam juice, and fish. Simmer, covered, 25 minutes. Clean shrimp; steam shrimp, scallops, and clams. Add shrimp, scallops, clams and crabmeat just before serving.

Wine suggestions: Gewurztraminer - Alsace
Beaujolais - Fleurie

FROGMORE STEW

This unusual sounding recipe gets its name from the small town of Frogmore, S.C. There are endless variations. Each ingredient flavors the others and the result is delicious - a fun, casual meal!

Preparation: 20 minutes

Cooking: 1 hour
Servings: 8-10

3 pounds Polish sausage, cut into 2-inch pieces
2 lemons, sliced
2 large onions, coarsely chopped
2 Tablespoons crab boil or seafood seasoning mix

salt and pepper to taste
1 stick butter
12 ears corn, shucked
3 pounds raw shrimp in the shell

Fill large kettle or Dutch oven with 2 gallons water. Add sausage, lemons, onion, crab boil, salt, and pepper. Bring to a boil; simmer 45 minutes. Add butter. When butter has melted, add corn; cook for 5 minutes. Add shrimp and cook for about 8 minutes, or until shrimp are pink. Drain liquid and serve on large platter. Let each guest take some sausage and corn, then peel their own shrimp.

Wine suggestions: Gewurztraminer - Alsace
Chardonnay
Beaujolais - Fleurie

SHRIMP MANALLÉ
Delicious!

Preparation: 1 hour
Planning: Must prepare ahead
Marinating: 2 hours

Baking: 30 minutes
Broiling: 5 minutes
Servings: 4-6

2½ pounds large raw shrimp, peeled and deveined
3 sticks butter
6 Tablespoons Worcestershire sauce
2 teaspoons freshly ground pepper

6 drops Tabasco sauce
1½ teaspoons fresh lemon juice
3 cloves garlic
non-stick vegetable spray
French bread for dipping

Rinse shrimp; do not dry. Melt butter in large skillet. Add Worcestershire sauce, pepper, Tabasco, lemon juice and garlic. Mix well. Spray large baking dish with vegetable spray. Arrange shrimp in baking dish and cover with sauce. Marinate at least 2 hours. Bake, uncovered, at 400 degrees for 30 minutes. Broil for 5 minutes. Serve in bowls; invite guests to dip French bread in juices and eat shrimp with fork.

Wine suggestions: Chardonnay - Clos du Bois, Rutherford Hill
Sauvignon Blanc - Kenwood, Ehlers Lane

SHRIMP PERLO
The more seasonings, the better!

Preparation: 30 minutes
Planning: Can partially prepare ahead

Cooking: 10 minutes
Servings: 2-3

1 cup cooked rice
8-10 slices bacon
2 medium onions, chopped
1 pound raw shrimp, peeled and deveined
⅛ teaspoon salt

⅛ teaspoon pepper
¼ teaspoon seasoned salt
2 cloves garlic, minced
¼ teaspoon lemon-pepper seasoning

Cook bacon in large skillet. Pour off all but 2 Tablespoons of bacon drippings. Add rice, crumbled bacon, onions, and shrimp. Mix together, stirring constantly. Add salt, pepper, seasoned salt, garlic, and lemon-pepper seasoning. Cook about 10 minutes, or until shrimp are cooked and turn pink.

Wine suggestions: Chardonnay - Dry Creek, Rutherford Hill
Pouilly Fuisse

SHRIMP A LA GRECQUE

Preparation: 45 minutes

Cooking: 20 minutes
Servings: 4

½ cup minced onions
1 large green bell pepper,
cut in ½-inch squares
½ pound mushrooms, sliced
2 Tablespoons olive oil
2 Tablespoons butter
1 cup dry white wine
1 teaspoon salt
4 medium tomatoes, peeled,
seeded and chopped
1 small clove garlic,
minced, or ¼ teaspoon
garlic juice

½ teaspoon freshly ground
pepper
1 teaspoon dried whole
oregano
8 ounces feta cheese,
crumbled
1 pound large raw shrimp,
peeled and deveined
1 cup pitted black olives,
sliced
2 Tablespoons ouzo,
optional
½ cup chopped fresh parsley

In heavy skillet, sauté onion, pepper, and mushrooms in oil and butter until soft. Add wine, salt, tomatoes, garlic, pepper, and oregano. Bring to a boil; lower heat to medium and simmer until sauce is slightly thickened. Stir in cheese; simmer for 10-15 minutes. Adjust seasonings. Just before serving, add shrimp and olives to the hot sauce and cook for 5 minutes, or until shrimp are just tender; do not overcook. Lace with ouzo and stir thoroughly. Garnish with parsley and serve immediately in large bowls. Crusty thick French bread makes a good accompaniment for this dish.

*Wine suggestions: Sauvignon Blanc - Grgich Hills, Robert Mondavi
Sancere/Pouilly Fume*

PARMESAN SHRIMP SCAMPI

Preparation: 1 hour
Planning: Must partially prepare ahead
Marinating: 1 hour

Broiling: 10 minutes
Servings: 4

**2 pounds medium to large
 shrimp**
1 stick butter, softened
2 Tablespoons lemon juice
4 cloves garlic, minced
1 teaspoon salt
½ teaspoon pepper

¼ teaspoon dry mustard
**2 Tablespoons minced fresh
 parsley**
¼ teaspoon paprika
**⅓ cup freshly grated
 Parmesan cheese**

Peel and devein shrimp. Place in shallow baking dish. Mix butter, lemon juice, garlic, salt, pepper, mustard, and parsley; heat until butter is melted. Pour over shrimp; marinate at least one hour in refrigerator. Sprinkle with Parmesan cheese and paprika; broil 10 minutes until shrimp are tender and lightly browned. Scampi can be served with rice pilaf and steamed vegetables for a complete meal.

Wine suggestions: Chardonnay - Edna Valley, Raymond
Puligny Montrachet

SEAFOOD PECAN

Preparation: 30 minutes
Planning: Can partially prepare ahead

Baking: 10-15 minutes
Servings: 4

2 Tablespoons butter
**2 Tablespoons all-purpose
 flour**
1 cup milk
¼ teaspoon salt
**½ cup grated sharp Cheddar
 cheese**
½ cup sour cream

**4 fish fillets, flounder,
 snapper, or other fish**
1 cup crabmeat
**1 cup uncooked scallops,
 rinsed**
**1½ cups cooked rice or
 noodles**
¼ cup pecan pieces, toasted

Melt butter in saucepan over medium-low heat; blend in flour, then milk. Stir constantly until thickened. Add salt and cheese; stir until cheese melts. Set aside. When cool, add sour cream. Place fish fillets on bottom of greased, square, 1-quart casserole dish. Add crabmeat and scallops to cream sauce; pour over fish. Can be refrigerated at this point until ready to bake. Bake at 325 degrees until fish is done, about 10-15 minutes. Serve over cooked rice or noodles. Sprinkle with pecan pieces.

Wine suggestions: Chardonnay - Sonoma Cutrer, Deloach
Meursault - Premier Cru

BARBARA DOOLEY'S STIR-FRY SHRIMP WITH FRIED RICE
*A favorite of Vince Dooley, Athletic Director
and Head Football Coach at the University of Georgia*

Preparation: 30 minutes
Planning: Can partially prepare ahead

Cooking: 6 minutes
Servings: 4-6

3 Tablespoons peanut oil, divided, no substitutions
1 egg
4 green onions with tops, sliced
1 clove garlic, minced

¾ pound shrimp, peeled and deveined
½ cup sliced water chestnuts
4 cups cooked rice, chilled
¼ cup soy sauce

Pour 1 Tablespoon oil in skillet. Heat over medium heat. When oil is hot, add egg and scramble. Remove egg and set aside. Increase heat; add remaining 2 tablespoons oil, onion, and garlic. Stir-fry 1 minute. Stir in shrimp and water chestnuts; cook until shrimp turn pink, about 5 minutes. Stir in cold rice and soy sauce until well blended. Add scrambled egg; stir until heated through.

Wine suggestions: Gewurztraminer - Rutherford Hill, Mark West
Riesling - Trefethen

CURRIED SEAFOOD SALAD

Preparation: 45 minutes　　　　　　　　　　Chilling: 2-3 hours
Planning: Must prepare ahead　　　　　　　　　　Servings: 6

1 cup uncooked long-grain rice
1 pound large raw shrimp or 1 (12-ounce) package frozen shrimp
1 teaspoon salt
¾ cup mayonnaise
⅓ cup milk
2 Tablespoons lemon juice
2 Tablespoons olive oil or vegetable oil

1½ teaspoons curry powder
1 (6½-7-ounce) can tuna, drained and flaked, optional
2 stalks celery, diced
1 (4½-ounce) can pitted ripe olives, cut in quarters
lettuce or spinach leaves
optional condiments: chutney, peanuts, flaked coconut

At least 3 hours before serving, prepare rice according to package directions; chill cooked rice. Peel and devein shrimp. In 2-quart saucepan, add salt to 2 inches of water. Heat to boiling; add shrimp. Return to a boil; reduce heat to low; cook shrimp 1 minute until tender; drain. Place shrimp in large bowl; refrigerate, covered, until chilled. Mix mayonnaise, milk, lemon juice, oil, and curry powder with shrimp until well blended. Gently stir in rice, tuna, celery, and olives. Line platter with lettuce leaves or spinach leaves. Spoon seafood salad on top. Serve with condiments, if desired.

Wine suggestions: Gewurztraminer - Alsace
　　　　　　　　　　Riesling - Trefethen

 ## DELICIOUS BAKED FISH
So quick to make, yet you'll get raves!

Preparation: 10 minutes　　　　　　　　Baking: 15-25 minutes
Planning: Can partially prepare ahead　　　　　　Servings: 4-6

2 pounds fresh fish fillets, scrod, flounder, or grouper
1 cup mayonnaise
⅔ cup freshly grated Parmesan cheese

⅔ cup dry Italian bread crumbs

160

Preheat oven to 400 degrees. Place fish fillets in lightly oiled baking dish. Mix mayonnaise, Parmesan cheese, and Italian bread crumbs in bowl to form a thick paste. Spread on top of each fish fillet with spoon. Bake 15 minutes; fish will flake when done. If fillets are thick, additional baking time will be necessary.

Wine suggestions: Chardonnay - Deloach, Groth
Pouilly Fuisse

RED SNAPPER ALMONDINE

Preparation: 10 minutes
Frying: 10 minutes
Servings: 4

4 (6-8-ounce) red snapper
fillets
½ cup milk
¼ cup butter
¼ cup vegetable oil
½ cup all-purpose flour,
seasoned with salt and
pepper

¼ cup sliced almonds
1 Tablespoon lemon juice
1 Tablespoon chopped fresh
parsley

Wash and dry fillets thoroughly. Cut 2 or 3 gashes in skin side of fillet to prevent curling. Pour milk in shallow bowl. Put seasoned flour in another. Dip fillets into milk, then into flour; place on wax paper. Heat butter and oil in heavy skillet over medium-high heat. Place fillets in pan, skin side up. Fry 3-4 minutes on each side, turning gently. Remove fillets to warm serving platter. Place almonds and lemon juice in butter; brown, stirring constantly. Pour over fillets; garnish with parsley before serving.

Wine suggestions: Chardonnay - Clos du Bois, Lambert Bridge
Pouilly Fuisse

BAKED STUFFED SNAPPER
A specialty from Proof of the Pudding caterers in Atlanta

Preparation: 20 minutes   Baking: 30-40 minutes
Planning: Can partially prepare ahead   Servings: 4-6

1 (3-pound) snapper, cleaned and scaled
2 Tablespoons vegetable oil
½ cup chopped green onions
½ cup chopped green bell pepper
3 Tablespoons butter

1 medium tomato, peeled, seeded and chopped
1 teaspoon ground thyme
3 Tablespoons chopped fresh parsley
4 pitted black olives, sliced
juice of 1 lemon
lemon slices for garnish

Preheat oven to 350 degrees. Brush baking dish and fish with oil. Briefly sauté onion and pepper in skillet with butter. Add tomato, thyme, parsley and olives; mix well. Stuff mixture into fish cavity; diagonally slash skin of fish and place in pan. Can refrigerate at this point until ready to bake. Bake for 30-40 minutes until fish flakes. Serve in baking dish or remove to warm platter. Sprinkle with lemon juice and decorate with lemon slices.

Wine suggestions: Chardonnay - Robert Mondavi, Raymond
                   Chablis- Premier Cru

GRILLED MARINATED TUNA
WITH FRESH GINGER AND SOY-BUTTER SAUCE
From Pearl's Fish Cafe in Atlanta

Preparation: 5 minutes   Grilling: 20-30 minutes
Planning: Must partially prepare ahead   Servings: 6
Marinating: 2 hours

7½ cups soy sauce
1½ cups sesame oil
1½ cups dry sherry
9 ounces hoisin sauce
1¾ cups sugar

1 bunch green onions, thinly sliced
15 cloves garlic, minced
6 (9-ounce) fresh yellowfin tuna steaks

In large mixing bowl, combine soy sauce, sesame oil, sherry, hoisin sauce, and sugar. Whisk together until thoroughly blended. Add green onion and garlic; mix well. Place tuna steaks in pan and cover with marinade; marinate in refrigerator for at least 2 hours. Remove tuna from refrigerator and allow to return to room temperature, then grill until fish flakes with a fork, 20 to 30 minutes. Top tuna steaks with Ginger and Soy Butter sauce; serve.

Ginger and Soy-Butter Sauce:
¼ pound fresh ginger root, peeled and minced
2 shallots, peeled and minced
1½ cups white wine

2 cups heavy cream
1 pound unsalted butter, cubed
½ cup soy sauce
1 Tablespoon ground ginger

Combine fresh ginger, shallots, and white wine in saucepan. Over medium heat, reduce liquid until 2 Tablespoons of liquid remain. Add cream; reduce again until one-quarter of liquid remains. While reducing stages are in process, continuously whip with wire whisk. When liquid is reduced, add cubed unsalted butter, one piece at a time, whipping constantly. Continuous whipping will keep sauce from breaking. Add soy sauce and ground ginger, continuing to whip. Remove from heat; store in container until ready to use.

Wine suggestions: Chardonnay - Raymond
                     Cabernet Sauvignon - Beringer, Beaulieu Vineyard Rutherford

ZESTY GRILLED SWORDFISH

Preparation: 15 minutes   Grilling: 10 minutes
Planning: Must partially prepare ahead   Servings: 4
Marinating: 30 minutes

1 pound swordfish fillets,   **1 small clove garlic, minced**
   cut into 1-inch pieces   **½ teaspoon lemon juice**
2 Tablespoons soy sauce   **¼ teaspoon dried whole**
2 Tablespoons orange juice   **oregano, crumbled**
1 Tablespoon vegetable oil   **¼ teaspoon freshly ground**
1 Tablespoon ketchup   **black pepper**
1 Tablespoon chopped fresh   **hot cooked rice**
   parsley

Arrange swordfish cubes in single layer in shallow baking dish. Combine soy sauce, orange juice, oil, ketchup, parsley, garlic, lemon juice, oregano, and pepper in small bowl; mix well. Pour over fish, turning to coat well. Let marinate at room temperature, turning once, for at least 30 minutes. Preheat broiler or prepare barbeque grill. Broil or grill fish 4 inches from heat source, turn and continue to cook until fish flakes with fork, about 10 minutes. Serve over hot cooked rice.

Wine suggestions: Sauvignon Blanc - Robert Mondavi Reserve,
                      Grgich Hills

 # BONE'S SEAFOOD SEASONING
*A tasty addition to all seafood recipes, from Bone's
Steak and Seafood restaurant in Atlanta*

Preparation: 5 minutes   Yield: 2 cups
Planning: Can prepare ahead

⅓ cup salt   **2 Tablespoons dried whole**
¼ cup garlic salt   **thyme**
½ cup black pepper   **⅓ cup paprika**
¼ cup cayenne pepper   **3 Tablespoons onion salt**

Combine all ingredients; mix thoroughly. Pour into pint jar and cover.

Meats

Peach Blossom

MEAT

BEEF
Beef-Chicken Kabobs 171
Beef Stuffed Pork Roast 193
Beer Beef Steak Stroganoff 180
Brunswick Stew 168
Corned Beef and Cabbage, Irish Style . . 183
Flank Steak with Fresh Basil-Tomato
    Sauce 176
Ginger Grilled London Broil 177
Marinade for London Broil 177
Marinated Roast Beef Sandwiches 178
Munich "Sauerbraten" 179
Oriental Flank Steak with Rice 174
Roast Beef for Sandwiches 178
Roast Tenderloin 182
Scotched Filet Mignon with Fresh
    Mushroom Sauce 174
Steak in a Bag 180
Steak Tournedos 175
Sukiyaki. 173
Whiskey-Glazed Corned Beef 184
BEEF, GROUND
Bob's Brunswick Stew 167
Chili Seasoning 198
Enchilada Cheese Towers 170
Lasagnette 169
Picadillo 181
Po Boy Fillets 172

Salami 172
HAM
Crescent Squares 184
Honey-Glazed Baked Ham 186
Mandarin Ham Rolls 185
New Orleans Muffaletto 186
Veggie-Stuffed Ham Slices 187
LAMB
Butterflied Leg of Lamb 189
Princes Diana Roast Saddle of Lamb . . . 188
Sweet Lamb Chops 190
PORK
Bar-B-Que Spareribs and Meatballs 192
Beef Stuffed Pork Roast 193
Bob's Brunswick Stew 167
Braised Pork Tenderloin 190
Brunswick Stew 168
Chalupas 196
Mimi's Bar-B-Que 191
Pork Chops with Sour Cream 194
Porky's Revenge 194
Roasted Pork Loin with Prunes and
    Madeira 195
SAUSAGE
Hoppinjohn Jambalaya 196
VEAL
Veal Vermouth 198
Veal with Mustard Sauce 197

BOB'S BRUNSWICK STEW

True brunswick stew at its best, as prepared by
caterer Bob Harrell of Bob's Barbeque in Davisboro, Georgia

Preparation: 1½ hours   Boiling: 2 hours
Planning: Can prepare ahead   Servings: 60
Cooking: 1½ hours

1 **pound ground beef**	1 **Tablespoon lemon juice**
1 **(2-3 pound) fryer chicken**	1 **Tablespoon pepper**
1 **(2-3 pound) hog jowl**	1 **teaspoon cayenne pepper,**
1 **(2-3 pound) Boston butt**	**or to taste**
4 **pints tomatoes**	1 **Tablespoon**
2 **medium onions**	**Worcestershire sauce**
8 **cups cream-style corn**	2 **Tablespoons salt, or to**
1 **cup ketchup**	**taste**

Brown ground beef in skillet; drain excess fat. Boil chicken, hog jowl, and Boston butt in water in separate pans until very tender. Cool, remove bones: grind in food grinder or food processor. Process tomatoes and onions separately in food grinder or food processor. Combine all ingredients in very large pot. Cook, stirring, over low heat for 30 minutes. Continue cooking over medium heat for 1 hour, stirring frequently. Brunswick stew freezes well. If frozen, thaw stew and reheat slowly wih a small amount of water added to the pan. Stir constantly to avoid sticking. Brunswick stew can be served as a main dish stew or as a side dish with barbeque.

Note: The hog jowl is the essential ingredient to thicken the stew to a hearty consistency.

Wine suggestions: Zinfandel - Deloach, Joseph Phelps
Syrah - McDowell Valley Vineyards

BRUNSWICK STEW
Recipe inherited from Ruby Hight Burns
by Olive Ann Burns, author of COLD SASSY TREE

Preparation: 1 hour   Cooking: 6-7 hours
Planning: Can prepare ahead   Yield: 3 gallons

5 pounds lean beef
3 pounds lean pork
chicken can be substituted
   for part of beef or pork
2 (10-ounce) packages
   frozen lima beans
1 (10-ounce) package frozen
   whole okra
3 large Irish potatoes
9 large onions
5 (16-ounce) cans tomatoes
4 (10¾-ounce) cans cream
   of tomato soup, undiluted

3 (17-ounce) cans
   cream-style corn
1 pound butter
1 (16-ounce) bottle ketchup
1 (12-ounce) bottle chili
   sauce
⅛ teaspoon cayenne pepper
Worcestershire sauce, salt,
   pepper, vinegar, and
   lemon juice to taste

Cover meat with water and boil until very tender. Chill. If convenient, wait until the next day to grind cold. Save all broth for seasoning. Remove all or most of fat. Using food grinder, grind beans, okra, potatoes, onions, and all cold cooked meat. Add to broth. Add tomatoes, soup, and corn; simmer slowly, on low heat, at least six hours. Scorching can be a problem, especially as mixture thickens,so stir often. After stew has cooked about an hour, add butter, ketchup, chili sauce, and cayenne pepper. Add Worcesterhire sauce, salt, pepper, vinegar, and lemon juice, a little at a time; it is safer to add more seasonings later if necessary. Let stew cook down; taste and correct seasonings.

Note: "Every area of the South seems to have its own style of Brunswick Stew. This recipe is modernized, but it tastes exactly like what old-timers in Northeast Georgia cooked in big iron pots over an outdoor fire or a woodstove. The important thing is to grind all vegetables raw, and all meats after cooking and cooling. If not, the taste is good but not

the same. A Yankee friend says his Southern mother-in-law uses a hog's head for the pork; he insists this is essential. But Ruby Burns didn't mention cooking a hog's-head!"

Olive Ann Burns

Wine suggestions: Petit Sirah - Foppiano
Zinfandel - Deloach

LASAGNETTE

Preparation: 20 minutes
Planning: Can prepare ahead

Baking: 35 minutes
Servings: 6-8

1 teaspoon vegetable oil
1 pound ground round beef
1 (16-ounce) can tomatoes, undrained
1 (8-ounce) can tomato sauce
1 teaspoon salt
3 teaspoons sugar
2 garlic cloves, crushed

1 (5-ounce) package egg noodles
1 cup sour cream
1 (3-ounce) package cream cheese
6 green onions, chopped with tops
1 cup grated mozzarella cheese

Heat oil in skillet; add beef, breaking pieces with fork, and cook until lightly browned. Drain excess fat. Stir tomatoes and tomato sauce into meat. Add salt, sugar, and garlic. Simmer 5-10 minutes. Cook noodles; drain well and blend in sour cream, cream cheese, and onion. Pour half of meat sauce into lightly greased 3-quart casserole dish. Cover with half the noodle mixture, then ½ cup mozzarella. Repeat layers. Bake at 350 degrees for 35 minutes. Lasagnette can be frozen, then thawed before baking.

Wine suggestions: Chianti Clasico - Saccardi
Beaujolais Villages

ENCHILADA CHEESE TOWERS

Preparation: 20 minutes   Baking: 15-20 minutes
Planning: Can partially prepare ahead   Servings: 4

1 pound ground round beef
½ cup vegetable oil, divided
1 cup chopped green bell
  pepper
1 cup chopped red bell
  pepper
1 medium onion, chopped
1 large clove garlic, minced
1 teaspoon chili powder
¼ teaspoon ground cumin
1 (8-ounce) can tomato
  sauce

⅓ cup half and half
1 (16-ounce) can refried
  beans
1 medium tomato, chopped
¼ cup green chiles
6 corn tortillas, 7½ inches
  in diameter
3 cups shredded Jarlsberg
  cheese
sliced pitted ripe olives for
  garnish

In large skillet, brown beef in 2 Tablespoons oil. Add peppers, onion, garlic, chili powder, and cumin. Cook until peppers are just tender; stirring often. Add tomato sauce. Simmer 5 minutes, stirring occasionally. Blend in half and half. Remove from heat; keep warm. In second skillet, heat refried beans with tomato and chiles; Remove and keep warm. In 8-inch skillet, heat remaining oil. Fry tortillas quickly, one at a time, until golden and blistered; drain on paper towels. Place one tortilla in casserole dish that conforms to tortilla size. Top with 1/5 of bean mixture, meat mixture, and cheese. Repeat with 5 tortillas, placing one on top of another. Bake at 375 degrees for 15 minutes. Sprinkle with additional cheese. Bake until cheese melts; garnish with olives before serving.

Wine suggestions: Beaujolais Villages
                     Petit Sirah - McDowell Valley Vineyards

BEEF-CHICKEN KABOBS

Preparation: 1 hour
Planning: Must partially prepare ahead
Marinating: 12 hours

Grilling: 5 minutes
Servings: 12-15

3 pounds top sirloin
2 pounds boneless chicken
juice of 6 lemons
4 medium onions, chopped
¼ teaspoon pepper
8 teaspoons Worcestershire
  sauce
4 cloves garlic, crushed
12 Tablespoons vegetable
  oil
4 teaspoons salt

1 teaspoon ground ginger
2 bay leaves
2 teaspoons prepared
  mustard
20 new potatoes
4 green bell peppers
20 small white onions,
  peeled
1 pint cherry tomatoes
1 pound whole mushrooms

Cut meat and chicken into 2-inch cubes. Place in glass baking dish. Mix together lemon juice, onion, pepper, Worcestershire sauce, garlic, oil, salt, ginger, bay leaves, and mustard. Pour over meat; marinate in refrigerator 12 hours or overnight. Boil potatoes 5 minutes in salted water. Cut bell peppers into 2-inch chunks. Arrange marinated meat and all vegetables in bowls. Provide 12-15 skewers for guests to make their own kabobs. Grill over medium coals about 5 minutes, basting with marinade.

Wine suggestions: Pinot Noir - Sanford, Robert Mondavi
                    Volnay

PO BOY FILLETS

Preparation: 45 minutes
Planning: Must prepare ahead

Grilling: 16 minutes
Chilling: 2 to 3 hours
Servings: 6

1 pound ground beef
½ pound fresh mushrooms,
   chopped
3 Tablespoons finely
   chopped pimiento stuffed
   olives
2 Tablespoons finely
   chopped green bell pepper

2 Tablespoons finely
   chopped onion
¼ cup grated Parmesan
   cheese
½ teaspoon salt
½ teaspoon pepper
6 slices bacon

Shape ground beef into 12x7½-inch rectangle on waxed paper. Sprinkle remaining ingredients, except bacon, evenly over beef. Beginning at short end, roll jelly-roll style, lifting waxed paper to help support ground beef. Carefully slide roll onto baking sheet, seam side down. Smooth and shape beef roll. Refrigerate 2-3 hours. Cook bacon until transparent, not crisp; drain. Cut beef roll into 1½-inch thick slices. Wrap a bacon slice around outer edge of each fillet; secure with a wooden pick. Grill fillets 4-5 inches from hot coals 8 minutes on each side, or until desired degree of doneness is reached.

Wine suggestions: Beaujolais Villages
   Cabernet Sauvignon - B.V. Rutherford

SALAMI

Preparation: 5 minutes
Planning: Must prepare ahead

Marinating: 4 days
Baking: 12 hours
Yield: 4 pounds

5 pounds lean ground beef
5 teaspoons pickling salt or
   plain non-iodinized salt
2½ teaspoons garlic salt
1 teaspoon hickory smoked
   salt

2½ teaspoons coarsely
   ground black pepper
2½ teaspoons mustard seed
1 Tablespoon peppercorns,
   whole or cracked

Add seasonings to meat; knead well once a day for 4 days. Then form into four 1-pound rolls. Place rolls in pan; bake at 150 degrees for 12 hours. Baked rolls can be frozen.

Note: Foil on bottom of pan under rack saves clean-up.

Wine suggestions: Ajaccio Barbera

SUKIYAKI

Preparation: 30 minutes   Stir-frying: 20 minutes
Planning: Must partially prepare ahead   Servings: 4

3 Tablespoons vegetable oil
1 medium onion, thinly sliced
1 pound sirloin steak, very thinly sliced
½ pound fresh spinach, torn into bite-size pieces
6 (5-inch) stalks celery, halved and thinly sliced lengthwise
8 scallions, thinly sliced lengthwise
8 large fresh mushrooms, sliced
¼ cup soy sauce
¼ cup teriyaki sauce
4 Tablespoons sugar
1 (10½-ounce) can beef consommé
soy sauce to taste
hot cooked white rice

Heat oil in large skillet or wok over medium high heat. Add onion, steak, spinach, celery, scallions, and mushrooms, one at a time, stir-frying for 1 minute after each addition. Stir in soy sauce, teriyaki sauce, sugar, and consommé; cook 2 minutes. Additional soy sauce can be added, if desired. Serve over hot rice.

Note: Have all ingredients sliced, measured, and within easy reach before beginning cooking process.

Wine suggestions: Syrah - McDowell Valley Vineyards
                   Zinfandel - Deloach

SCOTCHED FILET MIGNON
WITH FRESH MUSHROOM SAUCE
A different way to serve filet!

Preparation: 30 minutes

Grilling: 10-20 minutes

Servings: 6

6 (6-ounce) Filet mignons
12 Tablespoons butter,
  divided
1 pound fresh mushrooms,
  sliced
2 teaspoons all-purpose
  flour

Salt and pepper to taste
1 cup heavy cream, heated
½ cup Scotch
6 slices French bread
Fresh parsley sprigs for
  garnish

In skillet, sauté filets in 3 Tablespoons butter for 2½ minutes on each side for rare, longer to desired doneness, or filets may be grilled instead. Remove filets; keep warm. In same skillet, sauté mushrooms in 3 Tablespoons butter; add flour, salt, and pepper. Blend well. Stir in warm cream, do not boil. Add Scotch to mushroom sauce and heat thoroughly. Meanwhile, sauté bread slices in 6 Tablespoons butter. Arrange bread slices on platter; top each with a cooked filet. Spoon sauce over meat. Garnish with fresh parsley. Serve additional sauce at table.

Wine suggestions: Cabernet Sauvignon - Beringer
Bordeaux - Medoc, St. Emilion

ORIENTAL FLANK STEAK WITH RICE

Preparation: 45 minutes
Planning: Must partially prepare ahead
Marinating: 30 minutes

Cooking: 1 hour
Servings: 4-6

1¼ pounds flank steak
½ cup soy sauce
¼ cup vegetable oil
2 Tablespoon molasses
2 teaspoons dry mustard
1 teaspoon ground ginger
1 clove garlic, minced
1 cup water

½ cup uncooked long-grain
  rice
1 medium carrot, shredded
½ cup sliced water
  chestnuts
½ cup green onions, sliced
onion slices for garnish

Cut pocket in flank steak. Combine soy sauce, oil, molasses, mustard, ginger, and garlic. Place meat in shallow dish, pour marinade into pocket of steak and over steak. Let marinate at room temperature for 30 minutes, turning occasionally. Meanwhile, in small saucepan combine water, rice, carrot, water chestnuts, and green onion. Bring to a boil, then simmer for 8 minutes. Remove from heat. Drain meat, reserving marinade. Add ¼ cup of marinade to rice mixture. Spoon rice stuffing into pocket of meat and secure ends with picks. Return meat to baking dish and cover with foil. Bake at 350 degrees for 1 hour, brushing occasionally with marinade. Garnish with onions. Slice across grain to serve.

Wine suggestions: Zinfandel - Deloach
Beaujolais - Morgon, Brouilly

STEAK TOURNEDOS

Preparation: 15-30 minutes
Planning: Can prepare ahead

Grilling: 15 minutes
Servings: 4

1-1½ pounds flank steak
meat tenderizer, optional
¼ teaspoon salt
½ teaspoon pepper
1 teaspoon garlic salt
2 Tablespoons chopped
fresh parsley
½ pound bacon, cooked and
drained

1 (10-ounce) package frozen
spinach, cooked and
squeezed dry
2 cups hollandaise sauce
(see Index)
¼ teaspoon dried tarragon

Pound steak until thin. Sprinkle with tenderizer, salt, pepper, garlic salt, and parsley. Put cooked bacon on top of spices. Spread spinach over all ingredients. Roll up steak, jelly-roll style, and skewer with toothpicks to hold together. Cut into thick slices with sharp knife. Grill about 15 minutes, or until desired doneness. Serve with Hollandaise sauce flavored with tarragon

Wine suggestion: Cabernet Sauvignon - Lyeth, Far Niente, Raymond
Merlot - St. Francis, Clos du Bois
Bordeaux - Pauillac/Margaux

175

FLANK STEAK WITH FRESH BASIL-TOMATO SAUCE

This recipe comes from Elise Griffin,
Peasant Restaurants, Inc., Atlanta

Preparation: 30 minutes

Cooking: 20-30 minutes
Servings: 4-6

**2 pounds tomatoes, peeled
  and seeded**
1 (1½-2 pound) flank steak
salt and pepper to taste
1 clove garlic, halved
**6 Tablespoons olive oil,
  divided**
**1½ Tablespoons red wine
  vinegar**

1 clove garlic, minced
1 teaspoon salt
**½ teaspoon freshly ground
  pepper**
**2 Tablespoons chopped
  fresh basil**
**2 Tablespoons minced fresh
  parsley**

Purée tomatoes in food processor or blender. Strain pulp and juice through sieve with wooden spoon, reserving juice and discarding seeds and remaining bits of pulp. In skillet, reduce tomato juice over medium heat until 1½ cups remain. Remove from heat. Meanwhile, season flank steak with salt and pepper; rub with cut halves of garlic and 2 Tablespoons olive oil. With sharp knife, make 1-inch cuts around outer edge of steak at 2-inch intervals so steak lies flat while cooking. Preheat charcoal or gas grill to medium hot; grill steak until medium-rare. While steak is cooking, transfer reduced tomato juice to food processor or blender. Purée with remaining 4 Tablespoons oil, vinegar, garlic, salt, pepper, and basil. Slice steak on the diagonal into very thin slices. Spoon tomato sauce on warmed plates, lay slices of steak in a row down center of sauce; garnish with parsley and dust with freshly ground pepper.

Wine suggestion: Zinfandel - Deloach

GINGER GRILLED LONDON BROIL

Preparation: 15 minutes   Grilling: 15-20 minutes
Planning: Must partially prepare ahead   Servings: 4-6
Marinating: 12 hours

1½-2 pounds London broil
  steak
¼ teaspoon ground ginger,
  divided

¼ cup soy sauce
½ cup lemon juice

Score both sides of steak in diagonal pattern and place in large shallow pan. Sprinkle half of ginger over steak and rub into meat, turn over and repeat. Mix soy sauce and lemon juice; pour over steak. Marinate, covered, 12-24 hours, turning at least once. Remove from marinade and grill over medium to hot coals, varying height and time to preferred doneness. Let steak rest for a few minutes before cutting. Slice across grain in thin slices to serve.

Wine suggestions: Cabernet Sauvignon - Groth, Robert Mondavi,
                    B.V. Private Reserve
                    Merlot - Rutherford Hill
                    Bordeaux - Margaux/St. Emilion

MARINADE FOR LONDON BROIL

Preparation: 5-10 minutes   Marinating: 3 hours
Planning: Can prepare ahead   Yield: ¾ cup

½ cup soy sauce
¼ cup vegetable oil
2 Tablespoons molasses
2 teaspoons ground ginger

2 teaspoons dry mustard
6 cloves garlic, minced
1 medium onion, thinly
  sliced

Mix soy sauce, oil, molasses, ginger, mustard, and garlic; add onion. After marinating meat at least 3 hours, or overnight, strain marinade and serve warm with sliced meat.

ROAST BEEF FOR SANDWICHES

Preparation: 15 minutes
Planning: Can prepare ahead

Baking: 3-4 hours
Servings: 6-8

4 slices bacon
3-4 pound beef pot roast
1 cup cream of mushroom
soup, undiluted
½ cup white wine

2 Tablespoons
Worcestershire sauce
1 Tablespoon lemon-pepper
seasoning
¼ cup chopped dill pickles

In Dutch oven, cook bacon. Drain, reserving 2 Tablespoons drippings. Crumble bacon; set aside. Brown meat in drippings. Skim off grease. Combine soup, wine, Worcestershire sauce, and lemon pepper; add to meat. Bake, covered, at 325 degrees for 3-4 hours. Add pickles half-way through baking. Add water if necessary. For a tasty open-face sandwich, warm beef can be placed on a halved onion roll and topped with pan gravy and crumbled bacon. Beef is also delicious served chilled and topped with crumbled bacon on an onion roll.

Wine suggestions: Zinfandel - Preston, Grgich Hills
Syrah - Joseph Phelps

MARINATED ROAST BEEF SANDWICHES
Great for a party buffet or outdoor picnic

Preparation: 15 minutes
Planning: Must prepare ahead
Marinating: 4 hours

Chilling: 12 hours
Servings: 10

5-6 pound sirloin tip or
rump roast, cooked
medium rare*
1 (16-ounce) bottle Italian
salad dressing

1 medium onion, chopped
1 cup tarragon vinegar
1 (3½-ounce) jar capers,
drained
1 (2-ounce) jar pimientos

* Cook roast on grill, or in oven, or purchase pre-cooked and sliced.

Chill cooked roast 12 hours or overnight. Slice roast very thin. Mix remaining ingredients and pour over meat. Marinate at least 4 hours. Serve cold with pita or other sandwich bread.

Wine suggestions: Cabernet Sauvignon - B.V. Beautour, Beringer, Estancia, Bordeaux - Medoc, St. Estephe

MUNICH "SAUERBRATEN"

Preparation: 20 minutes   Cooking: 3 hours
Planning: Must partially prepare ahead   Servings: 8
Marinating: 3 days

1 (4 pound) chuck or rump roast	4 whole cloves
salt and pepper	1 teaspoon finely chopped fresh parsley
½ cup sugar	½ teaspoon ground nutmeg
2 cups cider vinegar	all-purpose flour for browning
2 cups water	
1 medium onion, thinly sliced	vegetable oil for browning
4 bay leaves	16 ginger snaps, crushed
	1 Tablespoon sugar

Rub meat with salt and pepper. Place in large glass bowl or crock. Bring sugar, vinegar, and water to a boil in medium saucepan. Pour over meat. Add onion, bay leaves, cloves, parsley, and nutmeg. Refrigerate, covered, 2-3 days, turning daily. To cook, drain meat, reserving marinade. Pat meat dry; dust with flour. Brown in oil in Dutch oven. Strain marinade. Pour 1 cup marinade into pan with meat. Simmer, covered, 3 hours. Add more marinade as needed. Remove meat. To make gravy, add ginger snaps and sugar to 1 cup pan juices. Cook, stirring, 5-10 minutes. Serve hot gravy with meat. Side dishes of red cabbage, rye bread, and potato pancakes can be served to compliment this meal.

Wine suggestions: Syrah - McDowell Valley Vineyards
Cotes du Rhone

BEER BEEF STEAK STROGANOFF
Heavenly!

Preparation: 30 minutes

Cooking: 30 minutes
Servings: 6-8

**2 pounds sirloin steak, cut
into 1-inch strips**
2 Tablespoons vegetable oil
1½ teaspoons salt
⅛ teaspoon pepper
2 medium onions, sliced
**1 (3-ounce) can mushrooms,
undrained**

**2 Tablespoons all-purpose
flour**
¼ teaspoon paprika
1 (12-ounce) can beer
**1 teaspoon Worcestershire
sauce**
1 cup sour cream
hot buttered noodles

In large skillet, quickly brown meat in hot oil, a third at a time. Season
with salt and pepper. Remove from skillet and keep warm. In same skillet, cook onion and undrained mushrooms, covered, 3-4 minutes, or
until onion is tender. Push to one side. Blend flour and paprika into pan
drippings. Add beer and Worcestershire sauce. Cook, stirring, until
thick and bubbly. Return beef to skillet. Stir in sour cream and heat only
until sour cream is heated through. Do not boil. Serve immediately over
hot noodles.

Wine suggestions: Cabernet Sauvignon/Merlot - Raymond/Groth,
Clos du Bois/ St. Francis
Bordeaux - St. Emilion, Haut-Medoc

STEAK IN A BAG
Easy but elegant

Preparation: 45 minutes
Planning: Can partially prepare ahead

Baking: 30-50 minutes
Servings: 6

**1 cup egg bread crumbs (3-4
slices egg bread)**
**1 (2-3 pound) top sirloin
steak, 2½ inches thick**
**4 Tablespoons butter,
softened**
4 Tablespoons vegetable oil

1 teaspoon crushed garlic
2 teaspoons seasoned salt
**2½ teaspoons seasoned
pepper**
**1 cup grated sharp Cheddar
cheese**

Preheat oven to 375 degrees. Prepare bread crumbs in food processor; set aside. Remove excess fat from steak. Mix butter, oil, garlic, salt, and pepper until blended. Spread on all sides of steak. Mix bread crumbs and cheese; press into butter mixture on steak, coating well. Place steak in brown bag, securing end with staples or paper clips. At this point, steak may be refrigerated several hours. Before cooking, bring steak back to room temperature. Place bag on baking sheet and bake for 30 mintues; steak will be rare. For medium-rare steak, adjust oven to 425 degrees and bake 15 minutes longer. For medium-well steak, adjust heat to 375 degrees and bake 5 minutes longer for a total of 50 minutes. Remove steak from bag; let stand 5 minutes before carving into thin slices.

Wine Suggestions: Beaujolais - Morgon, Moulin a Vent
Zinfandel - Preston

PICADILLO

Preparation: 25 minutes
Planning: Can prepare ahead

Cooking: 30 minutes
Servings: 4-6

1 medium onion, diced
1 green bell pepper, diced
2 Tablespoons vegetable oil
1 clove garlic, crushed
1 pound ground beef
2/3 cup raisins
2 Tablespoons capers
1/4 cup pimiento stuffed
  olives, chopped

2 fresh tomatoes, peeled,
  seeded, and chunked
1/8 teaspoon salt
1/8 teaspoon pepper
hot cooked white rice
bacon bits for garnish

Sauté onion and pepper in oil until onion is transparent. Add garlic. Add ground beef; cook; drain excess oil. Add raisins, capers, olives, tomatoes, salt, and pepper. Cook over low to medium heat for 30 minutes. Serve over white rice; sprinkle with bacon bits.

Wine suggestions: Zinfandel - Deloach
Beaujolais - Morgon, Brouilly

ROAST TENDERLOIN

Preparation: 15 minutes
Planning: Must partially prepare ahead
Marinating: 12 hours

Baking: 20 minutes
Broiling: 15 minutes
Servings: 10-12

**1 (5½ pound) beef
  tenderloin
seasoned salt
freshly ground black pepper
Worcestershire sauce
½ cup red wine
1 heaping Tablespoon
  all-purpose flour**

**3 Tablespoons butter,
  softened
salt and pepper to taste
1 pound mushroom caps,
  optional**

Trim fat and cartledge from meat. Rub with seasoned salt, pepper, and Worcestershire sauce, coating well with each. Place meat in plastic bag and refrigerate overnight. A few hours before serving, remove meat from refrigerator. Preheat oven to 550 degrees on broil. Place meat in iron skillet on rack in lower ⅓ of oven; roast for 15 minutes. Reduce heat to 350 degrees and roast for an additional 20 minutes. Remove from oven and let stand 15 minutes before carving. Add wine to skillet and bring to a boil, scraping browned bits from pan. Mix flour and butter and whisk into wine sauce, adding more water or wine if needed. Add salt and pepper to taste. Stir mushroom caps into gravy mixture and heat through. Serve with sliced tenderloin.

Wine suggestions: Cabernet Sauvignon - Robert Mondavi, Pine Ridge
Bordeaux - Margaux, Pauillac

CORNED BEEF AND CABBAGE, IRISH STYLE

Preparation: 15 minutes   Baking: 20 minutes
Cooking: 4½ hours   Servings: 12

1 (4-pound) corned beef
   brisket
3 medium onions, sliced
3 cloves garlic, minced
8 whole cloves
3 bay leaves
16 small to medium
   potatoes, pared

16 medium carrots, pared
1 large head cabbage, cut
   into 8 wedges
prepared mustard
¼ cup dark brown sugar
¼ teaspoon ground cloves
Horseradish Sauce

Place corned beef in Dutch oven; barely cover with hot water. Add onion, garlic, cloves, and bay leaves. Simmer, covered, but do not boil, one hour per pound, or until fork tender. Remove meat from liquid; add potatoes and carrots. Cover, bring to a boil, and cook 10 minutes. Add cabbage wedges; cook 20 minutes longer, or until vegetables are done. Meanwhile, glaze corned beef by lightly spreading fat side of meat with mustard. Combine brown sugar and cloves; sprinkle over meat. Place in shallow pan. Bake at 350 degrees 15-20 minutes or until nicely glazed. To serve corned beef, carve at slight angle across the grain, slicing thinly. Serve with Horseradish Sauce.

Horseradish Sauce:
6 Tablespoons prepared
   horseradish
2 cups sour cream
2 Tablespoons red wine
   vinegar

2 teaspoons Worcestershire
   sauce
1 teaspoon salt
6 drops hot sauce

Mix all ingredients well; refrigerate.

Wine suggestion: Gewurztraminer

183

WHISKEY-GLAZED CORNED BEEF

Preparation: 15 minutes
Cooking: 3½ hours
Baking: 30 minutes

Planning: Can prepare ahead
Servings: 4-6

6-7 pound
  corned beef brisket
½ cup blended whiskey
1 clove garlic
2 bay leaves
4 whole cloves
4 white or black
  peppercorns

¼ cup orange juice
¾ cup light brown sugar
2 Tablespoons corned beef
  stock
1 teaspoon prepared
  mustard
¼ cup whiskey

Place corned beef in Dutch oven; cover with water. Add whiskey and seasonings; bring to a boil. Simmer, covered, 3-4 hours, or until tender. Remove corned beef and place in roasting pan; cut fat cross-hatched fashion. Combine orange juice, sugar, corned beef stock, mustard, and whiskey in saucepan. Cook over low heat stirring until blended; boil 1 minute. Pour over corned beef. Bake at 400 degrees for 30 minutes, basting every 10 minutes. Serve warm with cabbage and acorn squash or cold for sandwiches.

Wine suggestions: Zinfandel - Deloach
Cote du Rhone

 # CRESCENT SQUARES

Preparation: 20 minutes
Planning: Can partially prepare ahead

Baking: 35 minutes
Servings: 4

7½ Tablespoons butter,
  divided
1 Tablespoon onion,
  chopped
3 ounces cream cheese
2 Tablespoons milk
⅛ teaspoon chives
⅛ teaspoon ground oregano

¼ teaspoon salt
¼ teaspoon curry powder
2 cups cooked chicken, ham
  or turkey, cubed
1 can crescent rolls
1 teaspoon celery salt
¾ cup Parmesan cheese

Slowly boil ham with cinnamon sticks for 3½ hours. Marinate in stock for 4 hours. Remove ham; place on broiler pan. Slice criss-cross cuts on top side of ham; stud with cloves. Mix mustard, lemon juice, cloves, and orange juice. Stir in sugar and honey. Baste with ⅓ glaze; bake at 350 degrees for 25 minutes. Baste with ⅓ glaze; bake 25 minutes more. Baste with remaining glaze; bake an additional 5-10 minutes.

Wine suggestion: Tavel

VEGGIE-STUFFED HAM SLICES

Preparation: 30 minutes   Baking: 10 minutes
Planning: Can partially prepare ahead   Servings: 8
Broiling: 5 minutes

1 (½-pound) eggplant (small)   ½ cup celery, finely chopped
6 Tablespoons butter,   ½ cup sliced scallions
  divided   1 medium tomato, peeled
4 Tablespoons all-purpose   and chopped
  flour   2 cups grated mozzarella
3 cups half and half   cheese
salt and pepper to taste   8 thinly sliced pieces boiled
⅛ teaspoon ground nutmeg   ham
⅛ teaspoon cayenne pepper   2 cups grated Swiss or
1 egg yolk, slightly beaten   Gruyere cheese

Peel eggplant; trim off stem and bottom. Cut into ¼-inch cubes and soak in salted water. Meanwhile, melt 3 Tablespoons butter in saucepan. Add flour, stirring. Add half-and-half. Cook 5 minutes, until thickened. Add salt, pepper, nutmeg, cayenne, and egg yolk. Beat briskly with wire whisk; set aside. Melt 3 Tablespoons butter in skillet. sauté eggplant, celery, onion, and tomato; Cool briefly; add mozzarella cheese to eggplant mixture. Arrange ham on flat surface. Spoon cheese and vegetable mixture on ham slices. Roll up slices jelly-roll style; place seam-side down in buttered baking dish. Spoon sauce over ham slices; sprinkle with grated Swiss cheese. Can refrigerate at this point until ready to bake. Bake at 350 degrees for 10 minutes, or until bubbly. Broil 5 minutes to brown.

Wine suggestion: Beaujolais

PRINCESS DIANA ROAST SADDLE OF LAMB

Preparation: 20 minutes   Roasting: 1¼-1½ hours
Planning: Can partially prepare ahead   Servings: 12-16

1 teaspoon salt
½ teaspoon freshly ground
  pepper
2 cloves garlic, minced
⅓ cup chopped fresh mint
⅓ cup chopped fresh basil

1 (5-pound) boneless saddle
  of lamb or 1 (7-pound)
  boneless leg of lamb,
  butterflied, trimmed,
  and tied
red currant jelly, optional

In small bowl, combine salt, pepper, garlic, and herbs. With fingers and handle of wooden spoon, stuff into openings in lamb. This can be prepared ahead. Let stand at room temperature up to 3 hours. Preheat oven to 500 degrees. Place lamb fat side up on rack in roasting pan. Roast 15 minutes. Reduce temperature to 375 degrees; roast 40 minutes more for rare, 45 minutes for medium-rare. For the leg of lamb, roast 1 hour more for rare, 70 minutes more for medium-rare. Let stand 10 minutes before slicing. Serve with red currant jelly, if desired, and Lemon- Mustard sauce.

Lemon-Mustard sauce:

6 Tablespoons unsalted
  butter
2 large cloves garlic, minced
3 Tablespoons coarsely
  ground French mustard

juice of one lemon
salt and freshly ground
  pepper to taste
grated peel from 2 large
  lemons

Combine butter and garlic in small saucepan; cook over low heat 3-5 minutes. Just before serving, whisk in remaining ingredients; heat mixture briefly. Do not leave on heat because sauce will curdle.

Wine suggestions: Cabernet Sauvignon - Beringer Reserve, Ridge
                   Pomerol

BUTTERFLIED LEG OF LAMB
Guests will applaud your efforts!

Preparation: 25 minutes
Planning: Must partially prepare ahead
Marinating: 2 hours

Broiling: 10 minutes
Baking: 2⅓ hours
Servings: 6-8

¼ cup olive oil
3 teaspoons minced garlic
1 teaspoon dried tarragon
1 (7-pound) leg of lamb, boned and butterflied
⅓ cup spicy mustard, divided
½ cup grated Parmesan cheese

3 Tablespoons minced fresh parsley
2 Tablespoons fine dry bread crumbs
2 Tablespoons butter, melted

Blend oil with garlic and tarragon in small bowl. Brush over lamb; let marinate at room temperature for 2 hours. Preheat oven to broiling. Place lamb fat side down in shallow baking pan. Brush with half of mustard. Broil 6 inches from heat source for 5 minutes. Turn lamb, brush with remaining mustard; broil 5 minutes. Reduce oven to 450 degrees. Blend cheese, parsley, and bread crumbs in small bowl. Sprinkle over meat. Pat gently so crumb mixture will stick to lamb. Drizzle with butter. Roast until crumbs are crisp and brown and meat thermometer registers 130 degrees for rare; 160 degrees for medium (approximately 20 minutes per pound). Let stand 10 minutes before serving.

Wine suggestions: Merlot - Clos du Bois, Rutherford Hill
Bordeaux - Margaux, St Emilion

SWEET LAMB CHOPS

Preparation: 30 minutes
Planning: Must prepare ahead

Cooking: 1½ hours
Marinating: 8 hours
Servings: 4

4 lamb chops
½ cup brandy
½ cup soy sauce
½ cup honey
2 Tablespoons vegetable oil

2 Tablespoons butter
1 large onion, thickly sliced
1 (8-ounce) can water chesnuts, sliced and drained

Marinate lamb chops 8 hours in brandy, soy sauce, and honey. Remove lamb, reserving marinade. Brown chops in hot oil, turning to brown on both sides. Remove and set aside. Pour off oil; add butter to skillet. Cook onion over low heat until golden. Stir in water chesnuts. Return chops to pan and add marinade. Cook, covered, over low heat 1½ hours until tender.

Wine suggestions: Zinfandel - Clos du Val
Gewurztraminer

 # BRAISED PORK TENDERLOIN

Preparation: 20 minutes

Baking: 1 hour
Servings: 4-6

2 (1½-pound) pork tenderloins
salt, pepper, and dry mustard to taste
3½ Tablespoons butter
¼ teaspoon dried whole rosemary

1 large onion, sliced
½-¾ cup dry white wine
1 cup heavy cream
1 Tablespoon all-purpose flour

Rub meat with salt, pepper, and mustard. Brown in heavy skillet in butter. Transfer meat to shallow casserole dish with cover; sprinkle with rosemary. Lightly brown onion in skillet, adding more butter if needed. Add wine to skillet and bring to a boil, scraping browned bits from bottom of pan. Pour mixture over meat. Bake, covered, at 300 degrees for 45 minutes. Baste occasionally. Blend flour into cream. Stir into wine mixture and baste meat again. Continue baking 15 minutes more. This entree can be served with rice, using cream sauce as gravy.

Wine suggestions: Cabernet Sauvignon - Raymond, Lyeth
Bordeaux - Pauillac, Margaux

MIMMIE'S BAR-B-QUE

Preparation: 30 minutes   Cooking: 3-6 hours
Planning: Can prepare ahead   Servings: 10

**1 (5-pound) lean Boston   1 large onion, sliced
butt or 1 (5-pound) pork   ½ teaspoon salt
roast   Mimi's Barbeque Sauce**

Simmer pork in water with onion and salt. Cook until meat falls apart, about 3-6 hours. Shred meat and mix with bar-b-que sauce. Meat can be frozen with or without sauce.

Mimi's Barbeque Sauce:
**¼ cup light brown sugar   ¼ cup Worcestershire sauce
1½ teaspoons salt   2-4 drops Tabasco sauce
1 cup ketchup   1 teaspoon celery seed
¼ teaspoon pepper   1 cup stock or water
¼ cup cider vinegar   3 Tablespoons lemon juice
1 teaspoon chili powder**

Combine all ingredients and bring to a boil. Boil hard for 2-3 minutes. Sauce can be stored in refrigerator until ready to use.

Wine suggestions: Zinfandel - Deloach, Grgich Hills
Beaujolais Villages

BAR-B-QUE SPARERIBS AND MEATBALLS
A different way to serve spareribs

Preparation: 1 hour

Planning: Can partially prepare ahead

Baking: 1½ hours

Servings: 8

4 pounds spareribs or loin back ribs, cut into 8 pieces
2 Tablespoons butter
2 cloves garlic, crushed
2 Tablespoons prepared mustard
¼ cup light brown sugar
1 cup ketchup
¾ cup chili sauce

1 Tablespoon celery seed
2 Tablespoons Worcestershire sauce
2 dashes hot sauce
½ teaspoon salt
1½ cups water or red wine
1 medium onion, thinly sliced
1 lemon, thinly sliced
Fluffy Meat Balls

Salt ribs. Place in shallow roasting pan, meaty side down. Roast at 450 degrees for 30 minutes. Melt butter in saucepan. Add garlic and cook 4-5 minutes. Blend in mustard and sugar. Add ketchup, chili sauce, celery seed, Worcestershire sauce, hot sauce, salt and water; bring to boil. Drain off excess fat from ribs. Turn meaty side up. Pour sauce over ribs and top with onion and lemon slices. Bake at 350 degrees for 1½ hours, or until done, basting occasionally with sauce. During last 30 minutes of baking, add meatballs to pan. If sauce gets too thick, add more water. Sauce can be prepared ahead. Arrange ribs and meatballs on platter. Skim excess fat from sauce; drizzle sauce over meat.

Fluffy Meat Balls:
½ pound ground beef
½ pound ground pork or sausage
¼ cup fine dry breadcrumbs
¼ cup finely chopped onion

1 teaspoon salt
⅛ teaspoon pepper
⅓ cup milk
1 egg, slightly beaten

Mix ground beef, pork, breadcrumbs, onion, salt, pepper, milk and egg; mix well. Form into about 16 meatballs.

Wine suggestions: Beaujolais Villages
Zinfandel - Preston, Deloach

BEEF STUFFED PORK ROAST

Preparation: 1 hour　　　　　　　　　　Cooking: 2½ hours
Planning: Can prepare sauce ahead　　　　　　Servings: 6-8

**3 pounds boned pork loin,
　butterflied
Tangy Barbeque Sauce
½ pound ground sirloin
1 small onion, chopped
1 small clove garlic, minced
¼ teaspoon salt**

**⅛ teaspoon pepper
1 cup fresh sliced
　mushrooms
¼ cup fine dry breadcrumbs
¼ cup grated Parmesan
　cheese**

Pound meat into 15x10 rectangle about ¾-inch. Brush top with ¼ cup barbeque sauce. Combine ground sirloin, onion, garlic, salt, pepper, and ¼ cup barbeque sauce; spread evenly over roast. Press mushrooms into ground beef. Sprinkle with breadcrumbs and cheese. Starting at 10-inch side, roll up meat and tie. Place on rack in shallow roasting pan. Roast, uncovered, at 325 degrees for about 2½ hours. Baste with additional barbeque sauce for last 15-20 minutes of roasting. Remove meat to serving platter. Cover with barbeque sauce and arrange sliced mushrooms neatly on top. Serve remaining sauce.

Tangy Barbeque Sauce:
**1 (14-ounce) bottle ketchup
½ cup chili sauce
⅓ cup wine vinegar
¼ cup light brown sugar
2 Tablespoons lemon juice
1 clove garlic, minced
¼ teaspoon pepper**

**2 Tablespoons
　Worcestershire sauce
2 Tablespoons mustard
2 Tablespoons vegetable oil
2 Tablespoons steak sauce
1 teaspoon dry mustard
¼ teaspoon salt**

Combine all ingredients; simmer 30 minutes. Makes 2⅔ cups. Store sauce in refrigerator until ready to use.

Wine suggestions:　Syrah - McDowell Valley Vineyards
　　　　　　　　　　Cotes du Rhone

PORKY'S REVENGE

*"After my dear ex-husband, Lewis ("I do, 'least I thought I did")
Grizzard had heart surgery whereby they replaced a leaky valve with
one made of pig tissue, two things happened: First, he entered every
hog calling contest south of Hapeville with a final victory in Ludowici;
and second, he developed a penchant for pork. I experimented with
many recipes but the one below was his favorite (except for the Spam
soup he dearly loved)."*

Kathy Grizzard Schmook, author of HOW TO TAME A WILD BORE

Preparation: 30 minutes
Marinating: 12 hours

Roasting: 45 minutes
Servings: 16-20

1 cup chicken stock
1 (5-ounce) bottle soy sauce
3 Tablespoons sesame seeds
3 Tablespoons brown sugar
2 cloves garlic, crushed

1 onion, chopped
1 teaspoon ground ginger
5 pound pork tenderloin,
  deboned

Combine stock, soy sauce, sesame seeds, brown sugar, garlic, onion,
and ginger in small saucepan. Cook over medium-low heat for 30
minutes. Pour over pork; marinate 12 hours or overnight. Roast pork at
350 degrees for 45 minutes, reserving marinade. In small saucepan,
cook marinade about 30 minutes, until thickened. Slice pork thin; pour
sauce over meat and serve at room temperature. Pork can also be
served in sesame seed buns as sandwiches.

Wine suggestions: Chardonnay - Grgich Hills, Trefethen

PORK CHOPS WITH SOUR CREAM

Preparation: 20 minutes

Cooking: 1 hour
Servings: 2

2 pork loin chops, ¾-inch
  thick
vegetable oil for browning
1 small onion, sliced
¼ teaspoon caraway seeds
¼ teaspoon salt

¼ teaspoon paprika
⅛ teaspoon dried dill weed
⅛ teaspoon garlic powder
⅓ cup water
⅓ cup sour cream

Brown chops in oil; drain. Add onion, caraway seeds, salt, paprika, dill, garlic powder, and water to chops. Simmer, covered, over low heat for 1 hour. Remove pork chops to warm platter. Add sour cream to drippings. Heat thoroughly, but do not boil. Spoon sauce over chops before serving.

Wine suggestions: Cabernet Sauvignon - Beringer, Rutherford Hill
Bordeaux - Haut-Medoc, Pauillac

ROASTED PORK LOIN WITH PRUNES AND MADEIRA
Simple to do, and very pretty

Preparation: 30 minutes

Cooking: 2½ hours
Servings: 6-8

**1½ pounds pitted dried
 prunes
1 bottle dry Madeira wine
1 (4-5) pound well-marbled
 center loin roast, boned,
 rolled, and tied
½ teaspoon ground ginger**

**½ teaspoon salt
⅛ teaspoon freshly ground
 pepper
½ cup dry white wine
1 cup heavy cream
salt and freshly ground
 pepper to taste**

Combine prunes in medium bowl with enough wine to cover; let stand at room temperature 2-3 hours. Preheat oven to 325 degrees. Run long, sharp knife through center of roast to make opening. Stuff with 12-16 plumped prunes, pushing with handle of wooden spoon. Combine ginger, salt, and pepper; rub into roast. Place meat fat side up in narrow, deep dish that holds roast snugly. Roast 30 minutes. Drain remaining prunes, reserving wine, and set aside. Pour wine over meat. Continue roasting 1 hour, basting frequently with pan drippings. Add cream; continue roasting, basting often, until meat thermometer inserted in thickest part of roast registers 155-160 degrees, about 45-60 minutes. Remove roast from pan and keep warm. Strain pan juices into small saucepan if they have curdled. Skim fat from pan. Reduce juices over high heat until thickened. Add remaining prunes; toss to heat through. Season with salt and pepper. Keep warm. Slice pork; arrange in overlapping pattern on heated platter and drizzle with some of sauce. Serve immediately, passing remaining sauce at the table.

Wine suggestions: Sauvignon Blanc - Grgich Hills, Glen Ellen
Zinfandel - Simi, Burgess Cellars

195

CHALUPAS

Preparation: 15 minutes   Cooking: 5½ hours
Planning: Can partially prepare ahead   Servings: 6-8

1 (3-pound) boneless pork roast, trimmed
1 pound pinto beans, uncooked
1 (4-ounce) can chopped green chilies
1 cup chopped onions
3 cloves garlic, minced
1 Tablespoon ground cumin
2 Tablespoons chili powder
1 Tablespoon salt
1 teaspoon ground oregano
7 cups water
tortilla chips
assorted condiments:
 sour cream, hot picante sauce, chopped tomatoes, black olives, chopped avocado, chopped onion, shredded lettuce, grated sharp Cheddar cheese

In Dutch oven or crock pot, combine roast, beans, chiles, onion, garlic, cumin, chili powder, salt, oregano, and water. Simmer, covered, 5 hours, or until roast is very tender and falls apart. Uncover; cook an additional 30 minutes, or until mixture thickens. Stir thoroughly. Serve over tortilla chips with a variety of condiments. Chalupa mixture can be prepared in advance and reheated before serving.

Wine suggestion: *Petit Sirah - Foppiano*
                    Syrah - McDowell Valley Vineyards

HOPPINJOHN JAMBALAYA

Preparation: 1 hour   Cooking: 45 minutes
Planning: Can prepare ahead   Servings: 12

2 Tablespoons vegetable oil
2 large onions, chopped
1 green bell pepper, chopped
½ cup chopped fresh parsley
3 cloves garlic, minced
2 pounds smoked hot sausage, such as Polish kilbasa, cut into ½-inch pieces
1 pound hog jowl, cut into ½-inch pieces
1 pound dried black-eyed peas, half-cooked
6 cups chicken broth
3 cups uncooked long-grain rice
salt and pepper to taste
1 bunch green onions, chopped

Heat oil; add onion, green pepper, parsley, and garlic; sauté 10 minutes. Add sausage, hog jowl, peas, and broth; bring to a boil. Add rice and cook 45 minutes, or until rice is tender and water is absorbed. Season with salt and pepper, to taste. Add green onions and let stand 10 minutes before serving.

Wine suggestions: Syrah - McDowell Valley Vineyards
Beaujolais Villages

VEAL WITH MUSTARD SAUCE
This is rich and delicious!

Preparation: 20 minutes
Cooking: 15 minutes
Servings: 3-4

**2 Tablespoons unsalted
butter**
1 Tablespoon vegetable oil
2 green onions, chopped
**1 pound veal scallops,
pounded thin and cut into
serving pieces**

salt and pepper to taste
**¼ cup dry vermouth or white
wine**
¼ cup Dijon mustard
⅓ cup heavy cream
**1 medium tomato, seeded
and chopped**

Melt butter and oil in large heavy skillet. Add onions; cook over low heat until tender, about 5 minutes. Raise heat and add veal which has been seasoned with salt and pepper; cook scallops quickly, about 1 minute on each side. They do not have to brown. Remove veal from pan and keep warm while preparing sauce. Add vermouth to skillet and boil until mixture is reduced by half. Whisk in mustard and cream; cook 1 minute. Taste sauce and correct seasonings. Return veal to pan and coat with sauce. Arrange scallops on a platter; spoon remaining sauce over scallops and sprinkle chopped tomato on top. A green vegetable, such as broccoli, and rice pilaf compliment this dish.

Wine suggestions: Cabernet Sauvignon - Beringer, Raymond
Bordeaux - Haut-Medoc, Pauillac

VEAL VERMOUTH

Excellent entree for a dinner party - elegant in appearance, divine in taste!

Preparation: 15 minutes

Cooking: 20 minutes
Servings: 4-6

1½ pounds thin veal steak
2 Tablespoons all-purpose
   flour
¼ cup butter
1 clove garlic, minced
¾ pound fresh mushrooms,
   sliced

½ teaspoon salt
⅛ teaspoon pepper
1 Tablespoon lemon juice
⅓ cup dry vermouth
2 Tablespoons snipped fresh
   parsley

Flatten veal to ¼-inch thickness. Cut into 2-inch squares and dredge in flour. Melt butter and sauté veal, a little at a time, until golden brown on both sides. Return all meat to skillet; add garlic and heap with mushrooms. Sprinkle with salt, pepper, and lemon juice. Pour on vermouth; cover and cook over low heat for 20 minutes or until veal is fork tender. Add a little more vermouth if needed. Garnish with parsley just before serving.

Wine suggestions: Merlot - Clos du Bois, Pine Ridge
Chardonnay - Grgich Hills, Trefethen

 ## CHILI SEASONING

Preparation: 5 minutes
Planning: Can prepare ahead

Yield: ⅓ cup

1 Tablespoon chili powder
2 teaspoons ground cumin
1 teaspoon ground oregano
1 Tablespoon seasoned salt
1 dried chili pepper, seeds
   removed, crushed

1 teaspoon instant minced
   onion
¼ teaspoon instant minced
   garlic

Combine ingredients and store in container with tight-fitting lid. Use as seasoning in any chili recipe using 1 pound meat.

198

Poultry

Pink Dogwood

POULTRY

CHICKEN

Baked Chicken Breasts 201
Baked Swiss Chicken 201
Bessie's Chicken 202
Breast of Chicken Florentine 222
Chicken and Dumplings 218
Chicken and Peanuts in Hot Sauce 224
Chicken Artichoke Casserole 215
Chicken Breasts in Currant Jelly Sauce . 216
Chicken Carolina 225
Chicken Chaufroid 221
Chicken Curry Mousse 207
Chicken Florentine 226
Chicken in Champagne Sauce 204
Chicken Moravian 209
Chicken Nuggets 204
Chicken Scallopini 220
Chicken Sukh 228
Chicken with Mushroom-Wine Sauce . . 210
Chicken with Sherried-Cheese Sauce . . 212
Commander Burns' Barbeque Chicken . 208
Curried Chicken and Eggplant Stew . . . 224
Deviled Chicken 202
Fried Chicken with Cream Gravy 203
Lemon Chicken 205
Maple-Pecan Chicken 208
Orange Almond Chicken 217

Oriental Sesame Chicken Dinner 226
Pecan-Breaded Chicken 216
Poppy Seed Chicken 211
Poulet De Susie 228
Roast Chicken Stuffed with Orzo 213
Sherried Parmesan Chicken 211
Southern Chicken Pie 223
Soy Baked Chicken 227
Stuffed Chicken Breasts with Dill
    Butter Sauce 206
Stuffed Chicken Teriyaki 229
Swiss Chicken 219
Tangy Baked Chicken 214
Tarragon Chicken with Angel Hair
    Pasta 214

CORNISH HENS
Cornish Hens with Apricot Glaze 230

DOVES
Doves with Cream Gravy 231
Smothered Doves 231

DUCK
Roast Duck with Raspberry Sauce 232
Hot and Sweet Mustard 230

TURKEY
Roast Turkey with Wild Rice Stuffing . . . 233
Rotisserie Grilled Turkey for a Gas Grill . . 234

BAKED SWISS CHICKEN
Young and old delight when this dish is served

Preparation: 15 minutes   Baking: 45-55 minutes
Planning: Can prepare ahead   Servings: 8

8 chicken breast halves, skinned and boned
8 slices Swiss cheese
1 (10¾ ounce) can cream of chicken soup, undiluted
¼ cup dry white wine
¾ cup herb-seasoned stuffing mix, crushed
¼ cup butter, melted

Arrange chicken in greased 13x9x2 dish. Top each chicken breast with cheese slice. Combine soup and wine, mixing well. Spoon sauce over chicken; sprinkle with stuffing. Drizzle butter over stuffing. Bake at 350 degrees for 45-55 minutes. Chicken can be prepared ahead, then baked just before serving.

Wine suggestions: Sauvignon Blanc - Robert Mondavi, Kenwood
Sancere

BAKED CHICKEN BREASTS
Moist and flavorful, never dry

Preparation: 15 minutes   Baking: 1 hour
         Servings: 6

1 (8-ounce) carton sour cream
2 teaspoons Worcestershire sauce
½ teaspoon celery salt
½ teaspoon garlic salt
1 Tablespoon lemon juice
6 chicken breast halves, skinned and boned
½ (8-ounce) package herb-seasoned stuffing mix, crushed
butter

Combine sour cream, Worcestershire sauce, celery salt, garlic salt, and lemon juice. Coat chicken with mixture, then roll chicken in stuffing crumbs. Place chicken in buttered baking dish; dot with butter. Bake at 350 degrees for 1 hour.

Wine suggestions: Chardonnay - Iron Horse, Stratford
Meursault

BESSIE'S CHICKEN

This recipe comes from Bessie Johnson, the cook
at Manuel's Tavern in Atlanta for 15 years

Preparation: 40 minutes

Frying: 25 minutes
Servings: 4-6

1 fryer chicken, cut up
2 eggs
1 cup milk
1 cup all-purpose flour

1½ teaspoons seasoned salt
½ teaspoon monosodium
  glutamate
vegetable oil for frying

Soak chicken pieces in salted water for 30 minutes. Beat eggs; mix with milk. Drain chicken; dip chicken pieces in egg-milk mixture. Combine flour, seasoned salt, and monosodium glutamate; coat chicken in flour mixture. Heat frying oil to 375 degrees. Without covering, fry chicken in hot oil for 25 minutes until chicken feels tender when pierced with a fork, turning often.

 ## DEVILED CHICKEN

Preparation: 5 minutes

Baking: 1 hour
Servings: 4

1 (3-pound) broiler-fryer
  chicken, cut up
salt and pepper to taste
2 Tablespoons mayonnaise

¼ cup butter, melted
2 teaspoons vinegar
½ teaspoon paprika
2 teaspoons mustard

Place chicken pieces into lightly greased baking dish, skin side up. Sprinkle with salt and pepper to taste. Combine mayonnaise, melted butter, vinegar, paprika and mustard; pour over chicken. Bake at 350 degrees for 1 hour.

FRIED CHICKEN WITH CREAM GRAVY
Best fried chicken ever, just like mother and grandmother make!

Preparation: 15 minutes

Cooking: 40 minutes
Servings: 4

1 (3-pound) broiler-fryer
   chicken, cut up
1 cup self-rising flour
1½ teaspoons salt
¼ teaspoon pepper
⅛ teaspoon paprika
1 egg, slightly beaten
2 Tablespoons water

vegetable oil for frying
3-4 Tablespoons hot grease
   from drippings
¼ cup all-purpose flour
1½ cups water
1½ cups milk
salt and pepper to taste

Remove skin from chicken, wash and pat dry. Combine flour, salt, pepper, and paprika in plastic bag. Combine egg and water in pie plate. Dip one piece of chicken at a time into egg mixture, then place into flour bag, shaking to coat. In large skillet over medium-high heat, heat ¾-inch oil until oil begins to look like it is "cracking," or temperature reaches 350 degrees on deep-fat thermometer. Place chicken pieces into hot oil. Fry until browned, turning once, then reduce heat to medium. Continue frying, frequently turning pieces in pan. Total cooking time should be 25 minutes. Remove chicken pieces; drain on paper towels. Keep warm. Carefully pour off grease from skillet, leaving all the crusty pieces in pan. Measure 3-4 Tablespoons of grease and return to skillet. Blend flour into grease; cook over low heat, stirring constantly until mixture is bubbly, making sure to stir in crusty bits from bottom of pan. Combine water and milk; add all at once to mixture in skillet; blend well. Cook, over medium heat, stirring constantly with wooden spoon in figure-8 motion until mixture is thickened and bubbly and has a smooth and velvety consistency. Add salt and pepper to taste.

CHICKEN NUGGETS

Preparation: 10 minutes   Frying: 15 minutes
Planning: Must partially prepare ahead   Servings: 4
Marinating: 3 hours

4-6 chicken breast halves,   **2 cups all-purpose flour**
   skinned and boned   **2 teaspoons salt**
1½ cups buttermilk   **1 teaspoon pepper**
2 Tablespoons lemon juice   **1 teaspoon paprika**
½ teaspoon salt   **½ teaspoon poultry**
¼ teaspoon pepper   **seasoning**
¼ teaspoon celery salt   **vegetable oil for frying**

Cut chicken into 3-inch pieces. Combine buttermilk, lemon juice, ½ teaspoon salt, ¼ teaspoon pepper and celery salt. Pour over chicken; marinate in refrigerator 3 hours. Combine flour, salt, pepper, paprika, and poultry seasoning in paper bag. Shake chicken pieces in bag, one at a time, until well coated. Fry chicken pieces over medium heat in 1-inch of vegetable oil until lightly browned. Drain and serve immediately. Serve nuggets with Barbeque Sauce or Honey-Mustard Dressing for dipping (see Index).

Wine suggestions: Zinfandel - Preston
                     Petit Sirah - Foppiano

CHICKEN IN CHAMPAGNE SAUCE
Dining out when dining in!

Preparation: 5 minutes   Cooking: 25 minutes
                                       Servings: 4

2 Tablespoons all-purpose   **2 Tablespoons butter**
   flour   **1 Tablespoon olive oil**
½ teaspoon salt   **¾ cup champagne**
⅛ teaspoon pepper   **½ pound fresh mushrooms,**
4 chicken breast halves,   **sliced**
   skinned and boned   **½ cup heavy cream**

Peel lemons; cut peeling into slices and set aside. Squeeze juice from lemons into saucepan. Add bottled lemon juice, vinegar, butter, and salt; bring to a slow boil. Add sliced lemon peel and onion slices. Simmer, stirring occasionally, for 10 minutes. Meanwhile, have chicken cooking on grill over low coals. When sauce is ready, brush over chicken. Return sauce to low heat and simmer while chicken continues to cook. Baste chicken frequently with sauce. Total grilling time for chicken should be 45-50 minutes. Serve onions along with the chicken; they will have absorbed the sauce and taste heavenly!

Wine suggestions: Zinfandel - Deloach, Preston
Beaujolais - Morgon, Fleurie

CHICKEN MORAVIAN
Prepare this dish and bake during church for Sunday dinner

Preparation: 10 minutes

Baking: 3 hours
Servings: 8

1 (4-ounce) package dried
  beef, shredded
8 slices bacon
8 chicken breast halves,
  skinned and boned
1 (10¾ ounce) can cream of
  mushroom soup,
  undiluted

1 cup sour cream
1 teaspoon instant minced
  onion

Place shredded beef in bottom of greased 13x9x2 casserole. Fry bacon until half done; wrap around chicken pieces, securing with toothpicks. Place on top of beef. Mix soup, sour cream, and instant minced onion in medium bowl. Pour mixture over chicken. Bake, covered, at 275 degrees for 2½ hours. Remove cover; continue baking for ½ hour more.

Wine suggestions: Pinot Noir - Saintsbury, Hacienda
Volnay

CHICKEN WITH MUSHROOM-WINE SAUCE
Elegant for any entertaining

Cooking: 30 minutes   Servings: 8

4 Tablespoons butter
1 large clove garlic
1 bay leaf
1 small onion, halved
8 chicken breast halves,
   skinned and boned
salt to taste
lemon-pepper seasoning to
   taste

1 cup dry white wine
½ pound fresh mushrooms,
   sliced
1 cup chicken broth
2 teaspoons cornstarch,
   optional

Coat skillet with non-stick cooking spray. Melt butter in skillet over medium-high heat. Add 1 whole garlic clove, bay leaf, and onion halves; sauté 1 minute. Sprinkle each chicken breast with salt and lemon-pepper seasoning to taste. Place chicken in skillet. Sauté 5-8 minutes per side, or until done. Add additional butter if needed. Remove chicken from pan and keep warm. Remove and discard garlic, bay leaf and onion halves. Pour wine into skillet and deglaze bottom. Let wine simmer until reduced by half, about 5 minutes. Add sliced mushrooms; sauté 3-5 minutes. Add chicken broth and heat. If thicker sauce is desired, mix 2 teaspoons cornstarch with 1 Tablespoon water to make a smooth paste. While stirring sauce, add cornstarch paste until desired thickness is reached. Pour finished sauce over chicken and serve.

Wine suggestions: Chardonnay - Stratford, Innisfree
                            Chablis - Premier Cru

POPPY SEED CHICKEN

Preparation: 10 minutes
Planning: Can prepare ahead

Baking: 25 minutes
Servings: 8

5 whole chicken breasts, cooked and cubed
2 (10¾-ounce) cans cream of chicken soup, undiluted
1 (8-ounce) carton sour cream

1 roll butter-flavored crackers, crushed
½ cup butter, melted
2 Tablespoons poppy seeds

Place cubed chicken in lightly greased 13x9x2 baking dish. Combine soup and sour cream; pour over chicken. Sprinkle with cracker crumbs; pour melted butter on top, moistening all cracker crumbs. Sprinkle with poppy seeds. Bake at 350 degrees for 20 to 25 minutes, or until bubbly. Poppy seed chicken can be prepared ahead, then baked just before serving.

Wine suggestions: Chardonnay - Raymond, Dry Creek
Chablis Premier Cru

SHERRIED PARMESAN CHICKEN

Preparation: 25 minutes

Baking: 1 hour
Servings: 6

6 chicken thighs or breast halves
¼ cup vegetable oil
1 large onion, preferably Vidalia, thinly sliced

½ cup sherry
½ cup grated Parmesan cheese
½ cup seasoned bread crumbs

Brown chicken pieces in skillet in hot oil. Remove chicken from skillet. Sauté onion in drippings until transparent. In shallow baking dish, layer half the onion. Add chicken; top with remaining onion. Pour sherry over chicken and onion. Mix cheese with bread crumbs and sprinkle on top. Bake, covered, at 350 degrees for 30 minutes. Uncover and bake an additional 30 minutes.

Wine suggestions: Chardonnay - Grgich Hills, Farniente
Meursault Premier Cru

 ## CHICKEN WITH SHERRIED-CHEESE SAUCE

Preparation: 5 minutes

Microwaving: 20 minutes

Servings: 8

¼ cup butter	1 teaspoon paprika
1 cup dry bread crumbs	1 clove garlic, minced
2 Tablespoons Parmesan cheese	4 large whole chicken breasts, split and skinned
1 Tablespoon dried parsley	Sherried Cheese Sauce

Place butter in microwave-safe bowl or pie plate. Microwave at HIGH (100% power) for 45-60 seconds. In another plate, mix bread crumbs, Parmesan cheese, parsley, paprika, and garlic. Dip each chicken piece in butter, then coat with crumb mixture. Place in shallow baking dish; cover with waxed paper. Microwave at HIGH (100% power) for 10-14 minutes, or until chicken is no longer pink. Let stand, covered, until sauce is ready. Chicken can be cooked in conventional oven at 350 degrees for 55 minutes, if desired.

Sherried Cheese Sauce:

1 Tablespoon butter	⅝ cup milk
1 Tablespoon all-purpose flour	1 Tablespoon sherry
¼ teaspoon salt	½ cup grated Swiss cheese
⅛ teaspoon pepper	⅛ teaspoon ground nutmeg

Place butter in 2-cup measure. Microwave at HIGH (100% power) for 15-20 seconds; stir in flour, salt, and pepper. Blend in milk and sherry; microwave at HIGH (100% power) for 2-3 minutes, until thickened. Blend in Swiss cheese and nutmeg, stirring until cheese melts. Serve immediately over chicken.

Wine suggestions: Chardonnay - Pine Ridge, Robert Mondavi
Pulighy Montrachet

ROAST CHICKEN STUFFED WITH ORZO
This wonderfully flavored chicken is stuffed with rice-shaped pasta

Preparation: 1 hour

Baking: 2 hours
Servings: 8

4 cups water
3 teaspoons salt, divided
⅔ cup orzo (rice-shaped pasta)
2 Tablespoons butter
1 stalk celery, thinly sliced
½ pound fresh mushrooms, sliced
2 green onions, cut into ¼-inch pieces

¼ cup minced fresh parsley
¾ teaspoon dried basil
1 egg
1 (5-6 pound) roasting chicken
2 Tablespoons all-purpose flour
1¼ cups water

In 3-quart saucepan over high heat, boil water and 1 teaspoon salt. Add orzo; reduce heat to medium-high; cook 5 minutes. Orzo will be slightly undercooked. Drain and set aside. In large skillet over medium heat, melt butter and cook celery 5 minutes. Add mushrooms and green onion; cook until tender, stirring occasionally. In medium bowl, mix cooked orzo, celery mixture, parsley, basil, egg, and ½ teaspoon salt. Remove giblets and neck from chicken. Rinse chicken with cold water and pat dry.

With chicken breast side up, lift wings up towards neck, then fold under back of chicken so they stay in place. Spoon stuffing lightly into body cavity. Close by folding skin over opening; close with skewer. With string, tie legs and tail together. Rub chicken with 1 teaspoon salt. Place chicken, breast side up, on rack in open roasting pan. Roast at 350 degrees for 1¾ hours, or until meat thermometer registers 175 to 180 degrees. When done, remove to warm dish. To make gravy, combine flour, ½ teaspoon salt and water in covered jar; shake until blended well. Skim fat from drippings in pan and discard. Stir flour mixture into drippings, stirring to loosen brown bits from bottom of pan. Cook over medium heat, stirring constantly, until gravy thickens slightly and boils. Serve gravy with chicken and stuffing.

Wine suggestions: Sauvignon Blanc - Clos du Bois, Iron Horse
Pouilly Fume

 ## TARRAGON CHICKEN WITH ANGEL HAIR PASTA

Preparation: 10 minutes

Cooking: 25 minutes
Servings: 6

6 boneless chicken breast halves	**¾ cup grated Parmesan cheese**
3 Tablespoons butter	**¼ teaspoon salt**
2 cloves garlic, minced	**½ cup dry white wine**
1 teaspoon dried whole tarragon, crumbled	**¼ teaspoon cayenne pepper**
1 cup heavy cream	**1 pound angel hair pasta, cooked**

Lightly pound chicken between pieces of waxed paper. Sauté in butter over medium-high heat, about 1 minute on each side. Add garlic, tarragon, cream, Parmesan cheese, salt, wine, and cayenne pepper. Stir until blended; cook over medium heat until chicken is done and sauce is slightly reduced, about 15 minutes. Serve over angel hair pasta.

Wine suggestions: Sauvignon Blanc - Robert Mondavi, Pine Ridge Sancere

TANGY BAKED CHICKEN

Preparation: 10 minutes

Baking: 1 hour
Servings: 6

1 (3-pound) broiler-fryer chicken, cut up	**⅛ cup vinegar**
salt and pepper to taste	**⅛ cup lemon juice**
1 (10-ounce) jar tangy mustard-mayonnaise sauce (such as Durkee)	**½ cup sugar**
	2 Tablespoons Worcestershire sauce
1 cup water	**1 lemon, sliced**
½ cup butter, melted	**hot cooked rice**

Place chicken pieces, skin side up, in greased 13x9x2 baking dish. Sprinkle chicken with salt and pepper to taste. Bake, uncovered, at 425 degrees for 30 minutes; drain well. Combine sauce, water, butter, vinegar, lemon juice, sugar, and Worcestershire sauce; pour over chicken. Place lemon slices on top; bake, covered, at 350 degrees for 30 minutes. Serve over rice.

Wine suggestions: Sauvignon Blanc - Kenwood, Clos du Bois
Sancere

CHICKEN ARTICHOKE CASSEROLE

Preparation: 40 minutes   Baking: 30 minutes
Planning: Can partially prepare ahead   Servings: 8

1 cup butter
½ cup all-purpose flour
3½ cups milk
¼ teaspoon cayenne pepper
1 clove garlic, minced
1 cup grated sharp Cheddar cheese
1 (10-ounce) can button mushrooms, drained

8 boneless chicken breast halves, cooked and cut into bite-size pieces
2 (14-ounce) cans artichoke hearts, drained and quartered
2 cups fresh bread crumbs
4 Tablespoons butter, melted

Melt butter in saucepan; stir in flour and cook over low heat for 5-10 minutes until lightly browned. Gradually add milk; stir until thick and smooth. Add cayenne pepper, garlic, and cheese. Stir until cheese melts and mixture bubbles. Add mushrooms. Arrange chicken in greased 13x9x2 casserole dish. Top with artichokes and sauce. Mix bread crumbs with butter; sprinkle over dish. Bake at 350 degrees for 30 minutes. Casserole can be prepared ahead, then baked just before serving.

Wine suggestions: Chardonnay - Raymond, Deloach
Meursault

CHICKEN BREASTS IN CURRANT JELLY SAUCE
A dish to make a family dinner an occasion

Preparation: 10 minutes   Baking: 1¼ hours
                                                                   Servings: 6-8

6-8 chicken breast halves
salt and pepper to taste
2 (12-ounce) jars currant
  jelly
1 cup water
2 Tablespoons cornstarch

1 Tablespoon ground
  allspice
2 Tablespoons
  Worcestershire sauce
¼ cup lemon juice
hot cooked wild rice

Season chicken breasts with salt and pepper; place in lightly greased shallow baking dish. Combine jelly, water, cornstarch, allspice, Worcestershire sauce, and lemon juice in saucepan. Heat until ingredients are smoothly blended. Pour sauce over chicken. Bake, covered, at 350 degrees for 1 hour; uncover and bake 15 minutes longer. Baste several times while baking. Serve with wild rice. Serve additional sauce at the table.

Wine suggestions: Zinfandel - Storybook Mountain, Grgich Hills
                              Chardonnay - Raymond, Beringer

PECAN-BREADED CHICKEN

Preparation: 45 minutes   Cooking: 15 minutes
                                                                   Servings: 4

4 chicken breast halves,
  skinned and boned
10 Tablespoons butter,
  divided
3 Tablespoons Dijon
  mustard, divided

¾ cup ground pecans
2 Tablespoons vegetable oil
⅔ cup sour cream
¼ teaspoon salt
⅛ teaspoon pepper

Preheat oven to 200 degrees. Flatten chicken with meat mallet between pieces of waxed paper until ¼-inch thick. Melt 6 Tablespoons butter in large skillet. Remove from heat; whisk in 2 Tablespoons mustard. Dip chicken in butter-mustard mixture and heavily coat each piece with pecans. Melt 4 Tablespoons butter in large skillet; stir in oil. Sauté chicken pieces, 3 minutes each side. Place in casserole dish and keep warm in oven. Discard oil and butter; deglaze pan with sour cream, scraping up bits left in pan. Whisk in remaining mustard, salt, and pepper. Top each chicken breast with sauce before serving.

Wine suggestions: Chenin Blanc - Dry Creek, Quail Run
Vouvray - Monmousseau

ORANGE ALMOND CHICKEN

Preparation: 10 minutes

Cooking: 15 minutes
Servings: 6

⅔ **cup sliced almonds**
4 Tablespoons butter,
divided
6 chicken breast halves,
skinned and boned
⅛ teaspoon salt
⅛ teaspoon pepper

1½ cups heavy cream
4 teaspoons Dijon mustard
2 Tablespoons orange
marmalade
⅛ teaspoon cayenne pepper
hot cooked rice

Sauté almonds in 1 Tablespoon butter until crisp; set aside. Place chicken breasts between pieces of waxed paper and lightly pound with meat mallet. Season with salt and pepper. In 3 Tablespoons butter, sauté chicken over medium-high heat until golden brown, about 1 minute on each side. Add cream, mustard, marmalade, and cayenne pepper. Lower heat to medium; cook until sauce thickens and coats the back of a spoon and chicken is tender, about 10 minutes. Adjust seasonings, if necessary. Stir in almonds just before serving. Serve with rice.

Wine suggestions: Beaujolais Villages
Zinfandel - Preston
Gewurztraminer - Alsace

CHICKEN AND DUMPLINGS
An old Southern favorite

Preparation: 1½ hours   Cooking: 15 minutes
                                              Servings: 4

1 (3-pound) stewing chicken   **3 Tablespoons butter**
1 small onion, sliced   **3 Tablespoons all-purpose**
1 carrot, sliced   **flour**
1 stalk celery including   **⅛ teaspoon paprika**
** leaves**   **½ cup half and half**
6 peppercorns   **white pepper to taste**
1 teaspoon salt   **Dumplings**

Place chicken, onion, carrot, celery, peppercorns, and salt in water to cover; simmer 1 hour, or until tender. Remove from broth; when cool, remove meat from bones and cut into 1-inch cubes. Strain stock; add water if needed to make 2½ cups. Melt butter in Dutch oven; stir in flour mixed with paprika. Add chicken stock gradually, stirring until slightly thickened. Add half and half; season with pepper to taste. Add chicken; heat until mixture is slowly bubbling. Prepare dumpling pastry. Dip teaspoon into cold water, then into dumpling pastry. Spoon onto chicken mixture about ½ teaspoon at a time, pressing some of dumplings down into pot with back of spoon. Cook, covered, over medium-low heat for 15 minutes without lifting lid. The correct cooking temperature is critical at this point. It should be high enough to just bubble gently; if too high, chicken will stick and burn on the bottom.

Dumplings:
1 cup all-purpose flour   **½ Tablespoon shortening**
½ teaspoon salt   **⅓ cup milk**
2 teaspoons baking powder

Sift together flour, salt, and baking powder into large bowl. Blend in shortening until mixture resembles coarse crumbs. Add milk; mix well. If too dry, add 1 teaspoon more milk. Mixture should be consistency of biscuit dough.

SWISS CHICKEN
*A favorite recipe from "homerun king"
and former Atlanta Brave, Hank Aaron*

Preparation: 20 minutes
Cooking: 30-40 minutes

Broiling: 5 minutes
Servings: 6

6 Tablespoons butter, divided
2 Tablespoons vegetable oil
6 chicken breast halves, skinned and boned
¾ pound large fresh white mushrooms, stemmed
1 large bunch broccoli, stems peeled and trimmed, cut into spears and cooked al dente

lemon-pepper seasoning to taste
2 Tablespoons all-purpose flour
½ cup chicken stock
½ cup dry white wine
1½ cups grated Swiss cheese
Salt and white pepper to taste
grated Swiss cheese for garnish

Lightly butter large baking dish. Melt 2 Tablespoons butter with oil in large heavy skillet. Add chicken; cook until juices run clear when pricked with fork, about 3-5 minutes on each side; do not overcook. Remove chicken; set aside. Melt 2 Tablespoons butter in skillet. Add mushrooms; cook over medium-high heat until tender. Arrange cooked broccoli in single layer in bottom of dish. Season chicken with lemon-pepper and arrange in single layer over broccoli. Preheat broiler. Melt remaining 2 Tablespoons butter in 1-quart saucepan. Whisk in flour; cook over low heat, stirring constantly, about 3 minutes. Pour in chicken stock and wine, whisking until thoroughly blended. Continue cooking and stirring until sauce thickens enough to coat spoon. Add 1½ cups cheese; stir until melted. Taste and season with salt and pepper. Pour sauce over chicken; arrange mushrooms on top. Sprinkle additional cheese over dish to garnish. Broil about 6 inches from heat until top is bubbly and golden. Serve immediately.

Wine suggestions: Chardonnay - Stratford, Callaway
Chablis Premier Cru
Beaujolais Villages

CHICKEN SCALLOPINI
Quick and easy, yet elegant enough for company

Preparation: 10 minutes

Cooking: 20 minutes

Servings: 4

1 pound boneless chicken breasts
¾ cup Italian bread crumbs
1 egg
1 Tablespoon butter
1 Tablespoon olive or vegetable oil

1 (16-ounce) can tomatoes, undrained
½ teaspoon sugar
¼ teaspoon dried whole oregano

With meat mallet, pound chicken pieces until each is about ⅛-inch thick. Spread bread crumbs in pie plate. In second pie plate, beat egg slightly. Dip chicken in egg, then into bread crumbs to coat. In skillet over medium heat, heat butter and oil. Add chicken; cook about 1 minute on each side. Remove to platter and keep warm. In same skillet, stir tomatoes and their liquid, sugar, and oregano. Heat to boiling, stirring to break up tomatoes. Reduce heat to low; simmer 1 minute. Spoon over chicken. Chicken Scallopini can be served with Fettuccine Alfredo or other pasta.

Note: If seasoned bread crumbs are not available, substitute ¾ cup plain bread crumbs mixed with 1 teaspoon salt and ½ teaspoon dried whole oregano.

Wine suggestions: Sauvignon Blanc - Groth, Simi
Pouilly Fume

SESAME CHICKEN WITH HONEY DIP

Preparation: 30 minutes

Baking: 12 minutes

Servings: 6

½ cup mayonnaise
1 teaspoon dry mustard
1 teaspoon instant minced onion
½ cup fine dry bread crumbs

¼ cup sesame seeds
2 cups cubed cooked chicken or turkey
Honey Dip

Mix thoroughly mayonnaise, mustard, and onion; set aside. Mix crumbs with sesame seeds. Coat chicken with mayonnaise mixture, then crumb mixture. Place on baking sheet. Bake at 425 degrees for 12 minutes, or until lightly browned. Serve with Honey Dip.

Honey Dip:
1 Tablespoon mayonnaise   **2 Tablespoons honey**

Mix together mayonnaise and honey.

CHICKEN CHAUFROID
Nice for a summer luncheon

Preparation: 45 minutes   Cooking: 30 minutes
Planning: Must partially prepare ahead   Servings: 8
Chilling: 2 hours

**4 whole chicken breasts,
  split**
**2 (10-ounce) cans chicken
  broth**
**1 (3-ounce) package cream
  cheese, softened**
¼ cup mayonnaise
**2 Tablespoons snipped fresh
  dill, or 1 Tablespoon dried
  dill weed**
2 Tablespoons lemon juice

**½ teaspoon grated lemon
  rind**
¼ teaspoon salt
**lettuce leaves, preferably
  Romaine**
8 tomato slices
8 slices avocado
**½ cup toasted slivered
  almonds**
**1¾ cups bottled Italian
  dressing**

Place chicken breasts and broth in saucepan. Simmer, covered, 30 minutes or until tender. Refrigerate chicken in broth until cool; remove all skin and bones. Make a paste of cream cheese, mayonnaise, dill, lemon juice, rind, and salt. Coat rounded side of each breast with paste. Cover with plastic wrap and chill 2 hours. To serve, on each plate arrange a bed of lettuce; top with a chicken breast and tomato slice. Garnish long edges of breasts with avocado. Sprinkle with almonds; drizzle each serving with 3 Tablespoons dressing.

Wine suggestions: Sauvignon Blanc - Stratford, Groth
                     Chardonnay - Beringer
                     Chablis - French

BREAST OF CHICKEN FLORENTINE
This recipe comes from Jean Benton, caterer, of Benton and Associates, Inc.

Preparation: 1 hour

Baking: 20-30 minutes
Servings: 12

12 chicken breast halves
1 cup all-purpose flour
½ teaspoon salt
½ teaspoon pepper
9 Tablespoons butter
2 (10-ounce) packages frozen leaf spinach, thawed

½ teaspoon nutmeg
4 cups White Sauce, divided
1 cup grated sharp Cheddar cheese
½ teaspoon cayenne pepper
¼ teaspoon Worcestershire sauce

Roll chicken breasts in flour seasoned with salt and pepper. Melt butter in large skillet; sauté chicken until browned on both sides, about 20 minutes. Chicken needs to be cooked through, but still moist. Set chicken aside. Press liquid out of thawed spinach; chop slightly. Add nutmeg and spinach to 2 cups white sauce; set aside. Add cheese to 2 cups white sauce. Season with cayenne pepper and Worcestershire sauce; set aside. Spread spinach mixture in lightly greased 13x9x2 baking dish. Place chicken breasts on top. Spread cheddar cheese sauce over chicken. Bake at 350 degrees for 20 to 30 minutes, or until cheese sauce is browned and bubbly.

White Sauce:
½ cup butter
½ cup all-purpose flour

4 cups whole milk
1 teaspoon salt

Melt butter in 2-quart saucepan over low heat. Add flour, stirring constantly, until well blended. Slowly stir in milk; add salt. Simmer, stirring with wire whisk, until thickened, smooth, and hot.

Wine suggestions: Chardonnay - Chalone, Kalim
Meursault

SOUTHERN CHICKEN PIE
Always a favorite

Preparation: 45 minutes

Baking: 25 minutes
Servings: 8

6 Tablespoons butter
½ cup chopped green onion
½ cup chopped carrots
½ cup chopped celery
7 Tablespoons all-purpose
  flour
1 teaspoon salt
⅛ teaspoon pepper

¼ teaspoon poultry
  seasoning
3 cups chicken broth
3 cups cubed, cooked
  chicken or turkey
½ cup green peas, cooked
Biscuits

Melt butter in large saucepan. Add onion, carrots, and celery; cook over medium heat 2 minutes. Add flour, salt, pepper, and poultry seasoning; stir until blended. Add chicken broth all at once, stirring well. If using hot broth, add gradually, stirring to prevent lumping. Cook over medium heat, stirring constantly, until slightly thickened. Add chicken and peas; stir and heat until bubbly. Pour into 13x9x2 baking dish or individual ramekins. Place biscuits on hot pie mixture. Bake at 425 degrees for 20-25 minutes, or until biscuits are brown.

Biscuits:
2 cups all-purpose flour
1 Tablespoon sugar
1 teaspoon salt

4 teaspoons baking powder
¾ cup shortening
¾ cup milk

Sift together flour, sugar, salt, and baking powder into large bowl. Cut in shortening with pastry blender. Add milk, mixing well. Roll out to ½-inch thickness on floured board. Cut with floured biscuit cutter.

Wine suggestions: Sauvignon Blanc - Dry Creek, Stratford
                     Sancere

 ## CHICKEN AND PEANUTS IN HOT SAUCE

Preparation: 25 minutes
Stir-frying: 5 minutes   Servings: 4

2 pounds chicken breasts, boned, skinned, and cubed
4 teaspoons cornstarch, divided
4 teaspoons dry sherry
½ teaspoon salt
2 Tablespoons dry sherry
2 Tablespoons soy sauce
2 teaspoons sugar

2 teaspoons red wine vinegar
4 Tablespoons vegetable or peanut oil
3 whole Chinese chiles, cut in half and seeded
10 scallions, cut into ½-inch pieces
1 cup unsalted peanuts
hot cooked rice

Mix cubed chicken in bowl with 2 teaspoons cornstarch, 4 teaspoons dry sherry, and salt; set aside. Combine 2 Tablespoons dry sherry, soy sauce, sugar, vinegar, and 2 teaspoons cornstarch in separate bowl; set aside. Heat oil in wok or large skillet. Fry chiles in hot oil for a few seconds, stirring quickly; remove chiles. Add chicken; stir-fry until chicken turns white, about 2 minutes. Add scallions and soy sauce mixture. Stir quickly until thickened. Add peanuts and stir for a few seconds. Serve immediately over hot fluffy rice.

Wine suggestions: Gewurztraminer - Alsace
                    Beaujolais Villages

CURRIED CHICKEN AND EGGPLANT STEW

Preparation: 15 minutes   Cooking: 45 minutes
                                                  Servings: 8

2 Tablespoons vegetable oil
2 Tablespoons butter
½ cup diced onion
1 clove garlic, minced
1 medium eggplant, pared and cubed
1 (16-ounce) can stewed tomatoes, undrained

½ teaspoon curry powder
¼ teaspoon ground oregano
¼ teaspoon salt
2 large whole chicken breasts, cooked and cubed
1 cup chicken broth
2½ teaspoons chopped fresh parsley

In Dutch oven, heat oil and butter over medium heat; sauté onion and garlic. Add eggplant; sauté for 2 minutes. Add tomatoes and their liquid, curry powder, oregano, and salt; bring to boil. Cover; reduce heat and simmer for 15 minutes. Add chicken and broth; simmer 15 more minutes. Garnish with parsley before serving.

Wine suggestions: Chardonnay - Edna Valley, Robert Mondavi
Chablis Premier Cru

CHICKEN CAROLINA

A gourmet meal-in-one from Ted Turner, Atlanta's best-known entrepreneur and owner of the Atlanta Braves and Hawks

Preparation: 25 minutes

Baking: 1½ hours
Servings: 4

1 (2½-pound) whole broiler-fryer chicken
salt and pepper
1 medium cooking apple, peeled and quartered
2 medium onions, quartered
¼ cup olive oil
½ teaspoon paprika
4 medium potatoes, peeled and quartered

8 carrots, cut into 2-inch pieces
4 stalks celery, cut into 1-inch pieces
⅛ teaspoon salt
⅛ teaspoon pepper
1 cup white wine

Rub chicken inside and out with salt and pepper. Place apples and onion in cavity of chicken. Place chicken in Dutch oven; rub with mixture of oil and paprika. Arrange potatoes, carrots, and celery around chicken; season with salt and pepper to taste. Add white wine. Cover tightly; bake at 450 degrees for 1½ hours. Baste chicken and vegetables several times with cooking juices while baking. Spoon broth over each serving.

Wine suggestions: Pinot Noir - Saintsbury, Robert Mondavi
Beaujolais Villages
Chardonnay - Sterling

ORIENTAL SESAME CHICKEN DINNER
A meal in one with flare

Preparation: 10 minutes

Cooking: 20 minutes

Servings: 4

2 Tablespoons sesame seeds
6 chicken breast halves,
  boned and skinned
3 Tablespoons soy sauce
3 Tablespoons vegetable oil
1 bunch fresh broccoli, cut
  into flowerets

1½ Tablespoons lemon juice
½ teaspoon garlic powder
1 (8-ounce) package
  chicken-flavored rice mix,
  cooked

Toast sesame seeds at 350 degrees for 10 minutes, or until golden brown. Cut chicken into 2x½-inch strips. Toss with soy sauce and oil; set aside. Steam broccoli for 5 minutes. In large skillet or wok, cook chicken over medium heat, stir-frying until browned and tender, about 4 minutes. Stir in lemon juice and sprinkle with garlic powder; add broccoli and sesame seeds. Stir-fry 2 minutes. Serve over rice.

Wine suggestions: Gewurztraminer - Alsace
Beaujolais Villages

CHICKEN FLORENTINE
Enjoy, knowing each serving is only 297 calories!

Preparation: 10 minutes

Cooking: 45 minutes

Servings: 4

1 pound boneless chicken
  breasts, skinned
⅛ teaspoon pepper
¾ cup chicken broth
2 Tablespoons dry white
  wine
1 pound fresh spinach

1 Tablespoon water
2 teaspoons cornstarch
3 ounces Neufchatel cheese,
  cut into pieces
lemon juice
paprika for garnish

Place chicken in skillet. Sprinkle with pepper. Add broth and wine; bring to a boil. Reduce heat; simmer, covered, for 30 minutes. Remove chicken with slotted spoon. Cover and keep warm. Reserve broth in skillet. Wash spinach and place in large saucepan with only the water that clings to the leaves. Cook, covered, until tender, 3-5 minutes. Set aside, keeping warm. Combine water with cornstarch. Stir into broth in skillet. Cook, stirring, until blended; continue cooking for 2 minutes. Add cheese, stirring to melt. Arrange spinach on platter; sprinkle with lemon juice. Top with chicken and cheese sauce. Garnish with paprika.

Wine suggestions: Chardonnay - Dry Creek, Silverado
                              Meursault

SOY BAKED CHICKEN

Preparation: 5 minutes   Cooking: 1 hour
                                                          Servings: 4

2½-3 pounds chicken pieces   **paprika for garnish**
⅓ cup soy sauce   **1 (8-ounce) package wide**
2 Tablespoons lemon juice   **egg noodles**
¼ teaspoon onion powder   **2 Tablespoons chopped**
¼ teaspoon garlic powder   **fresh parsley**
¼ teaspoon poultry
**   seasoning**

Place chicken, skin side down, in lightly greased baking dish. Mix together soy sauce, lemon juice, onion powder, garlic powder, and poultry seasoning; pour over chicken. Turn chicken over, skin side up. Sprinkle with paprika. Bake at 375 degrees for 1 hour, basting once with juices. Transfer to serving dish. Meanwhile, cook noodles according to package directions. Drain noodles and add to juices in dish used for baking chicken. Toss. Sprinkle parsley over noodles; serve at once with chicken.

Wine suggestions: Pinot Noir - Sanford, Hacienda
                              Chardonnay - Beringer, Innisfree

CHICKEN SUKH

Preparation: 10 minutes

Cooking: 40 minutes
Servings: 4

**1 broiler-fryer chicken, cut
into pieces
1½ teaspoons salt
¼ teaspoon ground ginger
6 Tablespoons butter
2 cups chopped mild onion
1 (16-ounce) can chick peas,
drained**

**1 teaspoon ground cumin
1 Tablespoon ground
coriander
¾ teaspoon pepper
¾ cup uncooked long-grain
rice
3 cups hot chicken broth**

Dry chicken; rub with salt and ginger. In large skillet, brown chicken in butter with onion. Add chick peas, cumin, coriander, and pepper. Cook, covered, over low heat 10 minutes, shaking pan frequently. Transfer to large pot. Stir in rice and broth. Bring to a boil; reduce heat to low, cover and cook 20 minutes. Uncover, and cook 10 minutes longer.

Wine suggestions: Chardonnay - Robert Mondavi, Dry Creek
Pouilly Fuisse
Beaujolais - Brouilly

POULET DE SUSIE

Preparation: 30 minutes

Baking: 1 hour
Servings: 6

**6 chicken breast halves,
boned and skinned
all-purpose flour to coat
3 Tablespoons vegetable oil
2 (14-ounce) cans artichoke
hearts, drained
¼ cup butter**

**1 cup white wine
8 ounces fresh mushrooms,
sliced
1 (16-ounce) can pitted ripe
olives, drained and sliced
½ teaspoon dried tarragon**

Coat chicken with flour; brown in oil. Place chicken in lightly greased baking dish. Pour artichoke hearts over chicken; set aside. In 2-quart saucepan, melt butter; add wine and let simmer 5 minutes. Add mushrooms, olives, and tarragon; simmer 5 minutes longer. Pour sauce over chicken and artichokes. Bake, covered, at 350 degrees for 1 hour. Poulet de Susie can be served over rice.

Wine suggestions: Chardonnay - Sonoma Cutrer, Acacia
Meursault

STUFFED CHICKEN TERIYAKI
Explodes with flavor

Preparation: 15 minutes   Cooking: 1 hour
Planning: Must partially prepare ahead   Servings: 6
Marinating: 8 hours

**6 large whole chicken
  breasts, boned and
  butterflied**
½ cup bottled teriyaki sauce
½ pound lean ground pork
⅓ cup dry bread crumbs
**1 Tablespoon chopped green
  onion**

**1 Tablespoon chopped water
  chestnuts**
1 egg, slightly beaten
¼ cup milk
1 Tablespoon soy sauce
¼ teaspoon ground ginger
1 Tablespoon butter, melted
hot cooked rice

Marinate chicken in teriyaki sauce overnight, or at least 8 hours. Combine pork, bread crumbs, green onion, and water chestnuts in medium bowl. In small bowl combine beaten egg, milk, soy sauce, and ginger. Lightly stir egg mixture into pork mixture with fork. Fill each breast with stuffing and secure with skewers or kitchen twine. Place in lightly greased baking dish; brush with melted butter and bake at 350 degrees for 1 hour. Baste frequently with remaining teriyaki sauce. Serve on bed of fluffy rice.

Wine suggestions: Chardonnay - Deloach, Acacia
Pinot Noir - Sanford
Meursault

229

CORNISH HENS WITH APRICOT GLAZE

Preparation: 10 minutes

Grilling: 1 hour
Servings: 4

4 (1½-pound) Cornish hens
1 teaspoon salt
½ teaspoon pepper
¼ cup bottled French
   dressing

2 Tablespoons orange juice
2 teaspoons dry onion soup
   mix
4 Tablespoons apricot
   preserves

Prepare grill for cooking. Rinse hens with cold water and pat dry with paper towels. Season hens with salt and pepper, inside and out. Tie legs together. In small bowl, combine French dressing, orange juice, onion soup mix, and apricot preserves; set aside. Grill hens, covered, for 45-60 minutes, or until fork can be inserted easily in leg and hens are golden brown. Approximately 15 minutes before hens are done, baste with apricot glaze several times until all glaze is used.

Wine suggestions: Pinot Noir - Sanford
                    Chardonnay - Simi Reserve

 # HOT & SWEET MUSTARD
A great gift for men!

Preparation: 10 minutes
Planning: Must prepare ahead

Cooking: 20 minutes
Yield: 4 ½-pint jars

1 cup dry mustard
1 cup white vinegar
1¼ cup sugar
3 eggs, well beaten

¼ teaspoon cayenne pepper
⅛ teaspoon white pepper
4 Tablespoons butter

Mix mustard and vinegar and let sit overnight. The next day, add sugar, eggs, and peppers; cook in double boiler until mixture reaches the consistency of custard. Stir constantly over low heat, approximately 20 minutes. Add butter. Stir. Pour into ½ pint jars. Cool. Refrigerate.

DOVES WITH CREAM GRAVY

Preparation: 20 minutes

Baking: 30-45 minutes
Servings: 3-4

1 cup all-purpose flour
½ teaspoon salt
¼ teaspoon pepper
6-8 doves

vegetable oil for frying
3 Tablespoons all-purpose
flour
2 cups milk

Combine flour, salt, and pepper. Dredge doves in flour mixture; brown in hot oil in skillet. Remove doves. To prepare gravy, drain all but ¼ cup pan drippings. Add flour to pan, blending well. When smooth, add milk; cook over medium heat, stirring constantly, until gravy is thickened. Return doves to pan. Bake, covered, at 350 degrees for 30 to 45 minutes.

Wine suggestions: Cabernet Sauvignon - Stag's Leap
Sancere

SMOTHERED DOVES

Preparation: 5 minutes

Baking: 2 hours
Servings: 2

6 dove breasts
salt to taste
pepper to taste

garlic powder to taste
3 slices bacon

Sprinkle each dove breast with salt, pepper, and garlic powder to taste. Place a half slice of bacon on top of each breast; wrap breast in aluminum foil. Bake at 250 degrees for 2 hours.

Wine suggestions: Zinfandel - Storybook Mountain, Deloach
Pinot Noir - Acacia, Hacienda

ROAST DUCK WITH RASPBERRY SAUCE
Divine duck!

Preparation: 30 minutes　　　　　　　　　　Roasting: 1½ hours
　　　　　　　　　　　　　　　　　　　　　　Servings: 6

1 (4-5 pound) duck,
　trimmed of excess fat
1 medium carrot, chopped
1 medium onion, chopped
1 medium tomato, chopped
1 cup beef stock or thinned
　beef broth

1 Tablespoon butter
3 Tablespoons sugar
⅓ cup cider vinegar
1 (10-ounce) package frozen
　raspberries, thawed
¼ cup Chambord raspberry
　liqueur

Season duck with salt and pepper to taste. Prick skin over surface of duck. Chop giblets; place duck and giblets in roasting pan. Roast at 450 degrees for 1½ hours. Remove duck, set aside. Pour off all but 2 Tablespoons fat from roasting pan. Add chopped vegetables and place over medium heat; sauté, stirring, for 10 minutes. Add beef stock, scraping up brown bits left in pan. Strain into bowl; set aside. In medium saucepan, melt butter; stir in sugar. Cook, stirring, until mixture is brown. Add vinegar; cook until mixture is reduced by half. Add reserved sauce; reduce heat to simmer. Stir in raspberries and Chambord. Simmer for 10 minutes. Spoon sauce over duck.

Wine suggestions:　Zinfandel - Ridge, Buehler
　　　　　　　　　　　Cabernet Sauvignon - Ridge
　　　　　　　　　　　Pinot Noir - Eyrie

ROAST TURKEY WITH WILD RICE STUFFING
Delicious any time of the year

Preparation: 20 minutes   Baking: 5 to 5½ hours
Planning: Can partially prepare ahead   Servings: 16

2 (6-ounce) packages long-grain and wild rice mix
¼ cup butter
8 ounces Canadian-style bacon, diced
½ cup sliced green onion
2 cloves garlic, minced
¼ cup dry white wine, optional

¼ cup chopped fresh parsley
⅓ cup chopped walnuts or pecans
1 teaspoon salt
¼ teaspoon pepper
1 (14-16 pound) whole turkey

Prepare rice according to package directions. Melt butter in skillet; add bacon, onion, and garlic. Sauté until golden and tender. Add wine, parsley, nuts, salt, and pepper. Mix with rice. Stuff turkey with rice mixture. Brush oil over skin of turkey. Cover loosely with foil. Roast at 325 degrees for 5-5½ hours, or until meat thermometer registers 185 degrees. Uncover for last 45 minutes of baking time.

Note: Ingredients for stuffing can be halved and used to stuff an 8-10 pound turkey or 4-6 Cornish hens. Adjust cooking time accordingly. Dry ingredients for stuffing can be mixed ahead and refrigerated overnight; mix in wine and stuff turkey just before baking.

Wine suggestions: Pinot Noir - Sanford, Robert Mondavi
                       Chardonnay - Sonoma Cutrer, Saintsbury

ROTISSERIE GRILLED TURKEY FOR A GAS GRILL

Preparation: 20 minutes

Grilling: 2-2½ hours

Servings: 8

1 (8-10 pound) fresh turkey
¼ cup vegetable oil
½ cup salt
1 cup vinegar

2 Tablespoons coarsely
   ground pepper
¼ cup dried parsley

Before turning on gas grill, clear space in center for drip pan and arrange briquettes around pan. Adjust rotisserie so spit is positioned over pan. Preheat grill to medium-low temperature. Remove giblets, rinse turkey and pat dry. Truss with lightweight galvanized wire, securing wings tightly to body of bird. Mix oil and salt; use ¼ of mixture to coat cavity and body of bird. Secure turkey to spit as tightly as possible. Be sure prongs are inserted well into flesh. Tighten with pliers. Bird will slip on spit if not secure. Place turkey on rotisserie and close grill. After cooking for 1 hour, add vinegar, pepper, and parsley to remaining oil and salt mixture. Baste with mixture every 15 minutes until meat thermometer registers 185 degrees, about 60-90 minutes. Allow to cool before carving. This is a fairly messy operation, so wear an apron.

Note: Use a 13x9x2 aluminum baking pan for a drip pan. The pan will be black after using, so use an old one or cover completely with foil.

Wine suggestions: Pinot Noir - Sanford, Saintsbury
Chardonnay - Sonoma Cutrer, Edna Valley
Volnay

Casseroles

Red Clover

CASEROLES

BEEF
Beef Bourguignon 237
Beef Ragout 240
Chipped Beef Casserole 238
BEEF, GROUND
Cabbage Beef Casserole 240
Ground Beef Noodle Bake 239
One Dish Meal 241
Oriental Spaghetti 238
Polynesian Goulash 239
Zucchini-Ground Beef Bake 242
CHICKEN
Cashew Chicken 244
Chicken Casserole Delight 244
Chicken Lasagna for a Crowd 243
Chicken Provencale 245
Chicken Rice Elegante 246
Hot Chicken Salad Casserole 242
Poulet Au Frommage 246
EGGS AND CHEESE
Cheesy Egg Bake 248
Chili Relleno Casserole 247
FRUIT
Cranberry Conserve 264
HAM
Baked Ham Mornay 249
Company Ham Casserole 250
Ham and Artichoke Casserole 248

LAMB
Sweet and Sour Lamb 251
PORK
Favorite Chops in Casserole 250
SAUSAGE
Sausage Rice Casserole 252
SEAFOOD
Blend of the Bayou Seafood Casserole . 253
Company Seafood Dinner 254
Do-Ahead Seafood Bake 254
Seafood Casserole 255
Shrimp and Crab Rice Casserole 256
Shrimp with Artichokes 252
Tuna and Artichokes 256
VEAL
Sauté De Veau Marengo 258
Veal Stroganoff Casserole 257
VEGETABLE
Asparagus Casserole 259
Baked Rice 262
Cajun Maque Choux 260
Golden Eggplant Casserole 260
Green Bean Casserole 261
Hot Bean Dish 259
Onion Casserole 261
Scalloped Potatoes Au Gratin 262
Squash Casserole 263
Tomato Cheese Casserole 263
Vegetable Ratatouille 264

BEEF BOURGUIGNON

Preparation: 15 minutes
Planning: Must partially prepare ahead

Baking: 2½ hours
Marinating: 2 hours
Servings: 6-8

1½ cups burgundy wine
2 Tablespoons brandy, optional
2 Tablespoons vegetable oil
1 teaspoon salt
½ teaspoon pepper
½ teaspoon dried whole thyme
1 sprig fresh parsley
1 bay leaf
3 pounds beef round steak, cut into 2-inch cubes
6 Tablespoons butter, divided

2 cloves garlic, crushed
2 large onions, finely chopped
1 medium carrot, chopped
4 rounded Tablespoons flour
1 Tablespoon tomato paste
1 cup beef broth or consommé
1½ cups fresh pearl onions
¾ pound mushroom caps
hot cooked rice

Mix wine, brandy, oil, salt, pepper, thyme, parsley, and bay leaf; blend well. Marinate beef in mixture 2 hours or more in glass dish, turning occasionally. After marinating, drain beef, reserving marinade. Remove parsley and bay leaf. Pat meat dry. Brown meat in skillet in 3 Tablespoons butter and place in large, oven-proof dish. Melt 2 Tablespoons butter; sauté garlic, onion, and carrot. Blend in flour and tomato paste. Add reserved marinade and beef broth; stir until mixture boils. Pour over meat. Bake, covered, at 350 degrees for 2 hours. Casserole can be frozen at this point; remove from freezer and bake 1 hour. Heat 1 Tablespoon butter in skillet; sauté pearl onions and mushrooms for 2 minutes. Add to top of casserole; bake 30 minutes. Serve with rice.

CHIPPED BEEF CASSEROLE

Preparation: 25 minutes
Planning: Must partially prepare ahead
Chilling: 12 hours

Baking: 1 hour
Servings: 6-8

3 (2½-ounce) packages
  sliced smoked beef
1 (8-ounce) package elbow
  macaroni, cooked al dente
2 (10¾-ounce) cans cream
  of mushroom soup,
  undiluted
2 cups milk

1 medium onion, finely
  chopped
½ green bell pepper,
  chopped
4 hard-cooked eggs, sliced
2 cups grated Cheddar
  cheese

In large bowl, tear beef into bite-size pieces. Add macaroni, soup, milk, onion, and pepper; mix well. Place half of mixture in 13x9x2 casserole dish; layer eggs on top. Spread remaining mixture on top of eggs. Top with cheese. Refrigerate overnight. Remove from refrigerator 30 minutes before baking. Bake, uncovered, at 350 degrees for 1 hour.

ORIENTAL SPAGHETTI

Preparation: 45 minutes
Planning: Can partially prepare ahead

Baking: 45 minutes
Servings: 6-8

1 (8-ounce) package
  spaghetti
½ pound ground beef
½ pound ground pork
1 cup chopped celery
½ cup chopped onion
½ teaspoon salt

1 (15-ounce) can Chinese
  vegetables
1 (10-ounce) can tomato
  soup, sauce, or paste
¾ cup grated Cheddar
  cheese

Break up spaghetti; boil according to package directions. Brown beef, pork, celery, and onion; drain off fat. Add salt, vegetables, and soup. Pour into baking dish; cover with cheese. Casserole can be refrigerated or frozen at this point; return to room temperature before baking. Bake at 350 degrees for 35-45 minutes. This dish is delicious with green salad and French bread.

GROUND BEEF NOODLE BAKE

Preparation: 30 minutes

Baking: 10 minutes
Servings: 6

4 cups thin noodles
**2 (3-ounce) packages cream
cheese, softened**
½ cup evaporated milk
2 teaspoons lemon juice
¼ teaspoon garlic salt
**1 teaspoon Worcestershire
sauce**
½ cup chopped onion
**¼ cup chopped green bell
pepper**
1 Tablespoon butter
1 pound ground beef
**1 (8-ounce) can tomato
sauce**
½ cup ketchup

Cook noodles according to package directions. Combine cream cheese, evaporated milk, lemon juice, garlic salt, and Worcestershire sauce; add to noodles. Place in greased 11x7 dish; pat into smooth layer. Cook onion, green pepper, and ground beef in butter until onion and green pepper are soft; drain. Stir in tomato sauce and ketchup; cook until thickened. Spread over noodles. Bake at 375 degrees for 10 minutes, until bubbly.

 # POLYNESIAN GOULASH *Excellent*

Preparation: 30 minutes

Baking: 45 minutes
Servings: 6

**2 pounds ground beef,
browned and drained**
¾ cup chopped celery
**¾ cup chopped green bell
pepper**
¾ cup chopped onion
**1 (14-ounce) can bean
sprouts or 2 cups fresh
bean sprouts**
½ cup sliced mushrooms
**1 (10¾-ounce) can cream of
celery soup, undiluted**
1½ Tablespoons soy sauce
salt and pepper, to taste
**1 (5-ounce) can dried
Chinese noodles**

Combine ground beef, celery, green pepper, onion, bean sprouts, mushrooms, soup, soy sauce, salt, and pepper; mix well. Pour into large casserole dish; top with Chinese noodles. Bake at 350 degrees for 45 minutes.

BEEF RAGOUT

Preparation: 30 minutes   Cooking: 3 hours
Planning: Can prepare ahead   Servings: 6-8

2 pounds lean stew beef or
  brisket, cut into 2-inch
  pieces
2 Tablespoons butter
1 medium onion, chopped
2 carrots, diced
1 stalk celery, chopped
2 Tablespoons all-purpose
  flour
3 fresh tomatoes, chopped
1 clove garlic, finely
  chopped

1 teaspoon salt
¼ teaspoon black pepper
2 cups red wine
2½ cups water or beef
  consommé
1 Tablespoon chopped fresh
  parsley
¼ teaspoon dried whole
  thyme or savory
1 bay leaf

In Dutch oven, brown meat in butter; add onion, carrots, and celery;
cook until vegetables are slightly browned. Add flour; mix well. Add
tomatoes and remaining ingredients. Cook, covered, until beef is tender, about 3 hours, or bake at 300 degrees for 3 hours. Beef Ragout is
good served with boiled potatoes or noodles.

CABBAGE BEEF CASSEROLE
An alternative to the usual cabbage rolls

Preparation: 30 minutes   Baking: 1 hour
Planning: Can partially prepare ahead   Servings: 6

1½ pounds ground beef
1 Tablespoon vegetable oil
2 medium onions, chopped
1 clove garlic, minced
1 teaspoon salt
¼ teaspoon pepper
1 (14-ounce) can tomato
  sauce

1 cup water
½ cup uncooked long-grain
  rice
4 cups shredded cabbage (1
  small cabbage)
sour cream
dill weed

In large skillet, cook beef in oil until browned; drain off fat. Stir in onion, garlic, salt, pepper, tomato sauce, and water. Bring to a boil; stir in rice. Simmer, covered, about 20 minutes. Place half the shredded cabbage in buttered baking dish. Cover with half of rice mixture. Repeat layers. Casserole can be refrigerated at this point, then brought to room temperature before baking. Bake, covered, at 350 degrees for 1 hour. Serve with sour cream seasoned with a small amount of dill.

ONE MEAL DISH

A wonderful dish to take to a "pot luck" dinner
or share with a friend

Preparation: 1 hour

Planning: Can prepare ahead

Baking: 35 minutes

Servings: 6

2 cups cooked brown rice
¼ pound mushrooms, sliced
1 pound ground beef,
    browned
2 cups broccoli, cut into
    ½-inch pieces
2 carrots, sliced
1 zucchini, sliced

1 cup cut green beans
1 (16-ounce) jar spaghetti
    sauce
1 cup grated longhorn
    cheese
1 cup grated Monterey Jack
    cheese

Place cooked rice in 10x6x2 baking dish. Cover rice with mushrooms. Top with ground beef. Cook broccoli, carrots, zucchini, and green beans in boiling, salted water 5-7 minutes; drain and spoon over ground beef. Top with spaghetti sauce. Bake, covered, at 375 degrees for 30 minutes. Combine cheeses and sprinkle over casserole. Return to oven to melt cheese, approximately 5 minutes, or until bubbly.

 ## ZUCCHINI-GROUND BEEF BAKE

Preparation: 30 minutes   Baking: 45 minutes
Planning: Can partially prepare ahead   Servings: 6-8

3 pounds zucchini
4 cups coarsely grated
  Monterey Jack cheese,
  divided
4 eggs, beaten
½ cup half and half
1 (4-ounce) can green chiles,
  diced
¼ cup chopped fresh parsley

1 teaspoon salt
2 teaspoons baking powder
2 pounds cooked lean
  ground beef, thoroughly
  drained
1 cup bread crumbs or
  herb-seasoned stuffing
2 Tablespoons butter

Preheat oven to 350 degrees. Cube zucchini; steam until just tender. Reserve ⅓ cup grated cheese for topping. Combine eggs, half and half, chiles, parsley, remaining cheese, salt, and baking powder. Toss in zucchini and ground beef; mix well. Transfer mixture to buttered casserole dish that has been dusted with ½ cup bread crumbs. Sprinkle with remaining bread crumbs and dot with butter. Sprinkle top with reserved ⅓ cup cheese. Casserole can be refrigerated at this point, then returned to room temperature before baking. Bake for 45 minutes, or until cooked throughout and lightly browned.

HOT CHICKEN SALAD CASSEROLE

Preparation: 20 minutes   Baking: 20 minutes
Planning: Can partially prepare ahead   Servings: 10

4 cups cooked chicken,
  cubed
1 cup mayonnaise
1 cup slivered almonds
1 cup chopped celery
1 (10¾-ounce) can cream of
  chicken soup, undiluted
1 small onion, chopped

4 teaspoons lemon juice
3 hard-cooked eggs,
  chopped
salt and pepper, to taste
2 cups crushed potato chips
1 cup grated Cheddar
  cheese

Combine chicken, mayonnaise, almonds, celery, soup, onion, lemon juice eggs, salt, and pepper; mix well. If mixture is dry, add more mayonnaise. Top with potato chips mixed with cheese. Casserole can be refrigerated or frozen at this point; return to room temperature before baking Bake at 350 degrees for 20 minutes.

CHICKEN LASAGNA FOR A CROWD

Preparation: 45 minutes

Baking: 30 minutes
Servings: 20-25

1 pound lasagna noodles
3 cups sliced fresh
mushrooms
2 cups chopped onion
4-6 Tablespoons butter
3 cups Hollandaise sauce
(see Index)
2 pounds deboned chicken
or turkey breast, cooked,
skinned and sliced
¼ teaspoon salt

⅛ teaspoon pepper
1 teaspoon dried whole basil
1 teaspoon dried whole
oregano
3 cups grated mozzarella
cheese
1 cup grated Parmesan
cheese
2 (12-ounce) cans asparagus
tips

Cook noodles according to package directions; drain. Sauté mushrooms and onion in butter until soft. Layer ingredients in two 13x9x2 casserole dishes as follows: ½ cup Hollandaise sauce, ¼ of the noodles, ¼ of the chicken, ¼ of the salt and pepper, ¼ of the mushroom-onion mixture, ½ cup of Hollandaise sauce, ¼ teaspoon basil, ¼ teaspoon oregano, ¾ cup mozzarella cheese and ¼ cup Parmesan cheese. Arrange all of asparagus on top of cheese layers. Repeat layers in each pan, ending with cheese. Bake, uncovered, at 350 degrees for 30 minutes. Let stand before cutting. Lasagna can be served with a fresh green salad.

CHICKEN CASSEROLE DELIGHT

Preparation: 1½ hours   Baking: 30 minutes
Planning: Can partially prepare ahead   Servings: 8

1 (6-ounce) package
   long-grain and wild rice
2½ cups chicken broth
1 medium onion, chopped
½ cup chopped celery
butter
4 cups chopped cooked
   chicken
1 (10-ounce) can sliced
   water chestnuts, drained

1 (4-ounce) jar pimientos,
   drained
1 (6-ounce) can mushrooms,
   drained
1 (10¾-ounce) can cream of
   celery soup, undiluted
1 cup mayonnaise
⅔ cup crushed potato chips
paprika for garnish

Cook rice in chicken broth until done, set aside. Sauté onion and celery in butter. Mix chicken, rice, onion, celery, water chesnuts, pimientos, mushrooms, soup, and mayonnaise in large casserole dish. At this point casserole can be refrigerated and baked later. Sprinkle with crushed potato chips and paprika. Bake at 350 degrees for 30 minutes. Excellent with fruit salad and rolls for a luncheon.

 ## CASHEW CHICKEN

Preparation: 30 minutes   Baking: 1½ hours
         Servings: 6

2 pounds boneless chicken
   breasts or pork
¼ cup all-purpose flour
   seasoned with salt and
   pepper
1 Tablespoon butter
2 (10¾-ounce) cans cream
   of mushroom soup,
   undiluted

1 cup sliced mushrooms
juice of one lemon
1 teaspoon dried whole
   thyme
½ cup white wine
½ teaspoon salt
¼ teaspoon pepper
1 cup salted cashew nuts
hot cooked rice

Pound chicken to ¼-inch thickness. Coat with seasoned flour. In large skillet, melt butter; brown chicken. Add all remaining ingredients except cashews. Bring to a boil; reduce heat, cook 1½ hours, adding cashews during last 15 minutes of cooking time. Serve over rice.

CHICKEN PROVENCALE

Preparation: 1 hour

Baking: 30 minutes
Servings: 6

2 whole chicken breasts
4 chicken thighs
1 teaspoon salt
1 bay leaf
1 sprig fresh parsley
flour
4 Tablespoons butter,
** divided**
2 onions, sliced
4 carrots, cooked and sliced

3 potatoes, cooked and
** sliced**
2 Tablespoons all-purpose
** flour**
2 teaspoons lemon juice
2 egg yolks, beaten
white pepper to taste
8 slices bacon, cooked and
** crumbled**
¼ cup chopped fresh parsley

Place chicken, salt, bay leaf, and parsley in pot with enough water to cover; simmer 45 minutes. Remove chicken. Reduce liquid to 2 cups; set aside. Remove skin and bones from chicken, keeping pieces as large as possible. Dredge in flour; brown in 2 Tablespoons butter. Remove chicken; brown onion lightly in skillet drippings. Put layers of chicken, carrots, potatoes, and onion in casserole dish. Meanwhile, melt 2 Tablespoons butter, blend in 2 Tablespoons flour; gradually add 2 cups reserved broth. Cook until smooth. Add lemon juice. Pour mixture over egg yolks, beating constantly. Return egg mixture to saucepan over low heat. Season with white pepper. Pour sauce over chicken and sprinkle with bacon and parsley. Bake, covered, at 300 degrees for 30 minutes.

CHICKEN RICE ELEGANTE

Preparation: 45 minutes

Baking: 1¼ hours
Servings: 4

1 (6¼-ounce) package
long-grain and wild rice
1 (10¾-ounce) can cream of
mushroom soup,
undiluted
1 (4-ounce) can mushrooms,
undrained
1 (8-ounce) carton sour
cream
1 small onion, minced
1 cup chopped celery

¾ cup butter, melted,
divided
⅛ teaspoon salt
⅛ teaspoon pepper
1 Tablespoon lemon juice
1 teaspoon Worcestershire
sauce
½ cup evaporated milk
4 split chicken breasts or 8
chicken thighs

Cook rice according to package directions. Mix rice, soup, mushrooms, sour cream, onion, celery, ¼ cup melted butter, salt, and pepper. Pour into large casserole dish; set aside. Combine ½ cup melted butter, lemon juice, Worcestershire sauce, and milk. Dip chicken in lemon juice mixture. Arrange chicken in single layer over rice. Bake, uncovered, at 350 degrees for 1¼ hours, or until done. Serve on platter with rice in center and chicken pieces around edge.

POULET AU FROMMAGE

Preparation: 30 minutes

Baking: 45 minutes
Servings: 6

1 (8-ounce) package wide
noodles
1½ cups cottage cheese
2 cups grated Cheddar or
American cheese
½ cup grated Parmesan
cheese
½ cup chopped onion
½ cup chopped green bell
pepper

¾ cup sliced mushrooms
3 Tablespoons butter
¼ cup diced pimientos
1 (10¾-ounce) can cream of
chicken soup, undiluted
¾ cup milk
½ teaspoon Italian
seasoning
3 cups cooked chicken or
turkey, cubed

Cook noodles according to package directions; drain. Mix together cottage cheese, Cheddar cheese, and Parmesan cheese. Sauté onion, green pepper, and mushrooms in butter until onion is translucent. Mix pimientos, soup, milk and Italian seasoning; add to vegetables. In large greased casserole dish, layer half the noodles, half the chicken, half the cheese mixture, and half the sauce mixture. Repeat layers. Bake at 350 degrees for 40-45 minutes.

 ## CHILI RELLENO CASSEROLE

Preparation: 30 minutes
Planning: Can partially prepare ahead

Baking: 45 minutes
Servings: 4

1 (7-ounce) can whole green chiles	2 Tablespoons all-purpose flour
1 cup grated Cheddar cheese	½ teaspoon chili powder
8 ounces plain yogurt	⅛ teaspoon ground cumin
2 eggs	½ cup chili salsa

Split chiles and open flat. Cover bottom of 1-quart greased baking dish with half the chiles. Sprinkle with half the cheese. Repeat for a second layer. Beat together yogurt, eggs, flour, chili powder, and cumin until smooth; pour over chili-cheese layers. At this point casserole can be refrigerated and baked later. Bake at 350 degrees for 30 minutes, or until set. Pour chili salsa over casserole and bake 15 minutes longer. This dish is delicious with refried beans or rice, warm buttered tortillas, and green salad.

Note: For an extra spicy taste, add extra diced green chiles to yogurt mixture.

CHEESY EGG BAKE

Preparation: 20 minutes

Baking: 30-40 minutes

Servings: 6-8

¼ cup all-purpose flour
¼ teaspoon salt
4 Tablespoons butter, melted
4 eggs, beaten
1 cup cottage cheese
1 (4-ounce) can chopped green chiles, drained

2 cups grated Monterey Jack cheese
1 (4-ounce) jar whole pimientos, drained
1 small green bell pepper, thinly sliced

Combine flour, salt, and butter in large bowl; add eggs, cottage cheese, chiles, and cheese. Mix well. Pour mixture into greased casserole dish. Garnish with pimientos and thinly sliced green pepper. Bake at 375 degrees for 30-40 minutes.

 ## HAM AND ARTICHOKE CASSEROLE
A great brunch dish!

Preparation: 15 minutes
Planning: Can prepare ahead

Baking: 40 minutes
Servings: 4

1 bunch green onions
2 (6½-ounce) jars marinated artichoke hearts
1 clove garlic, minced, or ¼ teaspoon garlic juice
4 eggs, beaten

8 ounces cooked ham, cut into ½-inch squares
2 cups grated sharp Cheddar cheese
8 butter-flavored crackers, crushed

Finely mince onions including half of the green tops. Tear apart artichokes; reserve oil. Sauté onion and garlic in artichoke oil. In bowl, combine all ingredients. Transfer to greased 9-inch square dish. At this point casserole can be refrigerated and brought back to room temperature before baking. Bake at 350 degrees for 40 minutes. Casserole does not have to be kept hot while serving.

BAKED HAM MORNAY

Preparation: 1 hour
Planning: Can partially prepare ahead

Baking: 10 minutes
Servings: 6-8

3 Tablespoons butter, divided
3 Tablespoons all-purpose flour
3 cups milk
salt and freshly ground pepper, to taste
⅛ teaspoon ground nutmeg
⅛ teaspoon cayenne pepper
2 cups grated Cheddar cheese

1 cup heavy cream
½ cup chopped onion
2 cups sliced mushrooms
2 cups cooked ham, cut into ½-inch cubes
12 ounces broad egg noodles
4 Tablespoons port wine
½ cup freshly grated Parmesan cheese
¼ teaspoon paprika

Preheat oven to 450 degrees. Heat 2 Tablespoons butter in saucepan; add flour, stirring with wire whisk. When blended, add milk, stirring rapidly with whisk. Add salt, pepper, nutmeg, cayenne pepper, and cheese, stirring until cheese melts. Add cream; bring to a boil. Remove from heat. Melt remaining Tablespoon of butter; stir in onion. When onions are translucent, add mushrooms; cook until wilted. Add ham; heat through. Cook noodles according to package directions until tender. Do not overcook. Add cheese sauce to ham mixture; add wine. Bring to a boil. Drain noodles well; add to mixture, stirring gently to blend. Place mixture in 14x8 baking dish. Sprinkle with Parmesan cheese and paprika. At this point casserole can be refrigerated and baked later. Bake 5-10 minutes, then place under broiler until nicely glazed. Serve immediately.

Note: This recipe can easily be doubled for a crowd.

COMPANY HAM CASSEROLE
Compliments of Homer Rice, Director of Athletics at Georgia Tech

Preparation: 30 minutes   Baking: 45-60 minutes
Planning: Can partially prepare ahead   Servings: 8

**1 (6-ounce) package
long-grain and wild rice
1 (10-ounce) package frozen
chopped broccoli
3 cups cooked ham, cut in
½-inch cubes
1 (4½-ounce) can sliced
mushrooms
1 (8-ounce) can sliced water
chestnuts**

**1 cup grated Cheddar
cheese
1 (10¾-ounce) can cream of
celery soup
1 cup mayonnaise
2 teaspoons prepared
mustard
1 teaspoon curry powder
¼ cup grated Parmesan
cheese**

Cook rice and broccoli according to package directions. Spread rice in buttered 13x9x2 baking dish. Top with broccoli. Combine ham, mushrooms, water chestnuts, Cheddar cheese, soup, mayonnaise, mustard, and curry; spread over broccoli layer. Sprinkle with Parmesan cheese. Casserole can be refrigerated until ready to bake. Bake at 350 degrees for 45-60 minutes.

FAVORITE CHOPS IN CASSEROLE
This has a wonderful aroma while cooking

Preparation: 15 minutes   Baking: 1 hour
                                           Servings: 4

**6 thick pork chops
vegetable oil for browning
¼-½ teaspoon dried tarragon
salt and pepper, to taste
4 apples, unpeeled and
chopped
4 medium onions, sliced**

**½ cup light brown sugar
2 Tablespoons ground
cinnamon
2 Tablespoons butter
juice of 1 lemon
¼ cup water**

Say "Goodbye" to Clipping with

Southern Living
2008 Annual Recipes

Enjoy old-style Southern food al...

✓ Insider tips for today's cook

✓ New twists on your trie true favorites

✓ Simple h...

et more than 850 of the Sweetest, Most Succulent, and Savory Recipes in the South!

Southern Living
2008 ANNUAL RECIPES
Every Single Recipe From 2008 — Over 850!

...hen-tested recipe from the 2008 issues of
...than 850 in all!

...ern Living Cooking School and
...cipe below for a yummy sample!)

...and serving suggestions

No

Rub chops with oil; sprinkle with tarragon, salt, and pepper. Brown over high heat. Arrange a bed of apples and onion in deep casserole dish. Mix sugar and cinnamon; sprinkle half of mixture over apples and onion. Arrange chops in casserole; sprinkle with remaining sugar and cinnamon; dot with butter. Combine lemon juice and water; pour over chops. Bake, covered, at 325 degrees for 1 hour. Uncover during last 10 minutes of baking.

SWEET AND SOUR LAMB
A lamb dish to remember

Preparation: 40 minutes

Cooking: 1½ hours
Servings: 6

3½ pounds lamb shoulder, cut into 1-inch cubes
2 Tablespoons vegetable oil
1 cup water
1 teaspoon salt
1 cup apple juice
⅓ cup vinegar
3 Tablespoons light brown sugar
¼ teaspoon dry mustard
½ teaspoon chili powder
⅛ teaspoon ground ginger

1 clove garlic, crushed
1 large onion, finely chopped
1 large green bell pepper, chopped
1 cup celery, chopped
3 Tablespoons cornstarch
¼ cup water
1 teaspoon soy sauce
1 cup peeled, chopped tomatoes
hot cooked rice or noodles

In large skillet, brown lamb well on all sides in oil. Add water and salt; simmer, covered, for 30 minutes. Add apple juice, vinegar, sugar, mustard, chili powder, ginger, and garlic; cook, covered, on low heat for 45 minutes. Add onion, green pepper, and celery; simmer 15 minutes on low heat. Combine cornstarch, water, and soy sauce; slowly add to meat mixture. Cook slowly, stirring until thickened. Add tomatoes; heat through. Serve immediately over hot rice or noodles.

251

SAUSAGE RICE CASSEROLE

Preparation: 30 minutes

Baking: 1 hour
Servings: 4-6

1 pound bulk sausage, hot
or mild
2 Tablespoons butter
1 small onion, chopped
¼ green bell pepper,
chopped
¼ cup celery, chopped
¾ cup sliced fresh
mushrooms
1 cup uncooked long-grain
rice

1 (10½-ounce) can
condensed beef broth or
consommé
10½ ounces water
½ scant teaspoon dried
whole thyme
1 teaspoon dried parsley
½ teaspoon salt
¼ teaspoon pepper
⅓ cup blanched almonds

Brown sausage in skillet. Remove from pan; drain and set aside. Melt butter; sauté onion, green pepper, and celery. Add mushrooms, cover, and cook 2-3 minutes. Mix rice, sautéed vegetables, broth, and water in casserole dish; add seasonings. Bake, covered, at 350 degrees for 40 minutes. Add sausage and almonds; bake 15-20 minutes longer.

SHRIMP WITH ARTICHOKES

Preparation: 45 minutes

Baking: 20 minutes
Servings: 6

1 (14-ounce) can artichoke
hearts
¾-1 pound cooked shrimp,
peeled and deveined
8-10 fresh mushrooms,
sliced
4 Tablespoons butter
4 Tablespoons chopped
onion
4 Tablespoons all-purpose
flour

1¼ cups half and half
1 Tablespoon
Worcestershire sauce
⅛ teaspoon salt
⅛ teaspoon pepper
3 Tablespoons dry sherry
¼ cup grated Parmesan
cheese
paprika for garnish

Drain artichokes; slice in half and arrange in buttered 13x9x2 casserole dish. Spread shrimp over artichokes. Sauté mushrooms in butter until soft; layer on top of shrimp and artichokes. Cook onion in same butter until transparent; stir in flour. Add half and half; stir until thickened. Add Worcestershire sauce, salt, pepper, and sherry; pour over casserole. Sprinkle with Parmesan cheese and paprika. Bake at 375 degrees for 20 minutes.

BLEND OF THE BAYOU SEAFOOD CASSEROLE

Can serve as a dip with crackers as well as a main dish

Preparation: 45 minutes   Baking: 30 minutes
Planning: Can prepare ahead   Servings: 8

- 1 (8-ounce) package cream cheese
- 10 Tablespoons butter, divided
- 1 pound shrimp, peeled and deveined
- 1 large onion, chopped
- 1 green bell pepper, chopped
- 2 stalks celery, chopped
- 1 (10¾-ounce) can cream of mushroom soup, undiluted
- 1 (4-ounce) can sliced mushrooms, drained
- 1 Tablespoon garlic salt
- ½ teaspoon cayenne pepper
- 1 teaspoon Tabasco sauce
- 1 pint crabmeat
- ¾ cup cooked rice
- 1 cup grated sharp Cheddar cheese

In double boiler, melt cream cheese and 8 Tablespoons butter. In skillet, sauté shrimp, onion, green bell pepper, and celery in 2 Tablespoons butter. Add to cream cheese mixture. Add soup, mushrooms, seasonings, crabmeat, and rice; mix well. Place in greased 2-quart casserole dish; top with cheese. Bake at 350 degrees for 20-30 minutes, until bubbly. This casserole freezes well.

COMPANY SEAFOOD DINNER

Preparation: 45 minutes

Baking: 45 minutes
Servings: 4

**12 Tablespoons butter,
 divided**
⅓ cup chopped green onion
1 clove garlic, minced
**½ green bell pepper,
 chopped**
**2 tomatoes, peeled and
 chopped**
10 sliced mushrooms
**1 (5-ounce) can ripe olives,
 sliced, drained**

⅛ teaspoon cayenne pepper
½ cup all-purpose flour
½ cup half and half
1 cup sour cream
½ cup white wine
**2 pounds cooked shrimp,
 peeled and deveined**
hot cooked rice

Melt 4 Tablespoons butter in large saucepan; sauté onion, garlic, green pepper, tomatoes, mushrooms, and olives. Add cayenne pepper; set aside. In small saucepan, melt 8 Tablespoons butter; add flour. Gradually add half and half and sour cream, stirring constantly. Add wine. Place shrimp in bottom of large casserole dish. Top with sauce and sautéed vegetables. Bake, covered, at 350 degrees for 45 minutes. Serve casserole over hot rice.

 ## DO-AHEAD SEAFOOD BAKE

Preparation: 15 minutes
Planning: Must partially prepare ahead
Chilling: 8 hours

Baking: 1 hour
Servings: 6-8

**1 (7-ounce) package frozen
 crabmeat or shrimp,
 thawed**
**1 cup macaroni shells,
 uncooked**
**1 cup grated Cheddar
 cheese**
**2 cups chopped
 hard-cooked eggs**

**1 (10¾-ounce) can cream of
 mushroom soup,
 undiluted**
1 cup milk
**1 Tablespoon chopped
 chives**

Combine crabmeat, macaroni, cheese, eggs, soup, milk, and chives; mix thoroughly. Place in casserole dish. Refrigerate 8 hours or overnight. Bake at 350 degrees for 1 hour.

SEAFOOD CASSEROLE

Preparation: 30 minutes

Baking: 45 minutes
Servings: 8

1 green bell pepper, diced
½ cup diced onion
1 cup diced celery
2 Tablespoons butter
1½ teaspoons pepper
1 teaspoon seasoned salt
1 (7-ounce) can crabmeat, drained
2 (6-ounce) cans shrimp, drained and rinsed
1 cup mayonnaise

3 cups cooked rice
1 (10¾-ounce) can cream of mushroom soup, undiluted
1 cup milk
1 (4-ounce) can mushrooms, stems and pieces, drained
1 Tablespoon lemon juice
⅓ cup fine bread crumbs or saltine cracker crumbs

Sauté green pepper, onion, and celery in butter with pepper and seasoned salt. Mix vegetables with crabmeat, shrimp, mayonnaise, rice, soup, milk, mushrooms, and lemon juice. Place in casserole dish. Top with bread crumbs. Bake at 350 degrees for 45 minutes.

Note: This recipe can be doubled for a crowd.

SHRIMP AND CRAB RICE CASSEROLE

Preparation: 45 minutes
Planning: Can partially prepare ahead

Baking: 45 minutes
Servings: 8

1 (6¼-ounce) package
  long-grain and wild rice
1 cup diced green bell
  pepper
1 cup diced onion
1 cup sliced celery
2 Tablespoons butter
1½ pounds cooked shrimp,
  peeled and deveined
1 teaspoon curry powder
1 teaspoon Worcestershire
  sauce

¾ cup mayonnaise
salt and pepper, to taste
½ cup white wine
1 (8-ounce) can sliced water
  chestnuts, drained
1 pound crabmeat
1 medium pimiento,
  chopped, optional
minced fresh parsley for
  garnish

Preheat oven to 350 degrees. Cook rice according to package directions; set aside. Sauté green pepper, onions, and celery in butter until tender; combine with rice. Add remaining ingredients, except parsley. Pour into greased 13x9 casserole dish. At this point casserole can be refrigerated and baked later. Bake, covered, for 45 minutes until thoroughly heated. Sprinkle with minced parsley before serving.

 # TUNA AND ARTICHOKES

Preparation: 15-20 minutes

Baking: 20 minutes
Servings: 6

5 Tablespoons butter,
  divided
2 Tablespoons chopped
  onion
1 Tablespoon all-purpose
  flour
½ teaspoon salt
⅛ teaspoon pepper

1¼ cups milk
2 (6½-ounce) cans tuna,
  drained
1 (10-ounce) package frozen
  artichoke hearts, thawed
¼ cup soft bread crumbs
1 cup grated Parmesan
  cheese

Melt 3 Tablespoons butter in skillet over medium heat. Sauté onion until tender; stir in flour, salt, and pepper. Gradually add milk; stir until thickened. Add tuna and artichoke hearts. Place in 1-quart casserole dish. Melt remaining 2 Tablespoons butter; combine with bread crumbs and Parmesan cheese. Sprinkle mixture over casserole. Bake at 350 degrees for 20 minutes.

VEAL STROGANOFF CASSEROLE
A company favorite

Preparation: 40 minutes
Planning: Can prepare ahead

Cooking: 1 hour
Baking: 15 minutes
Servings: 6

½ cup butter, divided
1½ cups sliced fresh mushrooms
1 (2-pound) veal shoulder, cut into 1-inch cubes
1 medium onion, finely chopped
1 small clove garlic, crushed
¼ cup all-purpose flour
2 cups water
½ cup dry sherry or chicken stock

1 teaspoon Worcestershire sauce
½ teaspoon paprika
1 teaspoon salt
¼ teaspoon pepper
12 ounces wide noodles, cooked
1 cup sour cream, warmed
½ cup grated Parmesan cheese

Melt ¼ cup butter in large skillet; add mushrooms. Cook slowly for 3 minutes; set aside. Melt remaining butter; brown meat with onion and garlic. Sprinkle in flour; blend well. Remove from heat; stir in water and sherry. Return to medium heat; bring to a boil, stirring constantly. Add Worcestershire sauce, paprika, salt, and pepper. Simmer, covered, for 1 hour. Remove from heat. Mix cooked noodles, mushrooms, and sour cream with meat mixture. Spoon into greased 2½-quart casserole dish. Sprinkle with Parmesan cheese. Bake at 400 degrees for 15 minutes.

SAUTÉ DE VEAU MARENGO
A brown veal stew with tomatoes and mushrooms

Preparation: 1 hour

Baking: 2½ hours
Servings: 6

3 pounds veal stew meat, cut into 2-inch pieces
2-3 Tablespoons olive oil
1 cup minced yellow onions
1 teaspoon salt
¼ teaspoon pepper
2 Tablespoons all-purpose flour
2 cups dry white wine or white vermouth
1 pound ripe tomatoes, peeled, seeded, juiced, and coarsely chopped
½ teaspoon dried whole basil or tarragon

½ teaspoon dried whole thyme
3x½-inch strip orange peel or ½ teaspoon bottled orange peel
2 cloves garlic, mashed
½ pound fresh mushrooms, quartered
½ Tablespoon cornstarch mixed with 1 Tablespoon water, optional
hot cooked rice

Preheat oven to 325 degrees. Dry veal on paper towels. Heat oil until almost smoking; brown veal. Arrange in casserole dish that can be used on stove surface unit. Drain all but 1 Tablespoon oil from skillet; brown onions 5-6 minutes over medium heat. While onions are browning, toss veal with salt, pepper, and flour in casserole dish. Stir over medium heat for 3-4 minutes to brown flour. Remove from heat. Add wine to onion; boil for 1 minute. Pour wine mixture into casserole and bring to simmer, stirring to mix liquid and flour. Stir in tomatoes. Add basil, thyme, orange peel, and garlic. Bring to simmer and correct seasonings. Bake, covered, at 350 degrees for 1½ to 2 hours, or until meat is tender. Add mushrooms to casserole. Bring to simmer on top of stove. Cover, return to oven for 15 minutes. Blend cornstarch in casserole if needed to thicken. Serve stew over rice.

 ## ASPARAGUS CASSEROLE

Preparation: 15 minutes

Baking: 30 minutes
Servings: 4-6

1 pound cooked fresh
  asparagus or 1 (15-ounce)
  can asparagus, drained
1 teaspoon white pepper
2 (2-ounce) jars pimientos,
  drained
2 eggs, beaten
1 cup butter-flavored
  cracker crumbs

1 cup milk
1 cup grated Cheddar
  cheese
¼ cup butter, melted
asparagus spears and
  pimientos for garnish

Combine all ingredients; spoon into 8-inch baking dish. Bake, uncovered, at 400 degrees for 30 minutes. Garnish with additional asparagus spears tied with a pimiento bow.

 ## HOT BEAN DISH

Preparation: 20 minutes

Baking: 1½ hours
Servings: 15-20

1 cup canned green beans
1 cup canned kidney beans
1 cup canned white or navy
  beans
1 cup canned pork and
  beans
2 Tablespoons barbeque
  sauce
1 onion, chopped

1 pound ground beef,
  browned and drained
½ pound bacon, cut into
  fourths, cooked
1 cup ketchup
1 teaspoon salt
¾ cup light brown sugar
1 teaspoon prepared
  mustard

Combine all ingredients; mix well. Spoon into casserole dish. Bake at 350 degrees for 1½ hours.

259

CAJUN MAQUE CHOUX

Preparation: 15 minutes
Planning: Can prepare ahead

Cooking: 45 minutes
Servings: 6

8 ears fresh white or yellow corn
3 Tablespoons vegetable oil
1 (14½-ounce) can whole tomatoes, undrained and chopped

¼ cup chopped green bell pepper
1 medium onion, chopped
salt and pepper, to taste

Into large bowl, cut corn from cob using sharp knife; scrape milk from cob into bowl. Heat oil in heavy saucepan. Add tomatoes; cook 5-10 minutes over medium heat. Add corn, green pepper, and onion. Cook, covered, on medium-high heat for 5 minutes. Lower heat. Cook 30-35 minutes on low heat.

 # GOLDEN EGGPLANT CASSEROLE

Preparation: 30 minutes

Baking: 45 minutes
Servings: 6

2½ cups peeled, cubed eggplant
18 saltine crackers, crumbled
½ cup grated sharp Cheddar cheese
¼ cup chopped celery

2 Tablespoons chopped pimientos
1 Tablespoon melted butter
½ teaspoon salt
⅛ teaspoon pepper
1 cup half and half or evaporated milk

Cook eggplant in boiling, salted water for 10 minutes; drain. Combine with remaining ingredients. Pour into 1-quart buttered casserole dish. Bake at 350 degrees for 45 minutes.

GREEN BEAN CASSEROLE

Embarassingly easy, yet guests never fail to request the recipe!

Preparation: 20 minutes

Baking: 30 minutes
Servings: 12

1 large onion, chopped
½ cup butter
¼ cup all-purpose flour
1½ cups milk
3 cups grated Cheddar
cheese
⅛ teaspoon Tabasco sauce
2 teaspoons soy sauce
½ teaspoon pepper

1 teaspoon salt
3 (10-ounce) packages
frozen french-style green
beans, cooked and drained
1 (4¼-ounce) can
mushrooms, drained
1 (8-ounce) can sliced water
chestnuts, drained
½ cup chopped almonds

Sauté onion in butter; add flour and milk. Stir in cheese, Tabasco, soy
sauce, pepper, and salt. Add beans, mushrooms, and water chesnuts.
Pour into casserole dish; sprinkle with chopped almonds. Bake at 350
degrees for 25-30 minutes, or until thoroughly heated.

ONION CASSEROLE

Preparation: 10-15 minutes
Planning: Can partially prepare ahead

Baking: 30 minutes
Servings: 8

5 jumbo sweet onions,
preferably Vidalia, thinly
sliced
½ cup butter

1 cup Parmesan cheese,
grated
20 saltine crackers, crushed

Sauté onion in butter until soft. In 2-quart casserole dish, layer half the
onion, half the cheese, and half the crackers. Repeat layers. Casserole
can be refrigerated at this point and baked later. Bake at 325 degrees
for 30 minutes. This dish is delicious with roast beef.

SCALLOPED POTATOES AU GRATIN

Preparation: 20 minutes   Baking: 1 hour
Planning: Can partially prepare ahead   Servings: 2

2 medium potatoes, peeled and thinly sliced	**1 clove garlic, crushed**
1 medium onion, thinly sliced	**½ teaspoon dry mustard**
	½ teaspoon salt
	¼ teaspoon pepper
2 Tablespoons butter	**1 cup milk**
2 Tablespoons all-purpose flour	**2-3 Tablespoons grated Parmesan cheese**

Layer potatoes and onion in baking dish. Melt butter in saucepan; add flour, garlic, mustard, salt, and pepper. Add milk gradually; cook until thickened. Pour over potatoes; sprinkle with cheese. Potatoes can be refrigerated at this point and baked later. Bake at 350 degrees for 45 minutes to 1 hour.

BAKED RICE

Preparation: 30 minutes   Baking: 30 minutes
                                                        Servings: 6

1 cup mixture of wild rice and brown rice	**½ pound fresh mushrooms, sliced**
2 cups water	**⅓ cup blanched sliced almonds**
8 slices bacon	
3 stalks celery, finely chopped	**1 teaspoon dried whole oregano**
1 large onion, finely chopped	**⅛ teaspoon salt**
	⅛ teaspoon pepper
2 Tablespoons chopped green bell pepper	**⅓ cup beef consommé**

Cook rice in water according to package directions. Cook bacon; crumble and set aside. Sauté celery, onion, green pepper, and mushrooms in bacon drippings; mix with rice. Add almonds, oregano, salt, pepper, bacon, and consommé. Bake at 325 degrees for 30 minutes.

SQUASH CASSEROLE

Preparation: 20 minutes   Baking: 45 minutes
Planning: Can partially prepare ahead   Servings: 6

1½-2 pounds fresh, small, yellow squash
1 (10¾-ounce) can cream of chicken soup, undiluted
1 medium carrot, grated
1 small onion, grated

1 (8-ounce) carton sour cream
1½ cups herb-seasoned stuffing
⅓ cup butter, melted

Wash and slice squash. Cover squash with water and cook 3-5 minutes; drain. Mix squash, soup, carrots, onion, and sour cream. Place in casserole dish. Combine stuffing and butter; sprinkle on casserole. At this point casserole can be refrigerated and baked later. Bake at 350 degrees for 45 minutes.

TOMATO CHEESE CASSEROLE
This recipe comes from Skip Caray, voice of the Atlanta Braves

Preparation: 20 minutes   Baking: 40 minutes
           Servings: 6-8

¼ cup butter
2 large onions, sliced
1 (6-ounce) package plain croutons
6 large tomatoes, sliced

½ teaspoon crumbled fresh or dried whole basil
½ teaspoon salt
3 cups grated Danish havarti cheese

In skillet, heat butter; sauté onion for 5 minutes. Add croutons; sauté 3 minutes. In greased 3-quart casserole dish, layer half of crouton-onion mixture and half of tomato slices; sprinkle with ¼ teaspoon basil, ¼ teaspoon salt, and half of cheese. Repeat layers, ending with cheese. Bake at 350 degrees for 40 minutes.

VEGETABLE RATATOUILLE
The perfect stretch dish when expecting an unknown number of guests

Preparation: 30 minutes

Baking: 20 minutes
Servings: 8

½ cup olive oil
4 cups cubed, peeled
 eggplant
4 cups cubed zucchini
½ cup green bell pepper, cut
 into squares
¼ cup red bell pepper, cut
 into squares
½ cup chopped onion
2 Tablespoons minced garlic
½ cup dry white wine
4 medium tomatoes, peeled
 and quartered

⅛ teaspoon ground thyme
1 bay leaf
1 teaspoon dried whole basil
⅛ teaspoon dried whole
 rosemary
1 Tablespoon salt
1 teaspoon pepper
¼ teaspoon cayenne pepper
½ cup pitted small ripe
 olives
2 Tablespoons dried parsley
¼ cup grated Parmesan
 cheese

In large skillet, heat oil; sauté eggplant and zucchini for 8 minutes. Add peppers and onion; simmer, uncovered, for 6 minutes. Add garlic; simmer 2 minutes. Add wine, tomatoes, herbs, salt, pepper, and olives. Pour into casserole dish and bake, uncovered, at 350 degrees for 20 minutes, or until eggplant is tender. Sprinkle with parsley and Parmesan cheese before serving.

 # CRANBERRY CONSERVE
A tangy treat!

Preparation: 5 minutes
Planning: Must prepare ahead

Cooking: 15 minutes
Yield: 5 cups

2 (16-ounce) cans whole
 cranberry sauce
1 cup sugar
½ cup vinegar
2 teaspoons salt
1 Tablespoon curry powder

1 Tablespoon
 Worcestershire sauce
2 Tablespoons molasses
1 teaspoon Tabasco sauce
½ teaspoon ground ginger

Combine all ingredients and boil 15 minutes. Pour into sterilized jars and seal.

Vegetables
and Side Dishes

Rose

VEGETABLES AND SIDE DISHES

SIDE DISHES
Almond Curried Fruit 290
Baked Stuffed Pumpkin 291
Hot Apricot Casserole 290
My Mother's Apples and Cornflakes 289
Party Pineapple Casserole 291
Plum Chutney 268
VEGETABLES
ARTICHOKES
Scalloped Artichokes. 267
ASPARAGUS
Asparagus Mornay 268
Marinated Asparagus 267
BROCCOLI
Broccoli Puff 271
Broccoli-Stuffed Tomatoes 269
Broccoli-Stuffed Vidalia Onions 270
Special Broccoli 271
BRUSSELS SPROUTS
Deviled Brussels Sprouts 269
CARROTS
Carrot Mold 273
Carrots Lyonnaise 272
Scalloped Carrots 273
CAULIFLOWER
Curried Baked Cauliflower 272
CHILES
Baked Green Chiles 274
CORN
Corn and Zucchini 275
Grandma's Corn Pudding 275
Savory Baked Corn Pie 274
EGGPLANT
Eggplant-Tomato Bake 278
GREEN BEANS
Green Beans-Open Sesame 276
Herbed Green Beans 277
Hot Marinated Green Beans 277

LIMA BEANS
Barbecued Lima Beans 278
MUSHROOMS
Mushrooms in Mustard Cream 279
OKRA
Okra Pilaf 281
Okra Tomato Bake 280
PEAS
Cremed Onions and Peas 281
Green Pea Medley 287
Peas Scoville 283
POTATOES
Cheesy Potato Casserole 283
Garlic Roasted Potatoes 284
Overnight Potatoes 284
Peachtree Potato Balls 282
Potatoes Parisienne 282
SPINACH
Cheesy Spinach Casserole 285
Sautéed Spinach 286
Spinach Squares 285
SQUASH
Cheesy Squash Dressing 286
SWEET POTATOES
Sherried Sweet Potatoes 288
Sweet Potato Soufflé 288
TOMATOES
Mimi's Tomato Relish 280
TURNIP GREENS
Grandma's Turnip Greens 289
VEGETABLE COMBINATIONS
Chiffy Chaffy 287
Sautéed Fresh Vegetables 270
Spring Vegetable Sauté 276
VEGETABLE SAUCES
"Hunker Down" Foolproof
Hollandaise Sauce 292
Neta's Chive Sauce 292

 ## *SCALLOPED ARTICHOKES*

Preparation: 15 minutes
Planning: Can partially prepare ahead

Cooking: 20 minutes
Servings: 6

1 small onion, finely chopped
¾ green bell pepper, finely chopped
5 Tablespoons vegetable oil
2 (14-ounce) cans quartered artichoke hearts, drained
1 egg, slightly beaten
¾ cup sour cream

⅛ teaspoon ground thyme
⅛ teaspoon dried whole basil
⅛ teaspoon Tabasco sauce
10 round buttery crackers, crushed
¼ cup grated Parmesan cheese

Cook onion and green pepper in oil until soft; turn into greased 2-quart casserole dish. Add artichoke hearts to dish. Combine egg, sour cream, thyme, basil, and Tabasco in bowl. Pour over ingredients in casserole. At this point, artichokes can be refrigerated and baked later. Sprinkle with cracker crumbs and Parmesan cheese. Bake at 375 degrees for 20 minutes.

MARINATED ASPARAGUS

Preparation: 10 minutes
Planning: Must prepare ahead
Marinating: 12 hours

Cooking: 5 minutes
Servings: 4

1 (15-ounce) can asparagus, drained
¼ cup white vinegar
½ cup sugar
¼ cup water

3 whole cloves
1 stick cinnamon
½ teaspoon celery seed
½ teaspoon salt

Place asparagus in serving dish. Combine remaining ingredients in saucepan; bring to a boil. Cool; pour over asparagus. Refrigerate, covered, at least 12 hours before serving.

267

ASPARAGUS MORNAY

Preparation: 10 minutes

Cooking: 10-15 minutes

Servings: 6

2 pounds fresh asparagus spears, rinsed and ends cut off
2 Tablespoons butter
1 Tablespoon all-purpose flour
⅛ teaspoon salt

⅛ teaspoon pepper
1 cup milk
½ cup grated sharp Cheddar cheese
¼ cup slivered almonds, toasted

Cover asparagus spears with small amount of boiling, salted water; cook 10-15 minutes; drain. Place in warm serving dish; keep warm. Meanwhile melt butter in small saucepan over low heat. Combine flour, salt, and pepper; blend into melted butter. Add milk, stirring constantly until mixture thickens and boils. Reduce heat, cook and stir 2 minutes. Add cheese; stir until melted. Pour cheese sauce over hot asparagus. Top with toasted almonds. Serve immediately.

 ## PLUM CHUTNEY

Preparation: 1 hour
Planning: Must prepare ahead

Cooking: 1½ hours
Yield: 6 ½-pint jars

3 pounds Italian plums
1 teaspoon salt
1½ pounds tart apples
1 teaspoon whole cloves
1 pound onions
3 chili peppers
1½ cups raisins

2 cups cider vinegar
2 cups light brown sugar
1 Tablespoon ground ginger
1 Tablespoon dried whole allspice
1 Tablespoon dry mustard

Pit and coarsely chop plums. Peel, core, and coarsely chop apples. Peel and chop onions. Place plums, apples, onion, and raisins in very large enameled pan. Add vinegar and brown sugar. Tie ginger, allspice, mustard, salt, cloves, and peppers in a cheesecloth bag; add to pan. Simmer gently, stirring occasionally, for 1½ hours. Ladle into sterilized jars and seal.

 ## *DEVILED BRUSSELS SPROUTS*

Preparation: 10 minutes

Cooking: 10 minutes
Servings: 5-6

**2 cups fresh or frozen
brussels sprouts**
½ cup butter
**2 Tablespoons minced
onion**
**1 Tablespoon prepared
mustard**

½ teaspoon salt
**1 teaspoon Worcestershire
sauce**
⅛ teaspoon cayenne pepper

Cook brussels sprouts until just tender crisp in boiling, salted water; set aside. In skillet, melt butter; cook onion until soft but not browned. Blend in mustard, salt, Worcestershire sauce, and cayenne pepper. Drain sprouts; turn into hot vegetable dish. Pour sauce over sprouts and serve at once. If not served immediately, sauce will separate.

BROCCOLI-STUFFED TOMATOES

Preparation: 40 minutes

Baking: 30 minutes
Servings: 6

6 medium tomatoes
½ teaspoon salt
½ teaspoon pepper
**1 (10-ounce) package frozen
chopped broccoli**
**1 cup shredded Swiss
cheese**

1 cup soft bread crumbs
½ cup mayonnaise
**2 Tablespoons chopped
onion**
**2 Tablespoons grated
Parmesan cheese**

Wash tomatoes thoroughly. Cut tops off tomatoes; remove pulp leaving shells intact. Mix salt with pepper; sprinkle insides of tomato shells with mixture, invert on wire rack and drain for 30 minutes. Cook broccoli according to package directions; drain well. Combine broccoli, Swiss cheese, bread crumbs, mayonnaise, and onion. Arrange tomato shells in shallow baking dish. Stuff with broccoli mixture. At this point, tomatoes can be refrigerated and baked later. Sprinkle tops with Parmesan cheese. Bake at 350 degrees for 30 minutes.

BROCCOLI-STUFFED VIDALIA ONIONS

Preparation: 30 minutes   Baking: 20 minutes
Planning: Can partially prepare ahead   Servings: 6

3 medium Vidalia onions or other sweet onions
1 (10-ounce) package frozen chopped broccoli
⅓ cup Parmesan cheese
¼ cup mayonnaise
2 teaspoons lemon juice

2 Tablespoons butter
2 Tablespoons all-purpose flour
¼ teaspoon salt
⅔ cup milk
1 (3-ounce) package cream cheese, softened

Peel and halve onions. Parboil in salted water for 12 minutes. Remove centers, leaving ¾-inch edges. Place onion cups in 13x9x2 pan. Chop center portions to equal 1 cup. Cook broccoli according to package directions; drain. Combine chopped onion, broccoli, Parmesan cheese, mayonnaise, and lemon juice. Spoon into onion cups. At this point, onions can be refrigerated until ready to bake. Melt butter; blend in flour and salt. Add milk; cook until thick, stirring constantly. Remove from heat; blend in cream cheese. Spoon sauce over onions; bake, uncovered, at 375 degrees for 20 minutes.

 ## SAUTÉED FRESH VEGETABLES

Preparation: 10 minutes   Cooking: 10-15 minutes
         Servings: 6

6 new potatoes
2-3 medium carrots
2 medium zucchini, yellow squash, or other seasonal vegetable

¼ cup butter
¼ teaspoon Italian seasoning

Wash vegetables; thinly slice. Potato skins may be left on, if potatoes are thoroughly scrubbed. Melt butter in large skillet. Add sliced vegetables and sprinkle with Italian seasoning. Sauté for 5 minutes, turning occasionally. Cook vegetables, covered, over low heat for an additional 5-10 minutes, or until vegetables are tender.

SPECIAL BROCCOLI
Quick, easy, and delicious!

Preparation: 30 minutes
Planning: Can partially prepare ahead

Baking: 35-40 minutes
Servings: 8

1 cup mayonnaise
1 cup sour cream
½ cup finely chopped onion
½ cup finely chopped green bell pepper
4 cups fresh broccoli or 2 (10-ounce) packages frozen broccoli, cooked and drained

1 cup sliced water chestnuts, drained
2 cups grated sharp Cheddar cheese
¾ cup crushed round buttery crackers

Preheat oven to 350 degrees. Blend mayonnaise with sour cream, onion, and green pepper in bowl. In greased 2-quart casserole dish, layer broccoli, water chestnuts, and sour cream mixture. Cover with grated cheese; top with cracker crumbs. At this point, broccoli can be refrigerated and baked later. Bake 35-40 minutes.

BROCCOLI PUFF
Rises like a soufflé

Preparation: 30 minutes

Baking: 30 minutes
Servings: 8

2 (10-ounce) packages frozen chopped broccoli
3 eggs, separated
1 Tablespoon all-purpose flour
⅛ teaspoon ground nutmeg
1 cup mayonnaise

1 Tablespoon butter, softened
¼ teaspoon salt
¼ teaspoon pepper
¼ cup plus 1 Tablespoon grated Parmesan cheese

Cook broccoli according to package directions; drain well. Beat egg yolks; add flour, mixing well. Stir in nutmeg, mayonnaise, butter, salt, pepper, and Parmesan cheese. Add broccoli, mixing lightly. Beat room temperature egg whites until stiff but not dry; gently fold into broccoli mixture. Pour into lightly buttered 9-inch square dish. Bake at 350 degrees for 30 minutes. Cut into squares to serve. Serve immediately.

CURRIED BAKED CAULIFLOWER

Preparation: 20 minutes
Planning: Can partially prepare ahead

Baking: 30 minutes
Servings: 8-10

1 large head cauliflower
½ teaspoon salt
1 (10½-ounce) can cream of
  chicken soup, undiluted
1 cup shredded sharp
  Cheddar cheese

⅓ cup mayonnaise
1 teaspoon curry powder
¼ cup dried bread crumbs
2 Tablespoons butter,
  melted

Preheat oven to 350 degrees. Break cauliflower into flowerets. Cook cauliflower, covered, in 1 inch boiling, salted water in large saucepan for 10 minutes; drain well; set aside. In 2-quart casserole dish, stir together cream of chicken soup, cheese, mayonnaise, and curry powder. Add cauliflower; mix well. Toss bread crumbs with melted butter; sprinkle on top of cauliflower. Bake 30 minutes, or until hot and bubbly.

Note: To freeze and serve up to one month later, prepare dish, but do not bake. To serve, thaw overnight in refrigerator. Preheat oven to 350 degrees. Bake, uncovered, for 40 minutes, or until hot and bubbly.

CARROTS LYONNAISE

Preparation: 20 minutes

Cooking: 10 minutes
Servings: 6

1 chicken bouillon cube
½ cup boiling water
1 pound carrots
¼ cup butter
3 medium onions, sliced
1 Tablespoon all-purpose
  flour

¼ teaspoon salt
⅛ teaspoon pepper
¾ cup water
⅛ teaspoon sugar

Dissolve bouillon cube in boiling water. Pare carrots; cut in julienne strips. Cook carrots, covered, in bouillon, for 10 minutes. Melt butter in large saucepan. Add onion; cook, covered, 15 minutes, stirring occasionally. Stir in flour, salt, pepper, and ¾ cup water. Bring to a boil. Add carrots and stock. Simmer, uncovered, for 10 minutes. Stir in sugar and serve.

SCALLOPED CARROTS
A practical all-purpose vegetable dish

Preparation: 20 minutes

Baking: 30 minutes
Servings: 10-12

**6 cups carrots (about 12-14)
cut into ½-inch slices
1 small onion, finely
chopped
¼ cup butter
¼ cup all-purpose flour
1 teaspoon salt
¼ teaspoon dry mustard**

**2 cups milk
¼ teaspoon pepper
¼ teaspoon celery salt
2 cups buttered bread cubes
½ pound grated sharp
Cheddar cheese
1 cup bread crumbs**

Cook carrots until tender; drain and set aside. Cook onion in butter for 2-3 minutes. Stir in flour, salt, dry mustard, and milk. Cook over medium heat, stirring until smooth and thick. Stir in pepper and celery salt; remove from heat. In 3-quart casserole, layer half the carrots, bread cubes, and cheese; layer remaining carrots. Pour sauce over carrots; top with bread crumbs. Bake at 325 degrees for 30 minutes, or until bread crumbs are browned. A 13x9x2 glass dish can be used by placing all the carrots on the bottom layer.

CARROT MOLD

Preparation: 10 minutes

Baking: 45-50 minutes
Servings: 4-6

**2 cups grated raw carrots
½ cup plain bread crumbs
2 eggs
1 teaspoon salt**

**2 Tablespoons corn oil
½ cup milk
2 Tablespoons grated onion,
optional**

Combine carrots and bread crumbs. Beat eggs in bowl; add salt, corn oil, milk, and onion. Add to carrot mixture. Pour into well-greased ring mold. Set in pan of hot water and cover mold with aluminum pie tin. Bake at 350 degrees for 45-50 minutes. Remove pie tin during final 10 minutes of baking time to allow carrot mold to crisp. Unmold on serving platter. For a colorful dish, this can be served with English peas in the center of the mold.

273

BAKED GREEN CHILES
An excellent side dish with Mexican food

Preparation: 15 minutes

Baking: 30-45 minutes
Servings: 6

1 cup cottage cheese
1 cup sour cream
1 (8-ounce) can tomato
  sauce
2 (4-ounce) cans chopped
  green chiles, drained

6 corn tortillas
8 ounces sharp Cheddar
  cheese, grated
8 ounces Monterey Jack
  cheese, grated

Blend cottage cheese, sour cream, tomato sauce, and green chiles in bowl. Bake tortillas at 500 degrees for 3-5 minutes, or until tortillas are pliable. Working quickly, dip tortillas into mixture, folding them into rolls. Place into greased baking dish. Alternate layers of Cheddar cheese, Monterey Jack cheese, and sauce mixture over rolled tortillas. Bake at 350 degrees for 30-45 minutes.

 ## SAVORY BAKED CORN PIE

Preparation: 20 minutes

Baking: 45 minutes
Servings: 6

1 small onion, minced
2 Tablespoons butter
2 Tablespoons all-purpose
  flour
2 Tablespoons light brown
  sugar
1 teaspoon salt

¼ teaspoon pepper
¼ teaspoon ground nutmeg
1 cup milk
2 eggs, beaten
1 (15-17-ounce) can whole
  kernel sweet corn, drained

Cook onion in butter until soft; blend in flour, brown sugar, salt, pepper, and nutmeg. Add milk; cook until thickened, stirring constantly. In bowl, beat eggs slightly. Add small amount of hot milk mixture to eggs, stirring constantly to prevent eggs from cooking. Gradually add remaining hot milk mixture, stirring constantly. Stir in corn. Pour into 9-inch pie pan; bake at 325 degrees for 45 minutes.

CORN AND ZUCCHINI
A marvelous dish!

Preparation: 20 minutes

Baking: 1 hour
Servings: 6

6 zucchini, thinly sliced
1 cup water
½ teaspoon salt
½ cup butter, divided
1½ cups finely chopped onion
1 clove garlic, minced

1 green bell pepper, finely chopped
1 cup grated sharp Cheddar cheese
3 eggs, slightly beaten
1 (12-ounce) can white corn, drained

Place zucchini in pan with water and salt; cover. Boil 10 minutes, or until tender; drain. Chop zucchini when cool enough to handle. Melt 3 Tablespoons butter in skillet. Add onion, garlic, and green pepper; sauté until soft. Stir in zucchini, remaining 5 Tablespoons butter, cheese, eggs, and corn; mix well. Pour into greased casserole dish and bake at 350 degrees for 1 hour.

 ## GRANDMA'S CORN PUDDING

Preparation: 5 minutes

Baking: 30 minutes
Servings: 6

1 (15-17-ounce) can whole kernel corn, drained or 2 cups fresh corn, cut from the cob
2 Tablespoons all-purpose flour
1 teaspoon salt

1 Tablespoon sugar, optional
2 eggs
1 cup milk, warm
3 Tablespoons butter, melted

Combine corn, flour, salt, and sugar. Beat together eggs and milk in bowl; add butter. Combine corn mixture and egg mixture. Pour into greased 1½-quart dish; bake at 350 degrees for 30 minutes. Too hot an oven will curdle pudding.

275

SPRING VEGETABLE SAUTÉ

Preparation: 20 minutes

Cooking: 15 minutes
Servings: 6-8

1 pound carrots
1½ to 2 pounds fresh
  asparagus
10 cups water
1 Tablespoon salt
1 teaspoon sugar
6 Tablespoons butter
1 bunch green onions, finely
  chopped

1 clove garlic, minced
⅛ teaspoon salt
⅛ teaspoon pepper or lemon
  pepper seasoning
⅛ teaspoon lemon juice,
  optional

Peel carrots; cut into 2- to 3-inch julienne strips. Wash asparagus; break off woody ends of stems. Cut green part into 1-inch pieces. Set vegetables aside. In large pot bring water to boil. Add salt and sugar. Add carrots to boiling water; boil about 5 minutes, then add asparagus. Boil 3 to 5 minutes, or until tender crisp. Drain vegetables well and rinse with cold water to stop cooking process. In skillet, melt butter. Sauté green onion and garlic until onion is tender. Add cooked vegetables; sauté until heated through. Add salt, pepper, and lemon juice. Serve immediately.

GREEN BEANS - OPEN SESAME

Preparation: 15 minutes

Cooking: 15 minutes
Servings: 6

1 pound fresh green beans,
  julienne cut
2 Tablespoons soy sauce
1 Tablespoon sesame oil

¼ teaspoon ground nutmeg
4 large mushrooms, sliced
½ cup sesame seeds,
  toasted

Steam beans until tender crisp, about 10 minutes; set aside. Combine soy sauce, sesame oil, and nutmeg in large skillet over low to medium heat. Add mushrooms; sauté until just tender. Add beans; toss lightly. Add sesame seeds, toss again. Serve immediately.

HOT MARINATED GREEN BEANS

Preparation: 15 minutes   Baking: 45 minutes
Planning: Must partially prepare ahead   Servings: 6
Marinating: 8 hours

2 (16-ounce) cans   **1 pound bacon, fried,**
  French-style green beans,   **drained, and crumbled**
  drained and rinsed   **½ cup bacon drippings**
2 large onions, sliced and   **½ cup vinegar**
  broken into rings   **½ cup light brown sugar**

In 2-quart casserole dish, layer beans and onions twice. Top with bacon. Combine bacon drippings, vinegar, and brown sugar; pour over beans. Marinate in refrigerator 8 hours or overnight. Bake at 350 degrees for 45 minutes.

·HERBED GREEN BEANS

Preparation: 15 minutes   Cooking: 30 minutes
                                  Servings: 4-6

1 pound fresh green beans   **1 teaspoon dried whole**
4 Tablespoons butter   **rosemary**
½ cup chopped green onion   **¼ teaspoon dried whole**
½ clove garlic, minced   **basil**
¼ cup chopped celery   **¾ teaspoon salt**
½ cup chopped fresh parsley

Wash and trim beans. Cook in 2 inches of boiling water in covered pan for 15-20 minutes; drain and keep warm. Meanwhile, melt butter; sauté onion, garlic, and celery in skillet until soft. Add parsley, rosemary, basil, and salt. Simmer, covered, for 10 minutes. Just before serving, combine beans and herbed butter mixture. Serve hot.

BARBECUED LIMA BEANS
Male guests will love this dish!

Preparation: 1¼ hours
Baking: 20 minutes
Planning: Can partially prepare ahead
Servings: 8

1 pound fresh, shelled lima beans or frozen lima beans
½ pound bacon, cut into ¼-inch pieces
1 medium onion, chopped
1 medium green bell pepper, chopped

1 (15-ounce) can tomato sauce
1 (14½-ounce) can stewed tomatoes
1 teaspoon salt
½ cup grated Monterey Jack cheese

Cover beans with cold water in large saucepan. Bring to a boil, skimming surface. Simmer until tender, 5-6 minutes, adding more water if necessary; drain thoroughly. Grease deep 12-inch casserole. Cook bacon in heavy skillet over medium-low heat until transparent, about 10 minutes. Drain all but 3 Tablespoons of drippings. Add onion and green pepper; cook until tender, stirring frequently, about 10 minutes. Add lima beans; cook until hot, stirring frequently, about 5 minutes. Mix in tomato sauce and stewed tomatoes. Simmer, covered, 15 minutes. Uncover and simmer until most of tomato juice is absorbed, stirring frequently, about 20 minutes. Add salt; pour into casserole dish. At this point, beans can be refrigerated. When ready to bake, bring to room temperature. Sprinkle top with grated cheese; bake at 450 degrees for 20 minutes. Serve immediately.

EGGPLANT-TOMATO BAKE

Preparation: 30 minutes
Baking: 25 minutes
Servings: 6

6 slices bacon
1 green bell pepper, chopped
1 medium onion, chopped
1 large eggplant, peeled and chopped
4 medium tomatoes, peeled and chopped

½ teaspoon salt
¼ teaspoon pepper
½ cup grated medium Cheddar cheese
½ cup bread crumbs or cracker crumbs

Cook bacon in large skillet until crisp; drain and crumble. Sauté green pepper and onion in 2 Tablespoons bacon drippings. Add eggplant and tomatoes; cook 5-7 minutes; add salt and pepper. Place in 2-quart casserole dish and top with bacon. Sprinkle with cheese and bread crumbs. Bake, uncovered, at 350 degrees for 25 minutes.

MUSHROOMS IN MUSTARD CREAM
Excellent cold vegetable for a summer picnic

Preparation: 15 minutes   Servings: 4
Planning: Can partially prepare ahead

**2 Tablespoons tarragon
  vinegar
2 Tablespoons Dijon
  mustard
¼ teaspoon Worcestershire
  sauce
1 teaspoon sugar
½ teaspoon salt
½ teaspoon ground white
  pepper**

**1 egg
½ cup vegetable oil
3 Tablespoons heavy cream
½ pound large mushrooms,
  sliced
chopped fresh parsley for
  garnish**

In small bowl, combine vinegar, mustard, Worcestershire sauce, sugar, salt, and white pepper. In electric blender, blend egg at high speed until light colored. Add oil in a slow, steady stream. Blend in mustard-vinegar mixture. Pour into medium bowl; beat in cream with whisk or electric beater. If not serving immediately, chill. To serve, divide mushroom slices among small, individual plates. Pour sauce over mushrooms and sprinkle with chopped parsley. This is a good accompaniment for grilled steaks.

OKRA TOMATO BAKE

Preparation: 15 minutes
Planning: Can partially prepare ahead

Baking: 30-45 minutes
Servings: 8-10

½ pound bacon
1 medium onion, finely chopped
2 (10-ounce) packages frozen okra or 3-4 cups cut fresh okra
2 Tablespoons uncooked instant rice
1 small green bell pepper, finely chopped

1 (16-ounce) can tomatoes, undrained
1 Tablespoon sugar
¼ teaspoon salt
⅛ teaspoon garlic salt
⅛ teaspoon pepper
1 Tablespoon grated Parmesan cheese
¼ cup dry bread crumbs
1 Tablespoon butter

In large skillet, cook bacon until crisp. Drain on paper towel; crumble; set aside. Cook onion and okra in drippings left in skillet. Drain; place in greased 11x7 casserole dish. Add rice, green pepper, and crumbled bacon; mix well. Blend tomatoes, sugar, salt, garlic salt, and pepper in mixer or food processor on low speed 1 to 2 minutes. Pour mixture over okra. At this point, casserole can be refrigerated and baked later. Top with Parmesan cheese. Combine bread crumbs and butter, mixing well; sprinkle over casserole. Bake at 350 degrees for 30-45 minutes, or until hot and bubbly.

 ## MIMI'S TOMATO RELISH
This is a tasty accompaniment for vegetables and pork!

Preparation: 45 minutes
Planning: Must prepare ahead

Cooking: 2½ hours
Yield: 6 pints

12 large ripe tomatoes, peeled and chopped
2 large onions, chopped into large pieces
2 green bell peppers, chopped into medium pieces

¼ cup finely chopped hot peppers
2 cups apple cider vinegar
2 cups sugar
2 Tablespoons salt

Combine all ingredients in order listed. Cook on low heat for 2 to 2½ hours, stirring occasionally. Pour into sterilized jars and seal.

OKRA PILAF

Preparation: 10 minutes

Cooking: 20 minutes
Servings: 6-8

3 slices bacon, diced
2 cups sliced okra, fresh or
frozen
¼ cup chopped green bell
pepper, optional
1 cup chopped onion

1 cup uncooked long-grain
rice
2 cups chicken broth
1 teaspoon salt
1 (16-ounce) can tomatoes,
drained and chopped

Cook bacon in Dutch oven until limp. Add okra and sauté until bacon is lightly browned. Add pepper and onion; cook until tender. Stir rice, broth, and salt into vegetables. Bring to a boil and stir once. Simmer, covered, 20 minutes or until rice is done. Stir in tomatoes; serve immediately.

CREAMED ONIONS AND PEAS

Preparation: 30 minutes

Baking: 20 minutes
Servings: 8

3 pounds small white
onions or quartered yellow
onions
1 (10-ounce) package frozen
green peas, slightly
thawed
¼ cup butter

¼ cup all-purpose flour
2 cups milk
½ cup chicken broth
1½ teaspoons salt
⅛ teaspoon pepper
½ teaspoon sugar
buttered bread crumbs

Peel onions; cut a small "x" in bottom of each to prevent splitting while cooking. Cook onions in boiling, salted water until almost tender; add peas and continue cooking until onions are just tender and peas are cooked, about 5 minutes; drain well. Meanwhile, prepare cream sauce by melting butter; stir in flour. Add milk and chicken broth. Cook until smooth and thick. Add salt, pepper, and sugar; cook sauce gently, about 10 minutes. Carefully mix in onions and peas. If sauce seems too thick, thin with additional chicken broth. Pour into baking dish. Top with buttered bread crumbs; bake at 325 degrees until hot, about 20 minutes.

PEACHTREE POTATO BALLS
Men love these!

Preparation: 1½ hours   Frying: 10 minutes
Planning: Can partially prepare ahead   Yield: 60 potato balls

2½ pounds baking potatoes, unpeeled, no substitutions
2 Tablespoons butter, softened
2 egg yolks, beaten
1½ teaspoons salt
½ teaspoon freshly ground pepper
⅛ teaspoon ground nutmeg

2 eggs
1 Tablespoon water
1 Tablespoon vegetable oil
½ cup fresh bread crumbs
1 Tablespoon poppy seeds
½ cup all-purpose flour
½ cup coarsely ground almonds
vegetable oil for deep frying

Cook potatoes in boiling water until soft, about 45 minutes. Peel potatoes when cool enough to handle. Force through ricer or sieve into large bowl. Beat in butter, egg yolks, salt, pepper, and nutmeg. Roll into 1-inch balls. Recipe can prepared to this point, covered, and refrigerated; let stand at room temperature for 30 minutes before frying. In large bowl, beat eggs with water and oil. In medium bowl, combine bread crumbs and poppy seeds. Roll balls lightly in flour. Dip in egg mixture. Roll half the balls in bread crumb mixture and the other half in ground almonds. Let stand on waxed paper 10 minutes. Heat oil in deep fryer to 375 degrees. Fry almond coated balls 45 seconds, crumb coated balls 30 seconds; drain on paper towels. Potato balls can be kept warm in a 200 degree oven for up to 30 minutes. This is a different potato dish to serve with a meat entree.

POTATOES PARISIENNE

Preparation: 15 minutes   Baking: 1½ hours
      Servings: 8

6 cups potatoes, unpeeled and sliced
salt and pepper to taste
2 cups heavy cream
2 Tablespoons Dijon mustard

2 cloves garlic, finely chopped
2 Tablespoons butter
½ cup grated Parmesan cheese

Layer potatoes in lightly greased baking dish; season with salt and pepper, to taste. In medium saucepan, combine cream, mustard, garlic, and butter; heat to boiling. Pour over potatoes. Bake, covered, at 350 degrees for 1 hour. Uncover; top with Parmesan cheese. Bake 30 minutes longer, or until potatoes are fork tender.

PEAS SCOVILLE

Preparation: 30 minutes

Cooking: 15 minute
Servings: 6

1 cup small pearl onions or
½ cup chopped shallots
2 (10-ounce) packages
  frozen green peas or 2
  cups shelled green peas
½ pound small white
  mushrooms

lemon juice for washing
  mushrooms
4 Tablespoons olive oil
⅛ teaspoon salt
⅛ teaspoon pepper

Place onions in cold water, bring to a boil; drain. Blanche peas the same way. Wash mushrooms in lemon juice and water. Slice mushrooms; sauté in hot olive oil. Add peas, onions, salt, and pepper. Cook, covered, over low heat for 10-15 minutes, stirring occasionally until peas are soft but not mushy.

CHEESY POTATO CASSEROLE

Preparation: 2 hours
Planning: Must partially prepare ahead

Baking: 45 minutes
Servings: 4

3 large red potatoes
2 Tablespoons butter
1 cup grated sharp Cheddar
  cheese

1 cup sour cream
¼ cup chopped green onion
¼ teaspoon salt
⅛ teaspoon pepper

Boil potatoes; chill; peel and grate into large bowl. In saucepan over low heat, combine butter and cheese; stir until melted. Remove from heat; blend in sour cream and green onion. Add to potatoes, mixing well; add salt and pepper. Place mixture in buttered casserole dish; dot with additional butter. At this point, potatoes can be refrigerated and baked later. Bake at 350 degrees for 45 minutes. This is a good side dish for beef or lamb.

GARLIC ROASTED POTATOES

Preparation: 10 minutes

Baking: 25 minutes
Servings: 4

**1-2 large cloves garlic,
  peeled and chopped**
4 Tablespoons butter
½ cup water

**1½ pounds small potatoes,
  peeled and quartered**
⅛ teaspoon salt
⅛ teaspoon pepper

Preheat oven to 450 degrees. Place garlic, butter, and water in small saucepan; simmer until water evaporates and garlic is tender. Strain butter; mash soft garlic through very fine strainer. Toss potatoes in garlic butter; place in single layer in large baking dish. Bake for 25 minutes, turning potatoes occasionally, until they are tender and browned. Remove potatoes from baking dish with slotted spoon. Season with salt and pepper before serving.

OVERNIGHT POTATOES

Preparation: 15 minutes
Planning: Must partially prepare ahead
Chilling: 8 hours

Baking: 45 minutes
Servings: 8

**6 medium potatoes, boiled,
  peeled, and sliced**
**1 (10¾-ounce) can cream of
  mushroom soup,
  undiluted**
2 cups sour cream

½ cup butter, melted
**½ cup chopped green onion
  with tops**
**1½ cups grated Cheddar
  cheese**
½ cup crushed cornflakes

Mix together potatoes, soup, sour cream, butter, onion, and cheese; pour into lightly greased 1½-quart baking dish. Refrigerate, covered, 8 hours or overnight. Before baking, bring to room temperature. Bake at 350 degrees for 45 minutes. Top potatoes with cornflake crumbs during last 20 minutes of baking.

SPINACH SQUARES
Makes spinach fun to eat!

Preparation: 15 minutes

Baking: 30 minutes
Yield: 16 squares

**2 (10-ounce) packages
  frozen chopped spinach,
  thawed and drained
1 stick butter
3 eggs, beaten
1 teaspoon salt**

**1 teaspoon ground thyme
garlic powder, to taste
1 cup biscuit baking mix
1 pound shredded Monterey
  Jack cheese**

Mix all ingredients. Spread into greased 13x9x2 pan. Bake at 350 degrees for 30 minutes. Cut into squares.

CHEESY SPINACH CASSEROLE

Preparation: 20 minutes
Planning: Must partially prepare ahead

Baking: 30 minutes
Chilling: 8 hours
Servings: 6

**2 (10-ounce) packages
  frozen chopped spinach
1 cup sour cream
2 Tablespoons dry onion
  soup mix**

**1 cup shredded medium or
  sharp Cheddar cheese**

Cook spinach according to package directions, omitting salt; drain well. Combine spinach, sour cream, and onion soup mix; mix well. Spoon into lightly greased 1-quart casserole dish. Sprinkle cheese over spinach mixture. Refrigerate, covered, 8 hours or overnight. Remove casserole from refrigerator 30 minutes before baking. Bake at 350 degrees for 30 minutes.

285

SAUTÉED SPINACH

Preparation: 10-15 minutes

Cooking: 10-15 minutes

Servings: 6

2 (10-ounce) packages
  frozen spinach
¼ cup butter
1-2 Tablespoons chopped
  green chiles, canned or
  fresh

½ teaspoon salt
2 Tablespoons chopped
  green onion
¼ teaspoon garlic powder

Cook spinach according to package directions; drain. Melt butter in large skillet; add spinach, green chiles, salt, onion, and garlic powder; stir well. Heat through; serve hot.

CHEESY SQUASH DRESSING

Preparation: 15-20 minutes
Planning: Can prepare ahead

Baking: 45 minutes
Servings: 10

4 pounds yellow squash,
  sliced
2 medium onions, chopped
1 stick butter
1 cup processed cheese,
  melted

2 eggs, beaten
1 (8-ounce) package
  herb-seasoned stuffing
  mix, divided
2 cups grated Cheddar
  cheese

Cook squash and onion in boiling water until tender; drain. Add butter and melted processed cheese, stirring gently. Fold in beaten eggs and half of stuffing mix. Pour into greased 13x9x2 baking dish. Sprinkle cheese over squash mixture; sprinkle remaining stuffing mix on top. Bake at 350 degrees for 45 minutes. This dish is great to serve at large dinner parties as an accompaniment for smoked meats.

GREEN PEA MEDLEY
An excellent cold vegetable for a picnic

Preparation: 10-15 minutes
Planning: Must prepare ahead

Chilling: 2 hours
Servings: 6-8

2 (10-ounce) packages
  frozen green peas
1 cup sour cream
2 green onions, chopped
6 slices bacon, cooked and
  crumbled

½ teaspoon salt
⅛ teaspoon pepper
1 Tablespoon dried dill
  weed
½ cup salted cashew nuts,
  optional

Thaw and drain peas. Mix remaining ingredients; combine with peas. Chill at least 2 hours before serving.

CHIFFY CHAFFY

Preparation: 15 minutes
Planning: Can prepare ahead

Cooking: 10 minutes
Servings: 6

1 large clove garlic, pressed,
  or ⅛ teaspoon garlic
  powder
2 Tablespoons olive oil
½ pound fresh mushrooms,
  sliced
1 onion, coarsely chopped
1 green bell pepper, coarsely
  chopped
2 medium zucchini or
  yellow squash, sliced

1 (16-ounce) can tomatoes,
  drained
1 Tablespoon chopped fresh
  parsley
⅛ teaspoon salt
⅛ teaspoon pepper
2 Tablespoons freshly grated
  Parmesan cheese
⅛ teaspoon cayenne pepper

Sauté garlic in olive oil. Add mushrooms, onion, bell pepper, and zucchini; cook until tender. Stir tomatoes into mixture; cook until hot. Add parsley, salt, pepper, Parmesan cheese, and cayenne pepper. Vegetables can be served hot or cold. Serve with French bread and red wine for a delicious meatless meal.

SHERRIED SWEET POTATOES
Try these at your next Thanksgiving dinner

Preparation: 20-30 minutes
Planning: Can prepare ahead

Baking: 30 minutes
Servings: 10

8 medium sweet potatoes
½ teaspoon salt, optional
1 cup light brown sugar,
  packed
2 Tablespoons cornstarch
½ teaspoon orange peel

2 cups orange juice
½ cup raisins
6 Tablespoons butter
⅓ cup dry sherry
¼ cup chopped walnuts

Cook whole sweet potatoes in salted water. Cool and peel; slice length-wise. Arrange in long baking dish. Sprinkle with salt, if desired. In saucepan, cook sugar, cornstarch, orange peel, orange juice, raisins, butter, and sherry until smooth and creamy. Pour sauce over sweet potatoes. Sprinkle with nuts. At this point, potatoes can be refrigerated until ready to bake. Bake at 325 degrees for 30 minutes.

SWEET POTATO SOUFFLÉ
This is Lt. Governor Zell Miller's favorite sweet potato soufflé

Preparation: 35 minutes

Baking: 45 minutes
Servings: 6

3 medium unpeeled sweet
  potatoes
½ cup half and half
⅓-½ cup firmly packed light
  brown sugar
2 Tablespoons butter,
  melted

¼ teaspoon salt
⅛ teaspoon ground nutmeg
⅛ teaspoon ground
  cinnamon
3 egg whites, room
  temperature
1 teaspoon baking powder

Cook sweet potatoes in boiling water 20-25 minutes, or until tender. Let cool to the touch; peel and mash. Combine potatoes, half and half, sugar, butter, salt, nutmeg, and cinnamon; set aside. Beat egg whites until foamy; add baking powder, beating until stiff, but not dry. Gently fold into sweet potato mixture. Spoon into greased 5-cup souffle dish. Bake at 325 degrees for 45 minutes.

GRANDMA'S TURNIP GREENS

Preparation: 1 hour   Cooking: 1 hour
Planning: Can prepare ahead   Servings: 6-8

5 pounds fresh turnip greens
    with roots
½ pound salt pork
6-8 cups water
2 teaspoons bacon drippings

chopped green onions for
    garnish
chopped banana peppers for
    garnish

Pick and wash turnip greens; tear into bite-size pieces. Peel turnip roots, and slice. Rinse salt pork; cut into 2-inch pieces. Combine salt pork and water in large Dutch oven; bring to a boil. Cover, reduce heat, and simmer 30 minutes. Add turnip greens; cover and cook 10 minutes. Add turnip roots and bacon drippings; cover and cook 15-20 minutes, or until greens and roots are tender. Serve with green onions or banana peppers. These are easily cooked and reheated later or frozen, thawed and reheated. Turnip greens can be served with hot buttered cornbread. The cornbread is often dunked into the "pot likker," the liquid from the greens.

 # MY MOTHER'S APPLES AND CORNFLAKES

Preparation: 15 minutes   Baking: 45 minutes
Planning: Can partially prepare ahead   Servings: 6

6 pared Granny Smith
    apples
3 Tablespoons sugar
ground cinnamon to
    taste

6 Tablespoons butter
1 cup cornflakes
½ cup water

Peel and slice apples. Arrange one layer of apples in greased casserole dish. Sprinkle with sugar and cinnamon; dot with butter. Cover with layer of cornflakes. Alternate layers until all apples are used. Add water; Bake, covered, at 350 degrees for 45 minutes. Ingredients can be placed in layers several hours before cooking, water added just before baking. This is delicious with game or ham.

 ## ALMOND CURRIED FRUIT

Preparation: 10 minutes   Baking: 1 hour
Planning: Can prepare ahead   Servings: 8-10

1 (29-ounce) can peaches
1 (16-ounce) can pears
1 (15½-ounce) can
   pineapple chunks
1 (16-ounce) can apricots
1 (6-ounce) jar maraschino
   cherries
½ cup slivered almonds,
   toasted

1 stick butter, melted
¾ cup light brown sugar,
   firmly packed
3 teaspoons curry powder
⅛ teaspoon lemon juice
⅛ teaspoon ground
   cinnamon
⅛ teaspoon ground nutmeg

Drain all fruit thoroughly. Arrange fruit in shallow baking dish. Sprinkle fruit with almonds. Combine butter, brown sugar, curry, lemon juice, cinnamon, and nutmeg in small bowl. Pour over fruit. Bake at 350 degrees for 1 hour. Fruit can be served hot or cold.

HOT APRICOT CASSEROLE
A nice holiday dish

Preparation: 15 minutes   Baking: 45 minutes
Planning: Can partially prepare ahead   Servings: 8

3 (16-ounce) cans apricots
2 rolls butter-flavored
   crackers
¼ cup sugar
2 Tablespoons light brown
   sugar
1 teaspoon ground
   cinnamon

1 (6-ounce) jar cherries,
   drained
1 cup chopped pecans
3 Tablespoons butter
ground cinnamon

Drain apricots, reserving liquid from 1 can. Crumble one roll of crackers. Mix cracker crumbs, apricot liquid, sugar, brown sugar, and cinnamon. Add apricots, cherries, and pecans; mix well. Pour in casserole dish. Top with second roll of crackers, crumbled. Dot with butter; sprinkle with cinnamon. At this point, casserole can be refrigerated and baked later. Bake at 375 degrees for 45 minutes.

 ## PARTY PINEAPPLE CASSEROLE

Preparation: 10 minutes   Cooking: 30 minutes
Planning: Can partially prepare ahead   Servings: 4-6

**1 (20-ounce) can pineapple
  chunks**
½ cup sugar
**3 Tablespoons all-purpose
  flour**

1 stick butter, melted
**1 cup shredded sharp
  Cheddar cheese**
**¾ to 1 cup round buttery
  crackers, crushed**

Drain pineapple, reserving 3 Tablespoons juice. Combine sugar, flour, melted butter, and cheese. Add pineapple juice; mix well. Gently fold in pineapple chunks. Pour into greased casserole dish. Casserole can be refrigerated at this point and baked later. Bake at 350 degrees for 20 minutes. Remove from oven and sprinkle with cracker crumbs; dot with additional butter. Return to oven; cook 10 additional minutes.

BAKED STUFFED PUMPKIN
A festive accompaniment to a fall dinner

Preparation: 20 minutes   Baking: 1¼ hours
Planning: Can prepare ahead   Servings: 4-6

**1 small pumpkin, 7 inches
  in diameter**
**2 cups peeled, chopped
  apples**
1 cup raisins
1 cup chopped pecans
**⅓ cup sugar or light brown
  sugar**

1 teaspoon lemon juice
¼ teaspoon ground nutmeg
**¼ teaspoon ground
  cinnamon**
**1 Tablespoon butter,
  softened**
sour cream for garnish

Wash pumpkin; cut off top; set aside. Scrape out seeds. Combine apples, raisins, pecans, sugar, lemon juice, spices, and butter in mixing bowl; toss gently. Spoon mixture into pumpkin shell. Replace top; place pumpkin on lightly greased cookie sheet. Bake at 350 degrees for 1¼ hours. Remove from oven and top stuffing with sour cream. Serve hot or cold.

"HUNKER DOWN" FOOLPROOF HOLLANDAISE SAUCE
A fool-proof recipe of G. Clisby Clarke, writer/performer
of "Hunker Down Hairy Dogs" and "Let the Big Dog Eat"

Preparation: 15 minutes   Cooking: 3-5 minutes
Planning: Can prepare ahead   Servings: 4-6

3 eggs   **2 lemons**
1 teaspoon salt   **1 stick butter, melted**
⅛ teaspoon cayenne pepper   **2 Tablespoons boiling water**

Beat eggs in blender; add salt, pepper, and juice of 2 lemons. Blend until well mixed. Very slowly, pour in butter; add boiling water. Pour mixture into heavy saucepan. Cook over low heat until it reaches consistency of loosely scrambled eggs. Return to blender and blend until smooth. Sauce can be prepared ahead and stored in an airtight container. To reheat, warm over low heat. Sauce will keep up to 3 weeks in the refrigerator.

NETA'S CHIVE SAUCE
A delicious sauce over any fresh vegetable

Preparation: 15 minutes   Cooking: 15 minutes
                                               Servings: 6

1 stick butter   **2 Tablespoons fresh or**
1 (8-ounce) package cream   **frozen chopped chives or**
  cheese, softened   **finely chopped green**
½ cup sour cream   **onion tops**
2 cups grated sharp Cheddar   **lemon juice, to taste,**
  cheese   **optional**

Melt butter over low heat. Add cream cheese, sour cream, cheese, chives, and lemon juice. Let simmer until smooth, stirring often with wire whisk. Serve hot over fresh vegetables.

Desserts

Southern Magnolia

DESSERTS

Amaretto Mousse 338
Apricot Wafer Dessert 341
Baked Pears with Caramel 351
Biscuit Tortoni 341

CAKES
  Amalgamation Cake 295
  Angel Strawberry Cake 309
  Banana Split Cake 296
  Cheesecake
    Black Forest Cheesecake 298
    Cappuccino Cheesecake 299
    Cara's Cheesecake 298
    Chestnut Cheesecake 300
    Chocolate Velvet Cheesecake 297
    German Brownie Cheesecake 331
  Chess Cake 304
  Chocolate-Cinnamon Cake 305
  Chocolate Truffle Cake 304
  Cocoa-Nut Layer Cake 302
  Colonial Strawberry Cake 308
  Flower Potcakes 300
  Lane Cake 306
  ½ Pound Cake 296
  Peach-Glazed Almond Cake 303
  Pineapple-Banana-Nut Cake 301
  Walnut Yule Log 310
  White Chocolate Cake 312
  Wonderful Spice Cake 307

CANDY
  Chocolate Truffles 337
  Colored Popcorn Balls 352
  English Toffee 336
  Haystack 295
  Lollipops 308
  Peanut Logs 336
  Pecan Pralines 337
  Red Candy Apples 339
Caramel Apple Fondue 354
Cardinal Strawberries 352
Charlotte Au Chocolate 344
Chocolate Chocolate Crepes 345
Chocolate Ice Cream Roll 346
Chocolate Marquis 348
Chocolate Snowball 349

COOKIES & BARS
  Brownies
    Creme De Menthe Brownies 332
    German Brownie Cheesecake 331
    Marshmallow-Fudge Brownies 330
  Candy Cane Cookies 342
  Cherry Squares 335
  Chocolate Amaretto Bars 333
  Chocolate Bon Bons 335
  Chocolate Kiss Cookies 329
  Chocolate Meringues 334
  Chocolate Pinwheel Cookies 328
  Chocolate Wows 327
  Christmas Tree Cones 312
  Crispy Chip Cookies 329
  Filled Butterscotch Cookies 326
  Gingerbread Men 324
  Great-Grandmother's Tea Cookies 328
  Honey Puffs 327
  Melting Moments 332

Orange Date-Nut Bars 331
Orange-Pecan Shortbread 325
Pumpkin Squares 334
Fancy Fruit Kabobs 352
Fresh Strawberries in Grand Marnier
  Sauce 353

FROSTINGS AND FILLINGS
  Amaretto Frosting 333
  Chocolate-Cinnamon Frosting 305
  Chocolate Glaze 311
  Cream Cheese Frosting 312
  Cream Frosting 295
  Lane Frosting 306
  Lemon Frosting 332
  Orange Frosting 325
  Pecan Cream Cheese Frosting 307
  Sweet Chocolate Frosting 302
  Sweet Cream Cheese Frosting 301
  Walnut Filling 310
Frozen Chocolate Parfait 347
Frozen Lemon Delight 350
Ginger Souffle 343
Kahlua Supreme 350
Nutty Buddy 348

PIES
  Amaretto Pie 314
  Angel Pecan Pie 322
  Apple Pecan Upside-Down Pie 316
  Baker's Chocolate Pie 314
  Black Bottom Pie 315
  Chocolate Rum Pie 317
  Classic Chess Pie 317
  Clay's Favorite Ice Cream Pie 319
  Coconut Cream Pie 318
  Easy Egg Custard Pie 319
  Easy Pie Crust 315
  Key Lime Pie 320
  Lemon Ice Box Pie 322
  Mystery Pecan Pie 323
  No-Fail Pecan Pie 321
  Pineapple Chess Pie 318
  Pistachio Ice Cream Pie 321
  Quick Mud Pie 320
  Sour Cream-Pumpkin Pie 323
  Sweet Potato Pie 326
  Wonderful Peach Cobbler 324
Pineapple Cream Delight 351

PUDDINGS
  Noodle Pudding with Fruit 339
  Rum Pudding Kristine 340
  Yia Yia's Rice Pudding 338
Rosebud's Bavarian Cream 342

SAUCES AND TOPPINGS
  Amaretto Sauce 353
  Chocolate Sauce 346
  Ginger Whipped Cream 343
  Grand Marnier Sauce 353
  Praline Parfait Sauce 354
  Raspberry Sauce 340
Strawberry Bavarian Cream 344

TORTES
  Almond Torte 313
  Coffee Brownie Torte 311
Vanilla Cream Custard 347

AMALGAMATION CAKE
A holiday favorite that will delight year 'round!

Preparation: 2½ hours
Planning: Can prepare ahead
Cooking: 1¾ hours

Baking: 30 minutes
Servings: 10

1 cup butter, softened
2 cups sugar
3 cups all-purpose flour
2 teaspoons baking powder

1 cup milk
2 teaspoons vanilla extract
8 egg whites, beaten
Cream Frosting

Preheat oven to 350 degrees. Cream butter and sugar. Add flour and baking powder alternately with milk. Add vanilla; mix well. Fold in beaten egg whites. Pour batter into three 8-inch round greased and floured cake pans. Bake for 30 minutes, or until center is completely set. Cool. Spread Cream Frosting between layers, on top, and around sides of cake. Frosted cake can be frozen for later use.

Cream Frosting:
8 egg yolks, beaten
1 cup butter, softened
2 cups sugar

1 cup chopped nuts
1 cup coconut
1 cup raisins

Cream egg yolks, butter, and sugar. Cook in double boiler for 1¾ hours over medium-low heat, stirring often, or microwave at HIGH (100% power) for 8 minutes, stirring every 2 minutes. Cool. Add nuts, coconut, and raisins; mix well.

 ## *HAYSTACKS*

Preparation: 15 minutes
Planning: Can prepare ahead

Cooking: 15 minutes
Yield: 6 dozen

2 (6-ounce) packages
  butterscotch chips
6 Tablespoons peanut butter

4 (1¾-ounce) cans
  shoestring potatoes

Melt butterscotch chips in top of double boiler; add peanut butter. Remove from heat and mix in potatoes. Drop by spoonfuls onto waxed paper.

BANANA SPLIT CAKE
A light dessert for a hearty appetite

Preparation: 25 minutes
Planning: Must prepare ahead

Chilling: 8 hours
Servings 14-16

3 sticks butter, divided, softened
2 cups graham cracker crumbs
2 eggs
2 cups powdered sugar
5 bananas
1 (16-ounce) can crushed pineapple, drained

1 (12-ounce) carton whipped topping
½ cup pecans for garnish
maraschino cherries for garnish
Chocolate Sauce (see Index), optional

Melt 1 stick butter; combine with graham cracker crumbs. Press into 12x8x2 glass dish. Refrigerate 20 minutes. In mixer, beat eggs, 2 sticks butter, and powdered sugar for 15 minutes. Spread mixture on top of graham cracker crust. Slice bananas on top of butter mixture. Spread crushed pineapple on top of sliced bananas; cover with whipped topping. Garnish with nuts; arrange cherries on top. Refrigerate 8-10 hours before serving. Chocolate sauce can be drizzled over individual servings, if desired.

½ POUND CAKE

Preparation: 30 minutes
Planning: Can prepare ahead

Baking: 1 hour
Servings: 12

2 cups all-purpose flour
1¾ cups sugar
1 cup butter

5 eggs
1 teaspoon vanilla extract

Sift flour 3 times and measure 2 cups. Cream sugar and butter 10 minutes with mixer at medium-high speed. Add flour and eggs alternately, one egg at a time. Add vanilla. Pour into greased and floured loaf pan. Bake at 350 degrees for 1 hour.

CHOCOLATE VELVET CHEESECAKE

Preparation: 30 minutes   Baking: 90 minutes
Planning: Must prepare ahead   Servings: 8
Chilling: 3 hours

⅓ cup plus 2 Tablespoons
  unsalted butter
1 (8½-ounce) package
  chocolate wafer cookies
⅛ teaspoon salt
⅛ teaspoon ground
  cinnamon
12 ounces semi-sweet
  chocolate, broken in
  pieces
2 Tablespoons unsalted
  butter, softened

3 (8-ounce) packages cream
  cheese
1½ cups heavy cream
1 teaspoon vanilla extract
1 cup sugar
3 large eggs, room
  temperature, slightly
  beaten
3 Tablespoons unsweetened
  cocoa

In food processor or blender, process 2 Tablespoons butter and cookies; add salt and cinnamon. With processor running, gradually add ⅓ cup butter. Press into bottom and sides of 9-inch springform pan. Refrigerate until ready to fill. Combine chocolate and 2 Tablespoons butter in top of double boiler. Melt chocolate until smooth; set aside, uncovered, at room temperature. Cube cream cheese and place into very large bowl. Beat with mixer at medium speed until smooth. Gradually beat in chocolate. Add cream and vanilla; beat until blended. Continue to beat at low speed; gradually adding sugar. Add eggs, one at a time, beating well. Sieve cocoa over batter; blend well. Pour into prepared crust. Bake at 350 degrees for 30 minutes. Reduce temperature to 325 degrees and bake for 30 minutes. Turn off oven; let sit 30 minutes with oven door slightly open. Refrigerate until well chilled before serving.

CARA'S CHEESECAKE
Award-winning recipe

Preparation: 20 minutes
Planning: Must prepare ahead
Chilling: 3 hours

Baking: 3 hours
Cooling: 2 hours
Servings: 12

**2 (8-ounce) packages cream
  cheese, softened**
1½ cups sugar
4 eggs, slightly beaten
3 Tablespoons cornstarch
**3 Tablespoons all-purpose
  flour**

juice of ½ lemon
1 teaspoon vanilla extract
**½ cup butter, melted and
  cooled**
4 cups sour cream

Preheat oven to 325 degrees. Grease 9-inch springform pan. With electric mixer, beat cream cheese at high speed. Gradually beat in sugar; beat in eggs, one at a time, at low speed. Add cornstarch, flour, lemon juice, and vanilla. Beat in butter and sour cream. Pour cheese mixture into greased pan. Bake one hour, or until firm around the edges. Turn off oven. Let pan stand in closed oven 2 hours. Remove; let cake cool at least 2 hours. Refrigerate cake for 3 hours, or until well chilled. To remove cake from pan, run spatula around sides of cheesecake, then release clasps of springform pan. Leave bottom of pan intact and set on serving plate.

BLACK FOREST CHEESECAKE
It's heavenly!

Preparation: 45 minutes
Planning: Must prepare ahead
Chilling: 2 hours

Baking: 1 hour
Servings: 12

**1½ cups chocolate cookie
  crumbs**
¼ cup butter, melted
**3 (8-ounce) packages cream
  cheese, softened**
1¾ cups sugar, divided
4 eggs
**⅓ cup cherry-flavored
  liqueur**

**4 (1-ounce) squares
  semi-sweet chocolate**
½ cup sour cream
1 cup heavy cream
**maraschino cherries
  for garnish**

Combine cookie crumbs and butter, mixing well. Press into bottom and 1 inch up sides of 9-inch springform pan. Beat cream cheese with mixer until light and fluffy. Gradually add 1½ cups sugar. Add eggs, one at a time, beating well. Stir in liqueur, blending well. Pour into prepared pan. Bake at 350 degrees for 1 hour. Let cake cool to room temperature on wire rack for at least 1 hour. Melt chocolate in top of double boiler and cool slightly. Stir in sour cream; spread mixture over top of cake. Chill thoroughly. Beat heavy cream until thickened; blend in ¼ cup sugar. Spread over chocolate layer and garnish with cherries.

CAPPUCCINO CHEESECAKE
A crowd pleaser

Preparation: 30 minutes
Planning: Must prepare ahead
Chilling: 24 hours

Baking: 1½ hours
Servings: 12

½ cup graham cracker crumbs
9 egg yolks
1¾ cups sugar, divided
1 teaspoon fresh lemon juice
½ teaspoon vanilla extract
¼ teaspoon salt
¼ teaspoon finely grated lemon peel

5 (8-ounce) packages cream cheese, softened
¾ cup butter, softened
½ cup sour cream
½ cup all-purpose flour
6 ounces semi-sweet chocolate chips, melted
½ cup sliced almonds, toasted

Butter and flour 10-inch springform pan, shaking out excess flour. Sprinkle bottom with graham cracker crumbs. Combine egg yolks, 1 cup sugar, lemon juice, vanilla, salt, and lemon peel in medium bowl. Beat until light and fluffy; set aside. Combine cream cheese, butter, remaining ¾ cup sugar, sour cream, and flour in large bowl; beat until smooth and creamy. Stir in chocolate and almonds. Gradually add egg mixture to cream cheese mixture, stirring constantly until just blended. Do not over mix. Pour batter into prepared pan to within ¾-inch of rim. Set pan in baking dish. Add enough warm water to come halfway up sides of pan. Bake at 325 degrees for 1½ hours, or until set. Remove from water; cool completely. Remove springform. Refrigerate cake 24 hours. Let stand at room temperature 30 minutes before serving.

CHESTNUT CHEESECAKE
A wonderful dessert from Trotters Restaurant in Atlanta

Preparation: 30 minutes
Planning: Must prepare ahead
Chilling: 1 hour

Baking: 1¾ hours
Servings: 10

1½ cups graham cracker crumbs
1¾ cups sugar, divided
⅓ cup melted butter
2¼ pounds cream cheese, softened
¼ cup all-purpose flour
½ Tablespoon lemon juice
½ Tablespoon vanilla extract
4 eggs
2 egg yolks
½ cup whipped cream
8 ounces unsweetened chestnut purée
2 ounces Frangelica liqueur

Mix cracker crumbs, ¼ cup sugar, and butter; press into 10-inch spring-form pan covering bottom and sides. In large bowl, combine cream cheese, flour, 1½ cup sugar, lemon juice, and vanilla, beating until thoroughly blended. In separate bowl, combine eggs and egg yolks, whipping until well blended. Fold in whipped cream; mix thoroughly. Combine with cream cheese mixture; blend well. In separate bowl, mix chestnut purée and Frangelica liqueur. Add ¼ cup of cheesecake filling to purée; blend thoroughly. Pour batter into pan, layering as follows: cheesecake filling, chestnut purée, remaining cheesecake filling. Bake, uncovered, at 400 degrees for 10 minutes. Lower oven temperature to 225 degrees, cover cheesecake with tented foil and continue to bake at 225 degrees for 1½ hours. Cool completely. Chill before serving.

FLOWER POTCAKES
Fun idea for school birthday parties

Preparation: 20 minutes
Planning: Can prepare ahead

Baking: 20 minutes
Yield: 10

1 (18½-ounce) package devil's food cake mix
1 (16½-ounce) can green frosting, if not available tint white frosting
large colored marshmallows
gum drops
colored sugars
10 (2½-inch) new clay flowerpots

Preheat oven to 350 degrees. Line flowerpots with foil. Grease and flour foil-lined pots. Prepare cake batter according to package directions. Spoon ½ cup batter into each flowerpot. Place flowerpots in muffin pans to steady; bake 15-20 minutes, or until toothpick inserted in center comes out clean. Remove from oven and place on wire racks until completely cool. Frost cakes with green icing. Decorate by cutting marshmallows and gum drops into slices and dipping in colored sugar. Or use a real flower, insert stem in plastic straw, and stick straw in center of cupcake.

PINEAPPLE-BANANA-NUT CAKE
Simply scrumptious!

Preparation: 15 minutes   Baking: 25-30 minutes
Planning: Must prepare ahead   Servings: 12
Chilling: 2 hours

3 cups all-purpose flour
2 cups sugar
1 teaspoon salt
1 teaspoon baking soda
3 eggs, beaten
1½ cups vegetable oil
1½ teaspoons vanilla extract

1 (8-ounce) can crushed pineapple, undrained
2 cups bananas, chopped
1½ cups pecans, chopped
Sweet Cream Cheese Frosting

Preheat oven to 350 degrees. Combine flour, sugar, salt, and baking soda; add eggs and oil. Stir to moisten, but do not beat. Add vanilla, pineapple, bananas, and pecans. Pour into three greased and floured cake pans. Bake for 25-30 minutes. Cool in pans. Set aside on wire rack. Spread Sweet Cream Cheese Frosting between layers and on top and sides of cake. Chill.

Sweet Cream Cheese Frosting
1 (8-ounce) package cream cheese, softened
1 (16-ounce) box powdered sugar

1 (8-ounce) carton whipped topping
1 teaspoon vanilla extract
½ cup chopped pecans

Mix together all ingredients until smooth.

COCOA-NUT LAYER CAKE
Impressive and different!

Preparation: 1 hour   Baking: 30-35 minutes
Planning: Must partially prepare ahead   Servings: 12

½ **cup unsweetened cocoa**
½ **cup boiling water**
1¾ **cups unsifted**
   all-purpose flour
1 **teaspoon baking powder**
1 **teaspoon baking soda**
⅛ **teaspoon salt**
½ **cup butter, softened**
2 **cups sugar**

2 **eggs**
1 **teaspoon vanilla extract**
1½ **cups buttermilk**
½ **cup finely chopped**
   pistachio nuts or walnuts
1 **cup heavy cream**
Sweet Chocolate Frosting
¼ **cup chopped pistachio**
   nuts or walnuts

In small bowl, mix cocoa with boiling water. Cool completely. Preheat oven to 350 degrees. Grease and flour three 8-inch round cake pans. Sift flour, baking powder, baking soda, and salt. In large bowl, combine butter, sugar, eggs, and vanilla; beat 5 minutes, or until fluffy. Blend in flour mixture, in fourths, alternately with buttermilk, beginning and ending with flour mixture. Beat just until smooth. Measure 1⅔ cups of batter into small bowl. Stir in ½ cup nuts; pour into one cake pan. Add cocoa mixture to remaining batter; mix and divide into other two cake pans. Bake 30-35 minutes, or until tests done. Cool completely. Whip heavy cream until stiff; refrigerate. To assemble cake, place chocolate layer first; spread with ½ of whipped cream. Place nut layer next; spread with remaining whipped cream. Top with last chocolate layer. Frost cake with Sweet Chocolate Frosting and garnish top edge with nuts. Store in refrigerator.

Sweet Chocolate Frosting:
⅓ **cup half and half**
⅓ **cup butter**
⅔ **cup unsweetened cocoa**
2⅔ **cups sifted powdered**
   sugar, divided

1 **teaspoon light corn syrup**
1 **teaspoon vanilla extract**

Heat half and half in saucepan until bubbles form; remove from heat. Add to butter, cocoa, 1½ cups powdered sugar, syrup, and vanilla. Beat until smooth. Add remaining powdered sugar, beating until smooth.

PEACH-GLAZED ALMOND CAKE

Preparation: 30 minutes   Baking: 45 minutes
Planning: Can prepare ahead   Servings: 10

2¾ cups all-purpose flour, divided

¾ cup plus 2 Tablespoons sugar, divided

¼ teaspoon salt

½ cup butter

1 Tablespoon water

3 eggs, separated

¾ cup peach preserves, divided

⅛ teaspoon cream of tartar

½ cup unblanched almonds, finely chopped

½ cup milk

⅓ cup vegetable oil

1½ teaspoons baking powder

1¼ teaspoons almond extract

½ teaspoon salt

1 (28-ounce) can cling peach slices, drained

Preheat oven to 350 degrees. In large bowl, mix 1½ cups flour, 2 Tablespoons sugar, and ¼ teaspoon salt. With pastry blender or two knives used scissor-fashion, cut butter into flour mixture until mixture resembles coarse crumbs. Stir in water and one egg yolk. With hands, work dough until smooth. Press dough evenly and firmly on bottom and sides of 9-inch round cake pan. Brush dough with ¼ cup peach preserves. In small bowl with mixer at high speed, beat 3 egg whites and cream of tartar until stiff peaks form; set aside. In large bowl, with mixer at low speed, beat almonds, milk, oil, baking powder, almond extract, salt, 2 egg yolks, 1¼ cups flour, and ¾ cup sugar until smooth; fold in beaten egg whites. Pour into dough-lined cake pan, spreading batter evenly. Bake 45 minutes, or until cake springs back when touched with finger. Cool cake 20 minutes on wire rack, or until side of cake shrinks from pan. Remove cake from pan and cool completely on rack. Place cake on platter. Brush top of cake with ¼ cup peach preserves. Arrange peach slices on top of cake; brush with remaining ¼ cup peach preserves.

CHOCOLATE TRUFFLE CAKE
Compliments of Elise Griffin, Peasant Restaurants,
Inc. of Atlanta; sinfully rich!

Preparation: 30 minutes
Planning: Must partially prepare ahead
Chilling: 2 hours

Baking: 15 minutes
Servings: 8-12

16 ounces semi-sweet
 chocolate
1 stick unsalted butter
1½ teaspoons all-purpose
 flour

1½ teaspoons sugar
1 teaspoon hot water
4 eggs, separated
1 cup heavy cream

Preheat oven to 425 degrees. Grease bottom of 8-inch springform pan. Melt chocolate and butter in top of double boiler. Add flour, sugar, and water; blend well. Add egg yolks, one at a time, beating well after each addition. Beat egg whites until stiff, but not dry; fold into chocolate mixture. Turn into pan; bake 15 minutes. Cake will look very undercooked in center. Let cool completely; as cake cools, middle will sink a bit. Chill or freeze cooled cake. Whip cream until soft peaks form. Spread very thick layer over top of cake, smoothing with spatula. Cut cake while cold, but let stand at room temperature about 15 minutes before serving.

 ## CHESS CAKE

Preparation: 10 minutes
Planning: Must prepare ahead
Chilling: 1 hour

Baking: 30-40 minutes
Servings: 12

1 (18½-ounce) box yellow
 cake mix
1 egg
½ cup butter, softened
1 (16-ounce) box powdered
 sugar

1 (8-ounce) package cream
 cheese, softened
2 eggs
fresh strawberries for
 garnish

Mix cake mix, egg, and butter with electric mixer until blended. Press into greased 13x9x2 pan. Combine powdered sugar, cream cheese, and eggs; pour over first mixture. Bake at 350 degrees for 30-40 minutes. Cool before serving. Garnish with fresh strawberries.

CHOCOLATE-CINNAMON CAKE
Not too sweet, but just right!

Preparation: 25 minutes
Planning: Must partially prepare ahead

Baking: 20-25 minutes
Servings: 12

¾ cup butter, softened
1½ cups sugar, divided
¾ teaspoon salt
1 Tablespoon vanilla extract
¾ cup unsweetened cocoa
3½ cups cake flour, unsifted

2 teaspoons baking soda
2½ cups water
4 egg whites, room
   temperature
Chocolate-Cinnamon
   Frosting

Preheat oven to 350 degrees. Grease and flour three 9-inch round cake pans. In large bowl, beat butter, ¾ cup sugar, salt, and vanilla until fluffy. Combine cocoa, flour, and baking soda in sifter. Sift into bowl on top of butter mixture. Add water; beat with mixer at low speed just until smooth. In medium bowl with clean beaters, beat egg whites until fluffy. Gradually add remaining ¾ cup sugar. Continue beating until stiff peaks form. Fold, a third at a time, into chocolate batter. Divide batter evenly among pans. Bake for 20-25 minutes, or until centers spring back when touched. Cool 5 minutes in pans; remove to cooling rack; cool completely, at least 1 hour. Spread Chocolate-Cinnamon Frosting between layers and on top and sides of cake.

Chocolate-Cinnamon Frosting:
⅓ cup butter, softened
1½ pounds powdered sugar
⅓ cup unsweetened cocoa
1 teaspoon ground
   cinnamon

¾ teaspoon vanilla extract
⅓-½ cup milk

In medium mixing bowl, beat together all ingredients until smooth.

LANE CAKE
A holiday favorite

Preparation: 30 minutes
Planning: Can prepare ahead

Baking: 20 minutes
Cooking: 15-20 minutes
Servings: 12

8 egg whites
1 cup butter
2 cups sugar
1 teaspoon vanilla extract
3¼ cups all-purpose flour

3½ teaspoons baking
   powder
¾ teaspoon salt
1 cup milk
Lane Frosting

Preheat oven to 375 degrees. Line four buttered 9-inch cake pans with waxed paper. Beat egg whites until stiff; set aside. Cream butter until fluffy. Add sugar gradually, beating well after each addition. Add vanilla, continue beating until consistency of whipped cream. Add flour, baking powder, and salt, alternately with milk, blending until smooth. Gently fold in egg whites. Pour batter into prepared pans. Bake for 20 minutes. Let cakes cool before removing from pans. Spread Lane Frosting between layers and on top and sides of cake. This cake is best if assembled, then covered in a cake box for at least one day before serving.

Lane Frosting:
½ pound butter
1½ cups sugar
8 egg yolks
¼ cup bourbon
1½ cups dark seedless
   raisins, soaked in hot
   water 5 minutes and
   drained

1½ cups shredded fresh
   coconut
2 cups chopped pecans

Cream butter. Add sugar and egg yolks, beating well. Cook in double boiler over simmering water for 15-20 minutes until thick. Remove from heat; add bourbon and beat 1 minute. Add raisins, coconut, and pecans. Cool.

WONDERFUL SPICE CAKE

Preparation: 30 minutes
Planning: Can prepare ahead

Baking: 25 minutes
Servings: 12

1 cup vegetable oil
1 cup firmly packed light
  brown sugar
1 cup sugar
2 eggs
2½ cups all-purpose flour
½ teaspoon salt
1 teaspoon baking soda
1 teaspoon ground
  cinnamon

1 teaspoon ground nutmeg
1 cup buttermilk
1 teaspoon vanilla extract
¾ cup flaked coconut
¾ cup chopped pecans
Pecan Cream Cheese
  Frosting
flaked coconut for garnish
pecan halves for garnish

Combine oil, brown sugar, and sugar; beat well. Add eggs, one at a time, beating well. Combine flour, salt, baking soda, cinnamon, and nutmeg. Add to first mixture alternately with buttermilk, beginning and ending with flour mixture. Stir in vanilla, coconut, and pecans. Pour batter into two greased and floured 9-inch cake pans. Bake at 350 degrees for 25 minutes. Cool cake in pans for 10 minutes, then cool on wire racks. Spread Pecan Cream Cheese Frosting between layers, on top, and around sides of cake. Garnish with coconut and pecan halves.

Pecan Cream Cheese Frosting:
1 (8-ounce) package cream
  cheese, softened
¼ cup butter, softened
1 (16-ounce) box powdered
  sugar

½ teaspoon vanilla extract
¾ cup chopped pecans

Beat cream cheese and butter until fluffy. Add powdered sugar and vanilla; beat until smooth. Stir in pecans.

COLONIAL STRAWBERRY CAKE

Preparation: 30 minutes
Planning: Must prepare ahead
Chilling: 2 hours

Baking: 30-35 minutes
Servings: 8

½ cup unsalted butter,
  softened
1 cup sugar
2 cups cake flour, sifted
  twice
½ teaspoon salt
2 teaspoons baking powder
⅔ cup milk

1 teaspoon vanilla extract
¼ teaspoon almond extract
4 egg whites
1 pint fresh strawberries or
  1 (10-ounce) box frozen
  sliced strawberries,
  drained
1 cup heavy cream

Preheat oven to 350 degrees. Grease and flour two 8-inch cake pans.
Line bottom of each pan with circle of waxed paper. Cream butter and
sugar until light and fluffy. Sift together cake flour, salt, and baking
powder. Add flour mixture and milk alternately to butter mixture,
beating constantly. Add vanilla and almond extracts. Beat egg whites
until stiff peaks form; fold into batter. Pour into prepared pans. Bake
for 30-35 minutes. Cool in pans for 10 minutes; turn out on wire racks.
Cool. Slice strawberries, reserving a few for garnish. Whip cream until
stiff. Cover bottom cake layer completely with ¼-inch of whipped
cream. Cover with strawberries leaving a margin of 1½ inches around
the outer edge. Cover strawberries with thin layer of whipped cream.
Place second cake layer on top; frost cake with whipped cream. Garnish with strawberries. Chill before serving.

 # LOLLIPOPS

Preparation: 30 minutes
Planning: Can prepare ahead

Cooking: 20 minutes
Yield: 10-20 lollipops

2 cups sugar
⅔ cup light corn syrup
½ cup water
food coloring

1 teaspoon vanilla, fruit, or
  peppermint flavoring
⅛-inch diameter dowel, cut
  to 5-inch lengths

In large saucepan, combine sugar, corn syrup, and water. Stir over low heat until sugar is dissolved; raise heat and cook quickly, without stirring, to just past the hard crack stage, 310 degrees on candy thermometer. Grease a cookie sheet while syrup is boiling. Stir in a few drops desired food color and flavor. Spoon by tablespoons onto greased sheet. Press into each lollipop a wooden dowel or twisted paper loop. Remove lollipops when cold. Or pour onto cookie sheet in thin layer. When cold and brittle, break into chunks to resemble broken glass. Or, pour into greased lollipop molds, insert sticks, and remove when cool. Store on waxed paper in airtight containers.

Note: Use fruit oils (orange, lemon, peppermint, etc.), available from a pharmacist, as they are tastier and the flavors last longer.

ANGEL STRAWBERRY CAKE
A surprising treat in the center!

Preparation: 45 minutes
Planning: Must partially prepare ahead
Chilling: 8 hours
Baking: 40 minutes
Servings: 12

1 (14½-ounce) package angel food cake mix
1 (8-ounce) package cream cheese, softened
1 (14-ounce) can sweetened condensed milk
¼ cup lemon juice
1 teaspoon almond extract
2¼ cups sliced fresh strawberries
1½ cups heavy cream
¼ cup sugar
whole strawberries for garnish

Prepare batter and bake cake in 10-inch tube pan according to package directions; cool well, about 1½ hours. Remove cake from pan. Cut a 1-inch slice crosswise from top of cake and set aside. Make cuts 1 inch from center and 1 inch from side of cake. With fingers, carefully remove cake within cuts, leaving a 1-inch base. Reserve cake pieces. Beat cream cheese until fluffy; add condensed milk, blending well. Stir in lemon juice and almond extract. Fold in reserved cake pieces and sliced strawberries; spoon into cake cavity. Replace top of cake; chill 8 hours or overnight. Whip cream, adding sugar. Frost cake with sweetened whipped cream; garnish with strawberries.

WALNUT YULE LOG

Preparation: 1¾ hours   Baking: 12 minutes
Planning: Must prepare ahead   Servings: 12
Chilling: 8 hours

¾ cup cake flour, sifted   **3 Tablespoons water**
¼ cup unsweetened cocoa   **1 teaspoon vanilla extract**
1 teaspoon baking powder   **Walnut Filling**
3 eggs   **Chocolate Glaze**
¾ cup sugar

Grease 15x10x1 jelly-roll pan. Line bottom with greased waxed paper. Sift flour, cocoa, and baking powder into small bowl. Beat eggs in medium bowl with electric mixer until thick and creamy. Gradually add sugar, beating constantly until mixture is very thick. Stir in water and vanilla; fold in flour mixture. Spread batter in prepared pan. Bake at 375 degrees for 12 minutes, or until center springs back when lightly touched. Loosen cake around edges and invert pan onto clean towel lightly dusted with powdered sugar. Peel off waxed paper. Starting at one of the short sides, roll cake and towel up together. Place seam side down on wire rack; cool completely. Unroll cake carefully; spread with about ⅔ of Walnut Filling. Roll, lifting cake with end of towel. Place, seam side down, on small platter. Spread remaining Walnut Filling over roll. Chill 8 hours or overnight. Spread Chocolate Glaze over roll or drizzle it on top. Garnish with chopped walnuts. Chill until time to serve.

Walnut Filling:
2 egg yolks   **1 teaspoon powdered**
2 Tablespoons sugar   ** instant coffee**
1 teaspoon cornstarch   **1 teaspoon vanilla extract**
½ cup half and half   **1 cup very finely chopped**
¾ cup unsalted butter   ** walnuts**
1 cup powdered sugar

Combine egg yolks, 2 Tablespoons sugar, and cornstarch in small saucepan. Blend in half and half. Cook, stirring constantly, over medium heat until mixture comes to a boil. Remove from heat; cool; chill. Meanwhile, in medium bowl of electric mixer, beat butter until soft and smooth. Add powdered sugar; beat until smooth. Dissolve coffee

in vanilla; add to filling. Gradually add chilled egg-yolk mixture, 1 Tablespoon at a time, beating constantly until light and fluffy. Fold in nuts.

Chocolate Glaze:

4 (1-ounce) squares semi-sweet chocolate

3 Tablespoons unsalted butter

1 Tablespoon half and half

In double boiler over hot, not boiling, water, melt chocolate with butter and milk, stirring occasionally until smooth. Let stand 5 minutes.

COFFEE BROWNIE TORTE

Preparation: 25 minutes
Planning: Must prepare ahead
Chilling: 1 hour

Baking: 20 minutes
Servings: 12

1 (15½-ounce) package fudge brownie mix
¼ cup water
2 eggs
½ cup finely chopped nuts
1½ cups heavy cream, chilled

½ cup light brown sugar, packed
1 Tablespoon powdered instant coffee
shaved chocolate for garnish

Preheat oven to 350 degrees. Grease and flour two 9-inch cake pans. blend brownie mix, water, and eggs; stir in nuts. Spread in pans. Bake 20 minutes. Cool 5 minutes. Remove from pans and cool on wire racks. In chilled bowl, beat cream until it begins to thicken. Gradually add sugar and instant coffee. Continue beating until stiff. Place one cake layer on serving dish, cover with 1 cup cream mixture. Top with second cake layer; frost top with remaining cream mixture. Garnish with shaved chocolate. Chill at least 1 hour before serving.

WHITE CHOCOLATE CAKE
A company cake they won't forget!

Preparation: 30 minutes
Planning: Must partially prepare ahead

Baking: 30 minutes
Servings: 12

2 cups sugar
1 cup butter, softened
4 eggs
½ pound white chocolate,
   melted and cooled
1 teaspoon vanilla extract

2½ cups all-purpose flour
1 cup buttermilk
1 cup chopped pecans
1 can coconut
Cream Cheese Frosting

Cream sugar with softened butter. Add eggs, one at a time, beating well after each addition. Add melted chocolate and vanilla; beat, blending well. Alternately add flour and buttermilk, beginning and ending with flour. Blend in nuts and coconut. Pour batter into two 9-inch greased and floured pans. Bake at 350 degrees for 30 minutes. Cool in pan, then remove to wire rack. Cool completely, at least 1 hour. Frost all layers, top, and sides of cake with Cream Cheese Frosting.

Cream Cheese Frosting:
1 (8-ounce) package cream
   cheese, softened
¼ cup butter, softened

1 (16-ounce) box powdered
   sugar
1 teaspoon vanilla extract

Blend together all ingredients; mix well until smooth.

 # CHRISTMAS TREE CONES
Children love to make these!

Preparation: 45 minutes
Planning: Can prepare ahead

Servings: 6

2 cups powdered sugar
3 Tablespoons butter
1 Tablespoon milk
3 teaspoons green food
   coloring

2½ teaspoons vanilla extract
6 sugar ice cream cones
candy pieces (M&M's,
   red-hots, sprinkles, etc.)

Sift sugar into large bowl. Add butter, milk, vanilla, and food coloring. Mix together until frosting is creamy. Stand the cones, inverted, on waxed paper. Spread the frosting all over the cones with a butter knife. Leave tops of cones bare so children can turn cones while trimming. Decorate trees with candy ornaments. Spread frosting on the tops.

ALMOND TORTE

Preparation: 15 minutes
Planning: Can prepare ahead

Baking: 50 minutes
Servings: 12

**1½ cups plus 2 Table-
  spoons all-purpose flour,
  divided**
**⅓ cup plus 2 Tablespoons
  sugar, divided**
½ cup butter, softened
1 egg yolk, lightly beaten
**7 ounces almond paste,
  crumbled**

2 eggs
1 egg white
½ teaspoon almond extract
**½ cup sliced almonds,
  toasted**
1 cup powdered sugar
2 Tablespoons milk

Preheat oven to 325 degrees. Combine 1½ cups flour and ⅓ cup sugar; cut in butter until evenly mixed. Stir in egg yolk. Mixture should be crumbly. Using fingers, press mixture on bottom and up sides of fluted 10-inch tart pan with removable bottom. Blend almond paste, 2 Tablespoons sugar, 2 Tablespoons flour, and 2 eggs in mixer or blender. Add egg white and almond extract; blend well. Pour into pastry shell. Bake 50 minutes, or until top is a rich golden-brown color. Cool 10 minutes before glazing. Toast almonds in a 325 degree oven for 10 minutes, or until lightly browned. Combine powdered sugar and milk; spread on top of torte. Garnish with almonds. Cool and remove sides of pan before serving. Torte will keep several days in refrigerator.

AMARETTO PIE

Elegant and easy - no pie crust necessary!

Preparation: 10 minutes

Baking: 45 minutes

Servings: 8

¼ cup butter, softened
1 cup sugar
2 eggs
¾ cup milk

¼ cup amaretto
¼ cup self-rising flour
½ (3½-ounce) package
    flaked coconut

Preheat oven to 350 degrees. Cream butter and sugar with food processor or mixer. When smooth, add eggs, blending well. Add milk, amaretto, and flour, beating constantly. Stir in coconut by hand. Pour mixture into greased 9-inch pie plate. Bake for 45 minutes, or until center is firm.

BAKER'S CHOCOLATE PIE

Preparation: 30 minutes
Planning: Must partially prepare ahead

Freezing: 2 hours
Servings: 8

1 cup powdered sugar
½ cup butter, softened
6 (1-ounce) squares
    semi-sweet chocolate,
    melted and cooled
1 teaspoon vanilla extract
4 eggs

1 (9-inch) pastry shell,
    baked
1 cup heavy cream, chilled
2 Tablespoons powdered
    sugar
chocolate curls for garnish

In small bowl, mix powdered sugar and butter with mixer on low speed until fluffy. Blend in chocolate and vanilla. On high speed, add eggs, one at a time, beating thoroughly after each. Pour into baked pie shell; cover with plastic wrap. Freeze 2 hours, or until firm. Remove from freezer 15 minutes before serving; remove plastic wrap. Beat cream and 2 Tablespoons powdered sugar in chilled bowl until stiff. Spread on pie. Garnish with chocolate curls.

BLACK BOTTOM PIE
An old family recipe with spectacular results

Preparation: 30 minutes
Planning: Must prepare ahead
Chilling: 4 hours

Baking: 8 minutes
Cooking: 20 minutes
Servings: 8

15 ginger snaps
7 Tablespoons butter,
divided
4 eggs, separated
2 cups milk
3 Tablespoons all-purpose
flour
1 cup sugar, divided

1 (1-ounce) square
unsweetened chocolate
1 Tablespoon unflavored
gelatin
4 Tablespoons cold water
2 Tablespoons bourbon
1 cup heavy cream, whipped
chocolate shavings

Crush ginger snaps; add 5 Tablespoons butter; blend well. Press into 9-inch pie plate. Bake at 375 degrees for 8 minutes. Cool. Beat egg yolks until creamy. Scald milk. Combine egg yolks, flour, ½ cup sugar, and 2 Tablespoons butter in top of double boiler. Pour milk over mixture; cook, stirring constantly, until custard becomes fairly thick and will coat a spoon. Set aside. Remove 1 cup custard and add chocolate. Stir until melted. Pour over crust. Chill. Soften gelatin in water; set aside. Beat egg whites until frothy; add ½ cup sugar; beat until stiff. To remaining custard, add gelatin and bourbon; beat. Fold in egg whites. Pour over chocolate layer. Top with whipped cream. Sprinkle chocolate shavings on top of pie, if desired. Chill.

 ## *EASY PIE CRUST*
There's no bowl or rolling pin to clean!

Preparation: 5 minutes
Planning: Can prepare ahead

Baking: 10-15 minutes
Yield: 1 8-inch pie crust

1½ cups all-purpose flour
1½ teaspoons sugar

½ cup vegetable oil
2 Tablespoons milk

Combine flour, sugar, oil, and milk in pie pan. Press mixture thinly on bottom and up sides of pan. Fill with a favorite pie filling. If crust needs to be pre-baked for recipe, bake at 400 degrees for 10-15 minutes.

APPLE PECAN UPSIDE-DOWN PIE

Preparation: 30 minutes   Baking: 45-55 minutes
Planning: Must partially prepare ahead   Servings: 8
Chilling: 1 hour

3 cups all-purpose flour	1¼ cups chopped pecans
2 sticks unsalted butter, cut into small pieces	2½ pounds Rome Beauty apples, peeled, cored, thinly sliced
¼ teaspoon salt	1 teaspoon ground cinnamon
½ teaspoon sugar	
⅓ cup ice water	¼ cup sugar
6 Tablespoons unsalted butter	1 Tablespoon plus 1 teaspoon all-purpose flour
⅔ cup firmly packed dark brown sugar	

Blend flour, butter, salt, and sugar in food processor until mixture resembles meal. With processor running, add ice water in a stream; process until mixture just forms a ball. Divide dough into 2 balls, one slightly larger than the other. Dust balls with flour; wrap in waxed paper. Chill for 1 hour. Roll into a ¼-inch round on a floured surface. The larger round should be 12 inches, and the smaller one 10 or 11 inches.

Preheat oven to 350 degrees. To prepare filling, heat 6 Tablespoons butter in skillet over low heat until hot. Stir in brown sugar and pecans; stir 1 minute. Pour into 9-inch pie plate; let cool slightly. Place larger round of dough on top of mixture, leaving a ½-inch overhang. In medium bowl, toss apples, cinnamon, sugar, and flour; combine well. Spread apple mixture on top of dough in pie plate. Brush one side of 10-inch round with water. Place wet side down over apple mixture. Press dough edges together; trim excess dough. Make several incisions for steam escape. Bake in center of oven for 45-55 minutes. Let cool 5 minutes. Invert on serving plate. Serve warm or at room temperature.

CHOCOLATE RUM PIE

*You'll love this recipe from Jeff Van Note, longtime
center for the Atlanta Falcons*

Preparation: 25 minutes
Planning: Must partially prepare ahead

Chilling: 2 hours
Servings: 6-8

½ ounce unsweetened
   chocolate
6 ounces semi-sweet
   chocolate chips
2 eggs, separated
1 egg

1½ Tablespoons rum
2 cups heavy cream,
   whipped, divided
1 (9-inch) graham cracker
   pie crust

Melt chocolate in top of double boiler; remove from heat. Stir in 2 egg yolks, 1 egg, and rum. Beat 2 egg whites until stiff; fold into chocolate. Cool. Fold in 1 cup heavy cream. Pour into crust; refrigerate 2 hours. Top with remaining whipped cream.

Note: For a sweeter pie, omit unsweetened chocolate and use 6½ ounces semi-sweet chocolate.

 # CLASSIC CHESS PIE

A quick and easy pie - you'll have all the ingredients on hand

Preparation: 10 minutes
Planning: Can prepare ahead

Baking: 45 minutes
Servings: 8

3 eggs, beaten
1½ cups sugar
½ cup butter, melted
1 Tablespoon cornmeal
2 Tablespoons buttermilk

½ teaspoon white vinegar
¼ teaspoon lemon juice
½ teaspoon vanilla extract
1 (9-inch) pastry shell,
   unbaked

In mixing bowl, beat eggs; mix in sugar, butter, cornmeal, buttermilk, vinegar, lemon juice, and vanilla; mix well. Pour into pastry shell. Bake at 350 degrees for 45 minutes. Cool completely.

PINEAPPLE CHESS PIE
The pineapple is a nice addition to an old favorite

Preparation: 10 minutes   Baking: 45 minutes
Planning: Can prepare ahead   Servings: 8

2 cups sugar
½ cup butter, softened
4 eggs
3½ Tablespoons all-purpose
   flour

1 (8-ounce) can crushed
   pineapple, drained
1 teaspoon vanilla extract
1 (9-inch) pastry shell,
   unbaked

Cream sugar and butter; add eggs and flour, mixing well. Stir in pineapple and vanilla. Pour into pastry shell. Bake at 350 degrees for 45 minutes. Cool completely.

COCONUT CREAM PIE

Preparation: 35 minutes   Chilling: 8 hours
Planning: Must prepare ahead   Servings: 8

¼ cup cornstarch
1 Tablespoon all-purpose
   flour
3 cups half and half, divided
3 eggs
3 egg yolks
¾ cup sugar

2 teaspoons vanilla extract
1½ cups coconut, divided
1 (9-inch) pastry shell,
   baked
1 cup heavy cream
2 Tablespoons powdered
   sugar

Dissolve cornstarch and flour in ½ cup half and half; stir well. Beat eggs, egg yolks, and sugar until light and fluffy. Heat 2½ cups half and half to boiling point; add cornstarch mixture, stirring constantly. Cook over medium heat until thickened. Remove from heat. Add vanilla and 1 cup coconut. Cool completely. When filling is cold, spoon into pastry shell. Whip cream until stiff; add powdered sugar. Spread over pie filling. Garnish with remaining ½ cup coconut. Refrigerate 8 hours or overnight.

 ### *EASY EGG CUSTARD PIE*

Preparation: 5 minutes Baking: 45 minutes
Planning: Can prepare ahead Servings: 6

4 egg yolks, slightly beaten **4 egg whites, optional**
1½ cups milk **4 Tablespoons sugar,**
½ cup sugar **optional**
1 teaspoon vanilla extract
1 (9-inch) pastry shell,
unbaked

Combine yolks, milk, sugar, and vanilla. Pour mixture into pie shell. Bake 10 minutes at 400 degrees. Reduce heat to 325 degrees; bake an additional 35 minutes. If desired, prepare meringue by beating egg whites until very stiff; slowly adding sugar. Spread meringue over custard; bake at 325 degrees for 15 minutes until browned.

CLAY'S FAVORTIE ICE CREAM PIE
Cool and delicious - great for summertime!

Preparation: 1½ hours Freezing: 14 hours
Planning: Must prepare ahead Servings: 8

1½ cups ginger snap crumbs **1 Tablespoon apricot**
¼ cup powdered sugar **liqueur or Grand Marnier**
⅓ cup plus 1 Tablespoon **½ cup sliced almonds,**
butter, melted, divided **toasted**
¾ cup chocolate syrup **½ teaspoon ground**
½ gallon vanilla ice cream, **cinnamon**
softened **1 Tablespoon sugar**
1 cup heavy cream

Mix crumbs, powdered sugar, and ⅓ cup butter. Press into bottom and sides of 9-inch deep dish pie plate. chill 1 hour. Pour chocolate syrup over bottom of crust. Fill crust with ice cream; freeze. Whip heavy cream; add liqueur and blend well. Spread over top of ice cream. For a more decorative appearance, fill pastry bag with whipped cream; with star tip on bag, cover top of pie with whipped cream stars. In small saucepan, stir almonds, 1 Tablespoon melted butter, cinnamon, and sugar over medium heat until toasted. Sprinkle almonds on top of whipped cream. Freeze overnight before serving.

QUICK MUD PIE

Contributed by Mrs. Kim Swindall,
wife of Georgia Congressman Pat Swindall

Preparation: 10 minutes   Freezing: 1 hour
Planning: Must partially prepare ahead   Servings: 8

**½ gallon pecan ice cream,
  softened**
**⅓ cup amaretto-flavored
  powdered instant coffee**
**1 teaspoon powdered
  instant coffee**

1 chocolate crumb pie crust
1 cup whipped topping
shaved chocolate for garnish

Put softened ice cream in large bowl; stir in coffees. Spoon mixture into pie crust; freeze. Before serving, top with whipped cream; garnish with shaved chocolate.

KEY LIME PIE

Preparation: 30 minutes   Baking: 5 minutes
Planning: Can prepare ahead   Servings: 8

1 cup sugar
¼ cup all-purpose flour
3 Tablespoons cornstarch
¼ teaspoon salt
2 cups water
3 eggs yolks, beaten
1 Tablespoon butter
**¼ cup lime juice, fresh or
  bottled**

**grated rind of 1 lime or
  lemon**
**1 (9-inch) pastry shell,
  baked**
3 egg whites
¼ teaspoon cream of tartar
6 Tablespoons sugar

Combine sugar, flour, cornstarch, and salt in saucepan; gradually stir in water. Cook over low heat, stirring, until thickened. Gradually stir mixture into beaten egg yolks. Return to low heat and cook, stirring, 2 minutes. Stir in butter, lime juice, and rind; cool slightly. Pour into baked pastry shell and cool. Beat egg whites until light and frothy. Add cream of tartar; continue beating until egg whites are stiff enough to peak. Gradually beat in sugar; beat until meringue is stiff and glossy. Spread meringue over cooled pie filling. Bake at 425 degrees for 5-6 minutes until meringue is lightly browned. Chill.

PISTACHIO ICE CREAM PIE
This pie is beautiful with thick ice cream layers!

Preparation: 30 minutes
Planning: Must prepare ahead
Freezing: 2-3 hours

Baking: 4-6 minutes
Servings: 10

1½ cups chocolate wafer crumbs
½ stick butter, melted
½ cup plus 2 Tablespoons sugar, divided
1 (6-ounce) can evaporated milk
2 (1-ounce) squares unsweetened chocolate

⅛ teaspoon salt
½ gallon pistachio or pistachio-chocolate -almond ice cream, softened
1 (8-ounce) carton whipped topping

Combine chocolate wafer crumbs, butter, and 2 Tablespoons sugar; press into 9-inch deep dish pie plate. Bake at 350 degrees for 4-6 minutes; cool. Cook milk, chocolate, ½ cup sugar, and salt over low heat until thickened, stirring constantly. Cool thoroughly; set aside. Spoon half of ice cream into crust. Pour half of chocolate sauce on top of ice cream. Let chill, covered, in freezer 30 minutes or more until frozen. Spread half of whipped topping over pie; chill again. Repeat layers, reserving 2 Tablespoons chocolate sauce to drizzle on top of whipped topping. Freeze, covered, until firm.

Note: Any flavored ice cream can be substituted for an equally delicious pie.

NO-FAIL PECAN PIE

Preparation: 5 minutes
Planning: Can prepare ahead

Baking: 45-50 minutes
Servings: 6

3 eggs, slightly beaten
¾ cup sugar
¾ cup light corn syrup
1 Tablespoon vanilla extract

3 Tablespoons butter, cut into pieces
1 cup chopped pecans
1 (9-inch) pastry shell, unbaked

In large bowl, mix eggs, sugar, syrup, vanilla, butter, and pecans. Pour into pastry shell. Bake at 350 degrees for 45-50 minutes, or until set. Pie can be served with whipped cream or ice cream for an added treat.

ANGEL PECAN PIE

Preparation: 15 minutes   Baking: 30 minutes
Planning: Must prepare ahead   Servings: 8

3 egg whites	**1 cup crisp butter-flavored**
1 cup plus 2 Tablespoons	**cracker crumbs**
sugar, divided	**1½ cups chopped pecans**
2 teaspoons vanilla extract,	**1 cup heavy cream**
divided	**1 teaspoon almond extract**

Preheat oven to 350 degrees. Grease 9-inch pie plate with butter. Beat
egg whites until foamy. Gradually add 1 cup sugar to egg whites, beating continuously. Add 1 teaspoon vanilla. Continue beating until mixture holds soft peaks. Fold cracker crumbs and 1 cup chopped pecans
into meringue mixture. Spoon mixture into pie plate, pulling up around
edge of pan with back of spoon, spreading evenly in center. Bake 30
minutes; cool completely on wire rack. Mix cream, 2 Tablespoons
sugar, 1 teaspoon vanilla, and almond extract. Whip until thick and
shiny. Spoon onto cooled pie. Sprinkle with remaining pecans. Chill
before serving.

LEMON ICE BOX PIE
Lovely and light

Preparation: 30 minutes   Chilling: 2 hours
Planning: Must prepare ahead   Servings: 6

1 (14-ounce) can sweetened	**3 egg yolks**
condensed milk	**1 cup heavy cream, divided**
½ cup fresh lemon juice	**1 (9-inch) graham cracker**
rind of 1 lemon, finely	**pie crust**
grated	**lemon slices for garnish**
2 Tablespoons sugar	

Beat condensed milk; slowly beat in lemon juice. As mixture thickens,
add rind, sugar, and yolks. Beat until mixture forms peaks. In chilled
bowl, whip cream. Slowly fold half of cream into pie filling. Pour filling
into pie crust. Chill for 2 hours. Before serving, top with remaining
whipped cream; garnish with thin lemon slices.

MYSTERY PECAN PIE

Preparation: 30 minutes
Planning: Can prepare ahead

Baking: 35-40 minutes
Servings: 8

**1 (8-ounce) package cream
  cheese, softened**
**⅓ cup plus ¼ cup sugar,
  divided**
4 eggs
**2 teaspoons vanilla extract,
  divided**

¼ teaspoon salt
**1 (9-inch) pastry shell,
  unbaked**
**1 cup pecans, whole or
  chopped**
1 cup light corn syrup

Beat cream cheese, ⅓ cup sugar, 1 egg, 1 teaspoon vanilla, and salt
until thick and creamy; set aside. Beat 3 eggs until blended; add ¼ cup
sugar, corn syrup, and 1 teaspoon vanilla. Spread cream cheese mixture in pastry shell. Top with pecans. Gently pour corn syrup mixture
over pecans. Bake at 375 degrees for 35-40 minutes. Serve warm or
cold.

SOUR CREAM-PUMPKIN PIE

Preparation: 30 minutes
Planning: Can prepare ahead

Baking: 65 minutes
Servings: 8

1 cup sugar
¼ teaspoon salt
½ teaspoon ground ginger
**1 teaspoon ground
  cinnamon**
¼ teaspoon ground nutmeg
¼ teaspoon ground cloves

1 (16-ounce) can pumpkin
**1 (8-ounce) carton sour
  cream**
3 eggs, separated
**1 (9-inch) pastry shell,
  unbaked**

Combine sugar, salt, ginger, cinnamon, nutmeg, and cloves in large
bowl; add pumpkin and sour cream; stir well. Beat egg yolks until thick
and lemon colored; stir into pumpkin mixture. Bring egg whites to room
temperature; beat until stiff peaks form. Fold into pumpkin mixture.
Pour into pastry shell. Bake at 450 degrees for 10 minutes. Reduce to
350 degrees; bake for 55 minutes, or until set.

WONDERFUL PEACH COBBLER
The almond flavoring makes this special!

Preparation: 40 minutes

Baking: 25 minutes
Servings: 8

8 cups sliced fresh peaches
(4-5 pounds)
2 cups sugar
3 Tablespoons all-purpose
flour
½ teaspoon ground nutmeg

1¼ teaspoons almond
extract
⅓ cup melted butter
pastry for double crust
8-inch pie

Combine peaches, sugar, flour, and nutmeg in large saucepan. Let sit 20 minutes until syrup forms. Bring peach mixture to a boil, reduce heat, and cook 10 minutes. Remove from heat; blend in almond extract and butter. Roll out half of pastry to fit 8x12x2 dish. Spoon half of peach mixture into buttered 8x12x2 dish; top with cut pastry. Bake at 475 degrees for 12 minutes. Spoon remaining peaches over baked pastry. Roll out remaining pastry and cut into ½-inch wide strips. Arrange over peaches in a lattice design. Bake at 475 degrees for 10-15 minutes until lightly browned.

GINGERBREAD MEN
The exceptional gingerbread man!

Preparation: 20 minutes

Baking: 30 minutes
Yield: 2 dozen

1 cup butter
1½ cups sugar
1 egg
4 teaspoons grated orange
peel
2 Tablespoons dark corn
syrup

3 cups all-purpose flour
2 teaspoons baking soda
2 teaspoons ground
cinnamon
1 teaspoon ground ginger
½ teaspoon salt
½ teaspoon ground cloves

Thoroughly cream together butter and sugar. Add egg; beat until light and fluffy. Add orange peel and corn syrup; mix well. In another bowl, stir together remaining ingredients; stir into creamed mixture. Chill thoroughly. On lightly floured surface, roll to ¼-inch thickness. Cut with gingerbread man cookie cutter. Place 1 inch apart on ungreased cookie sheet. Bake at 375 degrees for 8-10 minutes. Cool 1 minute; remove from pan. Cool on wire rack. Decorate gingerbread men with sugar and raisins, if desired.

ORANGE-PECAN SHORTBREAD COOKIES
Rich and tender, with a subtle orange flavor

Preparation: 20 minutes   Cooking: 8-13 minutes
Planning: Must partially prepare ahead   Yield: 5 dozen

1 cup powdered sugar
1 cup butter, softened
1 egg yolk
2 cups all-purpose flour
½ cup cornstarch

¾ cup chopped pecans
1 Tablespoon grated orange peel
sugar
Orange Frosting

In large bowl, combine powdered sugar and butter; cream until light and fluffy. Add egg yolk; blend well. Lightly spoon flour into 2-cup measuring cup; level off. Add flour and cornstarch to sugar mixture; stir until mixture forms smooth dough. Add pecans and orange peel; knead to blend. Shape dough in 1-inch balls. Place 2 inches apart on ungreased cookie sheet. Flatten balls with glass dipped in sugar. Bake at 350 degrees for 8-13 minutes, or until lightly browned and set. Immediately remove from cookie sheet; cool completely. Frost cookies.

Orange Frosting:
2 cups powdered sugar
3 Tablespoons butter
2-3 Tablespoons orange juice

1 teaspoon grated orange peel

Combine powdered sugar, butter, orange juice, and orange peel in small bowl; beat until smooth.

FILLED BUTTERSCOTCH COOKIES
These cookies improve with age when stored in an air-tight container

Preparation: 45 minutes
Planning: Must partially prepare ahead
Chilling: 8 hours

Baking: 8-12 minutes
Yield: 4 dozen

2 cups light brown sugar
½ cup shortening
3 eggs, beaten
1½ teaspoons vanilla extract
1½ teaspoons baking soda

4-6 cups flour, divided
1 pound dates
1 cup sugar
1 cup boiling water
1 cup pecans, chopped

Cream sugar and shortening; add eggs and vanilla. Add baking soda to 1 cup flour; add to sugar mixture. Add remaining flour as needed to make a batter which can be rolled. Turn onto floured board; knead until smooth and dry. Combine dates, sugar, and water; cook over low heat, stirring until thick. Cool thoroughly, then add pecans. Divide cookie dough into 6 parts; roll each part to ¼-inch thickness. Spread cooled date filling over dough in a thin layer. Roll jelly-roll style. Chill overnight, or freeze for later use. When ready to bake, slice the rolls about ¼-inch thick. Bake at 375 degrees for 8-12 minutes. These baked cookies will keep for weeks in an airtight container.

SWEET POTATO PIE
"Grandma's favorite"

Preparation: 15 minutes
Planning: Can prepare ahead

Baking: 20 minutes
Servings: 6

3 eggs, separated
2 cups mashed sweet
potatoes
2 Tablespoons butter,
melted
⅛ teaspoon salt

½ cup plus 6 Tablespoons
sugar, divided
½ teaspoon ground nutmeg
1 cup milk
1 (9-inch) pastry shell,
unbaked

Beat egg yolks into mashed potatoes; add butter, salt, ½ cup sugar, nutmeg, and milk. Pour into pastry shell. Bake at 350 degrees for 20 minutes, or until set. Beat egg whites until stiff, slowly adding remaining 6 Tablespoons sugar. Spread meringue over baked pie; brown in oven at 325 degrees for 15 minutes.

CHOCOLATE WOWS

Preparation: 15 minutes
Planning: Can prepare ahead

Baking: 10-12 minutes
Yield: 3 dozen

**6 (1-ounce) squares
  semi-sweet chocolate**
½ cup butter
2 eggs
¾ cup sugar
⅓ cup all-purpose flour
1 teaspoon baking powder

¼ cup cocoa
1½ teaspoons vanilla extract
¼ teaspoon salt
**2 cups coarsely chopped
  pecans**
**1 (6-ounce) package
  chocolate chips**

Preheat oven to 325 degrees. Heat chocolate and butter until melted. Remove from heat. Beat eggs and sugar with mixer at medium speed for 2 minutes, or until light colored. Reduce speed to low; add chocolate mixture, flour, baking powder, cocoa, vanilla, and salt. Beat 2 minutes at medium speed. Stir in pecans and chocolate chips. Drop by teaspoonfuls onto greased cookie sheet; flatten. Bake 10-12 minutes. Remove to wire rack and cool. Baked cookies may be frozen.

HONEY PUFFS

Preparation: 10 minutes

Frying: 30 minutes
Yield: 50

2 cups all-purpose flour
**4 Tablespoons baking
  powder**
⅛ teaspoon salt
1 egg, beaten
1½ cups milk

1 Tablespoon butter, melted
vegetable oil for deep frying
½ cup honey
ground cinnamon
walnut pieces

Sift flour, baking powder, and salt into mixing bowl. Add egg, milk, and melted butter; mix well until smooth and a thick batter is formed. Add additional flour if necessary. Heat oil to 350-360 degrees. Drop batter by Tablespoons into hot oil; fry until golden. To serve, dip hot puffs into warmed honey diluted with a little water, then sprinkle with cinnamon and walnut pieces.

CHOCOLATE PINWHEEL COOKIES
A good cookie that is not too sweet

Preparation: 30 minutes
Planning: Must partially prepare ahead
Chilling: 1 hour

Baking: 12 minutes
Yield: 3 dozen

½ cup butter, softened
1 (3-ounce) package cream
  cheese, softened
1 cup sugar
1 egg
1 teaspoon vanilla extract
2¼ cups all-purpose flour,
  divided

½ teaspoon baking powder
½ teaspoon salt
⅛ teaspoon baking soda
½ cup cocoa
powdered sugar, optional

In large mixing bowl, cream butter, cream cheese, sugar, egg, and vanilla. In large measuring cup, combine 1½ cups flour, baking powder, salt, and baking soda; blend into creamed mixture. Divide dough in half. Add cocoa to one half and ¾ cup flour to other half. Roll each half into 9-inch square. Place chocolate half on top of vanilla half; roll up like a jelly roll. Wrap dough in waxed paper; chill 1 hour or overnight. Slice dough in ¼-inch slices. Bake at 350 degrees for 12 minutes on ungreased cookie sheet. Remove to wire rack and cool. Sprinkle baked cookies with powdered sugar, if desired.

GREAT-GRANDMOTHER'S TEA COOKIES
All ages find these cookies irresistible

Preparation: 15 minutes
Planning: Can prepare ahead

Baking: 15 minutes
Yield: 4 dozen

1 cup butter
1 cup sugar
2 eggs

1 teaspoon vanilla extract
2 teaspoons baking powder
2 cups all-purpose flour

Cream butter and sugar. Add eggs, one at a time. Stir in vanilla. Sift together baking powder and flour; add flour to butter mixture, mixing to make soft dough. Roll dough and cut cookies, or drop by rounded teaspoons onto cookie sheet. Bake at 350 degrees for 15 minutes.

CRISPY CHIP COOKIES

Preparation: 10 minutes
Planning: Can prepare ahead

Baking: 15-20 minutes
Yield: 6 dozen

1 cup butter, softened
1 cup light brown sugar
1 cup sugar
2 eggs, beaten
1 teaspoon vanilla extract
2 cups all-purpose flour
1 teaspoon baking soda

1 teaspoon baking powder
1 cup oatmeal
1 cup cornflakes
1 cup chopped pecans
1 (6-ounce) package
  chocolate chips

Cream butter, brown sugar, and sugar. Add eggs; beat until smooth. Stir in vanilla. Combine flour, baking soda, and baking powder; add to sugar mixture; mix well. Stir oatmeal, cornflakes, pecans, and chocolate chips into mixture. Drop by large spoonfuls onto ungreased cookie sheet. Bake at 350 degrees for 15-20 minutes. Cookie dough can be frozen for later use.

CHOCOLATE KISS COOKIES

Preparation: 30 minutes
Planning: Must partially prepare ahead
Chilling: 1 hour

Baking: 10 minutes
Yield: 4½ dozen

1 cup butter, softened
⅔ cup sugar
1 teaspoon vanilla extract
1⅔ cups unsifted
   all-purpose flour
¼ cup cocoa

¾ cup finely chopped
  pecans
1 (9-ounce) package milk
  chocolate kisses
powdered sugar

Cream butter, sugar, and vanilla in large mixing bowl. Combine flour and cocoa; blend into creamed mixture. Add pecans; blend well. Chill dough 1 hour. Unwrap kisses. Shape a scant Tablespoon of dough around each kiss, covering completely. Shape into balls. Place on ungreased cookie sheet. Bake at 375 degrees for 10 minutes. Cool slightly; remove to wire rack; cool completely. Roll in powdered sugar.

MARSHMALLOW-FUDGE BROWNIES

Preparation: 30 minutes
Planning: Can prepare ahead

Baking: 30-35 minutes
Microwaving: 2½ minutes
Yield: 3½ dozen

1¼ cup butter, softened, divided
1¼ cup sugar, divided
1 (1-ounce) square unsweetened chocolate, melted
2 eggs, beaten
¾ cup chopped pecans, divided
½ cup plus 1 Tablespoon all-purpose flour, divided
2 (3-ounce) packages cream cheese, softened

1 egg, beaten
1 teaspoon vanilla extract, divided
¾ cup semisweet chocolate chips
1½ cups miniature marshmallows
2 (1-ounce) squares unsweetened chocolate
½ cup milk
1 (16-ounce) box powdered sugar

Cream ½ cup butter and 1 cup sugar. Add 1 square melted chocolate, 2 eggs, ½ cup pecans, and ½ cup flour; mix well. Spoon into greased and floured 13x9x2 pan; set aside.

Blend cream cheese, ¼ cup butter, and ¼ cup sugar. Add 1 egg, ¼ cup pecans, 1 Tablespoon flour, and ½ teaspoon vanilla; mix well. Spoon over chocolate layer in pan without mixing layers. Sprinkle chocolate chips over cream cheese layer. Bake at 350 degrees for 30-35 minutes. Cool slightly; top with marshmallows.

In large glass measuring cup, combine 2 squares chocolate, milk, and ½ cup butter. Microwave at HIGH (100% power) for 2 to 2½ minutes, until chocolate has melted. Stir in ½ teaspoon vanilla and powdered sugar. Stir until smooth. Spoon frosting over brownies. Cool. Cut into squares; store in refrigerator.

GERMAN BROWNIE CHEESECAKE

Preparation: 20 minutes
Planning: Must prepare ahead
Chilling: 8 hours

Baking: 20-25 minutes
Yield: 20 brownies

1 (18½-ounce) package
  German chocolate cake
  mix
½ cup shredded coconut
⅓ cup butter, softened
3 eggs

2 (8-ounce) packages cream
  cheese, softened
1 cup sugar, divided
5 teaspoons vanilla extract,
  divided
2 cups sour cream

Preheat oven to 350 degrees. In large mixing bowl, blend cake mix, coconut, butter, and 1 egg on low speed. Mixture should be crumbly. Press very lightly into ungreased 13x9x2 baking pan. Beat cream cheese, 2 eggs, ¾ cup sugar, and 2 teaspoons vanilla until smooth and fluffy. Spread over cake mixture. Bake 20-25 minutes. Mix sour cream, ¼ cup sugar, and 3 teaspoons vanilla until smooth. Spread over cheesecake. Cool. Refrigerate at least 8 hours. Cut into squares.

ORANGE DATE-NUT BARS

Preparation: 20 minutes
Planning: Can prepare ahead

Baking: 50 minutes
Yield: 21-28 bars

3 eggs
1 (6-ounce) can frozen
  orange juice concentrate
1 cup sugar
2 cups graham cracker
  crumbs
1 teaspoon baking powder
¼ teaspoon salt

¾ cup chopped nuts
1 (8-ounce) package pitted
  dates, chopped
1 teaspoon vanilla extract
1¼ cups powdered sugar
2½ Tablespoons orange
  juice

Preheat oven to 350 degrees. Grease and lightly flour 9-inch square pan. Beat eggs until light and fluffy; beat in orange juice concentrate. Stir in sugar, cracker crumbs, baking powder, salt, nuts, dates, and vanilla; mix well. Spoon mixture into prepared pan. Bake for 50 minutes. Cool in pan on wire rack. Combine powdered sugar and orange juice; beat until smooth. Frost date-nut mixture; cut into bars.

MELTING MOMENTS

Preparation: 15 minutes   Baking: 15 minutes
Planning: Must partially prepare ahead   Yield: 2-3 dozen
Chilling: 30 minutes

1 cup butter, softened
⅓ cup powdered sugar
¾ cup cornstarch

1 cup cake flour
Lemon Frosting

Preheat oven to 350 degrees. With food processor or mixer, combine butter, sugar, cornstarch, and flour. Chill dough 30 minutes. Roll into 1-inch balls; place on lightly greased cookie sheet. Press in center with thumb; bake 15 minutes, or until lightly browned. While still warm, spread with frosting.

Lemon Frosting:
2 Tablespoons butter,
  melted
1 cup powdered sugar
½ teaspoon lemon juice

½ teaspoon grated lemon
  peel
2 drops yellow food coloring
half and half

Mix butter, sugar, lemon juice, lemon peel, and food coloring. Add half and half by Tablespoons until frosting is smooth enough to spread.

CRÈME DE MENTHE BROWNIES

Preparation: 40 minutes   Baking: 22 minutes
Planning: Can prepare ahead   Yield: 48 brownies

2 sticks butter, softened,
  divided
1 cup sugar
4 eggs, beaten
1 cup all-purpose flour
½ teaspoon salt
1 (16-ounce) can chocolate
  syrup

1 teaspoon vanilla extract
2 cups powdered sugar,
  sifted
2 Tablespoons crème de
  menthe
1 cup chocolate chips
6 Tablespoons butter

Cream 1 stick butter and sugar. Add eggs, flour, salt, chocolate syrup, and vanilla; blend well. Pour into greased 13x9x2 pan. Bake at 350 degrees for 22 minutes. Cool in pan. Mix powdered sugar, 1 stick butter, and crème de menthe until fluffy. Spread over cooked brownies. Combine chocolate chips and butter in glass measuring cup. Microwave at HIGH (100% power) for 2-3 minutes until chocolate is melted, stirring twice. Cool until thickened, spread over crème de menthe layer. Chill brownies; cut into squares. Brownies can be frozen.

CHOCOLATE AMARETTO BARS

Preparation: 20 minutes   Baking: 20 minutes
Planning: Can prepare ahead   Yield: 30 bars

1 cup shortening   **1 Tablespoon amaretto**
4 (1-ounce) squares   **1½ cups all-purpose flour**
  unsweetened chocolate   **½ teaspoon salt**
2 cups sugar   **Amaretto Frosting**
4 eggs, beaten   **crushed almonds for garnish**

Combine shortening and chocolate in large glass bowl; microwave at HIGH (100% power) for 2-3 minutes, stirring twice, to melt. Add sugar, stirring until blended. Stir in eggs and amaretto. Combine flour and salt; add to creamed mixture, stirring well. Pour into lightly greased 13x9x2 baking pan. Bake at 400 degrees for 20 minutes; cool. Spread with Amaretto Frosting; sprinkle with almonds. Cut into squares. Bars can be frozen.

Amaretto Frosting:
¼ cup butter   **2½ cups powdered sugar**
1 (1-ounce) square   **⅛ teaspoon salt**
  unsweetened chocolate   **3 Tablespoons amaretto**
2 Tablespoons evaporated
  milk

Combine butter and chocolate in large glass bowl. Microwave at HIGH (100% power) for 1½-2 minutes, stirring once, to melt. Stir in milk. Add sugar, salt, and amaretto; stir until smooth.

PUMPKIN SQUARES

Preparation: 20 minutes
Planning: Can prepare ahead

Baking: 25-30 minutes
Yield: 24 squares

4 eggs
1 cup vegetable oil
1⅔ cups sugar
1 (16-ounce) can pumpkin
2 cups all-purpose flour
2 teaspoons baking powder
2 teaspoons ground
  cinnamon

1 teaspoon salt
1 teaspoon baking soda
1 (3-ounce) package cream
  cheese, softened
1 stick butter, softened
2 cups powdered sugar
½ cup chopped pecans

Beat together eggs, oil, sugar, and pumpkin. Blend together flour, baking powder, cinnamon, salt, and baking soda; add to egg mixture. Spread batter in ungreased 15x10x1 jelly-roll pan. Bake at 350 degrees for 25-30 minutes. Cool. Mix cream cheese, butter, and powdered suger; blend well. Spread frosting over baked cake. Garnish with chopped pecans. Cut into squares. Squares will freeze well.

CHOCOLATE MERINGUES

Preparation: 20 minutes
Planning: Can prepare ahead

Baking: 25 minutes
Yield: 2 dozen

2 egg whites
⅛ teaspoon salt
⅛ teaspoon cream of tartar
1 teaspoon vanilla extract

¾ cup sugar
1 (6-ounce) package
  chocolate chips
¼ cup chopped pecans

Beat egg whites, salt, cream of tartar, and vanilla until soft peaks form. Add sugar gradually, beating until peaks are stiff. Fold in chocolate chips and nuts. Cover cookie sheet with plain paper. Drop mixture by rounded teaspoonfuls onto cookie sheet. Bake at 300 degrees for 22-25 minutes. Cool slightly before removing from paper.

CHERRY SQUARES

Preparation: 1 hour
Planning: Can prepare ahead

Baking: 30 minutes
Yield: 15-20 squares

**1 cup plus 2 Tablespoons
all-purpose flour, divided
1 cup oats
1 cup light brown sugar
1 teaspoon baking soda
¾ teaspoon salt, divided
½ cup plus 3 Tablespoons
butter, softened, divided
2 eggs
¾ teaspoon almond extract,
divided**

**1 teaspoon baking powder
1 cup coconut
1 cup maraschino cherries,
chopped
¼ cup chopped pecans
2 cups powdered sugar
1½ Tablespoons juice from
cherries
1 Tablespoon milk**

Mix 1 cup flour, oats, brown sugar, baking soda, ¼ teaspoon salt, and ½ cup butter. Press into 9-inch square pan. Bake at 350 degrees for 10 minutes. Let cool completely. Mix eggs, ½ teaspoon almond extract, 2 Tablespoons flour, baking powder, ½ teaspoon salt, coconut, cherries, and pecans. Spread over baked crust. Bake at 350 degrees for 20 minutes. Cool. Mix 3 Tablespoons butter, sugar, cherry juice, ¼ teaspoon almond extract, and milk. Spread over baked layers. Cut into squares. Squares can be frozen.

 # CHOCOLATE BONBONS

Preparation: 30 minutes
Planning: Can prepare ahead

Yield: 50

**1 (6-ounce) package
semi-sweet chocolate
chips
1 (14-ounce) can sweetened
condensed milk**

**2 cups graham cracker
crumbs (30 crackers)
½ cup chopped pecans
8 ounces grated coconut**

Melt chocolate chips in top of double boiler. Remove from heat and stir in milk. Add cracker crumbs and nuts; stir until well blended. Drop by teaspoonfuls onto coconut. Roll into balls. Store in airtight container or freeze.

PEANUT LOGS

Preparation: 30 minutes
Planning: Can prepare ahead

Baking: 30 minutes
Yield: 100 logs

**1 (12-ounce) jar crunchy
  peanut butter**
1 cup butter, softened
**2 cups graham cracker
  crumbs**
1 pound powdered sugar
1 teaspoon vanilla extract

**1 cup chopped nuts,
  optional**
1 (4-ounce) bar parafin
**1 (12-ounce) package
  semi-sweet chocolate
  chips**

Mix peanut butter, butter, cracker crumbs, sugar, vanilla, and nuts; blend well. Hand roll into little finger-size logs. Melt parafin and chocolate chips in top of double boiler. With fork, dip logs, one at a time, into chocolate mixture. Place on waxed paper to harden chocolate.

Note: Logs are better if made one day, refrigerated, and dipped the next day. These logs will keep several weeks in an airtight container; they also freeze well.

ENGLISH TOFFEE

Preparation: 45 minutes
Planning: Must prepare ahead

Chilling: 10 minutes
Servings: 10-12

1 cup sugar
1 cup salted butter
**6 ounces semi-sweet
  chocolate chips**

1 cup chopped walnuts

In heavy saucepan, combine sugar and butter. Cook, stirring, until mixture reaches 310 degrees (hard crack stage) on a candy thermometer. Pour onto greased baking sheet. When cool enough to handle, flip toffee to prevent sticking. Melt chocolate in top of double boiler; spread over toffee. Sprinkle with nuts; press nuts into chocolate. Chill briefly to set chocolate, if necessary. Break into pieces.

CHOCOLATE TRUFFLES

Preparation: 30 minutes   Chilling: 1 hour
Planning: Must prepare ahead   Yield: 2 dozen

¼ cup heavy cream
2 Tablespoons Grand
  Marnier
6 ounces German sweet
  chocolate

4 Tablespoons butter,
  softened
powdered unsweetened
  cocoa for garnish

Boil cream until it is reduced to 2 Tablespoons. Remove from heat; stir in Grand Marnier and chocolate. Return to low heat to melt chocolate. Whisk in butter. When mixture is smooth, pour into bowl; refrigerate 1 hour. When mixture is firm, shape into 1-inch balls. Roll balls in cocoa. Store truffles, covered, in refrigerator. Let truffles stand at room temperature 1 hour before serving.

PECAN PRALINES
A favorite candy in New Orleans

Preparation: 30 minutes   Yield: 20-30

1 cup sugar
¼ teaspoon salt
1 cup light brown sugar
2 Tablespoons light corn
  syrup

½ cup evaporated milk
2 Tablespoons butter
1 teaspoon vanilla extract
2 cups chopped pecans

Combine sugar, salt, brown sugar, syrup, and milk in medium saucepan. Cook over medium heat until temperature reaches 234 degrees on candy thermometer. Add butter, vanilla, and pecans. Stir until thick. Drop by teaspoonfuls onto waxed paper. Cool.

YIA YIA'S RICE PUDDING

Preparation: 10 minutes
Planning: Must prepare ahead

Cooking: 1 hour
Chilling: 3 hours
Servings: 8

6 cups milk
1 cup uncooked
  medium-grain rice
½ cup sugar
2 Tablespoons butter

¼ teaspoon salt
2 teaspoons vanilla extract
¼ teaspoon ground nutmeg
  for garnish
½ cup raisins for garnish

Combine milk, rice, sugar, butter, and salt in medium saucepan. Heat over medium heat, stirring frequently, until tiny bubbles form around the edge. Reduce heat to low; simmer, covered, 1 hour, or until rice is very tender; stir occasionally. Stir in vanilla. Refrigerate, covered, until well chilled, about 3 hours. To serve, spoon rice pudding into dessert dishes. Garnish each serving with nutmeg and raisins.

 # AMARETTO MOUSSE

Preparation: 15 minutes
Planning: Must prepare ahead

Chilling: 4 hours
Servings: 6

½ cup sugar
½ cup water
2 eggs
⅛ teaspoon salt
1 (6-ounce) package
  chocolate chips

4 Tablespoons amaretto
1 cup heavy cream,
  whipped, divided

Heat sugar in water until dissolved; set aside. Mix eggs, salt, and chocolate in blender. Add sugar mixture slowly; blend until thickened. Cool. Add amaretto. Fold in ¾ of the whipped cream. Pour into small wine glasses. Chill 4 hours. Before serving, spoon a dollop of whipped cream on each serving.

NOODLE PUDDING WITH FRUIT
A traditional Jewish dessert

Preparation: 30 minutes   Baking: 1 hour
Planning: Can prepare ahead   Servings: 8-10

8 ounces medium noodles,   **4 apples, peeled and grated**
    cooked nearly tender,   **grated rind of ½ orange**
    drained   **½ cup yellow raisins**
salt to sprinkle   **2 teaspoons vanilla extract**
½ cup butter, melted   **2 Tablespoons cinnamon**
6 eggs   **sugar mixture**
1 cup sugar   **½ cup slivered almonds or**
½ cup milk   **chopped pecans**
2 cups sour cream

Sprinkle noodles lightly with salt. In 13x9x2 pan, toss noodles with butter until evenly coated. Beat together eggs, sugar, milk, and sour cream until well blended. Stir in apples, orange rind, raisins, and vanilla. Pour egg mixture evenly over noodles. Sprinkle top with cinnamon sugar; press almonds gently into custard. Bake at 350 degrees for 1 hour, or until top is browned and custard is set. Cut into squares; serve warm. After baking, dessert can be refrigerated and reheated prior to serving.

 ## *RED CANDY APPLES*
A fall treat that can't be beat!

Preparation: 30 minutes   Planning: Can prepare ahead
                                             Yield: 8 apples

3 cups sugar   **1 teaspoon red food**
½ cup light corn syrup   **coloring**
½ cup water   **8 apples**
1 teaspoon cinnamon   **wooden sticks**
    extract

Cook sugar, corn syrup, and water until it reaches 285 degrees on a candy thermometer. Remove from heat; add cinnamon and food coloring. Stir until color is blended. Insert wooden sticks into tops of apples; dip apples into mixture. Drain apples on waxed paper. Cool.

339

RUM PUDDING KRISTINE
This is well worth the trouble; sounds rich,
but tastes light and refreshing

Preparation: 1½ hours
Planning: Must partially prepare ahead

Cooking: 30 minutes
Chilling: 3 hours
Servings: 10

1½ envelopes unflavored gelatin	**¾ cup sugar**
⅓ cup cold water	**⅓ cup boiling water**
5 egg yolks	**⅔ cup light rum**
2 cups milk	**1 cup heavy cream, whipped**
	Raspberry Sauce

Soften gelatin in cold water. Mix egg yolks, milk, and sugar; bring to a boil over low heat, stirring to prevent scorching. Boil 1 minute; remove from heat. Add boiling water to softened gelatin and stir into milk mixture. Return to a boil; remove immediately from heat. Place in refrigerator, stirring occasionally, until mixture begins to thicken. Stir in rum. When mixture is quite thick, but not stiff, fold in whipped cream. Pour into serving bowl. Chill 3 hours. Serve with warm Raspberry Sauce.

NOTE: It will take about 30 minutes to bring egg, milk, and sugar mixture to a boil; if boil is rushed, custard will curdle. If custard is too thick, it will be lumpy when folding in whipped cream. However, a blender or food processor can be used at any disappointing stage and the pudding will become smooth again.

Raspberry Sauce:

1 (10-ounce) box frozen raspberries, thawed	**1 teaspoon cornstarch**
¼ cup sugar	**⅓ cup cold water**

Strain raspberries. Mix raspberry juice and sugar; heat to boiling. Mix cornstarch and water; add to raspberry juice; return to a boil. Remove from heat; stir in raspberries.

APRICOT WAFER DESSERT

Preparation: 50 minutes   Chilling: 12 hours
Planning: Must prepare ahead   Servings: 8-10

1½ cups dried apricots   ½ cup butter, softened
½ cup sugar   1½ cups powdered sugar,
1½ cups crushed vanilla   sifted
   wafers   2 eggs at room temperature
3 Tablespoons butter,   1 cup heavy cream, whipped
   melted

Place apricots in saucepan; cover with water. Simmer, covered, until tender, about 30 minutes. Drain. Sieve or purée; add sugar and set aside. Combine wafers with melted butter, reserving ½ cup for topping. Press remaining crumbs into 8x8 pan. Cream butter and powdered sugar until fluffy; beat in eggs. Spread on top of wafer crust. Top with apricot purée, spreading evenly. Spread whipped cream over apricot layer. Sprinkle with reserved crumb mixture. Chill 12 hours, or overnight.

BISCUIT TORTONI

This is a great dessert to have after a heavy meal

Preparation: 30 minutes   Freezing: 2 hours
Planning: Must prepare ahead   Servings: 6-8

½ cup crushed macaroons   2 cups heavy cream, divided
¾ cup crushed toasted   3 Tablespoons dark rum
   almonds, divided   4 maraschino cherries,
¼ cup powdered sugar   halved

Mix together macaroons, ½ cup almonds, sugar, and 1 cup cream. Whip remaining cream. Fold whipped cream and rum into first mixture. Spoon into paper muffin cups; freeze for 2 hours. To serve, sprinkle tops with remaining ¼ cup almonds, and garnish with cherry half in center of each cup.

ROSEBUD'S BAVARIAN CREAM

An elegant molded dessert from R. L. Mathis Dairy, Decatur, Georgia

Preparation: 30 minutes
Planning: Must prepare ahead

Chilling: 3 hours
Servings: 6

**1 envelope unflavored
  gelatin
½ teaspoon salt
¼ cup plus 2 Tablespoons
  sugar
2 eggs, separated**

**1¼ cups milk
1 cup heavy cream
1½ teaspoons vanilla extract
sliced strawberries and
  peaches**

In medium saucepan, stir gelatin, salt, and 2 Tablespoons sugar until well mixed. In small bowl, whisk egg yolks and milk with wire whisk. Stir milk mixture into gelatin mixture. Cook, over low heat, stirring constantly, until mixture coats spoon. Refrigerate until mixture mounds when dropped from spoon. In small bowl, beat egg whites at high speed of mixer until soft peaks form; at high speed, gradually beat in ¼ cup sugar until dissolved. Spoon egg whites over gelatin mixture. In same bowl, beat cream with vanilla until soft peaks form; add to gelatin mixture. With wire whisk, gently fold egg whites and cream into gelatin. Pour into 6-cup mold; refrigerate until set, about 3 hours. Carefully unmold onto chilled serving plate. Serve with sliced strawberries and peaches.

 ## CANDY CANE COOKIES
Children love to help make these!

Preparation: 30 minutes
Planning: Can prepare ahead

Baking: 10 minutes
Yield: 3 dozen

**2¾ cups sifted all-purpose
  flour
½ teaspoon salt
½ cup shortening
½ cup butter**

**1 cup sugar
1 egg
1 teaspoon vanilla extract
red paste food coloring**

Preheat oven to 325 degrees. Sift flour and salt and set aside. Cream shortening, butter, and sugar in an electric mixer; add egg, blending well. Add flour mixture and vanilla, blend well. Divide dough in half; add red color to one half. With fingers, roll ½ teaspoon of each color into a strip about 3 inches long. Place one white and one red strip side by side; press lightly together at one end and twist like a rope. Place on ungreased cookie sheet in a candy cane shape, at least 1½ inches apart. Bake for 10 minutes. Carefully remove from cookie sheet while warm; cool on a wire rack. Keep in airtight containers or freeze.

GINGER SOUFFLÉ

This recipe comes from Elise Griffin,
Peasant Restaurants, Inc. of Atlanta

Preparation: 30 minutes   Baking: 35-45 minutes
                                                        Servings: 4

3 Tablespoons butter
3 Tablespoons all-purpose
  flour
1 cup milk
⅓ cup sugar
⅛ teaspoon salt
1 Tablespoon cognac or
  brandy

¼ teaspoon ground ginger
½ cup crystallized ginger,
  finely chopped
4 eggs, separated
Ginger Whipped Cream

Preheat oven to 375 degrees. In saucepan, melt butter; add flour; stir with a wire whisk to blend. Bring milk to a boil, and add all at once to butter-flour mixture, stirring vigorously with whisk. Add sugar, salt, cognac, and gingers. Remove from heat. Beat in egg yolks, one at a time. Cool. Beat egg whites until soft peaks form; fold into mixture. Transfer to 2-quart casserole dish. Bake 35-45 minutes. Serve immediately with Ginger Whipped Cream.

Ginger Whipped Cream:
½ cup heavy cream
2 Tablespoons powdered
  sugar

2 teaspoons brandy
¼ teaspoon ground ginger

Whip cream until soft peaks form. Add remaining ingredients; beat only to combine. This will be the consistency of a custard sauce.

CHARLOTTE AU CHOCOLATE

Preparation: 45 minutes
Planning: Must prepare ahead

Chilling: 5 hours
Servings: 10

**1 (12-ounce) package
 chocolate chips**
6 eggs, separated
2 Tablespoons sugar
**2 cups heavy cream,
 whipped**

2 packages lady fingers
chocolate curls for garnish
whipped cream for garnish

Melt chocolate over low heat; cool. Beat in egg yolks, one at a time. Beat egg whites in small bowl until frothy. Beat sugar into egg whites until stiff peaks form. Beat ¼ of egg white mixture into chocolate. Fold in remaining egg white mixture. Fold in whipped cream. Line spring-form pan with lady fingers. Fill with half of chocolate filling. Put another layer of lady fingers on top of filling. Top with remaining chocolate filling. Garnish with chocolate curls and whipped cream. Refrigerate 5 hours before serving.

STRAWBERRY BAVARIAN CREAM

Preparation: 15 minutes
Planning: Must prepare ahead

Chilling: 2 hours
Servings: 6

**1 (10-ounce) package frozen
 sliced strawberries,
 thawed**
1 cup boiling water
**1 (3-ounce) package
 strawberry gelatin**

1 cup heavy cream, chilled
whipped cream for garnish
strawberries for garnish

Drain strawberries, reserving syrup; set aside. Pour boiling water over gelatin, stirring to dissolve. Add enough cold water to reserved syrup to measure 1 cup. Stir into dissolved gelatin; chill until almost set. In chilled bowl, beat cream until stiff. Beat gelatin until foamy. Fold gelatin and strawberries into whipped cream. Pour into 1-quart mold. Chill until firm, about 2 hours. Top with additional whipped cream and garnish with strawberries to serve.

CHOCOLATE CHOCOLATE CREPES
*This is Paul Albrecht's recipe from Pano's and Paul's Restaurant
in Atlanta for one of their most popular desserts*

Preparation: 45 minutes   Cooking: 15 minutes
Planning: Must partially prepare ahead   Servings: 4
Chilling: 1 hour

1 cup all-purpose flour
5 Tablespoons chocolate
  powder
1 cup milk
3 ounces sugar
1½ teaspoons vanilla
  extract, divided
3 eggs
1 Tablespoon clarified
  butter

8 ounces semi-sweet
  chocolate
1 cup heavy cream
1 ounce brandy
1 ounce Grand Marnier
chocolate syrup for garnish
whipped cream for garnish
pecans for garnish

Sift flour and chocolate powder. Mix with milk until batter is smooth. Add sugar, ½ teaspoon vanilla, eggs, and butter; blend well. Make very thin crepes with batter; allow to cool. Melt chocolate in double boiler. In saucepan, bring cream to a boil; blend into melted chocolate. Refrigerate 1 hour. When chilled, mix at medium speed 2 minutes until creamy. Add 1 teaspoon vanilla, brandy, and Grand Marnier. Fill crepes with chocolate mixture; lace with chocolate syrup and garnish with whipped cream and pecans.

Note: To make crepes, lightly oil 6-inch crepe pan; place over medium heat until hot. Pour 2 Tablespoons of batter into pan; turn pan until batter thinly covers the bottom. Cook 1 minute. Shake pan to loosen crepe; flip crepe and cook 30 seconds. Cool crepes on a towel. Stack between layers of waxed paper, if refrigerating or freezing.

CHOCOLATE ICE CREAM ROLL

Preparation: 45 minutes   Baking: 20-25 minutes
Planning: Must prepare ahead   Servings: 10
Freezing: 24 hours

6 eggs, room temperature,
   separated
¼ teaspoon cream of tartar
1 cup sugar, divided
1 teaspoon vanilla extract
¼ cup cocoa

¼ cup all-purpose flour
½ teaspoon salt
½ cup powdered sugar
1 quart vanilla ice cream,
   softened
Chocolate Sauce

Beat egg whites with cream of tartar; gradually add ½ cup sugar and beat until stiff and glossy. In another bowl, beat egg yolks; gradually add remaining ½ cup sugar and vanilla. Fold in egg white mixture. Mix cocoa, flour, salt, and powdered sugar; fold into yolk mixture, a little at a time. Pour into 10x15 jelly-roll pan, lined with foil and greased. Bake at 325 degrees for 20-25 minutes. Let cool slightly. Turn onto towel sprinkled with sifted powdered sugar, remove foil, and roll up jelly-roll style, small end to small end, until ready to fill. To fill, unroll log roll. Spread soft vanilla ice cream onto log roll surface. Roll back up and freeze, at least 24 hours. To serve, slice log roll into 10 pieces. Spoon Chocolate Sauce over individual slices or serve in a bowl. Whipped cream and nuts can be added for a special treat.

Chocolate Sauce:
1 cup sugar
2 rounded Tablespoons
   all-purpose flour
¼ cup cocoa

1 cup water
1 Tablespoon butter
1 teaspoon vanilla

Cook sugar, flour, cocoa, and water until thickened. Add butter and vanilla. Store in refrigerator and warm before serving. This will keep for some time and is good on other desserts.

FROZEN CHOCOLATE PARFAIT
This recipe is from Executive Chef Ray Farmer, Atlanta Athletic Club

Preparation: 20 minutes   Cooking: 15 minutes
Planning: Must prepare ahead   Servings: 12
Freezing: 6 hours

**4 ounces semi-sweet
  chocolate
3 eggs
3 egg yolks
1 cup sugar
3 cups heavy cream,
  whipped**

**Optional Toppings: whipped
  cream, toasted nuts,
  chocolate sauce, sliced
  bananas, sliced
  strawberries**

Melt chocolate in double boiler. Mix eggs, egg yolks, and sugar at high speed of mixer until ribbony, about 12-15 minutes; fold in melted chocolate, being careful not to over mix. Fold in whipped cream. Mold in any container or in 8-ounce plastic cups. Freeze until ready to serve, at least 6 hours. To unmold, use warm water and edge of a dull knife. Serve with whipped cream and other optional toppings.

VANILLA CREAM CUSTARD
A creamy and nutritious old favorite

Preparation: 5 minutes   Cooking: 15 minutes
Planning: Must prepare ahead   Yield: 1 quart
Chilling: 2 hours

**3 Tablespoons cornstarch
1 quart milk, divided
3 eggs, beaten
6 Tablespoons sugar**

**2 teaspoons vanilla extract
whipped cream for garnish
cherries for garnish**

Mix cornstarch with ⅓ cup milk. Add beaten eggs and sugar to remaining milk; stir to blend. Add cornstarch mixture to milk. Cook in top of double boiler until custard coats a spoon, about 15 minutes. Stir in vanilla. Chill for at least 2 hours. Serve in individual dishes; garnish with whipped cream and a cherry.

CHOCOLATE MARQUIS
From McKinnon's Louisiane Restaurant in Atlanta

Preparation: 1 hour   Freezing: 2-3 hours
Planning: Must prepare ahead   Servings: 24

**1 pound sweet or
  semi-sweet chocolate
6 egg yolks
10 ounces evaporated milk
  or heavy cream
2 teaspoons vanilla extract**

**1 ounce cognac, optional
1½ cups unsalted butter,
  melted
whipped cream
1 Tablespoon powdered
  sugar**

Melt chocolate in double boiler. Beat together egg yolks, milk, vanilla, and cognac. Add to chocolate; mix thoroughly. Simmer, stirring occasionally, until thickened, about 15 minutes. Remove from heat; let stand 30 minutes until mixture is warm. Stir in melted butter; mix thoroughly. Pour mixture into 9x5x3 loaf pan lined with clear plastic wrap; freeze 2-3 hours. When ready to serve, unmold and cut frozen chocolate into ¼- to ⅜-inch slices. Garnish with whipped cream sweetened with powdered sugar. Remaining chocolate can be wrapped and returned to freezer. A French sauterne is delicious with this chocolate dessert.

 ## NUTTY BUDDY

Preparation: 20 minutes   Baking: 10 minutes
Planning: Must prepare ahead   Servings: 10
Freezing: 10 minutes plus 8 hours

**2¼ cups corn square cereal,
  crushed
1 Tablespoon butter
¼ cup crunchy peanut butter
¼ cup chopped pecans
1½ Tablespoons light brown
  sugar**

**1 quart vanilla ice cream,
  softened
¼ cup hot fudge topping
10 (5-ounce) paper cups
10 popsicle sticks**

Bake crushed cereal at 325 degrees for 10 minutes or until toasted. Place cups in a 12-cup muffin pan. Mix cereal, butter, peanut butter, pecans, and brown sugar. Press 1 Tablespoon of mixture in each cup, going slightly up sides. Freeze 10 minutes. Spoon ice cream ¾ way up the cup; spoon 1 Tablespoon fudge topping on the ice cream; then spoon ice cream over fudge to the top of the cup. Cover with plastic wrap and insert a popsicle stick. Freeze until firm.

CHOCOLATE SNOWBALL

This is a favorite of Elise Griffin, Peasant Restaurants, Inc. of Atlanta

Preparation: 20 minutes　　　　　　　　　Baking: 45-60 minutes
Planning: Must prepare ahead　　　　　　　　　Servings: 8-12

8 ounces German sweet chocolate, broken in pieces
2 teaspoons powdered instant coffee
1 cup plus 2 Tablespoons sugar, divided

½ cup boiling water
2 sticks butter, softened, cut into 12 pieces
4 large eggs
1 Tablespoon plus 2 teaspoons cognac, divided
1 cup heavy cream

Preheat oven to 350 degrees. Line 5-cup soufflé dish wih double thickness of foil. Place chocolate, coffee granules, and 1 cup sugar in food processor. Turn in on/off bursts 4 times to get mixture started, then let processor run until chocolate is finely chopped. With processor running, add boiling water through feed tube. Let processor run until mixture is thoroughly blended and chocolate is melted. Add butter. Let processor run until butter is blended completely with chocolate. Add eggs and 1 Tablespoon cognac; run processor 10 seconds more. Pour mixture into prepared dish. Bake 45-60 minutes until thick crust forms on top. Mixture will recede as it cools. Cool completely. At this point, dessert can be wrapped airtight and refrigerated up to 2 weeks, or frozen. To serve, peel off foil; mixture will look sticky and irregular. Whip cream until thick; add 2 Tablespoons sugar and 2 teaspoons cognac. Fill pastry bag fitted with medium-size star tip. Cover mold completely with rosettes. Chill until ready to serve; cut into small pieces.

KAHLUA SUPREME
Simple but elegant - well suited for a gourmet dinner party

Preparation: 20 minutes   Microwaving: 1 to 1½ minutes
Planning: Must prepare ahead   Chilling: 1 hour
                                              Servings: 4-6

¼ cup Kahlua   **1 cup heavy cream**
¼ cup crème de cacao   **chocolate shavings for**
12 large marshmallows   **garnish**

Combine Kahlura, crème de cacao, and marshmallows in glass mixing bowl. Microwave at HIGH (100% power) for 1½ minutes, stirring every 15 seconds until marshmallows are melted and thoroughly combined with liqueurs. Cool completely. Whip cream; continue beating while slowly pouring cooled marshmallow mixture into whipped cream. Spoon into sherbet dishes; chill thoroughly, about 1 hour. Garnish with shaved chocolate.

FROZEN LEMON DELIGHT

Preparation: 30 minutes   Freezing: 3 hours
Planning: Must prepare ahead   Servings: 4

1 egg, separated   **½ cup heavy cream, very**
5 Tablespoons sugar,   **cold**
divided   **¼ cup graham cracker**
¼ teaspoon grated lemon   **crumbs**
rind
2½ Tablespoons lemon
juice, divided

In large bowl, mix egg yolk, 3 Tablespoons sugar, lemon rind, and 1 Tablespoon lemon juice. Beat egg white until stiff; beat 2 Tablespoons sugar into stiff egg white. Fold egg white mixture into egg yolk mixture. Whip cream until fluffy; add 1½ Tablespoons lemon juice; beat until stiff. Fold whipped cream into egg mixture; pour into airtight container. Sprinkle with graham cracker crumbs. Freeze.

PINEAPPLE CREAM DELIGHT
Guaranteed to be a hit!

Preparation: 25 minutes   Chilling: 3 hours
Planning: Must prepare ahead   Servings: 12-14

4 ounces slivered almonds   **4 egg yolks**
1 (16-ounce) can pineapple   **3 cups heavy cream, divided**
slices   **2 teaspoons rum**
¼ cup unsalted butter,   **3 packages lady fingers**
softened   **¼ cup sugar**
½ cup sugar

Grind almonds in food processor or blender until very fine. Drain pine-apple well, reserving juice; chop pineapple very fine. In mixing bowl, cream butter and sugar. Add egg yolks, one at a time. Whip 1 cup heavy cream until soft mounds form; add to butter mixture. Add almonds, pineapple, and rum, combining thoroughly. Oil 10-inch springform pan. Place 1 package lady fingers in bottom; drizzle with ⅓ of reserved pineapple juice. Spread with half of almond mixture. Repeat layers, ending with lady fingers drizzled with last of juice. Refrigerate, covered, 3 hours or overnight. A few hours before serving, remove sides of springform pan. Sweeten 2 cups heavy cream with ¼ cup sugar. Whip until stiff; spread over dessert. Chill before serving.

BAKED PEARS WITH CARAMEL

Preparation: 30 minutes   Baking: 15 minutes
                                                  Servings: 12

6 whole pears, peeled and   **2 Tablespoons butter**
halved   **1 cup half and half**
¾ cups sugar

Place pears, rounded side up, in shallow baking dish. Sprinkle pears with sugar; dot with butter. Bake at 475 degrees for 15 minutes. Add half and half; bake 2 minutes more. Broil briefly, if necessary, to caramelize pears.

Note: Canned pears can be used, but must be drained well and patted dry.

351

FANCY FRUIT KABOBS
Delicious and wonderfully different!

Preparation: 30 minutes   Marinating: 20 minutes
Planning: Must prepare ahead

assorted fresh fruits, cut   **Coco-Ribe liqueur**
  into bite-size pieces   **toothpicks or wooden kabob**
  (bananas, pineapple,   **sticks**
  seedless grapes,   **whipped cream sprinkled**
  strawberries, kiwi, melon,   **lightly with cocoa**
  etc.)

Make kabobs by alternating different fruits on toothpicks or wooden kabob sticks. Pour liqueur over kabobs and refrigerate at least 20 minutes. Serve marinated kabobs in a large bowl along with a bowl of cocoa-sprinkled whipped cream for dipping.

CARDINAL STRAWBERRIES

Preparation: 10 minutes   Chilling: 2 hours
Planning: Must partially prepare ahead   Servings; 8

3 pints fresh strawberries   **2 Tablespoons kirsch**
½ cup raspberry jam   **½ cup sliced almonds,**
4 Tablespoons sugar   **toasted**
¼ cup water

Wash and hull strawberries. Combine jam, sugar, and water in saucepan; simmer 2 minutes. Add kirsch; chill. Arrange berries in large, glass bowl; cover with sauce. Sprinkle with slivered almonds.

 # COLORED POPCORN BALLS

Preparation: 20 minutes   Cooking: 5 minutes
                                                  Yield: 12 balls

3 cups miniature   **12 cups unsalted, popped**
  marshmallows   **popcorn (about ½ cup**
6 Tablespoons butter   **uncooked kernels)**
3 Tablespoons dry gelatin
  (strawberry, orange, lime,
  etc.)

Combine marshmallows and butter in saucepan. Stir over medium-low heat until melted. Remove from heat; stir in gelatin. Pour over popcorn; stir to coat. Using buttered hands, form into balls. Store in individual plastic bags.

FRESH STRAWBERRIES IN GRAND MARNIER SAUCE

Preparation: 20 minutes   Cooking: 10 minutes
Planning: Can partially prepare ahead   Chilling: 30 minutes
                                                        Servings: 6

5 egg yolks   **1 cup heavy cream**
½ cup sugar   **2 pints fresh strawberries**
½ cup Grand Marnier or
**   other orange liqueur**

Combine egg yolks and sugar; blend well. Whip over very low heat, or in top of double boiler, until sauce is thick and creamy. Remove from heat; immediately plunge bottom of pan in cold water to stop cooking process. Add Grand Marnier; blend well. Whip cream until it becomes moderately thick, but not stiff. Combine whipped cream and egg mixture; blend and chill. Meanwhile clean and stem strawberries; slice in half. Divide berries into serving dishes; spoon chilled Grand Marnier sauce over berries.

AMARETTO SAUCE

Preparation: 45 minutes   Yield: 2 cups
Planning: Can prepare ahead

1 (3-ounce) package vanilla   **1 cup heavy cream, whipped**
**   pudding**   **¼ cup amaretto**
1 cup milk

Cook pudding with milk according to package directions; cover; cool to room temperature. With wire whisk, stir in whipped cream and amaretto, adding more of either ingredient according to individual taste. Sauce can be served as a dip for pound cake or assorted fruits (bananas, strawberries, apples, and mandarin oranges).

CARAMEL APPLE FONDUE
Your guests will love this wonderful, fun treat!

Preparation: 25 minutes   Cooking: 25 minutes
Planning: Can prepare ahead   Yield: 2 cups

¼ cup butter	**6 ounces sweetened**
1 cup dark brown sugar	**condensed milk**
½ cup light corn syrup	**½ teaspoon vanilla extract**
1 Tablespoon water	**Granny Smith apple slices**

Melt butter in double boiler; add sugar, syrup, water, and condensed milk, stirring until thickened. Add vanilla. Serve in chafing dish or fondue pot with apple slices for dipping. Fondue will keep up to 6 weeks in refrigerator.

Note: Dip apple slices in lemon juice to prevent browning.

PRALINE PARFAIT SAUCE

Preparation: 30 minutes   Cooking: 20 minutes
Planning: Can prepare ahead   Yield: 2 cups

1½ cups dark corn syrup	**¼ teaspoon salt**
½ cup dark brown sugar	**1½ teaspoons vanilla extract**
4 teaspoons all-purpose	**½ teaspoon ground**
flour	**cinnamon**
2 teaspoons butter	**¾ cup pecans, chopped**
1 cup water	

In saucepan, combine corn syrup, sugar, flour, butter, water, and salt; boil 10-20 minutes, until thickened; remove from heat. Add vanilla, cinnamon, and pecans. Cool. Serve over vanilla ice cream or pound cake. Store in airtight container in refrigerator.

Health and Diet

Hydrangea

HEALTH AND DIET

APPETIZERS
Ceviche 358
Garlic Shrimp in Lemon-Wine Sauce . . .359
Snappy Vegetable Dip 358
Tuna Spread 360
BREAD
Bran Muffins 362
DESSERTS
Brandied Poached Pears 375
Chocolate Silk 374
Strawberry Pie 376
Strawberry Surprise 366
White Wine Custard 376
Yellow Squash Pecan Pie 375
Yogurt Pops .361
FISH
Elegant Snapper 364
GIFTS AND SNACKS
Homemade Granola 365
Homemade Yogurt 366
MEATS
Beef Dijon 369
Chicken and Vegetable Sauté 371
Chicken Chow Mein 370
Veal Scallopini with Marsala Wine 372

PASTA
Low-Cal Macaroni and Cheese 373
Shrimp and Feta Cheese Linquine 363
Spinach Pasta with Mushroom-Cheese
    Sauce 372
SALAD
Curried Chicken Salad 370
Mandarin Orange and Almond Salad . .357
Orange and Lemon Salad 359
Sesame-Citrus Green Salad 371
Tarragon Chicken Salad 364
Tomato and Cheese Salad 363
Tomato-Zucchini Salad 373
SANDWICH
Glenda's Garden Sandwich 369
SOUPS
Chilled Gazpacho 362
Cold Cucumber Soup with Dill 361
Curried Fish Soup 360
VEGETABLES AND SIDE DISHES
Barley Pilaf 368
Broiled Zucchini 367
Garlic Squash 368
Stuffed Potatoes 367

MANDARIN ORANGE AND ALMOND SALAD
295 calories per serving...and men love it!

Preparation: 30 minutes   Servings: 6-8
Planning: Can partially prepare ahead

1 teaspoon sugar
1 teaspoon water
½ cup slivered almonds
8 cups lettuce, torn into
   bite-size pieces (romaine,
   Bibb, iceberg, or a
   mixture)

1 cup chopped celery
2 green onions, chopped
2 (11-ounce) cans mandarin
   oranges, drained
Sesame Oil and Vinegar
   Dressing

Mix sugar and water with almonds; spread in microwave safe dish. Microwave at HIGH (100% power) for 1 minute; stir. Microwave at HIGH (100% power) another minute; stir. Continue at one minute intervals until almonds are browned. Mix lettuce, celery, and onion; add oranges and almonds. Pour Sesame Oil and Vinegar Dressing over salad; toss.

Sesame Oil and Vinegar
   Dressing:
½ teaspoon salt
⅛ teaspoon pepper
4 Tablespoons sugar or
   sugar substitute
   equivalent

4 Tablespoons white vinegar
½ cup sesame oil

Combine salt, pepper, sugar, vinegar, and oil. Microwave at MEDIUM HIGH (70% power) for 1 minute to dissolve sugar. Cool. Dressing will keep up to 2 days in refrigerator.

CEVICHE
180 calories per serving

Preparation: 30 minutes   Marinating: 3 hours
Planning: Must partially prepare ahead   Servings: 4

1 pound raw shrimp, peeled, cut into ½-inch pieces
1 pound small scallops
1 large red onion, chopped
2 medium green bell peppers, chopped
1 medium red bell pepper, chopped
¾ cup chopped fresh parsley

2 cloves garlic, crushed
⅛ teaspoon dried cilantro, optional
⅛ teaspoon dried dill weed, optional
juice of 6-10 fresh limes
4 Tablespoons olive oil
salt and pepper, to taste

Cover seafood, onion, peppers, parsley, garlic, cilantro, and dill with lime juice. Let stand 3 hours, tossing occasionally. Drain; add olive oil and salt and pepper to taste. Toss; serve on salad plate with French bread as a first course or in a bowl with a basket of French bread cubes as an appetizer.

 ## SNAPPY VEGETABLE DIP
35 calories per Tablespoon

Preparation: 10 minutes   Chilling: 30 minutes
Planning: Must prepare ahead   Yield: 1½ cups

1 cup cream style cottage cheese
1 Tablespoon chopped fresh chives
1 (3-ounce) package cream cheese, softened

2 Tablespoons cocktail sauce
1 teaspoon dry mustard
4 drops hot sauce

Combine all ingredients in container of electric blender; process until thoroughly blended. Chill for 30 minutes. Serve with assorted raw vegetables.

GARLIC SHRIMP IN LEMON-WINE SAUCE
115 calories per serving

Preparation: 30 minutes

Cooking: 15 minutes
Servings: 6

2 shallots, finely chopped
4 cloves garlic, minced
4 Tablespoons low-calorie or low-cholesterol margarine
¼ cup dry white wine
2 Tablespoons lemon juice
1 Tablespoon chopped fresh chives
1 Tablespoon chopped fresh parsley

1 pound raw shrimp, peeled and deveined
½ teaspoon paprika
¼ teaspoon dried whole thyme
3 Tablespoons whole wheat bread crumbs
3 Tablespoons grated Parmesan cheese

In skillet, sauté shallots and garlic in margarine until shallots are softened. Add wine; cook until wine is reduced and almost evaporated. Add lemon juice, chives, parsley, shrimp, paprika, and thyme. Sauté shrimp, tossing and turning, over medium-high heat until shrimp are opaque and cooked through. Do not overcook. Sprinkle with bread crumbs and cheese. Cook and toss for another minute. Serve immediately with cocktail forks or on individual plates.

ORANGE AND LEMON SALAD
110 calories per serving...a refreshing salad

Preparation: 30 minutes

Servings: 4-6

4 large oranges
1 large lemon
½ cup sliced scallions
¼ cup chopped fresh mint
⅛ teaspoon salt

⅛ teaspoon freshly ground pepper
4 Tablespoons olive oil
1 head leaf lettuce, torn into bite-size pieces, chilled

Peel and section oranges and lemon; place in salad bowl. Add scallions, mint, salt, and pepper. Pour olive oil over fruit; mix thoroughly. Add chilled lettuce; toss lightly.

TUNA SPREAD
15 calories per Tablespoon

Preparation: 10 minutes

Planning: Must prepare ahead

Chilling: 1 hour

Yield: 2 cups

1 (10½-ounce) box Tofu

2 (6½-ounce) cans water packed tuna, drained

½ teaspoon garlic powder

3 teaspoons red wine vinegar

1 package powdered ranch salad dressing mix

1 to 2 Tablespoons reduced calorie mayonnaise

3 Tablespoons lemon juice

1½ teaspoons dried dill weed

¼ teaspoon celery seed

3 Tablespoons Dijon mustard

1 teaspoon liquid smoke, optional

Combine all ingredients; mix well; refrigerate about 1 hour. Serve on melba rounds or other crackers. Tuna spread can also be used to stuff celery or served as a dip for fresh vegetables.

CURRIED FISH SOUP
175 calories per serving

Preparation: 25 minutes

Planning: Can prepare ahead

Cooking: 12 minutes

Servings: 6

16 ounces fresh or frozen fish fillets (haddock, cod, grouper, snapper)

½ cup chopped onion

½ cup chopped celery

½ cup chopped carrot

2¼ teaspoons curry powder

2 Tablespoons butter or reduced-calorie margarine

2 (14½-ounce) cans chicken broth

1½ cups milk

4 teaspoons cornstarch

Cut fish into ½-inch pieces; set aside. In 3-quart saucepan, cook onion, celery, carrot, and curry powder in butter until vegetables are tender. Stir in broth all at once. Cook and stir about 5 minutes, or until bubbly; add fish. Cook and stir for 5 minutes more, or until fish flakes easily when tested with fork. Combine milk and cornstarch; stir into fish mixture. Continue cooking until thick and bubbly.

COLD CUCUMBER SOUP WITH DILL
50 calories per serving

Preparation: 45 minutes
Planning: Must prepare ahead
Chilling: 2 hours

Cooking: 20 minutes
Yield: 2 cups

1 Tablespoon unsalted butter
½ leek (white part only), chopped
¼ medium onion, chopped
2 cucumbers, peeled, seeded, and chopped
1 quart fresh or canned chicken broth

½ cup skim milk
freshly ground white pepper, to taste
2 teaspoons chopped fresh dill
cucumber slices for garnish
fresh dill for garnish

In saucepan, melt butter over medium heat; add leek, onion, and cucumber. Sauté 2 minutes. Add broth; bring to a boil. Reduce heat; simmer, uncovered, 20 minutes. Purée soup in blender or food processor in several batches. Cool to room temperature; chill for 2 hours. At this point, soup can be refrigerated for up to 1 week. Before serving, stir in skim milk, pepper, and dill. Ladle into chilled soup bowls; garnish each serving with cucumber slice and sprinkle of fresh dill.

 ## *YOGURT POPS*

Preparation: 10 minutes
Planning: Must prepare ahead

Servings: 8

2 cups plain low-fat yogurt
1 (6-ounce) can frozen orange juice concentrate, slightly thawed
1½ Tablespoons sugar, optional

8 (4 ounces each) waxed-paper cups
16 seedless grapes, halved, optional
8 popsicle sticks

Combine yogurt, orange juice concentrate, and sugar; stir until concentrate melts and sugar is dissolved. Pour into paper cups, dividing evenly. Drop handful of grape halves into each cup. Freeze until almost firm. Insert stick in center of each cup. Freeze until firm. Wrap each in plastic wrap. To serve, peel off paper cup.

361

CHILLED GAZPACHO
43 calories per serving

Preparation: 20 minutes   Chilling: 2 hours
Planning: Must prepare ahead   Servings: 6

1 (12-ounce) can tomato juice
3 medium tomatoes, peeled, seeded, and chopped
2 Tablespoons lemon juice
½ teaspoon garlic salt
⅛ teaspoon freshly ground pepper
hot sauce, to taste
1 medium cucumber, peeled, finely chopped
1 medium green bell pepper, finely chopped
½ cup finely chopped celery
⅓ cup minced green onion
cucumber slices for garnish

Combine tomato juice, tomatoes, lemon juice, garlic salt, pepper, and hot sauce in container of electric blender; blend until smooth. Combine tomato mixture, cucumber, green bell pepper, celery, and green onion; chill thoroughly, at least 2 hours. Ladle soup into bowls; garnish with cucumber slices.

BRAN MUFFINS
144 calories each

Preparation: 20 minutes   Cooking: 15 minutes
Planning: Can prepare ahead   Servings: 12 muffins

1 cup whole-wheat flour
2½ teaspoons baking powder
½ teaspoon baking soda
½ teaspoon salt
½ teaspoon ground cinnamon
¼ cup vegetable oil
1 cup skim milk
1 egg
1¼ cups 100% bran
½ cup sugar
½ cup unsweetened applesauce

Sift flour, baking powder, baking soda, salt, and cinnamon together; set aside. In larger bowl, whisk together oil, milk, and egg; stir in bran; let sit until bran is well moistened. Add sugar and applesauce to bran mixture; stir well. Add dry ingredients to bran mixture; mix well. Use low-calorie spray or low-calorie margarine to grease muffin tins. Fill greased tins ⅔ full. Bake at 400 degrees for 15 minutes. Remove muffins from tins and cool on wire rack. These muffins freeze well after baking.

SHRIMP AND FETA CHEESE LINGUINE
A fun dish for a picnic...425 calories per serving

Preparation: 30 minutes
Planning: Must partially prepare ahead

Standing: 1 hour
Servings: 4

¾ pound medium shrimp, cooked, peeled, and deveined

1 pound feta cheese, rinsed, patted dry, and crumbled

6 green onions, finely chopped

4 teaspoons minced fresh oregano or 1¼ teaspoons dried, crumbled oregano

4 tomatoes, peeled, cored, seeded, and coarsely chopped

salt to taste (feta cheese is very salty)

⅛ teaspoon freshly ground pepper

1 pound linguine, or other pasta, freshly cooked and drained

Combine shrimp, feta cheese, onion, oregano, tomatoes, salt, and pepper in large bowl. Let mixture stand at room temperature for at least 1 hour. Add pasta to sauce; toss to coat well. Serve immediately.

Note: To serve at a picnic, refrigerate before leaving. Let sit at room temperature en route. Dish will keep up to 2 hours unrefrigerated.

TOMATO AND CHEESE SALAD
86 calories per serving

Preparation: 15 minutes
Planning: Must prepare ahead

Chilling: 1 hour
Servings: 6

36 cherry tomatoes, halved

3 ounces mozzerella cheese, cubed

12 pitted ripe olives, sliced

6 teaspoons Italian salad dressing

½ teaspoon salt

2 thin slices red onion, optional

6 large iceberg or romaine lettuce leaves

Combine all ingredients, except lettuce, in bowl; toss lightly to coat with dressing. Refrigerate, covered, 1 hour until chilled. Serve on lettuce leaves.

ELEGANT SNAPPER
445 calories per serving

Preparation: 10 minutes   Baking: 15 minutes
Broiling: 2 minutes   Servings: 4

1 cup reduced-calorie or   **¼ cup grated Parmesan**
  sugarless mayonnaise   **cheese**
2 Tablespoons lemon juice
1 Tablespoon celery seeds
1½ pounds snapper fillets,
  or any mild fish, such as
  flounder, grouper, or
  orange roughy

Mix mayonnaise, lemon juice, and celery seed in small bowl. Wash fillets; blot dry with paper towel; arrange in shallow baking dish or on cookie sheet sprayed with non-stick cooking spray. Spread mayonnaise mixture on each fillet. Bake at 350 degrees for 8-12 minutes, or until fish is almost flaky when tested with fork. Remove fish; sprinkle with Parmesan cheese. Return to oven for 5 minutes. Broil 2 minutes to brown.

TARRAGON CHICKEN SALAD
350 calories per serving

Preparation: 15 minutes   Chilling: 2 hours
Planning: Must prepare ahead   Yield: 4 cups

⅓ cup olive oil   **⅛ teaspoon sugar**
3 Tablespoons red wine   **3 cups diced cooked**
  vinegar   **chicken**
2 Tablespoons chopped   **1 cup green seedless grapes**
  fresh tarragon or 1   **1 cup red seedless grapes**
  teaspoon dried tarragon   **lettuce leaves**
¼ teaspoon salt

Combine olive oil, vinegar, tarragon, salt, and sugar. Stir in chicken and grapes; refrigerate for 2 hours. Serve on lettuce leaves.

HOMEMADE GRANOLA
150 calories per ¼ cup serving

Preparation: 20 minutes
Planning: Can prepare ahead

Baking: 12 minutes
Yield: 12 cups

1 (42-ounce) box
   quick-cooking oats
14 ounces coconut
1 (12-ounce) jar wheat germ
1½ cups chopped pecans or
   walnuts

2 cups light brown sugar
1 teaspoon salt
1 cup water
1 cup vegetable oil
1 (1-ounce) bottle vanilla
   extract

Combine oats, coconut, wheat germ, nuts, sugar, and salt in large bowl or plastic container. Combine water, oil, and vanilla. Add oil mixture to oat mixture, mixing well. Spread granola in a thin layer on 6 cookie sheets. Bake at 350 degrees for 12 minutes. Turn out into large container and let cool. Store granola in airtight container and refrigerate. Granola can be kept in refrigerator for 1 month or can be frozen. To make granola bars, let mixture cool on cookie sheets, then cut into squares.

Note: To make a spiced variation, add 1½ teaspoons ground cinnamon and 1 teaspoon ground nutmeg to oat mixture. Stir in 1-½ cups raisins after granola is baked.

HOMEMADE YOGURT
230 calories per cup

Preparation: 10 minutes   Cooking: 25 minutes
Planning: Must prepare ahead   Incubating: 3-4 hours
Chilling: 6 hours minimum   Servings: 12

4 cups 2% milk, divided   **Toppings: Use fruit or add**
⅓ cup nonfat dry milk   **flavorings or extracts to**
½ cup plain yogurt   **yogurt mixture**

In small bowl, mix 1 cup milk with dry milk until dissolved. In saucepan, mix remaining 3 cups milk with milk mixture. Stirring, slowly heat to 190-210 degrees. Remove from heat; cool to 110 degrees. Remove protein film. In small bowl, stir plain yogurt until smooth; add ⅓ cup of warm milk mixture to yogurt, blending until creamy smooth. Add to remaining milk mixture; mix well. Pour into 1½-quart, wide mouth, insulated thermos or other container. Wrap container in towels or newspaper and incubate at room temperature for 3-4 hours, or until yogurt is thick and firm. Refrigerate at least 6 hours. Before serving, several layers of paper towels can be placed on top of yogurt to absorb most of the liquid that separates from the mixture.

Note: Made with whole milk, this is a very rich yogurt; skim milk makes a lower calorie yogurt.

 # STRAWBERRY SURPRISE
95 calories per serving

Preparation: 20 minutes   Chilling: 30 minutes
Planning: Must prepare ahead   Servings: 6

2 quarts strawberries,   **8 ounces yogurt**
cleaned, sliced or halved   **¾ teaspoon almond extract**

Place strawberries in individual serving dishes or stemmed, wide-mouthed glasses. Combine yogurt and almond extract; stir to blend. Pour yogurt mixture over strawberries. Chill for 30 minutes.

STUFFED POTATOES
70 calories per serving

Preparation: 1 hour
Planning: Can prepare ahead
Broiling: 2 minutes

Baking: 10 minutes
Servings: 4

2 large potatoes
¼ cup plain yogurt
2½ Tablespoons snipped
   chives
1 Tablespoon skim milk
1 teaspoon salt

¼ teaspoon garlic powder
⅛ teaspoon pepper
2 Tablespoons grated
   Parmesan cheese
paprika for garnish

Bake potatoes at 400 degrees for 45 minutes, or until done. Slice potatoes in half lengthwise; scoop out insides leaving shells intact. Mash potatoes; add yogurt, chives, milk, salt, garlic powder, and pepper. Spoon mixture into each shell. Sprinkle tops with cheese and paprika, return to oven. Bake at 350 degrees for 10 minutes, or until heated through. Place under broiler for 1-2 minutes to lightly brown tops. Potatoes can be frozen before baking.

BROILED ZUCCHINI
95 calories per serving

Preparation: 5 minutes
Planning: Can partially prepare ahead

Broiling: 12 minutes
Servings: 3-4

3 small zucchini, cut in half
   lengthwise
1½ Tablespoons butter,
   melted
⅛ teaspoon salt

⅛ teaspoon pepper
4 Tablespoons grated
   Parmesan cheese
paprika for garnish

Place zucchini, cut side up, on lightly greased broiler pan. Brush tops of zucchini with melted butter; sprinkle with salt, pepper, cheese, and paprika. Broil 6-8 inches from heat for 12 minutes, or until tender. Zucchini can be prepared in advance and broiled just before serving.

GARLIC SQUASH
85 calories per serving

Preparation: 10 minutes

Microwaving: 6 minutes
Servings: 4

½ pound baby zucchini, cut in half diagonally or regular zucchini, cut into small chunks
½ pound baby yellow squash, cut in half diagonally or regular squash, cut into small chunks

1 small carrot, thinly sliced
1 small clove garlic, minced
2 Tablespoons butter or reduced-calorie margarine
⅓ cup water

Place paper towel on microwave safe plate. Place zucchini, yellow squash, carrot, and garlic in center of towel; dot with butter. Fold corners over vegetables. Cover with another paper towel; tuck corners under packet. Pour water evenly over packet. Microwave at HIGH (100% power) for 5-7 minutes, or until vegetables are tender crisp, rotating plate once. Let stand 2 minutes before serving.

BARLEY PILAF
180 calories per serving...and a good fiber-rich dish

Preparation: 10 minutes

Cooking: 30 minutes
Servings: 6-8

2 Tablespoons butter
1 medium onion, chopped
1 cup pearl barley
2 cups chicken broth

½ teaspoon salt
½ cup chopped cashews, optional

In medium skillet or saucepan, melt butter. Add onion and barley; sauté until lightly browned. Add chicken broth and salt. Bring to a boil; reduce heat. Simmer, covered, 25-35 minutes. Turn into soufflé dish or casserole. Add cashews before serving.

368

BEEF DIJON

210 calories per serving - almost too good to be a diet dish!

Preparation: 35 minutes

Cooking: 6 minutes

Broiling: 8-10 minutes

Servings: 4

2 teaspoons whole black pepper
1 (1-pound) beef flank steak
½ teaspoon instant beef bouillon granules
¼ cup water
1¼ cup sliced fresh mushrooms
½ cup thinly sliced green onion

1 Tablespoon all-purpose flour
1 Tablespoon Dijon mustard
⅓ cup plain yogurt
1 (10-ounce) package frozen asparagus spears, cooked and drained, or fresh asparagus

Coarsely crack pepper; sprinkle half the pepper over steak. Rub over meat, pressing into steak. Turn steak; repeat. Place on broiler pan; broil 3 inches from heat. Allow 8-10 minutes total broiling time for medium rare, turning once. Carve meat diagonally across grain into thin slices. Dissolve bouillon granules in water; add mushrooms and green onion. Cook, uncovered, over medium heat for 5 minutes, or until mushrooms are tender. Stir flour and mustard into yogurt; add to mushroom mixture. Cook, stirring, 1 minute. Arrange beef slices on serving plates. Place cooked asparagus spears over beef slices. Spoon sauce over asparagus and beef.

GLENDA'S GARDEN

So good...from The Wright Gourmet Shoppe in Dunwoody, Georgia

Preparation: 15 minutes

Servings: 3-4

mustard sauce, available at Wright Gourmet
6-8 slices pumpernickle bread or 4 pita bread pockets
alfalfa sprouts

1 cucumber, chopped
1 tomato, chopped
1 red onion, chopped
1 avocado, sliced
¾ cup grated mozzarella cheese

Spread mustard sauce on bread slices or pita. Layer rest of ingredients on bread. Slice and serve.

369

CHICKEN CHOW MEIN
220 calories per serving

Preparation: 45 minutes

Stir-frying: 10 minutes
Servings: 4-6

1 cup chicken broth
1 Tablespoon soy sauce
⅛ teaspoon freshly ground
pepper
2 Tablespoons cornstarch
6 stalks celery
2 Tablespoons vegetable or
safflower oil
1 medium onion, very thinly
sliced

6 ounces bamboo shoots
1 cup sliced fresh
mushrooms
1 cup bean sprouts
3 chicken breasts, skinned,
cooked, and cubed
3 cups cooked rice

Mix chicken broth, soy sauce, and pepper. Stir in cornstarch until dissolved. Slice celery diagonally ⅛-inch thick. Heat oil in skillet or wok over high heat. When hot, stir-fry celery and onion 1-2 minutes. Add bamboo shoots, mushrooms, bean sprouts, and chicken broth mixture. Cook, stirring, until sauce thickens. Add chicken; stir-fry until hot and sauce is clear. Serve over hot cooked rice.

CURRIED CHICKEN SALAD
295 calories per serving without cashews

Preparation: 15 minutes
Planning: Must prepare ahead

Chilling: 2 hours
Yield: 4 cups

⅓ cup low-calorie
mayonnaise
⅓ cup plain yogurt
1 Tablespoon curry powder
1 Tablespoon lemon juice
3 cups diced cooked
chicken

1¼ cups sliced celery
1½ cups cubed cantaloupe
¼ cup raisins
¼ cup cashews, optional
lettuce leaves

Combine mayonnaise, yogurt, curry, and lemon juice in bowl. Add chicken, celery, cantaloupe, and raisins; stir. Refrigerate 2 hours. Garnish with cashews, if desired. Serve on lettuce leaves.

SESAME-CITRUS GREEN SALAD
115 calories per serving

Preparation: 25 minutes
Planning: Must partially prepare ahead

Chilling: 25 minutes
Servings: 4

1 clove garlic, split
2 cups Boston lettuce
2 cups romaine lettuce
5 leaves Belgian endive
1 cup fresh grapefruit
   sections, drained
½ cup fresh orange sections,
   drained

1 Tablespoon sesame seeds,
   toasted
2 Tablespoons vegetable oil
1 Tablespoon
   tarragon-flavored vinegar

Rub garlic inside medium salad bowl; discard garlic. Combine lettuces and endive in bowl; chill for 25 minutes. Top lettuce with grapefruit and oranges; sprinkle with sesame seeds. Combine oil and vinegar; pour over salad, toss gently.

 ## CHICKEN AND VEGETABLE SAUTÉ
287 calories per serving

Preparation: 20 minutes

Cooking: 15 minutes
Servings: 4

4 teaspoons vegetable oil
1½ pounds skinned and
   boned chicken, cut into
   1-inch pieces
4 cups sliced fresh
   mushrooms
2 cups zucchini, sliced into
   ⅛-inch thick pieces

8 Tablespoons diced red bell
   pepper
½ teaspoon salt
2 teaspoons chopped fresh
   parsley
2 teaspoons lemon juice

Heat oil in skillet. Sauté chicken over medium heat until lightly browned. Do not overcook. Remove chicken and keep warm. In same skillet , combine mushrooms, zucchini, bell pepper, and salt. Cook, covered, over low heat until vegetables are just tender. Add chicken, parsley, and lemon juice to vegetables. Toss and serve.

VEAL SCALLOPINI WITH MARSALA WINE
236 calories per 3-ounce serving

Preparation: 20 minutes

Cooking: 10 minutes

Servings: 4

**1 pound veal scallopini or 4
  veal cutlets**
**1 Tablespoon vegetable or
  olive oil**
**1 Tablespoon
  reduced-calorie margarine**

¼ cup Marsala wine
2 Tablespoons lemon juice
¼ teaspoon salt
**¼ teaspoon freshly ground
  pepper**
¼ cup chopped fresh parsley

Pound scallopini between waxed paper with flat side of cleaver until thin. Heat oil and margarine in heavy skillet. Over medium heat, sauté veal until browned on both sides, no more than 5 minutes per side. Remove veal to platter. Reduce heat; add wine, lemon juice, salt, and pepper to skillet. Bring to a boil; stir to lift drippings from bottom of skillet. Return veal and juices to skillet. Cook, turning and basting with warm sauce. Serve on platter; garnish with parsley.

SPINACH PASTA WITH MUSHROOM-CHEESE SAUCE
355 calories per serving

Preparation: 30 minutes
Planning: Can partially prepare ahead

Cooking: 15 minutes

Servings: 4

1 cup low fat cottage cheese
**⅓ cup chicken stock or
  bouillon**
**1 teaspoon Worcestershire
  sauce**
1 medium onion, minced

**½ pound mushrooms, thinly
  sliced**
1 Tablespoon vegetable oil
1 clove garlic, minced
**8 ounces spinach noodles,
  cooked**

In blender or food processor, blend cottage cheese, chicken stock, and Worcestershire sauce until smooth; set aside. In large skillet over medium heat, sauté onion and mushrooms in oil until soft. Add garlic; stir 1 minute. Remove from heat; stir in cheese mixture. Warm over medium-low heat. Sauce can be made up to 2 days ahead, then reheated. Serve over hot pasta.

TOMATO-ZUCCHINI SALAD
38 calories per serving using low fat yogurt

Preparation: 30 minutes   Chilling: 2 hours
Planning: Must prepare ahead   Servings: 6-8

3 small zucchini, thinly sliced
2 scallions, minced
½ teaspoon salt
⅔ cup (6 ounces) custard-style, low-fat plain or whole milk yogurt
1 very small clove garlic, minced

2 Tablespoons chopped fresh parsley
⅛-¼ teaspoons ground cumin
freshly ground pepper, to taste
2 cups (1 pint) cherry tomatoes, quartered

Toss zucchini, scallions, and salt in medium bowl until mixed. Let sit for 10 minutes; drain off any liquid. Meanwhile, place yogurt, garlic, parsley, and cumin in small bowl; mix until smooth. Season with salt and pepper to taste. Add cherry tomatoes and yogurt dressing to zucchini; toss again to combine. Chill for 2 hours. If needed, drain again before serving.

LOW-CAL MACARONI AND CHEESE
375 calories per serving

Preparation: 20 minutes   Baking: 30 minutes
Planning: Can partially prepare ahead   Servings: 4

2 cups uncooked macaroni
1⅓ cups low fat cottage cheese
½ cup grated Cheddar cheese

3 Tablespoons grated Parmesan cheese

Cook macaroni according to package directions; drain. Combine cottage cheese, Cheddar cheese, and Parmesan cheese. Add macaroni to cheese mixture. Turn into baking dish sprayed with non-stick vegetable spray. At this point, recipe can be refrigerated for up to 2 days and returned to room temperature before baking. Bake at 375 degrees for 30 minutes.

CHOCOLATE SILK
Better than mousse and only 160 calories per serving!

Preparation: 30 minutes   Chilling: 5 hours
Planning: Must prepare ahead   Servings: 4

6 Tablespoons sugar
¼ cup unsweetened cocoa,
  sifted
2 Tablespoons cornstarch,
  sifted
1 teaspoon unflavored
  gelatin
1 cup half and half
1 cup evaporated skim milk

⅔ cup milk
3 large egg yolks, lightly
  beaten
1½ teaspoons vanilla extract
¼ cup heavy cream,
  whipped, optional
1 Tablespoon chopped
  pistachio nuts, optional

In large heavy saucepan, combine sugar, cocoa, cornstarch, and gelatin; press out all lumps. Add half and half, evaporated skim milk, and whole milk; whisk vigorously to blend. Stirring with wooden spoon, cook over low heat until mixture just boils and is thickened and smooth, about 10 minutes. Blend a little of hot mixture into beaten egg yolks; stir warmed egg yolks back into saucepan. Cook over low heat 3-4 minutes. Do not let boil. Remove from heat; stir in vanilla. Cool 10 minutes, stirring frequently. Ladle mixture into 6 (4-ounce) pot de creme cups or remekins and let cool completely. Cover with plastic wrap; refrigerate at least 5 hours or overnight. Serve as is, or top with a dollop of whipped cream and chopped pistachio nuts.

YELLOW SQUASH PECAN PIE
395 calories per serving

Preparation: 45 minutes

Baking: 55 minutes
Servings: 6-8

2 eggs, slightly beaten
6-8 medium yellow squash, cubed
⅔ cup sugar
½ teaspoon salt
1 teaspoon ground cinnamon

½ teaspoon ground ginger
¼ teaspoon ground cloves
1 cup chopped pecans
1⅔ cup half and half or evaporated milk
1 (9-inch) pie shell, unbaked

Bake squash at 350 degrees for 30 minutes. Purée squash in blender or food processor. Blend 2 cups squash with eggs. Add sugar, salt, cinnamon, ginger, cloves, and nuts; mix well. Blend in half and half. Pour into pie shell. Bake at 400 degrees for 45-55 minutes, or until center is set. Cool before serving.

 ## *BRANDIED POACHED PEARS*
140 calories per serving

Preparation: 20 minutes
Planning: Must prepare ahead

Chilling: 3 hours
Servings: 4

4 fresh pears
lemon juice for brushing pears
½ cup water
2 Tablespoons sugar

1 Tablespoon lemon juice
1 Tablespoon peach brandy
5 teaspoons sliced almonds, toasted

Peel, core, and halve pears; brush with lemon juice. In 8-inch skillet, combine water and sugar. Bring to a boil over high heat. Add lemon juice and pear halves. Reduce heat; cook, covered, for 8-10 minutes, or until pears are tender. Remove from heat; add brandy. Cover; chill pears in poaching liquid. For each serving, place 2 pear halves standing upright and slightly overlapping in a stemmed glass. Pour 2 Table-spoons poaching liquid over each serving. Sprinkle with toasted almonds.

STRAWBERRY PIE
105 calories per serving, without topping

Preparation: 35 minutes   Chilling: 2-3 hours
Planning: Must prepare ahead   Servings: 8

16 graham cracker squares, crumbled
3 Tablespoons low-calorie margarine, melted
2 packets artificial sweetener (not Equal)
1½ cups water

1 (3-ounce) package strawberry gelatin with Nutrasweet
6 teaspoons cornstarch
4 cups sliced fresh strawberries
whipped topping, optional

Combine graham crackers, margarine, and sweetener. Spray 8- or 9-inch pie pan with non-stick vegetable spray. Press crust in bottom and up sides of pan. Bake at 350 degrees for 5 minutes. Put water in 2-quart saucepan. Dissolve gelatin and cornstarch over medium heat; do not boil. Continue stirring over heat until mixture thickens slightly, about 10 minutes. Cool. Place strawberries in bowl. Add cooled gelatin mixture; stir to combine. Pour into crust; chill until set. Top with whipped topping, if desired.

WHITE WINE CUSTARD
135 calories per serving

Preparation: 15 minutes   Baking: 40 minutes
         Servings: 6

4 eggs
⅓ cup sugar
⅛ teaspoon salt

2 cups skim milk, scalded
1 teaspoon vanilla extract
⅓ cup sweet white wine

Whip eggs slightly; add sugar and salt. Gradually pour in scalded milk, stirring constantly. Add vanilla and wine. Pour into individual custard cups. Set in larger dish; pour hot water around cups. Bake at 350 degrees about 40 minutes, or until knife inserted in center comes out clean. Do not overcook.

Peachtree Potpourri

Wild Rose

PEACHTREE POTPOURRI

Almond Roca 379
Bird Feeder Candles 384
Carmel Corn Jacks 382
Halloween Face Paint 384
Herb Rice Blend 381
Instant Non-Toxic Paste 384
Modeling Clay 383
No Cook Play Dough 383

Patriotic Pastries 380
Peachtree Potpourri 379
Peanut Play Dough 380
Popcorn Balls 382
Saltine Treats 380
Silly Putty 383
Vegetable Rice 381

 ### *PEACHTREE POTPOURRI*

Preparation: 15 minutes   Storage: 6 weeks
Planning: Must prepare ahead   Yield: 2 quarts

1 quart dried rose petals
1 quart other dried herbs
  and flowers (lilacs,
  honeysuckle, carnations,
  violets, geraniums,
  lavender, mint, marjoram,
  lemon thyme, rosemary)
1 Tablespoon orris root
1 teaspoon whole allspice

1 teaspoon whole cloves
1 teaspoon broken bay
  leaves
2 teaspoons dried, chopped
  lemon and orange rind
1-2 drops each of one or
  more fragrant oils
  (available at pharmacies)

Combine all ingredients. Store in sealed container in a dark place for 6 weeks. Divide among smaller containers for gift giving.

Note: Many variations are possible as long as the orris root is used in the same proportion to other ingredients. Orris root is the preserving ingredient and the secret to success.

 ### *ALMOND ROCA*

Preparation: 15 minutes   Cooking: 45 minutes
Planning: Must prepare ahead   Yield: 30-40 pieces

1 (½-pound) milk chocolate
  bar, shredded
½ pound almonds, sliced

1 pound lightly salted butter
2 cups sugar

Line cookie sheet with foil. Spread half of chocolate on sheet. Layer half of almonds over chocolate. Melt butter in skillet, stirring constantly. Gradually stir in sugar. Cook over medium heat until mixture reaches hard crack stage or 320 degrees. Working fast, pour over almonds and chocolate in pan. Top with remaining chocolate and almonds. When completely cool, break into pieces. Store at room temperature; do not refrigerate or freeze.

PEANUT PLAY DOUGH
Children can eat what they make!

Preparation: 15 minutes   Yield: 2 pounds

1 (18-ounce) jar peanut   cocoa, optional
** butter**   **raisins, chocolate chips,**
6 Tablespoons honey   ** nuts, etc. for decoration,**
non-fat dry milk   ** optional**

Mix peanut butter and honey. Gradually add dry milk and cocoa, mixing with hands, until it reaches consistency of commercial play dough. Store in airtight container until ready to use. Children can decorate their creations with raisins, chocolate chips, nuts, etc.

SALTINE TREATS

Preparation: 5 minutes   Baking: 3 minutes
                                               Servings: 4

4 saltine crackers   **butterscotch or chocolate**
20 miniature marshmallows   ** chips, optional**
peanut butter

Spread peanut butter on one side of each saltine; place 5 marsh-mallows on top. Place saltines on cookie sheet under broiler for 3-5 minutes.

Note: For a sweeter treat, use chips on top of peanut butter.

PATRIOTIC PASTRIES
Fun and delicious!

Preparation: 5 minutes

Sliced "day-old" bread   red jello
soft butter

Cut bread with star-shaped cookie cutter; spread with margarine. Sprinkle with red jello; toast.

 ## VEGETABLE RICE

Preparation: 10 minutes
Planning: Can prepare ahead

Yield: 2 gift packages
(4-5 servings in each)

4 packets instant vegetable broth or 4 vegetable bouillon cubes
1 teaspoon salt
2 teaspoons celery seeds
2 teaspoons onion flakes

2 teaspoons green pepper flakes
2 teaspoons sweet pepper flakes
2 cups uncooked long-grain rice

Combine all ingredients. Divide into 2 plastic bags or containers, putting about 1¼ cups rice mix in each. To cook, combine 1 package rice mix in saucepan with 2 cups water and 1 tablespoon margarine. Bring to a boil, cover tightly and cook over low heat until liquid is absorbed, about 25 minutes.

Note: When using as a gift, attach card with cooking instructions.

 ## HERB RICE BLEND

Preparation: 10 minutes
Planning: Can prepare ahead

Yield: 1 gift package
(4 servings)

1 cup uncooked long-grain rice
2 beef bouillon cubes, crushed
½ teaspoon salt
½ teaspoon dried whole rosemary

½ teaspoon dried whole marjoram
½ teaspoon dried whole thyme
1 teaspoon dried green onion flakes

Mix all ingredients. Put into plastic bag or container. To cook, combine rice mixture, 2 cups cold water, and 1 tablespoon butter in heavy saucepan. Bring to a boil, reduce heat to simmer. Cover tightly and simmer 12-14 minutes or until liquid is absorbed.

Note: When using as a gift, attach card with cooking instructions.

381

CARAMEL CORN JACKS

Preparation: 30 minutes
Planning: Can prepare ahead

Baking: 30 minutes
Yield: 2½ quarts

½ cup butter
1 cup packed, light brown
sugar
¼ cup light corn syrup
½ teaspoon salt
½ teaspoon vanilla extract

¼ teaspoon baking soda
3 quarts unsalted, popped
popcorn (about ½ cup
uncooked kernels)
1 cup salted peanuts,
optional

In a 1½-quart saucepan, combine butter, brown sugar, corn syrup, and salt. Bring mixture to a boil, stirring constantly. Boil over medium heat without stirring for 5 minutes. Remove from heat; stir in vanilla and baking soda. In large bowl, gradually pour hot syrup over popcorn, mixing well to coat the corn. Turn popcorn into greased 17x12x2-inch pan. Bake, uncovered, at 300 degrees for 30 minutes, stirring the popcorn after 15 minutes. Remove from oven; cool completely in pan. Loosen popcorn with spatula; break into pieces. Stir in peanuts. Store in a tightly covered container.

POPCORN BALLS
Fun activity for a rainy day!

Preparation: 10 minutes

Cooking: 20 minutes
Servings: 12

1 cup sugar
⅓ cup light corn syrup
⅓ cup water
¼ cup butter
½ teaspoon salt

1 teaspoon vinegar
1 teaspoon vanilla extract
3 quarts unsalted, popped
corn (about ½ cup
uncooked kernels)

In medium saucepan, combine sugar, syrup, water, butter, salt, and vinegar. Cook, stirring until sugar is dissolved. Continue cooking, without stirring, until syrup reaches 270 degrees or forms a brittle ball when dropped in cold water. Add vanilla. Pour syrup over popped corn, stirring until all kernels are covered. Grease hands and shape into balls. Do not double recipe. It is best to make several small batches.

SILLY PUTTY
A fun project for a rainy day!

Preparation: 10 minutes   Yield: ½ cup
Planning: Must prepare ahead

½ cup white glue   **4 Tablespoons liquid starch**

Mix glue and starch. Allow to dry slightly until workable. Use on smooth, dry surface. Store in an airtight container.

NO-COOK PLAY DOUGH

Preparation: 20 minutes   Yield: 1½ cups
Planning: Can prepare ahead

1 cup salt   **food coloring, optional**
1 cup all-purpose flour   **water**
1 Tablespoon vegetable oil

Mix salt and flour; add oil. Add food coloring to water, if desired. Slowly add water until desired consistency is reached. Store in an airtight container.

Note: An adult will have to knead dough at first.

MODELING CLAY

Preparation: 20 minutes   Yield: 2 cups
Planning: Can prepare ahead

1 pound baking soda   **1¼ cups water**
1 cup cornstarch   **food coloring, optional**

Mix soda and cornstarch in medium saucepan. Add water and food coloring, if desired. Cook over low heat, stirring constantly, until mixture resembles mashed potatoes. Remove from heat; cover with damp cloth. When clay is cool enough to handle, it is ready to use. Store clay in a sealed, plastic bag. Clay may be dried and painted with tempera paint.

INSTANT NON-TOXIC PASTE

Preparation: 5 minutes   Cooking: 5 minutes
Planning: Can prepare ahead   Yield: 2 cups

½ cup all-purpose flour   oil of peppermint
2 cups cold water

Mix together flour and cold water until creamy. Boil over low heat for 5 minutes, stirring constantly. Cool. Add a few drops oil of peppermint to prevent spoiling. Thin down if necessary with a few drops of cool water. Store covered in refrigerator.

HALLOWEEN FACE PAINT
Fun for Halloween or rainy-day dress up!

Preparation: 10 minutes   Yield: 2 teaspoons

1 teaspoon cornstarch   ½ teaspoon cold cream
½ teaspoon water   2 drops food coloring

In small mixing bowl, combine all ingredients; mix well.

BIRD FEEDER CANDLES
Place outside for our bird friends to enjoy!

Preparation: 15 minutes   Baking: 3 hours
                      Yield: 5-10 candles

5 pounds suet   red cherries
wild bird seed   small milk cartons or paper
sunflower seeds   cups
crunchy peanut butter   potpie pans

Place suet in covered roaster; bake at 300 degrees for 3 hours, or until all fat is rendered. Strain; measure, reserving 1 cup. Combine bird seed with sunflower seeds. Mix 2 cups warm fat to 1 cup seeds. Pour into 8-ounce cartons; refrigerate. When ready to use, melt reserved fat. Peel paper cartons off seed mixture. Set each "candle" into a potpie pan; pour melted fat around each candle to secure. Frost top with peanut butter and add a cherry for the flame.

ACKNOWLEDGMENTS

The members of the PEACHTREE BOUQUET Committee wish to express their appreciation to the following members and friends of the Junior League of DeKalb County, Inc. who contributed recipes to this cookbook.

Patricia Henson Adams
Molly London Ahlquist
Laura Akin
Sandy Allen
Nancy Emery Anderson
Karen Modisteff Anderson
Susan McCeney Anderson
Betty Mitchell Anderson
Jeanine Craig Andrews
Joan Smith Ansley
Martha Armstrong
Deborah Dendy Ashendorf
Ellen Wogon Austin
Barrie Clark Aycock
Cheryl Williams Baxter
LoraLee Abbazia Beard
Beverly Hall Beaudrot
Libby Conner Beckham
Patty Shotton Begnaud
Melinda Sumner Belote
Virginia Shannon Binion
Sandy Southwell Bishop
Wendy Spatz Bishop
Anne Kabel Blount
Judith Alexander Bobo
Wanda Boylston
Marcia Taylor Brent
Tricia Hulsey Bridges
Barbara Brockman
Carolyn Bennett Broucek
Jane Black Buckler
Nancy Parham Buckler
Catherine Chalk Builder
Nancy Stevens Burriss
Carol Preller Bush
Kathy Hastings Cable
Lynn Callahan Goodroe
Joye Baldwin Callaway
Betty Jeanne Ellison Candler
Karna Thomas Candler
Judy Rutland Carlsen
Victoria Willis Carpenter
Barbara Carson
Christina Carson
Virginia McSwain Carson
Katherine Triplitt Carter
Marge Davis Carter

Lyn Kilgo Cates
Mary Cawthon
Elaine Suess Chambers
Nancy Hooks Chambers
Missy Arnold Chapman
Julie Childs
Jeanne Chimelewski
Penn Weitnauer Clark
Jo Ann Fox Clark
Cissy Smith Cleveland
Charon Hodgens Clymer
Pam Thomas Colbenson
Jeannie Moore Conner
Janet McKnight Cook
Nancy Waring Corbitt
Caroline Moore Cribbs
Shelley Cross
Kate Livingston Cucchi
Joy Ballew Culbreth
Donna Fort Davidson
Nancy Palmer DeBaun
Sally Gay Dickey
Lynn Diversi
Whitney Dodd
Marlene Odom Duke
Cheryl Cooper Dunbar
Jeannie Nettles Dyson
Jane Fackler Edmonds
Deborah Patterson Edmonston
Beth McDaniel Edwards
Jan McCorkle Espy
Barbara Chandler Evans
Jennifer Slocumb Ewing
Becky Anderson Fern
Jan Fleischman
Liz Copelan Ford
Gayle Parks Forehand
Toni Fowler
Susan Fox
Elaine Byars Franklin
Donna Bastian Fullilove
Claire Perdue Furth
Janet Dorsett Gallagher
Meg Gates
June Gay
Eugenia Johnson Giles
Katherine Schob Glenn

Joanne West Goldman
Linda Vaughn Goldsmith
Susan Horton Gray
Rita Green
Shirley Markuson Guhl
Patricia Rives Haase
Marty Halyburton
Michele Hanft
Motsy Gregory Hanna
Jan Journey Harben
Betsy Aitken Harrell
Mary Ezell Harrington
Jane Fleming Harris
Jill Cofer Harris
Lynda Gardner Harris
Ellen Cottraux Head
Louise Hebbeler
Vivki Keck Hedrick
Laura Whelchel Henderson
Linda Dennon Herren
Nancy James Hilley
Cary Boyd Hobbs
Diane Bell Hobbs
Doug Holder
Joanne Kennamer Hood
Donna Hooker
Susan Snow Hope
Lynn Ely Hornsby
Sally Evans Hovis
Jane McMullan Howe
Darlene Huggins
Pam Parsons Hughes
Linda Campbell Hull
Pam Foell Hunt
Valerie Hunt
Becky Ericsson Hunter
Marianne Hunter
Laura Tomlinson Jackson
Lyn Young Jackson
Edna Kronebitter Jennings
Sandy Floyd Jernigan
Allison Thomas Johnson
Ginny Waters Johnston
Cindy Tolleson Jollay
Kathryn Tolleson Jollay
Mimi Thomas Kee
Paulette Childers Keith
Angel Diogo Keller
Chris Liles Kendrick
Lynn Cunningham Kessler
Nancy Bass Kirby
Julie Edwards Kitchen
Linda Holley Kjorlaug
Kathy Gunville Kline

Beryl Kramer
Mary Ellen Kubis
Cecilia Henry Kurland
Ellen Lappa
Carolyn Gatling Lassiter
Marianne Boylston Lassiter
Maggie Douglas Lawson
Nancy Whitten Leathers
Sandy Smith Lee
Becky Lewis Lester
Jill Hastings Letts
Alice Liles
Donna Raynor Livingston
Lynne Pickens Lock
Nancy Burns Luckey
Nancy Layton Lundstrom
Sally Daniel Maloof
Elizabeth Marsh
Mary McKee Martin
Joan Wynne Mathews
Anne McCoun
Barbara Smith McCoy
Ann Tee McCrory
Susan Rutland McCullar
Genet McIntosh
Sally Moffett McKenna
Betsi Britten McLure
Libby McMahan
Altine McQueen
Kathleen McWalters
Margaret McWalters
Rae Dennir McWhirter
Leslie Hughes Meiere
May Michalko
Carol Spruill Miller
Marty Kelley Mitchell
Flip Sthreshley Moehlman
Linda Gregory Moffett
Sally Morris
Susan Myers
Judith Ann Stish Nathan
Denise Fast Neely
Peggy New
Becky Reynolds Nicholson
Marsha Stevens O'Connor
Gay O'Neal
Johnnie Milam Oliver
Susan Dangler Ozburn
Lisa Pardue
Lissy Makay Parker
Ginny Williams Parks
Margaret Partridge
Sallie Garrison Paschal

Kathy Patterson
Sara Munch Paulk
Sally Jenkins Peavy
Nancy Reese Pecora
Corrine Peek
Mallory Divine Perdue
Dottie Lowery Phillips
Kimberly Bacon Pickens
Patricia Vandiver Powell
Karla Chamness Preston
Cindy Gregory Raines
Verna Mobley Rauschenberg
Nancy Meyers Ray
Nikki Kneale Reifeis
Dianne Ramey Reynolds
Robin Rhodes
Marsha Allen Richardson
Angie Nations Richardson
Betsy Painter Roberts
Carol Newsome Roberts
Susan Paul Roche
Nancy Levering Rozzelle
Hazel Risley Rutland
Lynn Sarpy
Evon Scales
Irene Scales
Margaret McWalters Scales
Ginn Spears Schmeelk
Nancy Kelly Schoeler
Barbara Rick Schuyler
Fran Lamby Scott
Lacey Scruggs
Carolyn Seidel
Cara Shaw
John Shaw
Sally McArthur Shigley
Mary Alice Shinall
Karen Vaughn Shinall
Lois Deutschberger Shingler
Marylee Glover Sleeth

Pat O'Callaghan Smith
Sallie Biggs Smith
Linda Mozley Smith
Ellen Phillips Smith
Dottie Haisten Spencer
Vicky Spruill
Vicki Kudlacz Stafford
Mary Leith Stanfield
Kay Wilson Stewart
Frances Carringer Stinson
Lisa Kirk Stovall
Bobbi Stuart
Anne Diveley Sumpter
Sally Beggs Thomas
Carolyn Thompson
Jane Huie Thrash
Claire Johnson Tolleson
Kathy Gillespie Tomajko
Kathy Spence Tribble
Pattie Jackson Tuggle
Hilde Beskin Van Houten
Gail Potter Vrana
June Lanier Wagner
Joanne Guardiani Warlick
Rita Warren
Ellen Warthen
Ginny Kellum Watt
Mary Jo Graham Wells
Linda Simpson Wells
Susan Harris West
Janis Whitehead
Ellen McHalffey Widener
Jeanne Keokenberg Williams
Barbara Scanlon Williams
Judy Kapp Winder
Deborah Long Wingate
Anne Workman
Kathy Mueller Wright
Judy Yates
Mary Carson Young

We want to express our special appreciation to Allen Lindley with Happy Herman's and Verney E. Bentley, III for their assistance in suggesting wines to complement the entrees.

The members of the PEACHTREE BOUQUET Committee also wish to express their appreciation to the following Special Contributors who submitted recipes that helped to make this a unique and outstanding cookbook.

Hank Aaron
The Abbey Restaurant
Affairs to Remember Caterers
Anthonys Restaurant
The Atlanta Athletic Club-
   Executive Chef Ray Farmer
Jean Benton, Benton and
   Associates, Inc. Caterers
Bone's Steak and Seafood
   restaurant
Bosco's Ristorante Italiano
Olive Ann Burns
Skip Caray
G. Clisby Clarke
Bill Curry
Barbara and Vince Dooley
Nathalie Dupree
East 48th Street Market
The Georgian Club - Chef Mohammad
   Bakhtiari
Joyce Gould, Caterer
Elise Griffin, Peasant
   Restaurants, Inc.
Bob Harrell, Bob's Barbeque
Hedgerose Heights Inn

Herren's restaurant
Houlihan's Restaurant
McKinnon's Louisiane Restaurant
The Mansion restaurant
Manuel's Tavern - Bessie
   Johnson
Marra's Seafood Grill
R. L. Mathis Dairy
Lt. Governor Zell Miller
Wayland Moore
Mortons of Chicago
Pano's and Paul's Restaurant
Pearl's Fish Cafe
Peasant Uptown restaurant
Pittypat's Porch
Proof of the Pudding Caterers
Homer Rice
Willard Scott
Kathy Grizzard Smook
Mrs. Pat Swindall
Trotters Restaurant
Ted Turner
Jeff Van Note
The Wright Gourmet Shoppe

-A-

ALMOND
and Mandarin Orange
Salad, 357
and Mushrooms with Wild
Rice, 131
Biscuit Tortoni, 341
Curried Fruit, 290
Honey Dressing, 92
Orange Chicken, 217
Peach-Glazed Cake, 303
Red Snapper Almondine,
161
Roca, 379
Torte, 313
AMARETTO
Chocolate Bars, 333
Freeze, 32
Mousse, 338
Pie, 314
Sauce, 353
Amberjack, Grilled, 141
Angel Strawberry Cake, 309
Antipasto, Holiday, 12
APPETIZERS
Cold
Candied Citrus Pecans,
16
Caviar Pie, 9
Cheese Straws, 17
Cream Cheese and
Bacon Tea Sandwiches,
10
Elegant and Easy Brie, 28
Garlic Olives, 24
Glazed Bacon with
Walnuts, 11
Glazed Nuts, 15
Hidden Treasure, 26
Holiday Antipasto, 12
Marinated Vegetables, 31
Pickled Shrimp, 29
Salmon Rolls, 28
Shrimp Pizza, 30
Dips
Almond-Honey Dressing,
92
Cheesy Dip Surprise, 15
Chili Relleno, 23
Clam, 19
Divine, 22
Ground Beef, 23
Honey, 221
Honey-Mustard
Dressing, 93
Hot and Sweet
Mustard, 230
Hot Nacho, 22
Miss Daisey's Crabmeat,
20
Onion Rye, 21
Rebecca Sauce, 27
Snappy Vegetable, 358
Tarama Salata, 31

Hot
Appetizer Gougère, 13
Blend of the Bayou
Seafood Casserole, 253
Bone's Beer-Battered
Shrimp, 153
Crab Grass, 20
Cranberry Meatballs, 9
Easy Fried Cheese, 11
Egg Rolls, 24
Far East Shrimp Balls, 30
Garlic Shrimp in Lemon-
Wine Sauce, 359
Hawaiian Chicken
Wings, 17
Hot Crabmeat Canapés,
19
Italian Cheese Rolls, 14
Mandarin Ham Rolls,
185
Mushroom Squares, 25
Parmesan Onion
Canapés, 21
Pearls' Fried Crabmeat
Puffs, 144
Phyllo Pastries, 18
Sausage Party Pizzas, 26
Sausage Pinwheels, 22
Sesame Chicken with
Honey Dip, 220
Shrimp Manallé, 156
Swiss Cheese Soufflé,
133
Spreads and Molds
Asparagus-Lobster
Cocktail Mousse, 10
Bacon Ball, 11
Ceviche, 358
Delicious Liver Pâté, 25
Garlic Cheese Ball, 16
Holiday Cheese Ball, 13
Hot Crab Spread, 20
Olive and Cream Cheese
Ball, 14
Oyster Log, 28
Salmon Mousse, 27
Shrimp Mousse, 29
Spicy Cheese Ball, 14
Strawberry Cheese Ball,
16
Tuna Spread, 360
APPLE(S)
and Cornflakes, My
Mother's, 289
Caramel Fondue, 354
Favorite Chops in
Casserole, 250
Molded Waldorf Salad, 89
Noodle Pudding with Fruit,
339
Orange-Anise Spice Bags,
38
Pecan Upside-Down Pie,
316

Red Candy, 339
Spiced Bourbon Punch,
32
Stuffed, 88
APRICOT(S)
and Prune Coffeecake,
116
Hot Casserole, 290
Wafer Dessert, 341
ARTICHOKE(S)
and Chicken Rice Salad,
63
and Ham Casserole, 248
and Ripe Olive Salad, 76
and Tuna, 256
Chicken Casserole, 215
Poulet De Susie, 228
Salmon in Foil, 148
Scalloped, 267
Soup, 51
with Shrimp, 252
ASPARAGUS
Beef Salad with Broccoli
and, 64
Casserole, 259
Fettuccini with, 124
Lobster Cocktail Mousse,
10
Marinated, 267
Mornay, 268
Spring Vegetable Sauté
276
AVOCADO
Avocado Soup, Chilled
Creamy, 60
Avocado Crab, 142
Green and Gold Salad, 72
-B-
BACON
Ball, 11
Cream Cheese Tea
Sandwiches, 10
Glazed with Walnuts, 11
Baked Chicken Breasts, 201
Baked Chicken, Tangy, 214
Baked Chicken, Soy, 227
Baked Fish, Delicious, 160
Baked Ham Mornay, 249
Baked Rice, 262
Baked Stuffed Pumpkin, 291
Baked Stuffed Snapper, 162
Baked Swiss Chicken, 201
BANANA(S)
Doris' Punch, 33
Pineapple-Nut Cake, 301
Split Cake, 296
BARBECUE
Bar-B-Que Spareribs and
Meatballs, 192
Beef Stuffed Pork Roast,
193
Chicken, Commander
Burn's, 208
Mimi's Bar-B-Que, 191

Barbecued Lima Beans, 278
Barley Pilaf, 368
Basic Steps to Making Bread, 97
Bavarian Cream, Rosebud's, 342
BEAN(S)
 Green Beans (See Separate Listing)
 Hearty Sausage Soup, 43
 Hot Dish, 259
BEEF
 Beer Steak Stroganoff, 180
 Bourguignon, 237
 Brunswick Stew, 168
 Chicken Kabobs, 171
 Chipped Casserole, 238
 Corned and Cabbage, Irish Style, 183
 Dijon, 369
 Flank Steak with Fresh Basil-Tomato Sauce, 176
 Ginger Grilled London Broil, 177
 Manuel's Greek Salad, 72
 Marinade for London Broil, 177
 Marinated Roast Sandwiches, 178
 Munich "Sauerbraten", 179
 Oriental Flank Steak with Rice, 174
 Ragout, 240
 Roast for Sandwiches, 178
 Roast Tenderloin, 182
 Salad with Broccoli and Asparagus, 64
 Scotched Filet Mignon with Fresh Mushroom Sauce, 174
 Steak in a Bag, 180
 Steak Tournedos, 175
 Stuffed Pork Roast, 193
 Sukiyaki, 173
 Whiskey-Glazed Corned, 184
BEEF, GROUND
 Baked Rotelle with, 125
 Bar-B-Que Spareribs and Meatballs, 192
 Bob's Brunswick Stew, 167
 Cabbage Casserole, 240
 Chili Seasoning, 198
 Cranberry Meatballs, 9
 Dip, 23
 Hot Nacho Dip, 22
 Enchilada Cheese Towers, 170
 Mexican Salad, 66
 Noodle Bake, 239
 One Meal Dish, 241
 Oriental Spaghetti, 238

Picadillo, 181
Po Boy Fillets, 172
Polynesian Goulash, 239
Salami, 172
Vegetable Medley Soup, 59
Zucchini Bake, 242
Beer Batter, 144
Beer Beef Steak Stroganoff, 180
BEVERAGES
 Amaretto Freeze, 32
 French Hot Chocolate, 34
 Ginger's Egg Nog, 36
 Hot Buttered Rum Mix, 32
 Hot Mocha Mix, 35
 Hot Spiced Wine, 40
 It's Almost Bailey's, 40
 Kahlua Velvet Frosty, 36
 Microwave Cappuccino, 34
 Orange-Anise Spice Bags, 38
 Punch
  Champagne, 35
  Doris' Banana, 33
  Pineapple-Champagne, 34
  Spiced Bourbon-Apple, 32
  Tequila-Champagne, 38
 Sherry Sour, 39
 Sneaky Petes, 37
 Tea
  Decaffinated Spiced Mix, 33
  Hot Florida, 39
  Long Island Iced, 39
  Perculator Hot Fruit, 37
  Spiced Iced, 38
  White Sangria, 36
Bird Feeder Candles, 384
BISCUITS
 Biscuits, 223
 Cheese, 111
 Quick, 111
 Tortoni, 341
Black Bottom Pie, 315
Blue Cheese Soufflé, 133
Braised Pork Tenderloin, 190
BRAN
 Muffins, 362
 Pineapple Muffins, 109
 Six Week Muffins, 110
Brandied Poached Pears, 375
Brazilian Rice, 129
BREADS
 Basic Steps to Making, 97
 Biscuits (See Separate Listing)
 Cheese Bread Sticks, 100
 Cheese Blintzes, 134
 Coffeecake and Sweet Breads

Apricot and Prune, 116
 Bishop's, 107
 Pluck It Cake, 112
 Sweet Rolls From Herren's, 115
 Corn Sticks, 110
 Dandy-Quicky Doughnuts, 102
 Dumplings and Chicken, 218
 Fabulous French Toast, 117
 Five Minute Microwave Croutons, 117
 Herb Butter, 118
 Homemade Croutons, 50
 Muffins (See Separate Listing)
 Patriotic Pastries, 380
 Quick
  Cheese French, 99
  Chocolate Zucchini, 100
  Cranberry Orange Tea, 101
  Ham and Cheese, 101
  Herb Tomato, 103
  Irish Raisin, 104
  Poppy Seed, 105
  Strawberry, 106
 Rolls (See Separate Listing)
 Soft Pretzels, 118
 Yeast
  Brown, 99
  Cheese Sticks, 100
  Herb Cheese, 98
  Proscuitto and Onion, 106
  Spinach, 104
  The Market's Crusty, 102
  White Batter, 103
BROCCOLI
 Cheese Soup Supreme, 44
 Chowder, 45
 Company Ham Casserole, 250
 Fresh Vegetable Marinade, 83
 Mold, 74
 Oriental Sesame Chicken Dinner, 226
 Puff, 271
 Special, 271
 Stuffed Tomatoes, 269
 Stuffed Vidalia Onions, 270
 Swiss Chicken, 219
 Tree Top Marinade, 82
Broiled Zucchini, 367
BROWNIE(S)
 Chocolate Amaretto Bars, 333
 Coffee Torte, 311
 Crème De Menthe, 332

German Cheesecake, 331
Marshmallow-Fudge, 330
BRUNCH
Cheese Blintzes, 134
Cheese Strata, 136
Creole Eggs, 122
Easy Swiss Cheese Pie, 138
Eggs, 121
Fancy Egg Scramble, 123
Herb Cheese Grits, 132
Irresistible Spinach Quiche, 135
Puff, 134
Shrimp Eggs, 122
Willard Scott's Cheese Grits Soufflé, 132
Brunswick Stew, 168
Brunswick Stew, Bob's, 167
Brussels, Sprouts, Deviled, 269
Butter, Herb, 118
Butter Rolls, 114
Butterflied Leg of Lamb, 189
Buttermilk-Garlic Dressing, 93
Butterscotch Cookies, Filled, 326
-C-
CABBAGE
and Corned Beef, Irish Style, 183
Beef Casserole, 240
Sweet and Sour Soup, 44
CAJUN
Crawfish Monica, 146
Hoppinjohn Jambalaya, 196
Maque Choux, 260
CAKE
Amalgamation, 295
Angel Strawberry, 309
Banana Split, 296
Cheesecake (See Separate Listing)
Chess, 304
Chocolate-Cinnamon, 305
Chocolate Truffle, 304
Cocoa-Nut Layer, 302
Colonial Strawberry, 308
Flower Potcakes, 300
1/2 Pound, 296
Lane, 306
Peach-Glazed Almond, 303
Pineapple-Banana Nut, 301
Pumpkin Squares, 334
Walnut Yule Log, 310
White Chocolate, 312
Wonderful Spice, 307
CANDY
Almond Roca, 379
Caramel Corn Jacks, 382

Chocolate Truffles, 337
Colored Popcorn Balls, 352
English Toffee, 336
Haystacks, 295
Lollipops, 308
Peanut Logs, 336
Peanut Play Dough, 380
Pecan Pralines, 337
Popcorn Balls, 382
Cappuccino Cheesecake, 299
CARAMEL
Apple Fondue, 354
Baked Pears with, 351
Corn Jacks, 382
CARROTS
Lyonnaise, 272
Mold, 273
Scalloped, 273
Spring Vegetable Sauté, 276
Cashew Chicken, 244
Cashews, Glazed, 15
CASSEROLE(S)
Cheesy Spinach, 285
Chicken Artichoke, 215
Chicken Lasagna for a Crowd, 243
Fruit
Almond Curried Fruit, 290
Cranberry Conserve, 264
Hot Apricot Casserole, 290
Party Pineapple, 291
Meat/Main Dish
Baked Ham Mornay, 249
Beef Bourguignon, 237
Beef Ragout, 240
Blend of the Bayou Seafood, 253
Cabbage Beef, 240
Cashew Chicken, 244
Cheesy Egg Bake, 248
Chicago-Style Crab, 142
Chicken Chow Mein, 370
Chicken Delight, 244
Chicken Provencale, 250
Chicken Rice Elegante, 246
Chili Relleno, 247
Chipped Beef, 238
Company Ham, 250
Company Seafood Dinner, 254
Do-Ahead Seafood Bake, 254
Enchilada Cheese Towers, 170
Favorite Chops in Casserole, 250
Ground Beef Noodle

Bake, 239
Ham and Artichoke, 248
Hot Chicken Salad, 242
Lasagnette, 169
One Dish Meal, 241
Oriental Spaghetti, 238
Oysters Rockefeller, 146
Polynesian Goulash, 239
Poulet Au Frommage, 246
Sausage Rice, 252
Sauté De Veau Marengo, 258
Scalloped Oysters, 148
Seafood, 255
Seafood Supreme, 152
Shrimp A La Grecque, 157
Shrimp and Crab Rice, 256
Shrimp with Artichokes, 252
Sweet and Sour Lamb, 251
Tuna and Artichokes, 256
Veal Stroganoff, 257
Zucchini-Ground Beef Bake, 242
Vegetable
Asparagus, 259
Baked Rice, 262
Cajun Maque Choux, 260
Cheesy Potato Casserole, 283
Corn and Zucchini, 275
Creamed Onions and Peas, 281
Eggplant-Tomato Bake, 278
Golden Eggplant, 260
Green Bean, 261
Hot Bean Dish, 259
Okra Tomato Bake, 280
Onion, 261
Overnight Potatoes, 284
Scalloped Potatoes Au Gratin, 262
Special Broccoli, 271
Squash, 263
Tomato Cheese, 263
CAULIFLOWER
Curried Baked, 272
Fresh Vegetable Marinade, 83
Tree Top Marinade, 82
Caviar Pie, 9
CELEBRITY
Barbara Dooley's Stir-Fried Shrimp with Fried Rice, 159
Brunswick Stew, 168
Chicken Carolina, 225
Chocolate Rum Pie, 317

Company Ham Casserole, 250
"Hunker Down" Foolproof Hollandaise Sauce, 292
Mexican Salad, 66
New Orleans Oyster Sandwich, 147
Porky's Revenge, 194
Quick Mud Pie, 320
Rosebud's Bavarian Cream, 342
Sweet Potato Soufflé, 288
Swiss Chicken, 219
Tomato Cheese Casserole, 263
Turnip Green and Cream Soup, 58
Willard Scott's Cheese Grits Soufflé, 132
Ceviche, 358
Chalupas, 196
Champagne Pineapple Punch, 34
Champagne Punch, 35
CHEESE
  and Ham Bread, 101
  and Macaroni, Deluxe, 136
  and Macaroni, Low-Cal, 373
  and Macaroni Salad, 78
  and Macaroni with Wine, 135
  and Tomato Salad, 363
  Appetizer Gougère, 13
  Bacon Ball, 11
  Biscuits, 111
  Blintzes, 134
  Bread Sticks, 100
  Broccoli Soup Supreme, 44
  Cheesy Egg Bake, 248
  Chicken Noodle Soup, 47
  Chowder, 57
  Cream Cheese and Bacon Tea Sandwiches, 10
  Dip Surprise, 15
  Easy Fried, 11
  Elegant and Easy Brie, 28
  Enchilada Cheese Towers, 170
  French Bread, 99
  Garlic Ball, 16
  Herb Bread, 98
  Herb Grits, 132
  Holiday Ball, 13
  Italian Rolls, 14
  Microwave Potato Soup, 54
  Olive and Cream Cheese Ball, 14
  Parmesan Onion Canapés, 21
  Queso, 138
  Spicy Ball, 14

Spinach Pasta with Mushroom Sauce, 372
Spinach Squares, 285
Strata, 136
Strawberry Ball, 16
Straws, 17
Tomato Casserole, 263
Willard Scott's Grits Soufflé, 132
CHEESECAKE
  Black Forest, 298
  Chocolate Velvet, 297
  Cappuccino, 299
  Cara's, 298
  Chestnut, 300
  German Brownie, 331
Cheesy Potato Casserole, 283
Cheesy Spinach Casserole, 285
Cheesy Squash Dressing, 286
Cherry Squares, 335
Chess Cake, 304
Chess Pie, Classic, 317
Chess Pie, Pineapple, 318
Chestnut Cheesecake, 300
CHICKEN
  and Artichoke Rice Salad, 63
  and Dumplings, 218
  and Peanuts in Hot Sauce, 224
  and Vegetable Sauté, 371
  Artichoke Casserole, 215
  Baked Breasts, 201
  Baked Swiss, 201
  Beef Kabobs, 171
  Bessie's, 202
  Bob's Brunswick Stew, 167
  Breast of Florentine, 222
  Breasts in Currant Jelly Sauce, 216
  Carolina, 225
  Cashew, 244
  Casserole Delight, 244
  Chaufroid, 221
  Cheesy Noodle Soup, 47
  Chow Mein, 370
  Chunky Corn Chowder, 48
  Commander Burns' Barbecue, 208
  Crescent Squares, 184
  Curried and Eggplant Stew, 224
  Curried Salad, 370
  Curry Mousse, 207
  Deviled, 202
  Enchilada Soup, 50
  Florentine, 226
  Fried with Cream Gravy, 203
  Gumbo, 48

Hawaiian Wings, 17
Hot Salad Casserole, 242
In Champagne Sauce, 204
Lasagna for a Crowd, 243
Lemon, 205
Main Dish Rice Salad, 66
Maple-Pecan, 208
Moravian, 209
Nuggets, 204
Orange Almond, 217
Oriental Salad, 63
Oriental Sesame Dinner, 226
Pecan-Breaded, 216
Phyllo Pastries, 18
Poppy Seed, 211
Poulet Au Frommage, 246
Poulet De Susie, 228
Provencale, 245
Rice Elegante, 246
Roast Stuffed with Orzo, 213
Scallopini, 220
Sesame Chicken with Honey Dip, 220
Sherried Parmesan, 211
Sopa De Pollo Y Maiz, 46
Southern Pie, 223
Soy Baked, 227
Stuffed Breasts with Dill Butter Sauce, 206
Stuffed Teriyaki, 229
Sukh, 228
Swiss, 219
Tangy Baked, 214
Tarragon Salad, 364
Tarragon with Angel Hair Pasta, 214
Waterzooi, 49
Wild Rice Salad, 64
with Mushroom-Wine Sauce, 210
with Sherried Cheese Sauce, 212
Chiffy Chaffy, 287
Chili Seasoning, 198
Chili Relleno Casserole, 247
Chive Sauce, Neta's, 292
CHOCOLATE
  Almond Roca, 379
  Baker's Pie, 314
  Black Bottom Pie, 315
  Black Forest Cheesecake, 298
  Bonbons, 335
  Brownies (See Separate Listing)
  Charlotte Au, 344
  Cinnamon Cake, 305
  Cocoa-Nut Layer Cake, 302
  Coffee Brownie Torte, 311
  Crepes, 345
  Crispy Chip Cookies, 329

Flower Potcakes, 300
French Hot, 34
Frozen Parfait, 347
Ice Cream Roll, 346
Kiss Cookies, 329
Marquis, 348
Meringues, 334
Nutty Buddy, 348
Pinwheel Cookies, 328
Rum Pie, 317
Silk, 374
Snowball, 349
Stuffed Apples, 88
Truffle Cake, 304
Truffles, 337
Velvet Cheesecake, 297
Walnut Yule Log, 310
White Cake, 312
Wows, 327
Zucchini Bread, 100
CHOWDER
Broccoli, 45
Cheese, 57
Chunky Corn, 48
Iowa Corn, 47
Chutney, Plum, 268
Cinnamon Chocolate Cake, 305
Cinnamon Sweet Rolls From Herren's, 115
Clam Dip, 19
Clam Sauce with Pasta, 126
Clay, Modeling, 383
Coconut Cream Pie, 318
COFFEE
Brownie Torte, 311
It's Almost Bailey's, 40
Kahlua Supreme, 350
Microwave Cappuccino, 34
Coffeecake (See Breads)
COOKIES
Brownies (See Separate Listing)
Candy Cane Cookies, 342
Cherry Squares, 335
Chocolate Bonbons, 335
Chocolate Kiss, 329
Chocolate Meringues, 334
Chocolate Pinwheel, 328
Chocolate Wows, 327
Christmas Tree Cones, 312
Crispy Chip, 329
Filled Butterscotch, 326
Gingerbread Men, 324
Great-Grandmother's Tea, 328
Honey Puffs, 327
Melting Moments, 332
Orange Date-Nut Bars, 331
Saltine Treats, 380
CORN
and Zucchini, 275
Cajun Maque Choux, 260
Chunky Chowder, 48

Corn Sticks, 110
Frogmore Stew, 155
Grandma's Pudding, 275
Iowa Chowder, 47
Salad, 71
Savory Baked Pie, 274
Sopa De Pollo Y Maiz, 46
Corned Beef and Cabbage, Irish Style, 183
Corned Beef, Whiskey-Glazed, 184
Cornish Hens, Roast with Wild Rice Stuffing, 233
Cornish Hens with Apricot Glaze, 230
CRAB(MEAT)
and Shrimp Rice Casserole, 256
Avocado, 142
Chicago-Style, 142
Grass, 20
Hot Canapés, 19
Hot Spread, 20
Miss Daisey's Dip, 20
Pasta Seafood Salad, 69
Pearl's Fried Puffs, 144
Seafood Soup, 56
Stuffed Fish Fillets, 149
Trotters' Linguini with, 143
CRANBERRY(IES)
Congealed Surprise, 84
Conserve, 264
Frozen Dream Salad, 83
Holiday Cranberry Mold, 84
Meatballs, 9
Orange Tea Bread, 101
Crawfish Monica, 146
Crawfish Soufflé, 145
Creole, Shrimp, 154
Creole Eggs, 122
Crème De Menthe Brownies, 332
Crepes, Chocolate Chocolate, 345
CROUTONS
Butter Toasted, 77
Five Minute Microwave, 117
Homemade, 50
CUCUMBER
Cold Soup, 54
Cold Soup with Dill, 361
Creamy Spinach Soup, 55
Crisp Pickles, 68
Curried, Baked Cauliflower, 272
Curried, Chicken and Eggplant Stew, 224
Curried Chicken Salad, 370
Curried Fish Soup, 360
Curried Fruit, Almond, 290

Curried Seafood Salad, 160
Curry Dressing, 73
Curry Mousse, Chicken, 207
Curry Rice Mix, Fruited, 130
CUSTARD
Pie, Easy, 319
Vanilla Cream, 347
White Wine, 376
-D-
Date Orange Nut Bars, 331
DESSERTS
Almond-Honey Dressing, 92
Amaretto Mousse, 338
Apricot Wafer, 341
Baked Pears with Caramel, 351
Biscuit Tortoni, 341
Brandied Poached Pears, 375
Cakes (See Separate Listing)
Candies (See Separate Listing)
Caramel Apple Fondue, 354
Cardinal Strawberries, 352
Charlotte Au Chocolate, 344
Chocolate Chocolate Crepes, 345
Chocolate Ice Cream Roll, 346
Chocolate Marquis, 348
Chocolate Snowball, 349
Cookies (See Separate Listing)
Fancy Fruit Kabobs, 352
Fresh Strawberries in Grand Marnier Sauce, 353
Frostings and Fillings (See Separate Listing)
Frozen Chocolate Parfait, 347
Frozen Lemon Delight, 350
Kahlua Supreme, 350
Nutty Buddy, 348
Pies (See Separate Listing)
Pineapple Cream Delight, 351
Pudding (See Separate Listing)
Rosebud's Bavarian Cream, 342
Sauces and Toppings (See Separate Listing)
Strawberry Bavarian Cream, 344
Strawberry Surprise, 366
Tortes (See Separate

Listing)
Vanilla Cream Custard, 347
White Wine Custard, 376
Deviled Brussels Sprouts, 269
Deviled Chicken, 202
Dips (See Appetizers)
Doughnuts, Dandy-Quicky, 102
Doves, Smothered, 231
Doves with Cream Gravy, 231
Duck, Roast with Raspberry Sauce, 232
Dumplings and Chicken, 218
-E-
Easy Egg Custard Pie, 319
Easy Pie Crust, 315
EGG(S)
Brunch, 121
Brunch Puff, 134
Cheese Strata, 136
Cheesy Bake, 248
Creole, 122
Easy Custard Pie, 319
Egg Nog, Ginger's, 36
Fancy Scramble, 123
Quiche (See Separate Listing)
Rolls, 24
Shrimp, 122
Soufflé (See Separate Listing)
EGGPLANT
and Curried Chicken Stew, 224
Golden Casserole, 260
Tomato Bake, 278
Vegetable Medley Soup, 59
Enchilada Cheese Towers, 170
-F-
Face Paint, Halloween, 384
Feta Cheese and Shrimp Linguine, 363
Feta Cheese Tart, 137
FETTUCCINI
Chicken Scallopini, 220
Scallops in Herb Sauce, 151
Spinach, 124
with Asparagus, 124
Filet Mignon with Fresh Mushroom Sauce, 174
FISH (Also See Individual Fish Listings)
Crunchy Fried, 141
Curried Fish Soup, 360
Delicious Baked, 160
Stuffed Fish Fillets, 149
FLANK STEAK
Tournedos, 175

with Fresh Basil-Tomato Sauce, 176
with Rice, Oriental, 174
Fondue, Caramel Apple, 354
French Bread, Cheese, 99
French Toast, Fabulous, 117
French Vinaigrette Dressing, 94
Fried Chicken with Cream Gravy, 203
FROSTINGS AND FILLINGS
Amaretto, 333
Chocolate-Cinnamon, 305
Chocolate Glaze, 311
Cream, 295
Cream Cheese, 312
Lane, 306
Lemon, 332
Orange, 325
Pecan Cream Cheese, 307
Sweet Chocolate, 302
Sweet Cream Cheese, 301
Walnut, 310
FRUIT (Also See Individual Fruit Listings and Salads: Fruit)
Almond Curried, 290
Kabobs, Fancy, 352
Plum Chutney, 268
Fudge, Marshmallow Brownies, 330
Fussilli Pescatore, 129

-G-

GAME (See Individual Game Listings)
GARLIC
Cheese Ball, 16
Olives, 24
Roasted Potatoes, 284
Shrimp in Lemon Wine Sauce, 359
Squash, 368
Gazpacho, Chilled, 362
Gazpacho Verde, 43
Ginger Grilled London Broil, 177
Ginger Soufflé, 343
Gingerbread Men, 324
Goulash, Polynesian, 239
Granola, Homemade, 365
GREEN BEANS
Bean Medley, 68
Casserole, 261
Herbed, 277
Hot Marinated, 277
Open Sesame, 276
Green Chiles, Baked, 274
GIFTS
Almond Roca, 379
Amaretto Sauce, 353

Bouquet Garni, 52
Candied Citrus Pecans, 16
Candy Cane Cookies, 342
Caramel Apple Fondue, 354
Caramel Corn Jacks, 382
Cheese Straws, 17
Chocolate Bonbons, 335
Chocolate Truffles, 337
Chocolate Zucchini Bread, 100
Cranberry Orange Tea Bread, 101
Crisp Cucumber Pickles, 68
Decaffinated Spiced Tea Mix, 33
English Toffee, 336
Five Minute Microwave Croutons, 117
Fruited Curry Rice Mix, 130
Garlic Olives, 24
Glazed Nuts, 15
Herbed Butter, 118
Herb Rice Blend, 381
Holiday Cheese Ball, 13
Homemade Croutons, 50
Homemade Granola, 365
Homemade Yogurt, 366
Hot and Sweet Mustard, 230
Hot Buttered Rum Mix, 32
Hot Mocha Mix, 35
Irish Raisin Bread, 104
Mimi's Bar-B-Que Sauce, 191
Mimi's Tomato Relish, 280
Orange-Anise Spice Bags, 38
Peanut Logs, 336
Peachtree Potpourri, 379
Pecan Pralines, 337
Plum Chutney, 268
Poppy Seed Bread, 105
Praline Parfait Sauce, 354
Strawberry Bread, 106
Vegetable Rice, 381
GREEK
Grecian Potato Salad, 73
Manuel's Salad, 72
Shrimp Ala Grecque, 157
Tomato and Pepper Salad, 82
GRILLED
Amberjack, 141
Cornish Hens with Apricot Glaze, 230
Ginger London Broil, 177
Marinated Tuna with Fresh Ginger and Soy Butter, 163
Po Boy Fillets, 172
Rotisserie Turkey for Gas

Grill, 234
Steak Tournedos, 175
Zesty Swordfish, 164
GRITS
Herb Cheese, 132
Willard Scott's Cheese
Soufflé, 132
GROUND BEEF (See Beef,
Ground)
-H-
Hollandaise Sauce, "Hunker
Down" Foolproof, 292
HAM
and Artichoke Casserole,
248
and Cheese Bread, 101
and Pasta Salad, 67
Baked Mornay, 249
Company Casserole, 250
Crescent Squares, 184
Honey-Glazed Baked, 186
Mandarin Rolls, 185
New Orleans Muffaletto,
186
Veggie Slices. 187
Hawaiian Chicken Wings,
17
Haystacks, 295
HEALTH AND DIET
Barley Pilaf, 368
Beef Dijon, 369
Bran Muffins, 362
Brandied Poached Pears,
375
Broiled Zucchini, 367
Ceviche, 358
Chicken and Vegetable
Sauté, 371
Chicken Chow Mein, 370
Chicken Florentine, 226
Chilled Gazpacho, 362
Chocolate Silk, 374
Cold Cucumber Soup with
Dill, 361
Curried Chicken Salad,
370
Curried Fish Soup, 360
Elegant Snapper, 364
Garlic Shrimp in Lemon-
Wine Sauce, 359
Garlic Squash, 368
Glenda's Garden, 369
Homemade Granola, 365
Homemade Yogurt, 366
Low-Cal Macaroni and
Cheese, 373
Mandarin Orange and
Almond Salad, 357
Orange and Lemon Salad,
359
Sesame-Citrus Green
Salad, 371
Shrimp and Feta Cheese
Linguine, 363

Snappy Vegetable Dip,
358
Spinach Pasta with
Mushroom Cheese
Sauce, 372
Strawberry Pie, 376
Strawberry Surprise, 366
Stuffed Potatoes, 367
Tarragon Chicken Salad,
364
Tomato and Cheese Salad,
363
Tomato-Zucchini Salad,
373
Tuna Spread, 360
Veal Scallopini with
Marsala Wine, 372
White Wine Custard, 376
Yellow Squash Pecan Pie,
375
Yogurt Pops, 361
Hearts of Palm Salad, 81
Herb Butter, 118
Herb Cheese Bread, 98
Herb Cheese Grits, 132
Herb Rice Blend, 381
Herb Tomato Bread, 103
Herbed Green Beans, 277
HONEY
Almond Dressing, 92
Dressing, 92
Glazed Baked Ham, 186
Mustard Dressing, 93
Puffs, 327
Wheat Rolls, 113
-I-
ICE CREAM
Chocolate Roll, 346
Clay's Favorite Pie, 319
Hot Buttered Rum Mix, 32
Kahlua Velvet Frosty, 36
Nutty Buddy, 348
Pistachio Ice Cream Pie,
321
Quick Mud Pie, 320
INTERNATIONAL (Also See
Greek, Irish, Italian,
Mexican and Oriental)
Brown Bread, 99
Chicken Waterzooi, 49
Munich "Sauerbraten",
179
Peloponnesian Pasta
Salad, 76
IRISH
Irish Raisin Bread, 104
Irish Style Corned Beef
and Cabbage, 183
ITALIAN
Italian Cheese Rolls, 14
Chicken Scalloppini, 220
Holiday Antipasto, 12
Risotto-"Italian Rice", 130
-J-
Jambalaya, Hoppinjohn, 196

-K-
Kabobs, Beef-Chicken, 171
Kabobs, Fancy Fruit, 352
Kahlua Supreme, 350
Key Lime Pie, 320
KIDS
Bird Feeder Candles, 384
Candy Cane Cookies, 342
Caramel Corn Jacks, 382
Cheese Bread Sticks, 100
Chicken Nuggets, 204
Chocolate Bonbons, 335
Christmas Tree Cones, 312
Colored Popcorn Balls,
352
Dandy-Quicky
Doughnuts, 102
Flower Potcakes, 300
Frozen Strawberry Yogurt
Salad, 91
Gingerbread Men, 324
Halloween Face Paint, 384
Haystacks, 295
Ice Cream Muffins, 98
Instant Non-Toxic Paste,
384
Lasagnette, 169
Lollipops, 308
Modeling Clay, 383
New Orleans Muffaletto,
186
No-Bake Play Dough, 383
Nutty Buddy, 348
Patriotic Pastries, 380
Peanut Play Dough, 380
Popcorn Balls, 382
Red Candy Apples, 339
Saltine Treats, 380
Silly Putty, 383
Soft Pretzels, 118
Spanish Squares, 285
Strawberry Surprise, 366
Stuffed Apples, 88
Super Salad, 86
Yogurt Pops, 361
Kiwi Orange Salad, 90
Korean Salad, Dressing for,
94

-L-
LAMB
Butterflied Leg of, 189
Princess Diana Roast
Saddle of, 188
Sweet and Sour, 251
Sweet Chops, 190
Lasagna, Chicken for a
Crowd, 243
Lasagnette, 169
LEMON
and Orange Salad, 359
Chicken, 205
Frozen Delight, 350
Ice Box Pie, 322

Lime Soufflé, 87
Tangy Mold, 85
Lima Bean Medley, 68
Lima Beans, Barbecued, 278
Lime-Lemon Soufflé, 87
LINGUINI
Feta Cheese and Shrimp, 363
Salad, 74
Trotters' with Crabmeat, 143
Liver, Delicious Pate, 25
LOBSTER
Asparagus Cocktail Mousse, 10
Pasta Seafood Salad, 69
Thermidor, 150
Lo-Cal Macaroni and Cheese, 373
Lollipops, 308
London Broil, Ginger Grilled, 177
London Broil, Marinade for, 177
-M-
MACARONI
and Cheese, Deluxe, 136
and Cheese, Low-Cal, 373
and Cheese Salad, 78
Do-Ahead Seafood Bake, 254
Million Dollar Salad, 78
with Wine and Cheese, 135
Maple-Pecan Chicken, 208
MARINADE
for Beef-Chicken Kabobs, 171
for Butterflied Leg of Lamb, 189
for London Broil, 177
for Roast Tenderloin, 182
for Sweet Lamb Chops, 190
Marinated Asparagus, 267
Marinated Green Beans, Hot, 277
Marinated Roast Beef Sandwiches, 178
Marinated Vegetables, 31
Meatballs and Bar-B-Que Spareribs, 192
Meatballs, Cranberry, 9
MEXICAN
Baked Green Chilies, 274
Chalupas, 196
Chili Relleno Dip, 23
Chili Relleno Casserole, 247
Chilled Gazpacho, 362
Enchilada Cheese Towers, 170
Enchilada Soup, 50

Hot Nacho Dip, 22
Queso, 138
Salad, 66
Sopa De Pollo Y Maiz, 46
MICROWAVE
Artichoke Soup, 51
Cheesy Potato Soup, 54
Chicken with Sherried Cheese Sauce, 212
MOUSSE
Amaretto, 338
Asparagus-Lobster Cocktail, 10
Curry Chicken, 207
Salmon, 27
Shrimp, 29
MUFFINS
Bran, 362
Ice Cream, 98
Peach, 108
Pineapple Bran, 109
Six Week Bran, 110
Sweet Potatoes, 108
Munich "Sauerbraten", 179
MUSHROOM(S)
and Almonds with Wild Rice, 131
and Leek Salad, 75
Chiffy Chaffy, 287
in Mustard Cream, 279
Marinated Mushroom Salad, 75
Phyllo Pastries, 18
Squares, 25
Mustard, Hot and Sweet, 230
-N-
New Orleans Muffaletto, 186
NOODLE(S)
Baked Ham Mornay, 249
Ground Beef Bake, 239
Poulet Au Frommage, 246
Pudding with Fruit, 339
Soy Baked Chicken, 227
Veal Stroganoff, 257
Nuts (Also See Individual Nut Listings)
Cocoa Layer Cake, 302
Orange Date Bars, 331
Pineapple Banana Cake, 301
-O-
OKRA
Chicken Gumbo, 48
Pilaf, 281
Tomato Bake, 280
Olive and Cream Cheese Ball, 14
Olives, Garlic, 24
ONION(S)
and Peas, Creamed, 281
and Proscuitto Bread, 106
Broccoli-Stuffed Vidalia, 270

Casserole, 261
Parmesan Canapès, 21
Rye, 21
ORANGE
Almond Chicken, 217
and Lemon Salad, 359
Anise Spice Bags, 38
Cranberry Tea Bread, 101
Date-Nut Bars, 331
Frosted Salad, 85
Kiwi Salad, 90
Mandarin and Almond Salad, 357
Marinated Salad, 90
Pecan Shortbread Cookies, 325
with Brown Rice-Pecan Salad, 80
ORIENTAL
Barbara Dooley's Stir-Fry Shrimp with Fried Rice, 159
Cashew Chicken, 244
Chicken and Peanuts in Hot Sauce, 224
Chicken Salad, 63
Chicken Chow Mein, 370
Chicken Sukh, 228
Egg Rolls, 24
Far East Shrimp Balls, 30
Flank Steak with Rice, 174
Mandarin Ham Rolls, 185
Sesame Chicken Dinner, 226
Soy Baked Chicken, 227
Spaghetti, 238
Stuffed Chicken Teriyaki, 229
Sukiyaki, 173
Orzo Stuffed Roast Chicken, 213
OYSTERS
Artichoke Soup, 51
Log, 28
New Orleans Sandwich, 147
Rockefeller Casserole, 146
Scalloped, 148
-P-
Parmesan Chicken, Sherried, 211
Parmesan Shrimp Scampi, 158
PASTA (Also See Individual Pasta Listings)
and Ham Salad, 67
Crawfish Monica, 146
Minestrone Alphabet Soup with Pesto, 53
Pesto and, 126
Seafood Salad, 69
Shrimp and Fresh Basil, 127
Tarragon Chicken with

Angel Hair, 214
Vegetable Medley, 128
with Clam Sauce, 126
Paste, Instant Non-Toxic, 384
PEAS
and Onions, Creamed, 281
Bean Medley, 68
Green Medley, 287
Scoville, 283
Split Soup with Smoked Ham, 52
Tangy English Mold, 81
PEACH(ES)
Glazed Almond Cake, 303
Molded Cream and, 88
Muffins, 108
Wonderful Cobbler, 324
Peachtree Potpourri, 379
PEANUT BUTTER
Nutty Buddy, 348
Peanut Logs, 336
Play Dough, 380
Saltine Treats, 380
Stuffed Apples, 88
Pears, Baked with Caramel, 351
Pears, Brandied Poached, 375
PECAN(S)
Angel Pie, 322
Apple Upside-Down Pie, 316
Breaded Chicken, 216
Candied Citrus, 16
Glazed Nuts, 15
Maple Chicken, 208
Mystery Pie, 323
No-Fail Pie, 321
Orange Shortbread Cookies, 325
Pralines, 337
Seafood, 158
Yellow Squash Pie, 375
Pepper and Tomato Salad, Greek, 82
Pepper and Tomato Soup, Roasted, 58
Pesto and Pasta, 126
Picadillo, 181
Pickles, Crisp Cucumber, 68
PICNIC
Beef Salad with Broccoli and Asparagus, 64
Bessie's Chicken, 202
Ceviche, 358
Cheese Bread Sticks, 100
Chicken and Artichoke Rice Salad, 63
Chicken Nuggets, 204
Chiffy Chaffy, 287
Chilled Gazpacho, 362
Cold Cucumber Soup, 54
Gazpacho Verde, 43
Green Pea Medley, 287

Honey Glazed Baked Ham, 186
Marinated Asparagus, 267
Marinated Roast Beef Sandwiches, 178
Mushrooms in Mustard Cream, 279
Salami, 172
Sesame Chicken with Honey Dip, 220
Shrimp and Feta Cheese Linguine, 363
Tree Top Marinade, 82
Tuna Spread, 360
PIE
Amaretto, 314
Angel Pecan, 322
Apple Upside-Down, 316
Baker's Chocolate, 314
Black Bottom, 315
Chocolate Rum, 317
Classic Chess, 317
Clay's Favorite Ice Cream, 319
Coconut Cream, 318
Easy Egg Custard, 319
Key Lime, 320
Lemon Ice Box, 322
Mystery, Pecan, 323
No-Fail Pecan, 321
Pineapple Chess, 318
Pistachio Ice Cream, 321
Savory Baked Corn, 274
Sour Cream-Pumpkin, 323
Strawberry, 376
Sweet Potato, 326
Wonderful Peach Cobbler, 324
Yellow Squash Pecan, 375
Pie Crust, Easy, 315
Pilaf, Barley, 368
Pilaf, Okra, 281
PINEAPPLE
Banana-Nut Cake, 301
Bran Muffins, 109
Champagne Punch, 34
Chess Pie, 318
Cream Delight, 351
Party Casserole, 291
Super Salad, 86
Pistachio Ice Cream Pie, 321
Play Dough, No-Cook, 383
Plum Chutney, 268
Po Boy Fillets, 172
Polynesian Goulash, 239
Popcorn Balls, 382
Popcorn Balls, Colored, 352
Poppy Seed Bread, 105
Poppy Seed Chicken, 211
PORK
Bar-B-Que Spareribs and Meatballs, 192
Beef Stuffed Roast, 193
Bob's Brunswick Stew, 167

Braised Tenderloin, 190
Brunswick Stew,, 168
Cashew Chicken, 244
Chalupas, 196
Chops with Sour Cream, 194
Favorite Chops in Casserole, 250
Mimi's Bar-B-Que, 191
Oriental Spaghetti, 238
Porky's Revenge, 194
Roasted Pork Loin with Prunes and Madeira, 195
Sausage (See Separate Listing)
Stuffed Chicken Teriyaki, 229
POTATO(ES)
Cheesy Casserole, 283
Cheesy Microwave, 54
Confetti Salad, 79
Garlic Roasted, 284
Grecian Salad, 73
Overnight, 284
Parisienne, 282
Peachtree Balls, 282
Salad with Sour Cream Dressing, 79
Scalloped Au Gratin, 262
Stuffed, 367
POULTRY (See Individual Poultry Listings)
Praline Parfait Sauce, 354
Pralines, Pecan, 337
Pretzels, Soft, 118
Prosciutto and Onion Bread, 106
Prunes and Apricot Coffeecake, 116
PUDDING
Chocolate Silk, 374
Grandma's Corn, 275
Noodle with Fruit, 339
Rum Pudding Kristine, 340
Yia Yia's Rice, 338
PUMPKIN
Baked Stuffed, 291
Sour Cream Pie, 323
Squares, 334
PUNCH (See Beverages: Punch)

-Q-
Queso, 138
Quiche, Easy Swiss Cheese, 138
Quiche, Irresistible Spinach, 135
Quick Mud Pie, 320
-R-
Raisin Bread, Irish, 104
Raisin Stuffed Apples, 88
Relish, Mimi's Tomato, 280

RESTAURANT
Baked Stuffed Snapper, 162
Bessie's Chicken, 202
Bob's Brunswick Stew, 167
Bone's Beer-Battered Shrimp, 153
Bone's Seafood Seasoning, 164
Breast of Chicken Florentine, 222
Chestnut Cheesecake, 300
Chocolate Chocolate Crepes, 345
Chocolate Marquis, 348
Chocolate Snowball, 349
Chocolate Truffle Cake, 304
Corn Sticks, 110
Crawfish Soufflé, 145
Creole Eggs, 122
Feta Cheese Tart, 137
Frozen Chocolate Parfait, 347
Fussilli Pescatore, 129
Ginger Soufflé, 343
Glenda's Garden 369
Grilled Amberjack, 141
Lobster Thermidor, 150
Manuel's Greek Salad, 72
Orange Marinated Fruit Salad, 90
Pasta Seafood Salad, 69
Pearl's Fried Crabmeat Puffs, 144
Potato Salad with Sour Cream Dressing, 79
Salmon Mousse, 27
Shrimp and Fresh Basil Pasta, 127
Stuffed Chicken Breasts with Dill Butter Sauce, 206
Sweet Rolls From Herren's, 115
Swiss Cheese Soufflé, 133
Tamara Salata, 31
The Georgian Club Caesar Salad and Dressing, 70
The Market's Crusty Bread, 102
Trotters' Linguini with Crabmeat, 143
Trotters' Seafood Soup, 56
RICE
Baked, 262
Barbara Dooley's Stir-Fry Shrimp with Fried, 159
Blend of the Bayou Seafood Casserole, 253
Brazillan, 129
Brown Rice-Pecan Salad with Oranges, 80
Cashew Chicken, 244

Chicken and Artichoke Salad, 63
Chicken and Peanuts in Hot Sauce, 224
Chicken Breasts in Currant Jelly Sauce, 216
Chicken-Casserole Delight, 244
Chicken Elegante, 246
Chicken Sukh, 228
Company Ham Casserole, 250
French Garden Soup, 55
Fruited Curry Mix, 130
Herb Blend, 381
Main Dish Salad, 66
One Meal Dish, 241
Orange Almond Chicken, 217
Oriental Sesame Chicken Dinner, 226
Risotto-"Italian Rice", 130
Sausage Casserole, 252
Seafood Casserole, 255
Shrimp and Crab Rice Casserole, 256
Shrimp Creole, 154
Shrimp Perlo, 156
Smoked Sausage Salad Medley, 71
Stuffed Chicken Teriyaki, 229
Tangy Baked Chicken, 214
Vegetable, 381
Wild Chicken Salad, 64
Wild Stuffing with Roast Turkey, 233
Wild with Mushrooms and Almonds, 131
with Green Chiles, 128
with Thyme, 131
Yia Yia's, 338
Ripe Olive and Artichoke Salad, 76
Roast Beef for Sandwiches, 178
Roast Chicken Stuffed with Orzo, 213
Roast Duck with Raspberry Sauce, 232
Roast Tenderloin, 182
Roast Turkey with Wild Rice Stuffing, 233
Roasted Pork Loin with Prunes and Madeira, 195
ROLLS
Butter, 114
Fan Up, 112
Honey Wheat, 113
Sweet From Herren's, 115
Rotelle with Ground Beef, Baked, 125
Rum Pudding Kristine, 340
-S-

SALAD(S)
Fruit
Green and Gold, 72
Kiwi Orange, 90
Mandarin Orange and Almond, 357
Orange and Lemon Salad, 359
Orange Marinated, 90
Sesame-Citrus Green Salad, 371
Super, 86
Fruit; Congealed
Congealed Cranberry Surprise, 84
Frosted Orange, 85
Holiday Cranberry Mold, 84
Lemon-Lime Soufflé, 87
Molded Peaches and Cream, 88
Molded Waldorf, 89
Pretzel, 86
Strawberry Rosé, 89
Tangy Lemon Mold, 85
Fruit; Frozen
Cranberry Dream, 83
Strawberry Yogurt, 91
Meat/Seafood
Beef Salad with Broccoli and Asparagus, 64
Chicken and Artichoke Rice, 63
Crab Avocado, 142
Curried Chicken, 370
Curried Seafood, 160
Ham and Pasta, 67
Hot Chicken Casserole, 242
Insalata Romana, 65
Main Dish Rice Salad, 66
Mexican, 66
Oriental Chicken, 63
Pasta Seafood, 69
Smoked Sausage Medley, 71
Tarragon Chicken, 364
Wild Rice Chicken, 64
Pasta/Rice
Brown Rice-Pecan with Oranges, 80
Chicken and Artichoke Rice, 63
Ham and Pasta, 67
Linguini, 74
Macaroni and Cheese, 78
Main Dish Rice, 66
Million Dollar Macaroni, 78
Peloponnesian Pasta, 76
Wild Rice Chicken, 64
Vegetable/ Tossed Green
Bean Medley, 68
Broccoli Mold, 74

Confetti Potato, 79
Corn, 71
Fresh Vegetable,
  Marinade, 83
Grecian Potato, 73
Greek Tomato and
  Pepper, 82
Hearts of Palm Salad, 81
Kiwi Orange, 90
Manuel's Greek, 72
Marinated Mushroom,
  75
Mimosa, 77
Mushroom and Leek, 75
Potato with Sour Cream
  Dressing, 79
Ripe Olive and
  Artichoke, 76
Strawberry Spinach, 91
The Georgian Club
  Caesar and Dressing,
  70
Tomato and Cheese, 363
Tomato-Zuccini, 373
Tree Top Marinade, 82
Vegetable: Congealed
  Broccoli Mold, 74
Tangy English Pea Mold,
  81
SALAD DRESSING
Almond-Honey, 92
Buttermilk-Garlic, 93
Curry, 73
Dill, 67
French Vinaigrette, 94
Ginger, 65
Honey, 92
Honey-Mustard, 93
Manuel's Greek, 72
Mimosa, 77
Oil and Vinegar, 76
Poppy Seed, 91
Rebecca Sauce, 27
Sesame Oil and Vinegar,
  357
Sweet and Sour, 94
The Georgian Club
  Caesar, 70
Salami, 172
Salmon In Foil, 148
Salmon Mousse, 27
Salmon Rolls, 28
SANDWICHES
Cream Cheese and Bacon
  Tea, 10
Glenda's Garden, 369
Marinated Roast Beef, 178
New Orleans Muffaletto,
  186
New Orleans Oyster, 147
Roast Beef for, 178
SAUCES
Amaretto, 353

Cheddar Cheese, 123
Chocolate, 346
Cream, 121
Currant Jelly Sauce, 216
Dill Butter Sauce, 206
Dill, 27
for Commander Burn's
  Barbecue Chicken, 208
Fresh Basil-Tomato, 176
Fresh Mushroom, 174
Ginger and Soy-Butter,
  163
Grand Marnier, 353
"Hunker Down" Foolproof
  Hollandaise Sauce, 292
Honey-Mustard Sauce,
  144
Horseradish, 183
Lemon-Mustard, 188
Lemon-Wine Sauce for
  Garlic Shrimp, 359
Mimi's Barbeque, 191
Mornay, 268
Mushroom-Wine for
  Chicken, 210
Neta's Chive, 292
Parmesan Cheese, 123
Praline Parfait, 354
Raspberry, 340
Rebecca, 27
Sherried-Cheese, 212
Sweet and Tangy Dipping
  153
Tangy Barbeque, 193
White, 125, 222
Sauerbraten, Munich, 179
SAUSAGE
Frogmore Stew, 155
Hoppinjohn Jambalaya,
  196
Hearty Bean Soup, 43
Party Pizzas, 26
Pinwheels, 22
Rice Casserole, 252
Smoked Salad Medley,, 71
Sautéed Fresh Vegetables,
  270
Sautéed Spinach, 286
Scallopini, Chicken, 220
Scalloped Artichokes, 267
Scalloped Carrots, 273
Scalloped Oysters, 148
Scalloped Potatoes Au
  Gratin, 262
SCALLOPS
Ceviche, 358
in Herb Sauce, 151
Fussilli Pescatore, 129
Seafood Pecan, 158
Seafood Stew, 154
Seafood Supreme, 152
Trotters' Seafood Soup, 56
Scotched Filet Mignon with

Fresh Mushroom Sauce,
  174
SEAFOOD (Also See
  Individual Seafood List-
  ings)
Blend of the Bayou
  Casserole, 253
Casserole, 255
Ceviche, 358
Curried Salad, 160
Do-Ahead Bake, 254
Fussilli Pescatore, 129
Pasta Salad, 69
Pecan, 158
Seasoning, Bone's, 164
Soup, 56
Stew, 154
Supreme, 152
Trotters' Soup, 56
SEASONINGS
Bone's Seafood, 164
Bouquet Garni, 52
Chili, 198
Sesame-Citrus Green Salad,
  371
Sherried Parmesan Chicken,
  211
Sherried Sweet Potatoes, 288
Sherry Sour, 39
SHRIMP
a la Grecque, 157
and Crab Rice Casserole,
  256
and Feta Cheese Linguine,
  363
and Fresh Basil Pasta, 127
Barbara Dooley's Stir-Fry
  with Fried Rice, 159
Bone's Beer-Battered, 153
Company Seafood Dinner,
  254
Crawfish Soufflé, 145
Creole, 154
Eggs, 122
Far East Balls, 30
Frogmore Stew, 155
Garlic in Lemon-Wine
  Sauce, 359
Hidden Treasure, 26
Main Dish Rice Salad, 66
Manallé, 156
Mousse, 29
Parmesan Scampi, 158
Pasta Seafood Salad, 69
Perlo, 156
Pickled, 29
Pizza, 30
Trotters' Seafood Soup, 56
SIDE DISHES
Almond Curried Fruit, 290
Baked Stuffed Pumpkin,
  291
Hot Apricot Casserole, 290

My Mother's Apples and
Cornflakes, 289
Party Pineapple Casserole,
291
Silly Putty, 383
SIRLOIN
Beer Beef Steak
Stroganoff, 180
Steak in a Bag, 180
Sukiyaki, 173
SNAPPER
Almondine, 161
Baked Stuffed, 162
Elegant, 364
Sneaky Petes, 37
SOUFFLE
Blue Cheese, 133
Crawfish, 145
Ginger, 343
Lemon-Lime, 87
Sweet Potato, 288
Swiss Cheese, 133
Willard Scott's Cheese
Grits, 132
SOUPS
Artichoke, 51
Bouquet Garni, 52
Broccoli-Cheese Supreme,
44
Cheesy Chicken Noodle,
47
Cheesy Microwave Potato,
54
Chicken Gumbo, 48
Chicken Waterzooi, 49
Chilled Gazpacho, 362
Chilled Creamy Avocado,
60
Chowder (See Separate
Listing)
Cold Cucumber with Dill,
361
Creamy Cucumber-
Spinach, 55
Curried Fish, 360
Cold Cucumber, 54
Enchilada, 50
French Garden, 55
Gazpacho Verde, 43
Hearty Sausage-Bean, 43
Minestrone Alphabet with
Pesto, 53
Roasted Pepper and
Tomato, 58
Seafood, 56
Sopa De Pollo Y Maiz, 46
Split Pea with Smoked
Ham, 52
Sweet and Sour, 44
Trotters' Seafood, 56
Turnip Green and Cream,
58
Vegetable Medley, 59
Sour Cream-Pumpkin Pie,
323

Southern Chicken Pie, 223
Soy Baked Chicken, 227
Spaghetti, Oriental, 238
SPINACH
Bread, 104
Breast of Chicken
Florentine, 222
Cheesy Casserole, 285
Chicken Florentine, 226
Crab Grass, 20
Creamy Cucumber Soup,
55
Fettuccini, 124
Irresistible Quiche, 135
Oysters Rockefeller
Casserole, 146
Pasta with Mushroom-
Cheese Sauce, 372
Sautéed, 286
Strawberry Salad, 91
Squares, 285
SQUASH
Casserole, 263
Cheesy Dressing, 286
Chiffy Chaffy, 287
Garlic, 368
Yellow Pecan Pie, 375
Zucchini (See Separate
Listing)
STEW
Bob's Brunswick, 167
Brunswick, 168
Chicken Waterzooi, 49
Curried Chicken and
Eggplant, 224
Frogmore, 155
Seafood, 154
STRAWBERRY(IES)
Angel Cake, 309
Bavarian Cream, 344
Bread, 106
Cardinal, 352
Cheese Ball, 16
Colonial Cake, 308
Fresh in Grand Marnier
Sauce, 353
Frozen Yogurt Salad, 91
Pie, 376
Pretzel Salad, 86
Spinach Salad, 91
Rosé, 89
Super Salad, 86
Stroganoff, Beer Beef Steak,
180
Stroganoff, Veal, 257
Stuffed Chicken Breasts with
Dill Butter Sauce, 206
Stuffed Potatoes, 367
Sukiyaki, 173
Sweet and Sour Dressing, 94
Sweet and Sour Lamb, 251
SWEET POTATO(ES)
Muffins, 108
Pie, 326
Sherried, 288

Soufflé, 288
SWISS CHEESE
Baked Chicken, 201
Chicken, 219
Easy Pie, 138
Soufflé, 133
Swordfish, Zesty Grilled, 164
-T-
Tarragon Chicken Salad, 364
Tarragon Chicken with Angel
Hair Pasta, 214
TEA (See Beverages: Tea)
Tenderloin, Roast, 182
Tequila-Champagne Punch,
38
Teriyaki, Stuffed Chicken,
229
Toffee, English, 336
TOMATO(ES)
and Cheese Salad, 363
and Pepper Salad, Greek,
82
and Roasted Pepper Soup,
58
Broccoli-Stuffed, 269
Cheese Casserole, 263
Eggplant Bake, 278
Herb Bread, 103
Mimi's Relish, 280
Okra Bake, 280
Zucchini Salad, 373
TORTES
Torte, Almond, 313
Torte, Coffee Brownie, 311
TUNA
and Artichokes, 256
Grilled Marinated with
Fresh Ginger and Soy-
Butter Sauce, 163
Insalata Romana, 65
Spread, 360
TURKEY
Crescent Squares, 184
Roast with Wild Rice
Stuffing, 233
Rotisserie Grilled for a Gas
Grill, 234
Southern, Pie, 223
Turnip Greens and Cream
Soup, 58
Turnip Greens, Grandma's,
289
-V-
VEAL
Sauté De Veau Marengo,
258
Scallopini with Marsala
Wine, 372
Stroganoff Casserole, 257
Vermouth, 198
with Mustard Sauce, 197
VEGETABLE(S) (Also See
Individual Vegetable List-
ings)

and Chicken Sauté, 371
Glenda's Garden, 369
Marinated, 31
Medley Soup, 59
Minestrone Alphabet Soup
  with Pesto, 53
Pasta Medley, 128
Ratatouille, 264
Rice. 381
Sautéed Fresh, 270
Snappy Dip, 358
Stuffed Ham Slices, 187
Vinaigrette Dressing, French,
  94
-W-
WALNUT(S)
  Glazed Bacon with, 11

Glazed Nuts, 15
Yule Log, 310
Whiskey-Glazed Corned
  Beef, 184
Wine, Hot Spiced, 40
Wine, White Custard, 376
Wine, White Sangria, 36
WOK
  Barbara Dooley's Stir-Fry
    Shrimp with Fried Rice,
    159
  Chicken and Peanuts in
    Hot Sauce, 224
  Chicken Chow Mein, 370
  Far East Shrimp Balls, 30
  Mandarin Ham Rolls, 185
  Oriental Sesame Chicken

Dinner, 226
Sukiyaki, 173
-Y-
YOGURT
  Frozen Cranberry Dream
    Salad, 83
  Frozen Strawberry Salad,
    91
  Homemade, 366
  Pops, 361
-Z-
ZUCCHINI
  and Corn, 275
  Broiled, 367
  Chocolate Bread, 100
  Ground Beef Bake, 242
  Tomato Salad, 373

Notes